EXPLORING THE
NATURAL
WONDERS
OF SOUTH AFRICA

EXPLORING THE
NATURAL
WONDERS
OF SOUTH AFRICA

Willie & Sandra Olivier

Struik Publishers (Pty) Ltd
(a member of The Struik Publishing Group (Pty) Ltd)
Cornelis Struik House, 80 McKenzie Street,
Cape Town 8001
Reg. No.: 54/00965/07

First published in 1996
Copyright © 1996 in published edition: Struik
Publishers (Pty) Ltd
Copyright © 1996 in text: Willie and Sandra Olivier
Copyright ©1996 in photography: As credited below
Copyright © 1996 in maps: Struik Publishers (Pty) Ltd

Managing editor: Annlerie van Rooyen
Editor: Lesley Hay-Whitton
Assistant editors: Inge du Plessis, Brenda Brickman
Designer: Darren MacGurk
Design manager: Petal Palmer
Design assistant: Lellyn Creamer
Cartography: Caroline Bowie, John Loubser
Indexer and proofreader: Sandie Vahl
Reproduction: cmyk Prepress
Printing/binding: Tien Wah Press (Pte) Ltd, Singapore
ISBN 1-86825-855-6

The travel routes, accommodation and other facilities described in this book were correct at the time of going to press. While every effort has been made to ensure accuracy, some of the information will become outdated during this edition's life-span. Travellers are advised to consult publicity associations and other sources before setting off. Details appear in the At a Glance boxes at the end of each tour.

The publishers would appreciate advice relating to new, upgraded or defunct facilities for incorporation into subsequent editions. Please write to: The Editor, *Exploring the Natural Wonders of South Africa*, Struik Publishers, P O Box 1144, Cape Town, 8000.

ACKNOWLEDGEMENTS
The publication of this book would not have been possible without the enthusiastic assistance and cooperation of numerous people. We would like to thank the following; should anyone have been omitted inadvertently we apologise for the oversight.

Staff members of the National Parks Board, notably Trevor Dearlove, Henriette Engelbrecht, Jill Gordon, Lucius Moolman, Kevin Moore, Otto von Kaschke, Corrie Pieterse, Christo van der Linde, Piet van Staden and Ettienne Fourie.

Our thanks to Peter Cattell, Gert Lombard and Anne Scott of Cape Nature Conservation, Jim Hallinan of the Cape of Good Hope Nature Reserve, Peter Burdett and Tertius Schoeman of Eastern Cape Conservation. Marena van Heemert of the Drostdy Museum in Swellendam provided historical background on the Breede River Pont and Dr Roger Smith of the South African Museum in Cape Town information on the Nieuwoudtville glacial pavements.

Thank you to Elizabeth Taylor of the Green Kalahari, Bernice Kotze of the Kalahari Regional Services Council, Leon Muller and Raymond Jessnitz

of Northern Cape Conservation. Peter Beaumont of the McGregor Museum in Kimberley and Jopie Kotze of Springbok assisted with information on Wonderwerk Cave and Namaqualand respectively.

In KwaZulu-Natal we were assisted by Natal Parks Board staff. Alexandra Miles enthusiastically arranged our visit to several parks and had to answer an endless list of queries; André and Jenny Deenik, Tony Drury, Barry James, Dick Nash and Rod and Alison Potter provided information. Our appreciation to Amber Millard, Wayne Matthews, Mark Stroud, Robbie Robberts and John Tinley of the KwaZulu Department of Conservation. A special word of appreciation to Menyuka (Jabulani) Mgqibelo, our guide at Tembe, Noah Indaba (Blessing) Ndglovu, our coxswain at Lake Sibaya, and Elliot Mathe, who took us on an unforgettable game walk at Umfolozi. Alison Duncan of the Harrismith Marketing Bureau and Tim Brown of Wilderness Safaris also assisted.

Aida van der Westhuizen of the Free State Department of Agriculture and Environmental Affairs, Rudolph de Vos of Northern Province Conservation, Cynthia Coetzee, Mike Crowther, Gustav Engelbrecht and Gus van Dyk of North-West Nature and Environmental Conservation, and Elna Haasbroek of Safcol's Sabie office and Marlies Liebenberg of Barberton Information Bureau deserve our appreciation.

Finally we wish to thank Struik's long-suffering editorial staff, especially Annlerie van Rooyen and Lesley Hay-Whitton, and all other staff members involved in the production of this book.

Willie and Sandra Olivier
Windhoek, Namibia

Front cover: The Amphitheatre, Drakensberg (top left); Lisbon Falls, Mpumalanga (top right); Maltese Cross, Cedarberg (bottom left); Zebra, Kruger National Park (bottom middle); Nature's Valley, end of Otter Hiking Trail (bottom right). **Spine:** Cheetah. **Back cover:** Boland Hiking Trail (top); Mountain-bike trail, De Hoop Nature Reserve (middle); Richtersveld (bottom). **Half-title page:** Lion, Kalahari. **Title page:** Nature's Valley.

CONTENTS

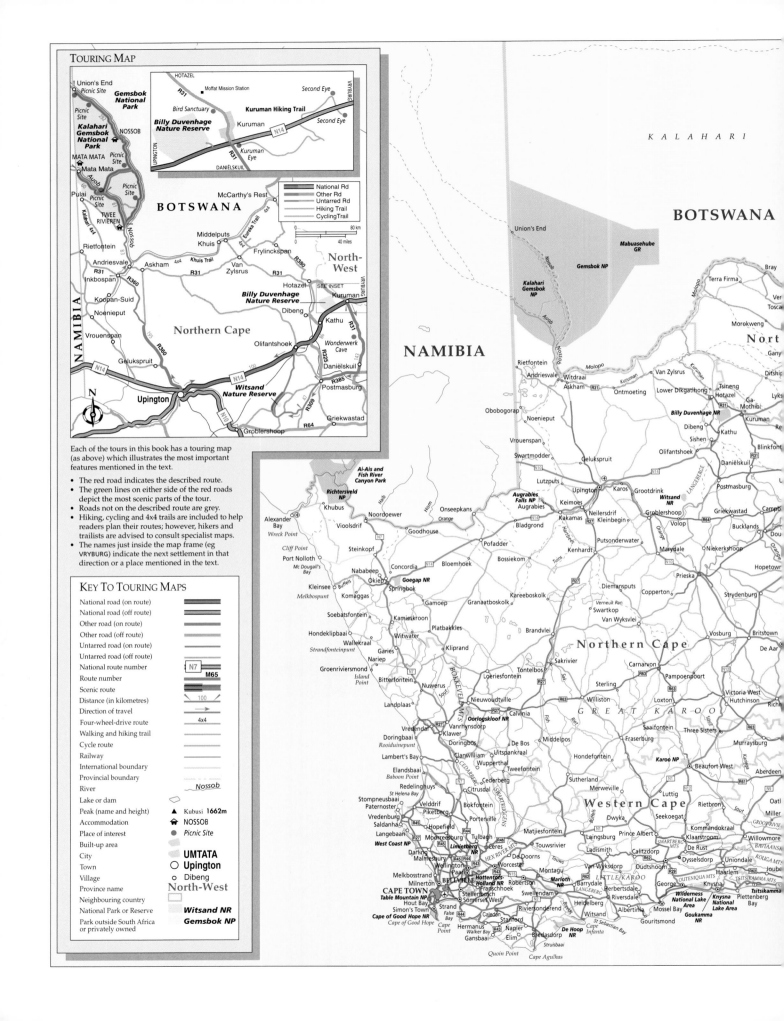

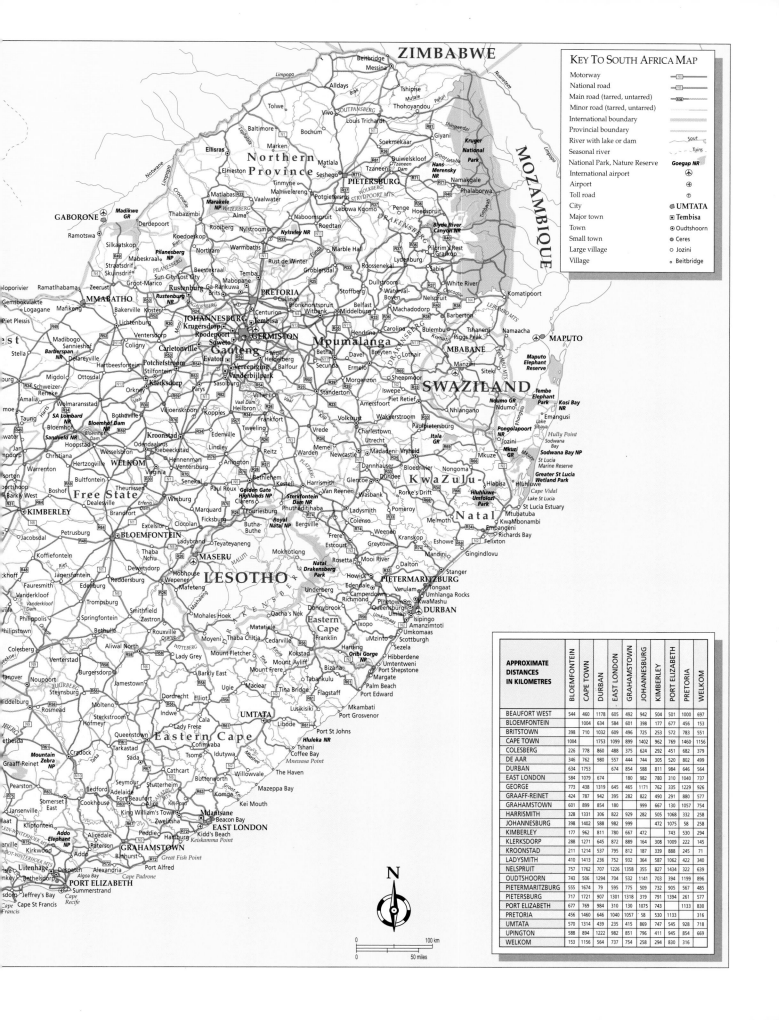

WESTERN AND SOUTHWESTERN CAPE

Few areas in the world have been so richly endowed by nature as the southwestern corner of Africa. Here, in the rugged mountains of this area, is a garden of exquisite beauty, dominated by ericas, proteas, Cape reeds and a profusion of other fynbos plants.

Nature has also fashioned two of Africa's most dramatic landmarks – the flat-topped Table Mountain with its breathtaking views, and, extending far into the Atlantic Ocean, the Cape Peninsula with Cape Point at its tip.

The ocean along Africa's most southerly point, Cape Agulhas, is one of the world's most important breeding grounds of the southern right whale. This sanctuary is overlooked by the cliffs of Potberg, home to the continent's southernmost breeding population of Cape vultures and the habitat of many plant species which are found nowhere else on earth.

Separating the coastal plains from the Little Karoo is the Langeberg range, a 400-km-long barrier of fynbos-covered slopes, contorted layers of rock, lofty mountain peaks and inviting pools.

On the West Coast, the sheltered lagoon at Langebaan is a sanctuary to thousands of waders that migrate southwards each year to escape the bitterly cold winters of the northern hemisphere, and the offshore islands attract myriads of raucous sea-birds. In spring, the surrounding Strandveld explodes into brilliant colours, when masses of plants burst into bloom.

To the northeast lies the Cedarberg, an untamed wilderness characterised by gnarled cedar trees, grotesquely weathered rock formations, and a multitude of caves and overhangs that bear testimony to the earlier inhabitants of this rugged land, the San people.

All this can be explored along countless walks and trails, scenic drives and impressive mountain passes, giving visitors the opportunity to appreciate the singular beauty of the Western and southwestern Cape.

Table Mountain, a magnificent backdrop to Cape Town, boasts a rich diversity of flower species, among them ericas, proteas and pincushions.

1 TABLE MOUNTAIN

Flanked by Devil's Peak and Lion's Head, Table Mountain, with its impressive vertical cliffs and characteristic 'table-cloth' of cloud, is one of Africa's most prominent landmarks and is in the process of being proclaimed a national park. Its floral diversity, long history, cableway, fascinating legends and sweeping views delight sightseers, trailists and botanists, earning Table Mountain a place as one of South Africa's top tourist attractions.

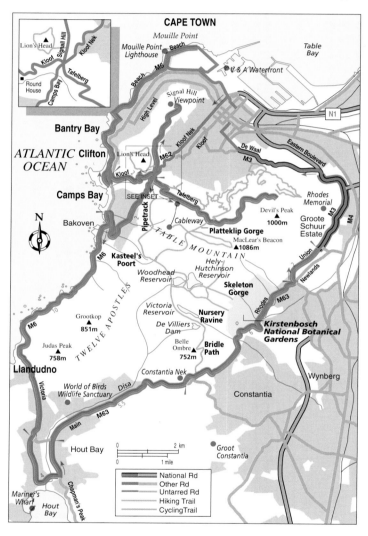

Mountain crevices are home to inquisitive rock dassies (hyrax).

How to get there
The only access point (besides footpaths) to the top of Table Mountain is from the Lower Cable Station (*see* below). To get there from the city centre, follow Kloof Nek Road to the traffic island on Kloof Nek. Turn left into Tafelberg Road; the Cable Station is 1,5 km beyond the turnoff. (Tafelberg Road continues for 5,5 km along the slopes of the mountain, providing superb views of the Mother City and Table Bay.)

Most of the 50-odd **mammal species** on the mountain are either small or nocturnal. Of these, rock dassie and baboon are most likely to be seen. Unfortunately, some of the baboons have become extremely aggressive as a result of being fed by visitors and, sadly, many have had to be put down.

More prolific by far is the mountain's **birdlife**, which includes grassbird, Cape sugarbird with its long tail, malachite, orangebreasted and lesser doublecollared sunbirds and Cape bunting. Inhabiting the dramatic cliffs and rocky areas are the magnificent black eagle, small blackshouldered kite, Cape rock thrush and redwinged starling.

TABLE MOUNTAIN'S CABLEWAY

The easiest, safest and quickest way to reach the top of Table Mountain is by cable car. From the Lower Cable Station visitors are hauled along a 1 240-m-long single-span cable to the upper station just above the sheer cliffs of Arrow Face – a journey of about 5 minutes. Since the cableway opened on 4 October 1929 more than ten million people have ascended the mountain in this

effortless way. The view from the summit arguably ranks among the most spectacular in the world. Over 1 000 m below lies Cape Town, sandwiched between the mountain and the gently sweeping curve of Table Bay, with Robben Island clearly visible. Towards the east lies False Bay and the Hottentots-Holland mountain range and to the west are the brilliant palm-lined white beaches of Camps Bay.

Watching the sunset and the flickering city lights far below from the mountain is an experience not easily forgotten, and a late-afternoon or early evening trip up the cableway in the summer is not to be missed.

For visitors there is a picnic area (wooden benches and tables) with magnificent views, a restaurant, curio shop and numerous footpaths to viewpoints along the edge of the mountain.

➡ *To get to Signal Hill, return to the traffic island on Kloof Nek and take the Signal Hill turnoff.*

LION'S HEAD AND SIGNAL HILL

The first stretch of this 3,5-km road to Signal Hill runs along the slopes of the 669-m-high Lion's Head, which became the site of a signalling station in 1673. In those early days a look-out man, posted on the summit, informed farmers of approaching ships that needed fresh provisions by firing a

---

The sandstone mass of Table Mountain began forming 125 million years ago when movements in the earth's crust thrust the sandstone sediments, deposited 125 million years earlier and underlain by granites and 900-million-year-old shales, upwards. Ice, wind, rain and extreme temperatures have since left only the mountain as a remnant of the sediments that once covered the entire False Bay and Cape Flats.

One of Table Mountain's most outstanding features is its rich **flora**. Covering only 6 000 ha, Table Mountain boasts more than 1 400 plant species – nearly as many as that of the British Isles. Among the flowering plants are red disas and giant proteas (*see* box, p. 12), watsonias, crassulas, mountain dahlias, nerines and amaryllis, while ericas provide a blaze of colour on the mountain slopes in spring and summer.

Table Mountain, viewed from Blouberg, watches over the restless waters of Table Bay at its foot.

small cannon. Visitors can climb to the summit along a relatively easy trail (*see* p. 15).

(*see* p. 15)

On your way to Signal Hill you pass a *kramat* (one of six holy shrines embracing the Cape Peninsula in a rough circle) where early Muslim religious leaders were buried. Muslims living within this 'sacred circle' believe that they will not be harmed by fire, famine, plague, earthquakes or tidal waves.

Further along the road one reaches the parking area and picnic site at Signal Hill. To most people the hill is synonomous with the gun that booms from its lower slopes each day (except Sunday) at precisely midday and the stunning views of Cape Town and its Atlantic suburbs.

➡ *To return to the city centre via Sea Point, retrace your steps to the traffic island on Kloof Nek and take a sharp turn to the right into Kloof Road (signposted Round House). This 17-km route takes you all the way round the lower slopes of Lion's Head and Signal Hill.*

The cableway provides easy access to the summit with its splendid views of Cape Town and the Peninsula.

11

RED DISA AND PROTEAS

Also known as The Pride of Table Mountain, the red disa (*Disa uniflora*) is probably the most exquisite of the nearly 100 disa species occurring in southern Africa.

Found throughout the Western and southwestern Cape, it favours stream banks, damp rock clefts and waterfalls. Each plant produces five or more flowers, usually

The red disa, Table Mountain's pride, in full bloom.

between December and February. Colours vary from carmine to pink and orange, although a rare yellow form also occurs.

Reigning over Table Mountain's floral kingdom is the unrivalled monarch of all flowers, the giant or king protea (*Protea cynaroides*). Up to 30 cm in diameter, these striking flowers range in colour from pale pink to deep crimson and a pale cream-green. One of the most widely distributed proteas, it occurs from the Cedarberg to the Cape Peninsula and eastwards to Grahamstown.

Other protea species growing here include wagon tree, strap-leaved sugarbush, real sugarbush and the red protea (*Protea grandiceps*). Conspicuous along the slopes of Lion's Head and Kirstenbosch is another member of the protea family, the silver tree, with its characteristic silvery-grey leaves which are covered in fine silky hairs.

LION'S HEAD CIRCULAR DRIVE

Soon after joining Kloof Nek Road, you pass the historic **Round House**, built on the foundations of an early fort. The present building (now a restaurant) dates back to around 1814 when it was built as a hunting lodge for the British Governor, Lord Charles Somerset.

On reaching the intersection with Lower Kloof Road, take a sharp turn to the left, and then turn right into Victoria Road (M6), which will take you past the **Clifton Scenic Reserve**. Stretching along the coastline between Camps Bay's exclusive Glen Beach and Clifton's Fourth Beach, this small reserve was declared a national monument in 1948 to preserve the scenic beauty of the area.

Wedged between the cold Atlantic and the looming bulk of Lion's Head is **Clifton**, with its four beaches that are famous for scantily clad sun-worshippers, and **Bantry Bay**. Both of these popular coastal resorts are characterised by luxury penthouse flats and mansions clinging to the mountain slopes.

Further along, at the parking area just off the junction of Queens and Beach roads, you can see an interesting geological feature below the sea wall. Known as the **Geological Exposure**, the rocks here show the intrusion of the lighter Cape granites into the dark Malmesbury shales, which took place some 500 million years ago. This is an interesting example of the contact between an igneous and a sedimentary rock.

From here, Beach Road makes its way past the **Sea Point Promenade** (popular with joggers and sunset strollers), Three Anchor Bay and Mouille Point to reach one of Cape Town's prime tourist drawcards, the Victoria and Alfred Waterfront. The city centre is then well signposted.

➡ *For another captivating drive from the traffic island at Kloof Nek, take the Camps Bay Drive turnoff. Affording magnificent sea and mountain views, this 50-km circular drive takes you along the Atlantic coastline to Hout Bay, over Constantia Nek to Kirstenbosch (see p. 14) and back to the city centre via De Waal Drive.*

Clifton, a millionaire's row, rises up from powder-white beaches while Table Mountain and the Twelve Apostles provide a dramatic backdrop.

Trailists relax as they gaze upon the tranquil waters of Hout Bay, which lies some 800 metres beneath them.

TABLE MOUNTAIN CIRCULAR DRIVE

As you make your way down Camps Bay Drive, you will be greeted by breathtaking views of the Atlantic Ocean and its delightful rocky bays and surf-fringed beaches.

Heading south from **Camps Bay**, the M6 (Victoria Road) takes you through Bakoven and from there along some 7 km of unspoilt coastline. Dominating the mountain-side scenery are a series of spectacular buttresses, commonly referred to as the **Twelve Apostles**.

The M6 then reaches the turnoff to **Llandudno** – a quiet residential area nestling among granite boulders – and the secluded beach of **Sandy Bay**. Clearly seen from the road is the wreck of the *Romelia*, a tanker which ran aground in 1977.

From here, the road ascends to **Hout Bay Nek** between the 758-m-high Judas Peak (left) and

Little Lion's Head (right), and a few hundred metres down the other side passes the turnoff to the popular Suikerbossie Restaurant, before reaching the fishing village of **Hout Bay**. A visit to the harbour, where you can buy fresh seafood, enjoy a seafood meal alfresco, or even take a launch trip to Duiker Island with its seal colony, is well worth your while. The M63 then continues through the lush Hout Bay Valley and, just before reaching Constantia Nek, passes **Orange Kloof**, one of the most extensive patches of indigenous forest on Table Mountain.

From **Constantia Nek** (the restaurant here affords fine views of the southern suburbs and False Bay in the distance), the M63 (Rhodes Drive) branches off to the left, following the lush, tree-shaded eastern slopes of Table Mountain. Continuing along Rhodes Drive, you pass the **Cecilia Conservation Area**,

Duiker Island is home to a colony of Cape fur seals.

13

KIRSTENBOSCH NATIONAL BOTANICAL GARDENS

One of the most famous botanic gardens in the world, Kirstenbosch is situated along the eastern slopes of Table Mountain and dominated by the imposing Castle Rock.

Covering 528 ha, it is home to nearly 6 000 indigenous plant species, ranging from tall yellowwood trees to cycads and dainty spring flowers. An area of about 36 ha in the lower part of the gardens features several footpaths that meander between the well-tended lawns and the many gardens of ericas, proteas, restios and succulents.

An enchanting corner of the gardens is The Dell, with its bubbling stream of crystal-clear water and verdant tree ferns. Other interesting features include the Cycad Amphitheatre, where a valuable collection of these 'living fossils' can be seen, the JW Mathews Rock Garden, and a

section of the bitter almond hedge planted by Jan van Riebeeck in 1660.

Visitors are free to explore the gardens by following the signposted walks, ranging from 45 minutes to 3 hours, or by joining one of the guided walks, conducted on Tuesdays and Saturdays. For the blind, a Fragrance Garden with aromatic plants and a Braille Trail are near the entrance complex.

There is an alfresco-style restaurant as well as a garden shop selling a wide variety of indigenous plants, seeds, books and gifts.

Not to be missed are the summer sunset concerts on Sundays, featuring music groups such as the Cape Town Symphony Orchestra. Many visitors use this opportunity to enjoy the superb scenery and music with a picnic on the lawns.

popular for its walks, before you reach the world-famous national botanical gardens of **Kirstenbosch** (*see* box, left).

After visiting the gardens, turn left into Rhodes Drive and left again at the traffic lights to join the M3. Towering high above the road are several spectacular buttresses, with the 1 000-m-high **Devil's Peak** prominent at the northeastern end. To the left lies **Newlands Forest** (much favoured by picnickers) and a little way on is the turnoff to Rhodes Memorial, which forms part of the Groote Schuur Estate (*see* below).

If time allows, drive up to **Rhodes Memorial**; the charming restaurant offers good value for money and the views from the memorial must rate as some of the best in Cape Town.

Beyond the **University of Cape Town**, the M3 skirts above **Groote Schuur Estate**, a bequest to the South African nation by Rhodes. Black wildebeest, eland and zebra are often seen grazing on the grassy slopes

adjoining the road. From here, **De Waal Drive** (M3) curves around Devil's Peak, with beautiful views of Cape Town and Table Bay on the right.

WALKS AND TRAILS

TABLE MOUNTAIN: Any outing, be it a short ramble or a longer walk, should not be taken lightly as it can change, as quickly as the weather, into tragedy. Comfortable footwear is essential, and it is advisable to carry a daypack with snacks, plenty of water and warm clothing (preferably waterproof). Listed below are a few of the most popular walks.

A pleasant walk from the Upper Cable Station is to **Maclear's Beacon**, at 1 085,9 m, the highest point on the mountain. Magnificent views of Cape Town, False Bay and the Hottentots-Holland range can be enjoyed along this 2-hour walk.

Also rewarding is the walk along Kasteelspoort, where a cableway was erected in 1893 to transport building materials for the construction of the

Woodhead Dam. The walk from Kloof Nek to the top of Kasteelspoort takes about 2½ hours and from there it is a further 2½ hours to the Upper Cable Station via the Valley of Red Gods or Echo Valley.

The most direct route up Table Mountain is **Platteklip Gorge**. This route is steep and exposed, and the climb from Tafelberg Road to the Upper Cable Station takes about 3 hours.

KIRSTENBOSCH: Both the **Skeleton Gorge** and **Nursery Ravine** walks lead through delightful forest scenery and they can be combined into a round trip of 3 to 3½ hours.

CONSTANTIA NEK: The easiest route to the top of Constantia Nek is to take the **Bridle Path**, which ascends gently along a jeep track for about 2½ hours before reaching Woodhead Dam. At the dam a pleasant diversion is a small, interesting Waterworks Museum; ask the resident Overseer for the key.

LION'S HEAD: An ascent of Lion's Head involves gaining about 350 m in altitude, but the magnificent view from the summit makes this round trip of 2 to 2½ hours worthwhile.

MOUNTAIN BIKE ROUTES

Mountain biking is permitted only along the lower slopes of Table Mountain (below Tafelberg Road) in the Van Riebeeck Park area. The routes are suitable for intermediate and experienced mountain bikers, who can cycle for as long as 3 hours without having to travel along the same route twice. No permits are required and access is from the top of Deer Park Drive West and Pin-oak Road in Vredehoek, and three points along Tafelberg Road.

Above: The many trails on Table Mountain take trailists on a journey through a kaleidoscope of ever-changing beauty.
Below: Kirstenbosch's setting and its floral displays make it one of the most fascinating botanical gardens in the world.

TABLE MOUNTAIN AT A GLANCE

MAIN ATTRACTIONS
Breathtaking mountain scenery, sweeping vistas of the Cape Peninsula and Atlantic Ocean, cableway, fynbos, Kirstenbosch, scenic drives and walks.

BEST TIMES TO VISIT
Although each season has its own attractions, the flowers are usually at their best between September and December. March and April are regarded as the two best months in the Cape, while September and October are also pleasant.

TABLE MOUNTAIN
Cableway tickets: At lower and upper cable stations, but it is advisable to use prebooking service during peak periods. Contact Captour, Tourist Rendezvous Travel Centre (*see* below), or the V&A Waterfront Information Centre, tel. (021) 418-2369, fax. 25-2165.
Operating times: Daily 07h00–22h30 (early December to mid-January) and 08h00–17h30 (May to October), weather permitting.

Permits/trail bookings: None required.
Facilities: Curio shop and restaurant (opening times change according to cableway schedule).

KIRSTENBOSCH
Permits/bookings: Entry fee payable at gate. No permits or bookings required for walks; guided walks depart 11h00 every Tuesday and Saturday from Information Centre near the entrance.
Opening times: Daily 08h00–19h00 (September to March) and 08h00–18h00 (April to August).
Facilities: Restaurant and shop (open daily 09h00–17h00; restaurant from 08h00 on weekends; closed on Christmas Day).
Music Concerts: No booking required; to confirm starting times contact the Information Centre, tel. (021) 762-1166, fax. 797-6570.

TOURIST INFORMATION
Captour, Tourist Rendezvous Travel Centre, PO Box 1403, Cape Town 8000; tel. (021) 418-5214, fax. 418-5227.

2 CAPE OF GOOD HOPE

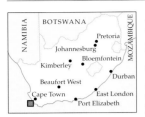

Described by the intrepid 17th-century British explorer Sir Francis Drake as 'the fairest cape ... in the whole circumference of the earth', the Cape Peninsula still provides one of the world's most spectacular viewpoints – rugged Cape Point. Rich in history and legend, its coastline is a rocky grave to several ships, while many of the over 2 600 fynbos plants growing in the Cape Peninsula occur nowhere else in the world.

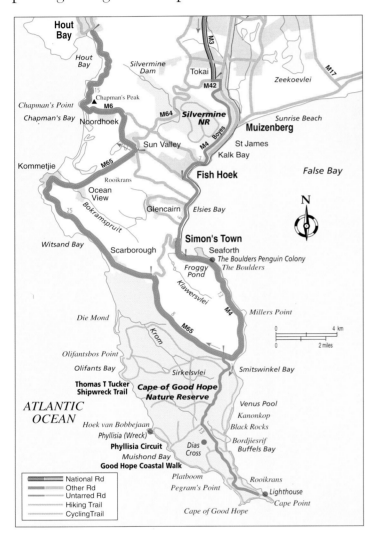

Fynbos flowers, such as this erica, are delicate and colourful.

How to get there
Cape Point is situated in the Cape of Good Hope Nature Reserve, within an hour's drive from Cape Town. The most direct route from the city is to take the M3, branch off to the M4 at the M42 junction and continue along the False Bay coast through Muizenberg, Fish Hoek and Simon's Town. Alternatively, take the slightly longer, but equally scenic, M6 route along the Atlantic coastline through Hout Bay (*see* p. 13) and along Chapman's Peak Drive. If, however, you wish to make a day of it, follow the Peninsula Circular Drive, which takes in both these routes (*see* p. 17).

Legend has it that the ill-fated ship the *Flying Dutchman* disappeared off Cape Point without a trace while trying to round the treacherous Cape of Good Hope in stormy weather in 1680. The captain, Hendrick van der Decken, swore he would ask the Devil to help him if God did not. As punishment he was doomed never to round the Cape.

Covering 7 750 ha, the Cape of Good Hope Nature Reserve boasts over 1 100 **plant species**, of which 14 are endemic and 38 are rare. No fewer than 25 protea, 39 erica and an astonishing 52 orchid species have also been recorded here.

Owing to the low nutritional value of the fynbos vegetation, the reserve cannot support large numbers of **animals**. However, species to look out for are Cape mountain zebra, bontebok, eland, red hartebeest, springbok, grey rhebok and grysbok.

Large numbers of baboon also find a sanctuary here in what is one of the last strongholds of these primates in the Peninsula. Numbering 250 in total, the four troops are resident at Cape Point, Buffels Bay, Olifantsbos and Smitswinkel Bay.

Interestingly, these baboons are among the few of their kind that supplement their normal

CAPE OF GOOD HOPE NATURE RESERVE

For most of the half a million visitors to the reserve each year, the highlight is the unrivalled vistas enjoyed from Cape Point Peak. From the Visitor Centre (a restaurant overlooking False Bay, a curio shop and an information centre), sightseers can either climb the 125 steps to the viewpoint on Cape Point Peak or ride there on the **funicular railway**.

The viewpoint is situated on the site of the original lighthouse, which came into operation in 1860. From this superb vantage point, 209,5 m above sea level, Cape Hangklip can easily be seen to the east, with Danger Point about 80 km away. Looking to the west, one may enjoy views of Dias Beach, Cape Maclear and the Cape of Good Hope – the southernmost tip of the Peninsula.

The Cape of Good Hope, the southernmost tip of the Peninsula.

diet of bulbs, grass seeds, flowers and insects with seafood such as limpets and small crustaceans. As a result of being fed by visitors (despite warning signs and fines) they can become extremely aggressive and some have had to be put down.

The reserve, with its 40 km of unspoilt coastline, also provides excellent opportunities for **outdoor recreation** – from walking trails (*see* p. 19) to watersports such as rock angling, diving, snorkelling and swimming. At Buffels Bay the rusting remains of the trawler *Tania* makes for an interesting dive, and there is a slipway for launching boats. The tidal pools at Bordjiesrif, Venus Pool and Buffels Bay are especially popular during the warm summer months, as are the numerous picnic and braai places dotted along the coast.

Whale-watching is yet another popular attraction, and during the spring and summer months local and overseas visitors can enjoy seeing, among others, the southern right whale from several viewpoints overlooking False Bay and the Atlantic Ocean.

➡ *A highly recommended drive that takes in Cape Point and the scenery of the Peninsula is the Peninsula Circular Drive, a 160-km round trip from Cape Town. The route follows De Waal Drive and Boyes Drive, continuing along the False Bay coast to the Cape of Good Hope Nature Reserve (see p. 16), and returning via Chapman's Peak and Hout Bay.*

PENINSULA CIRCULAR DRIVE

From the city centre head south along De Waal Drive (*see* p. 14) and then follow the M3, past the affluent suburb of Constantia, home to South Africa's oldest wine estate, Groot Constantia.

On reaching the M42 junction, turn left, then right into the M4 and then branch off onto **Boyes Drive**. This scenic alternative to the M4 winds along the slopes of the Muizenberg and Kalk Bay mountains, affording travellers breathtaking views over False Bay. Looking eastwards across the Cape Flats, you can see **Rondevlei Nature Reserve** (sanctuary to the Peninsula's only hippos and also noted for its

Four troops of baboons live at the Cape of Good Hope Nature Reserve.

excellent bird-watching opportunities from well-appointed hides) and Sandvlei, with its marina. Nestling at the foot of the mountains are the coastal resorts of Muizenberg, St James and the quaint fishing harbour of Kalk Bay, with Fish Hoek and Simon's Town tucked in the bays further south. Across the bay lies the Hottentots-Holland mountain range and Gordon's Bay.

From picturesque Kalk Bay, where Boyes Drive rejoins the M4, the road passes through Fish Hoek and, on entering the old naval town of Simon's Town,

reaches the turnoff to **Red Hill**. If you have the time for a short detour, you will be rewarded with spectacular views of False Bay from its summit.

Simon's Town, with its lovely old buildings lining the Historical Mile, is a popular stopping place for those en route to Cape Point, and a visit to **The Boulders** and its jackass penguin colony (*see* box, p. 18) is not to be missed.

Following the coastline closely, the road continues past Miller's Point (the restaurant here is known for its seafood) and Smitswinkel Bay, where you are likely

The waters of the 'fairest cape ... in the whole circumference of the earth' are reputed to be haunted by the ghost of the Flying Dutchman.

JACKASS PENGUINS AT BOULDERS

The waddling gait of the small jackass penguin has endeared this black-and-white sea-bird to thousands of people. Sadly, their numbers have decreased from one million breeding pairs at the beginning of the century to only about 20 000 breeding pairs worldwide. Factors responsible for this dramatic decline include the exploitation of guano, the collection of eggs, over-fishing and oil pollution.

The jackass penguin is endemic to southwestern Africa and breeds on 24 offshore islands (from Hollam's Bird Island along the Namibian coast to Bird Island in Algoa Bay) and at three mainland colonies. The protected colony at Boulders was established in 1985 and the population now numbers 340 breeding pairs. The most accessible of the three mainland colonies, it attracts thousands of local and overseas tourists every year.

These flightless birds spend most of their day at sea, swimming vast distances (non-breeding birds are known to cover up to 100 km in a single day) in search of pilchards, anchovy, maasbanker and squid.

Breeding occurs throughout the year, with a peak in November and December. Only two eggs are laid at a time, in a nest made in a burrow in the open, in guano or amongst boulders, and are incubated for 36 to 41 days.

Clinging to the rugged cliff's edge is the scenic Chapman's Peak Drive.

to encounter one of Cape Point's famous baboon troops, before reaching the turnoff to the **Cape of Good Hope Nature Reserve** (*see* p. 16).

From here, the route (now the M65) takes you through the seaside resorts of Scarborough and Kommetjie ('little basin') and then winds inland through the Noordhoek Valley, from where **Chapman's Peak Drive** (M6) is clearly signposted.

Regarded as one of the most scenic coastal drives in the world, Chapman's Peak Drive was built between 1915 and 1922. Blasted into the sheer cliffs of Chapman's

The jackass penguin colony at the Boulders, Simon's Town, provides a place of safety for these increasingly beleaguered birds.

Looking from Chapman's Peak Drive, with Chapman's Bay and the white sands of Noordhoek Beach to Kommetjie in the distance.

Peak, towering 450 m above, with a drop of 150 m to the ocean below, the drive follows the contact between Table Mountain sandstone and Cape granites.

As you ascend Chapman's Peak Drive, a magnificent view unfolds of the Peninsula's longest beach, **Noordhoek**, which stretches all the way to Kommetjie. Twisting and turning with the mountain folds, the road continues past several viewpoints where you can enjoy the dramatic coastal scenery – sheer cliff faces, crashing waves and, perhaps the most impressive of all, the towering bulk of **The Sentinel** guarding over Hout Bay.

Shortly before entering the town itself you can see fort and blockhouse ruins on your right, built by the British in 1796 to protect the bay.

From Hout Bay (*see* p. 13), continue along the M6, and then from Camps Bay either continue further along the coastal road through Sea Point (*see* p. 12), or follow Camps Bay Drive up to Kloof Nek (*see* p. 10).

WALKS AND TRAILS
One of the reserve's popular walks starts at Olifantsbos Bay, and follows the coast to the rusty stern and midship section of the *Thomas T Tucker*, an American Liberty ship which ran aground in 1942 with a cargo of war material. Nearby are the remains of another vessel, the coaster *Nolloth*, which came to grief in 1954. Both legs take about an hour, and can be linked to the 2- to 3-hour circular **Sirkelsvlei Trail**.

A popular longer route is the 12-km **Good Hope Coastal Walk** from Hoek van Bobbejaan to Cape Point. The 1½-hour circular **Kanonkop Walk** near Bordjiesrif offers panoramic views of False Bay from the summit of Kanonkop, named after the signalling cannon used by the Dutch East India Company.

CAPE OF GOOD HOPE RESERVE AT A GLANCE

MAIN ATTRACTIONS
Spectacular coastal views, unique fynbos vegetation, whale-watching, angling, snorkelling and diving.

BEST TIMES TO VISIT
March and April are regarded as the best months in the Cape, while September and October are also pleasant. The Cape's famous southeaster often blows in summer between November and February. However, each season has its own attraction, with the fynbos vegetation being at its best in spring and summer. August and September are good months for whale-watching.

PERMITS/BOOKINGS
Entrance fees payable at the gate. Special fishing permits obtainable from the office at Klaasjagersberg in the reserve, or from The Senior Nature Conservation Officer, PO Box 62, Simon's Town 7995; tel. (021) 780-9100, fax. 780-9525.

OPENING TIMES
Entry 07h00–18h00 (1 November to 30 April), 07h00–17h00 (1 May to 31 October). Closes at sunset.

FACILITIES
Viewpoint 209,5 m above sea level, restaurant, fast-food kiosk, curio shop, funicular railway, information centre.

TOURIST INFORMATION
Captour, Tourist Rendezvous Travel Centre, PO Box 1403, Cape Town 8000; tel. (021) 418-5214, fax. 418-5227.

3 HOTTENTOTS-HOLLAND MOUNTAINS

The Hottentots-Holland range with its more than 1 300 fynbos species lies at the heart of the world's richest botanical region, the Cape Floral Kingdom. Its rugged cliffs, mountain peaks, unspoilt kloofs and walks and trails are a delight to outdoor enthusiasts and flower lovers.

How to get there
Stellenbosch is a convenient base from which to explore the natural attractions of the Boland. The town is located about 50 km from Cape Town and can be approached via the N1 (take the R304 turnoff) or the N2 (take the R310 turnoff).

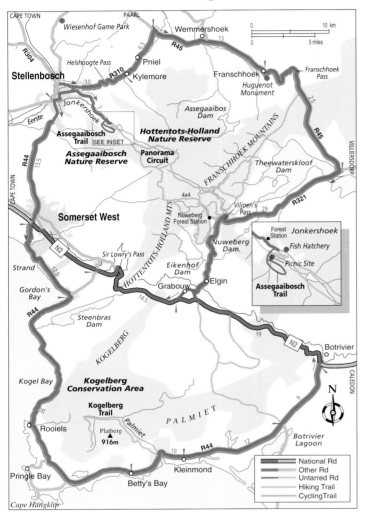

➡ *The Four Passes Drive is one of the most popular routes in the Cape (a 125/230-km round trip from Stellenbosch and Cape Town respectively). If you enter Stellenbosch from the R304, continue along Bird Street and turn left into Merriman. At the traffic circle, turn left into Cluver Road, and, at the junction, right into Helshoogte Road. If you enter town from the R310, pass the station on your left and turn right into Merriman. Continue as above.*

FOUR PASSES DRIVE

The first of the four passes, **Helshoogte** ('Hell's Heights'), twists its way up between the Jonkershoek Mountains and Simonsberg before it descends into the picturesque Drakenstein Valley. Here you'll find the mission village of Pniel (meaning 'face of God'), established in 1843, and, a little way on, Boschendal Wine Estate, known not only for its wines, but also for its superb meals and picnics.

A little further on (17 km from Stellenbosch), the road branches off to the right at the R45 junction, then continues along the Franschhoek Valley towards Franschhoek, where the French

Huguenots settled in 1688. The drive through the valley will take you past fruit orchards, vineyards, farm stalls and a score of wine estates (notably Bellingham) that open their doors to the public. Franschhoek itself is perhaps the highlight of the drive, boasting some of the best restaurants the Cape has to offer.

From the village, the R45 branches off to the left at the Huguenot Monument, then snakes up **Franschhoek Pass** in hairpin bends and sweeping curves, passing the original toll road between Franschhoek and Villiersdorp – the Cats Path – built in 1817. The summit of the pass, 733 m above sea level, rewards visitors with magnificent views of the valley below and the Drakenstein Mountains. Further along, the road crosses the Jan Joubertsgat Bridge, built in 1823 and reputedly the oldest bridge in the country. There is a parking area close by, and steps leading down the side of the bridge.

Approximately 24 km beyond Franschhoek, the route reaches the junction with the R321, then branches off to the right before crossing the Theewaterskloof Dam – a popular venue for bass anglers and watersports enthusiasts. It then makes its way through the Cape's apple country, where blossoming apple trees provide a stunning display in spring. The road continues up **Viljoen's Pass** to Nuweberg Forest Station, the entrance to the Hottentots-Holland Nature Reserve (*see* p. 21), on the summit of the pass.

After passing through Grabouw the N2 continues through pine plantations to reach the last of

Don't miss
No visit to the Fairest Cape is complete without a taste of the region's wines. Wine estates are clearly signposted along the Stellenbosch and Franschhoek wine routes, and offer anything from wine-tasting and cellar tours to picnics and excellent Cape cuisine. For more information and detailed maps, visit any tourist information bureau, or contact Captour at tel. (021) 418-5214, fax. 418-5227.

Assegaaibosch Nature Reserve.

The Cape sugarbird.

the four passes – the 427-m-high **Sir Lowry's Pass**, named after Sir Lowry Cole, Governor at the Cape in the early 19th century. The viewpoint on the summit provides sweeping vistas of False Bay and the Cape Peninsula. To return to Stellenbosch, follow the N2 and turn off onto the R44.

➡ *To get to Jonkershoek Valley, follow the directions to Helshoogte Pass (see p. 20), but instead of taking the left turning into Cluver Road, turn right into Marais Street, then left onto Jonkershoek Road. Continue along this road all the way into the valley. The turnoff to Assegaaibosch Nature Reserve is 9 km from town.*

ASSEGAAIBOSCH NATURE RESERVE

Located along the upper reaches of the Eerste River and adjoining the Hottentots-Holland Nature Reserve, Assegaaibosch covers 204 ha of mainly fynbos vegetation. To date some 135 bird species have been recorded in the area. Day visitors can enjoy walking a relaxing 2-km trail (*see* p. 23) or relax at the shady picnic sites (braai places and ablution facilities are provided) on the banks of the river.

Opposite the entrance to the reserve, along Jonkershoek Road, is the **Jonkershoek Fish Hatchery**, which was established in

The Franschhoek Pass offers breathtaking views of green cultivated farmlands and distant blue mountains.

1893 as a trout breeding station. Visitors are welcome to view the hatchery, the ponds and the freshwater aquarium.

➡ *The entrance gate to the Jonkershoek Plantation is at the end of Jonkershoek Road, about 1 km from Assegaaibosch.*

JONKERSHOEK PLANTATION

Surrounded by the Stellenbosch and Jonkershoek Mountains, the secluded Jonkershoek Valley, with its recognisable 1 504-m-high Twin Peaks, is a long-standing favourite with outdoor enthusiasts, who may indulge in anything

from challenging rock-climbing routes to easy walks. However, since these mountains are within the Hottentots-Holland Nature Reserve, entry permits for the reserve must be obtained from the Cape Nature Conservation Booking Office (*see* p. 23).

Starting at the entrance gate of the plantation is a **Circular Drive** along the valley carved by the Eerste River, and mountain-biking and horse-riding are permitted on the jeep tracks leading through the pine plantations. Picnic sites are provided for day visitors, and trout anglers can try their luck at the Jonkershoek Dam, near the entrance gate.

➡ *The entrance to the Hottentots-Holland Nature Reserve is situated on the summit of Viljoen's Pass at the Nuweberg Forest Station between Grabouw and Villiersdorp. It is 52 km from Stellenbosch via Sir Lowry's Pass and 71 km from Stellenbosch via Helshoogte Pass.*

HOTTENTOTS-HOLLAND NATURE RESERVE

This 42 000-ha reserve, which encompasses the Hottentots-Holland, Groot Drakenstein

Towering above the Jonkershoek Dam are the jagged peaks of the 1 494- and 1 504-m-high Twin Peaks.

The king protea is one of the most striking protea species.

FYNBOS

Fynbos is a collective name for the rich diversity of plants growing in the Cape Floral Kingdom. Although it is the smallest of the world's six floral kingdoms, covering a mere 0,04% of the earth's surface, it is also the richest, supporting some 8 500 plant species.

The most dominant families are the ericas (about 600 species), proteas (11 genera and over 300 species), and restios, which replace grasses in fynbos. Other fynbos plants include ground orchids, many types of lilies, a rich variety of plants belonging to the aster family, the cigar flower (*Retzia capensis*) and the ink-flower (*Harveya capensis*). The brunias and berzelias are especially striking during the spring and summer months.

Larger mammals are poorly represented in fynbos due to its low nutritional value. Among the most common species are grysbok (a fynbos endemic), grey rhebok, klip-springer, baboon and caracal. The leopard is the largest of the predators which occur in fynbos, but since it is nocturnal the most likely sign of its presence is its spoor. Likewise, the smaller mammal species such as honey badger, genets and porcupine, as well as other rodents, are nocturnal and thus also seldom seen.

Among the typical fynbos birds that you are likely to see are Victorin's warbler, Cape sugarbird, orangebreasted and malachite sunbirds, Cape siskin and protea canary.

Inhabiting this region's rivers are no fewer than 17 endemic fish species, among them Clanwilliam yellowfish, Twee River redfin, sawfin and fiery redfin.

and Franschhoek mountains, has as its main attractions breathtaking mountain scenery, a network of day and overnight hiking trails (*see* p. 23) and a rich diversity of fynbos plants. The Nuweberg Forest Station is the starting point for trails, and facilities for day visitors are limited to toilets and showers.

Although each season in the Boland mountains presents a dazzling display of flowers, August to December are generally the most spectacular. **Flowering plants** range from the gay lobelia and the inconspicuous sundew, with its sticky hairs, to the spectacular Cape bottle brushes (*Mimetes* sp.). In spring the mountain slopes are transformed into shades of pale pink, white and green when masses of ericas burst into bloom. Adding a splash of colour in late winter and spring are a bewildering variety of geophytes – watsonias, gladioli, aristeas and ixias. Also conspicuous are a rich diversity of daisies, from the yellow *Euryops* to the well-known everlastings with their paper-like petals.

The protea family is represented by species ranging from the king protea (*see* box, p. 12) to the dainty blushing bride (*Serruria florida*). The latter, once almost extinct, is also known as the Pride of Franschhoek and is restricted to the Franschhoek Mountains.

Birdlife is typical of the Cape mountains and so far more than 110 species have been recorded. The Cape sugarbird, with its long tail, is unlikely to escape attention, while the orangebreasted sunbird is another showy species.

Most of the **mammals** occurring in this fynbos habitat are either inconspicuous or nocturnal. Trailists are most likely to see baboon and rock dassie, while porcupine quills often betray the presence of this nocturnal animal. Grey rhebok, klipspringer, common duiker and grysbok also occur throughout the Hottentots-Holland Mountains, but are less frequently encountered.

➡ *An excursion to the unspoilt Kogelberg Conservation Area can be combined with one of the most spectacular coastal drives in the Cape (a 155-km round trip from Stellenbosch). From Stellenbosch, take the R44 through Strand, Gordon's Bay, Rooiels and Betty's Bay (a stop at the Harold Porter Botanic Reserve is a must if you have time). The entrance to Kogelberg is about 10 km from Betty's Bay, just before you enter Kleinmond. To return to Stellenbosch, follow the R44 to Botrivier, turn left onto the N2 and continue to Sir Lowry's Pass (see p. 21).*

The drive to the Kogelberg Conservation Area takes in some of the country's most spectacular coastal scenery.

KOGELBERG CONSERVATION AREA

The vegetation of this 16 537-ha area in the rugged mountains between Gordon's Bay and Kleinmond is an exceptional example of Cape fynbos.

The floral diversity here is underlined by the fact that nearly a fifth of all fynbos species are known to occur here, including 176 of South Africa's 600 erica species. Among the 1 600 plant species on the mountain slopes, peaks and in the deep river valleys are 150 endemics, many of them rare and endangered. Much of this diversity can be seen along the Kogelberg Trail (see below).

The reserve is also home to a variety of game, including klipspringer, grysbok and grey rhebok, and fish eagle, black eagle, sunbirds and kingfishers may also be spotted by keen birders. The Palmiet River, running through the reserve, provides good canoeing. The only facilities are toilets and a car-park near the gate.

WALKS AND TRAILS

ASSEGAAIBOSCH NATURE RESERVE:
The **Assegaaibosch Trail** is an easy 2-km walk from the wild flower garden, up Stellenbosch Mountain and along a contour path, from where there are views of Jonkershoek Valley.

JONKERSHOEK FOREST RESERVE:
One of the most popular routes in the Jonkershoek Valley follows the course of the Eerste River to the **First** and **Second waterfalls**. Far more demanding, but offering spectacular views of Assegaaiboschkloof, the valley and the Hottentots-Holland range, is the **Panorama Route**, a 20-km circular day walk; a permit is required from Cape Nature Conservation.

The rugged terrain of the Boland Hiking Trail is softened by fynbos.

HOTTENTOTS-HOLLAND NATURE RESERVE:
The popular 20-km **Buys se Pad** is a circular day walk from Grabouw Forest Station, while the **Boegoekloof** and **Groenlandsberg** day walks from Nuweberg Forest Station cover 17 km and 24 km respectively. Also starting at Nuweberg Forest Station is the 6-km circular **Palmiet Trail**, the first Cape hiking trail for the blind. The trail has logs on one side, guide rails at difficult sections and Braille labels marking points of interest.

The **Boland Hiking Trail** has overnight options from circular 2- and 3-day hikes to a 3-day traverse. A 2-day circular route takes you from Nuweberg to Landdroskop and back, or to Boesmanskloof and back. Both the Nuweberg-Franschhoek Pass and Nuweberg-Jonkershoek trails are linear.

KOGELBERG CONSERVATION AREA:
The **Kogelberg Trail**, a day route of 12 to 20 km along the valley of the Palmiet River, is a must for flower lovers.

HOTTENTOTS-HOLLAND MOUNTAINS AT A GLANCE

MAIN ATTRACTIONS
Fynbos, mountain scenery, unspoilt kloofs, Four Passes Drive, trails and walks, kloofing, canoeing, wine routes.

BEST TIMES TO VISIT
Scenic drives and day walks possible on clear days all year round. Hikers should prepare for sudden weather changes; routes can close at short notice. Winter restricts kloofing and overnight hikes (see below); June to September are best for canoeing on the Palmiet River. Fynbos is spectacular in spring and summer.

ASSEGAAIBOSCH NATURE RESERVE
Permits/bookings: Entry and trail permits at gate, but contact Cape Nature Conservation for prior reservation (see below).
Opening times: Open daily 08h00–18h00.

JONKERSHOEK FISH HATCHERY
Permits/bookings: No permit is required.
Opening times: Open Monday to Friday 08h00–16h00.

JONKERSHOEK PLANTATION
Permits/bookings: Entry and fishing permits at gate. Limited number of fishing permits issued on weekends, public holidays: contact SAF-COL, PO Box 6141, Uniedal 7612; tel. (021) 886-5715, fax. 886-6279.

Opening times: Open daily 07h30–17h00, but can be closed in summer because of the fire hazard.

HOTTENTOTS-HOLLAND NATURE RESERVE
Permits/bookings: For trails/kloofing, contact Cape Nature Conservation (see below).
Opening times: Open daily 07h30–17h00; Boland Hiking Trail and other overnight trails closed July to August. Kloofing routes closed 1 May to 31 October.
Accommodation: 4 overnight huts with bunks and mattresses on Boland Hiking Trail for overnight hikers only.

KOGELBERG CONSERVATION AREA
Permits/bookings: For trails and canoeing book in advance through Cape Nature Conservation (see below).
Opening times: Open daily 07h30–17h00. Canoeing day trips on Palmiet River from June to September only.

Cape Nature Conservation Booking Office, Private Bag X1, Uniedal 7612; tel. (021) 886-5858 or 886-6543, fax. 886-6575.

TOURIST INFORMATION
Captour, PO Box 1403, Cape Town 8000; tel. (021) 418-5214, fax. 418-5227.
Stellenbosch Publicity Association, PO Box 368, Stellenbosch 7600; tel. (021) 883-3584, fax. 883-8017.

KLOOFING

One of the most exhilarating ways of exploring the Hottentots-Holland Nature Reserve is on a kloofing trip down the Riviersonderend. A word of warning: kloofing involves rock scrambling, compulsory swims and nerve-racking jumps into pools, and once you start, there is no turning back. Either try the Riviersonderend Canyon, covering 17 km (8½ hours), or Suicide Gorge, a 17-km trip of about 9 hours. Both are circular routes starting at Nuweberg Forest Station.

If you're a beginner, first try the Riviersonderend Canyon, which requires two jumps, the highest being 7 m, before braving Suicide Gorge. The latter has three waterfalls, the most formidable being 14 m high.

It is advisable that you wear a wetsuit and lightweight hiking boots or running shoes with a good grip. Also carry a spare change of clothes, food, sunblock and first-aid items, and ensure that everything, particularly your camera, is properly waterproofed.

4 PAARL MOUNTAIN & LIMIETBERG

Paarl's famous granite domes – the three largest rocks in South Africa – have captured the attention of explorers, geologists, naturalists and travellers for over three centuries. The town is ideally situated for excursions into the surrounding mountains – be it a scramble up Bretagne Rock in the Paarl Mountain Nature Reserve, a scenic drive along the Bain's Kloof and Du Toit's Kloof passes, or a hike in the Limietberg Nature Reserve.

How to get there
To reach Paarl, take the N1 from Cape Town and after 53 km, turn onto the R45, which becomes the Main Street as you enter town.

Don't miss
The Berg River Valley around Paarl features many respected wine estates, notably the world-renowned Nederburg. These estates are clearly signposted along the motorways. For more details as well as a detailed map showing the Paarl Wine Route, contact Captour at tel. (021) 418-5214 or Paarl's tourist information bureau at tel. (02211) 2-3829 or 2-4842.

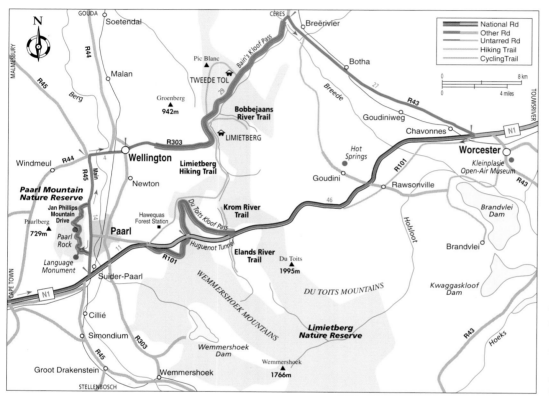

➤ To get to Paarl Mountain Nature Reserve follow the Main Street past Laborie Wine Estate and the headquarters of the KWV at La Concorde, then turn left into Jan Phillips Mountain Drive (the main road through the reserve which also provides access to the Afrikaans Language Monument). Continue along this road for about 6 km to reach the entrance gate. You could also approach the reserve from the northern side of town, via the same drive (see map).

PAARL MOUNTAIN NATURE RESERVE

The three imposing granite domes – Paarl Rock, Bretagne Rock and Gordon's Rock – are the most notable attractions of the 1 910-ha nature reserve on the slopes of Paarl Mountain, originally named the Diamond and Pearl Mountain because of the glistening appearance of its domes after rain (Paarl is the Dutch word for pearl).

Paarl Mountain originated some 500 million years ago when Cape granites intruded into the underlying Malmesbury shales. Subsequent erosion gradually stripped away the overlying rock, in a process that took millions of years, and exposed this 14-km-long, 6-km-wide mountain.

Paarl Mountain Nature Reserve offers various fynbos plants and lovely views of the surrounding mountains.

Chain handholds on the slopes of the steep Paarl Mountain enable visitors to enjoy the breathtaking views from the summit.

Paarl Rock, the easternmost dome, is the most accessible of the three, and an old ship's cannon, used in the days of the Cape Colony to inform farmers of approaching ships that required fresh produce, can still be seen on its summit. From here, the gravel road continues to a parking area at the foot of **Bretagne Rock** (left) and **Gordon's Rock** (right). A chain handhold helps visitors up the final ascent to the summit of Bretagne Rock, from where there is a bird's-eye view of the patchwork of vineyards, the jagged peaks of the Du Toit's Kloof Mountains, and Table Mountain in the distance. It is advisable not to attempt climbing Gordon's Rock, as the rock face is very slippery and steep.

Another feature of the reserve is the 15-ha **Meulwater Wild Flower Garden**, with its cultivated gardens of proteas, ericas and other fynbos plants. The stream that runs through the gardens originally provided water for a grain mill lower downstream, hence the name. Adjoining Meulwater are picnic sites with

Paarl's imposing granite domes glisten like pearls after rain.

braai places and ablution facilities for those who want to spend a relaxing day in the reserve.

A network of circular drives takes you to viewpoints along the edge of the mountain, and there are numerous footpaths crisscrossing the reserve (*see* p. 27).

Three dams on the mountain, which were built to supplement the town's drinking water supply, are kept well stocked with trout and black bass, and fishing is allowed, provided you have arranged for the necessary permit in advance (*see* p. 27).

➤ *Beyond Paarl, the mountains of the Limietberg Nature Reserve are traversed by the spectacular Bain's Kloof and Du Toit's Kloof passes. To reach Bain's Kloof, follow Paarl's Main Street, turn right into Optenhorst Street, then left to the R303, which leads to Wellington. From*

Wellington, the route takes in scenic Bain's Kloof Pass, returning via Worcester and Du Toit's Kloof Pass – a 130-km trip from Paarl.

BAIN'S KLOOF AND DU TOIT'S KLOOF DRIVE

One of South Africa's most impressive mountain passes and a national monument, Bain's Kloof is yet another of the renowned road-builder Andrew Geddes Bain's engineering feats. Using gunpowder to clear the way and reinforcing the road with dry-stone walls, 350 convict labourers took four years to complete the pass, which was opened in 1853. Despite these difficulties, Bain managed to retain some of the natural features along the way, such as **Montagu Rocks**, **Bell Rocks** and, perhaps most impressive of all, the massive rock arch known as **Dacres Pulpit**.

From Wellington the Bain's Kloof road snakes up the Hawequas Mountains to a vantage point just below the summit, offering expansive views of the Berg River Valley. However, the most spectacular section of the

pass is the descent from the highest point at **Eerste Tol**. Clinging to the slopes of the Limietberg, the road winds downwards, past the picnic and camp sites at **Tweede Tol**, into the wild valley of the Wit River.

The return route branches off onto the R43 to Worcester, and from there it makes its way through the winelands of the Breede River Valley and past the hot-water springs at Goudini before reaching the

27-km-long Du Toit's Kloof Pass, which was opened in 1949. Enhanced by protea-covered slopes, grey cliffs, secluded valleys and enchanting waterfalls in the winter months, the pass takes its

Harvesting waterblommetjies (Cape hawthorn), used in a traditional Cape stew, at Dal Josafat near Paarl.

The Du Toit's Kloof Pass crosses through some of South Africa's most spectacular scenery.

name from François du Toit, a Huguenot farmer who was granted a farm here in 1692.

Do not be tempted to take the shorter route through the Huguenot Toll Tunnel (opened in 1988); rather follow the windings of the old stone pass to the 820-m-high summit, where you will be amply rewarded with sweeping views of Paarl and the winelands of the Berg River Valley.

➡ *The only entrance road to the Limietberg Nature Reserve is at Tweede Tol near the foot of Bain's Kloof Pass, 25 km from Paarl. For those intent on exploring the reserve on foot, there are numerous entry points along the Bain's Kloof and Du Toit's Kloof passes (see below).*

LIMIETBERG NATURE RESERVE

Towering peaks, kloofs hemmed in by sheer cliffs, dramatic waterfalls and fynbos-covered slopes are only some of the elements of the 117 000-ha Limietberg Nature Reserve. Inhabiting the craggy peaks and mountain

A male Cape rockjumper, a shy bird, with its prey.

slopes are baboon, rock dassie and klipspringer, while the prolific fynbos attracts a wide variety of birds, among which are the Cape rockjumper, Cape sugarbird, sunbirds as well as the protea canary. At **Tweede Tol** day visitors can relax alongside the Wit River, surrounded by the Limietberg and the rugged Slanghoek Mountains. Picnic and camp sites are provided and there are several short walks to scenic spots and to natural pools that are irresistible in summer.

The reserve is criss-crossed by numerous trails, including an overnight hike for the more adventurous (*see below*).

Another notable feature of the Limietberg Nature Reserve is its trout-stocked rivers. The Smalblaar, Elandspad and Molenaars rivers in the Du Toit's Kloof Mountains are regarded as the best rainbow trout waters in the Western Cape, and the Wit River in Bain's Kloof also yields good catches. Certain stretches of these rivers are managed by the Cape Piscatorial Society, so ensure that you obtain their permission (*see* At a Glance) in addition to an entry permit before you fish these waters.

WALKS AND TRAILS

PAARL MOUNTAIN NATURE RESERVE: The **Klipkershout Trail** is an easy, circular ramble of just over 4 km in the southwestern corner of the reserve. The route is named after the rock candlewood, a conspicuous tree species occurring here. Branching off this route is a 1,2-km trail leading to the **Afrikaans Language Monument**, just outside the reserve.

LIMIETBERG NATURE RESERVE: Those wishing to explore the Limietberg Nature Reserve have a choice of eight day walks.

BAIN'S KLOOF SECTION: Starting at Eerste Tol, and featuring an inviting natural pool and three-tier waterfall (at the half-way point), is the **Bobbejaans River Trail**. The walk takes 6 hours to complete and is particularly popular in summer when the disas and giant proteas (*see* box, p. 12) are in bloom.

DU TOIT'S KLOOF SECTION: Equally popular in summer is the **Elands River Trail**, a 7-km round trip starting at the Worcester exit of the Huguenot Tunnel. Also starting here is the 5-km **Krom River Trail** which leads to two spectacular waterfalls and a magnificent pool.

The **Limietberg Hiking Trail** is a challenging 36-km overnight hike which goes from Du Toit's Kloof Pass to Tweede Tol in Bain's Kloof. The first day of the 17-km hike is characterised by several pools along the Wit River, and the second day of the hike leads to the 1 049-m-high Pic Blanc, the highest point along the route.

Streams tumbling down Bain's Kloof feed rivers in the valleys below.

PAARL MOUNTAIN & LIMIETBERG AT A GLANCE

MAIN ATTRACTIONS
Paarl Mountain, spectacular mountain scenery, Bain's Kloof and Du Toit's Kloof Drive, wine route, walks and trails, trout-fishing.

BEST TIMES TO VISIT
The Boland mountains are attractive throughout the year, being snow-capped in winter and colourful during the spring and summer months when the fynbos bursts into full bloom. The mountain streams and inviting pools are especially popular in summer.

PAARL MOUNTAIN NATURE RESERVE
Permits/bookings: Entry permits obtainable at gate; fishing permits in advance from Paarl Municipality, PO Box 12, Paarl 7622; tel. (021) 872-3658.
Opening times: Open daily 07h00–18h30 (1 April to 30 September) and 07h00–19h00 (1 October to 31 March).

LIMIETBERG NATURE RESERVE
Permits/bookings: **Hiking permits:** Contact Cape Nature Conservation (*see* below). **Fishing permits:** Contact Piscatorial Society, tel. (021) 24-7725 or 24-5602.
Opening times: Open daily 07h30–18h00 (but Tweede Tol camp site is closed from May to August).
Accommodation: Tweede Tol: 21 camp sites with hot/cold-water ablutions; book through Cape Nature Conservation (*see* below). Basic hut (sleeping 24 people) on Limietberg Hiking Trail; no fires permitted.

Cape Nature Conservation Booking Office, Private Bag X1, Uniedal 7612; tel. (021) 886-5858 or 886-6543, fax. 886-6575.

TOURIST INFORMATION
Paarl Publicity Association, PO Box 47, Paarl 7622; tel. (021) 872-4842, fax. 872-3841.

5 WEST COAST NATIONAL PARK

The West Coast National Park is a coastal kaleidoscope of lagoon, Strandveld flowers, mudflats, salt marshes, rocky shores and desolate beaches. Known for its spring flowers and large numbers of waders and sea-birds, the park's sheltered lagoon is also a popular watersporting venue.

Covering 27 600 ha, the park comprises the 15-km-long lagoon (which opens into Saldanha Bay), most of the land around the lagoon, Sixteen Mile Beach (from Yzerfontein to Langebaan), and the Malgas, Jutten, Marcus and Schaapen islands.

The park's rich marine life and diverse habitats – ranging from salt marshes (the largest in South Africa) to reedbeds, Strandveld vegetation (*see* p. 29) and rocky shores – attract an astonishing number and variety of **birds**, in fact, some 250 different species.

Sanctuary to over a quarter million birds, the offshore islands offer protection from predators and provide roosting and breeding grounds for several species of sea-bird. Approximately 70 000 Cape gannets (nearly 25% of the world's population) breed on **Malgas Island**, which is also home to the second-largest colony of bank cormorants in South Africa. **Schaapen Island** supports 7,4% of the world's breeding crowned cormorants and the largest colony of southern black-backed gulls. **Marcus Island** has the largest jackass penguin colony in the world, and more than 50% of the world's population of the southern African sub-species of the swift tern breed here. The largest of the four, **Jutten Island**, provides nesting sites for 25 000 Cape cormorant pairs, and the Langebaan/Saldanha Bay area supports 12% of the world's population of African black oystercatchers.

A visit to Malgas Island with its thousands of Cape gannets is not to be missed. Visitors are taken to the island in a double-hull catamaran and can view the birds at close quarters. The lagoon also provides superb **bird-watching** opportunities from strategically

How to get there
The entrance to the West Coast National Park is situated off the West Coast road (R27), some 85 km north of Cape Town (take the N1 from the city centre and turn off at the Paarden Eiland exit, which leads to the R27). There are two entrance gates to the park – one is in the southern section of the park (off the R27) and the other is in the park's northern section (take the signposted route from Langebaan village).

placed secluded hides. Two of these overlook the salt marshes at the southern end of the lagoon, and another, known as the Bottelary hide, is situated alongside the mudflats on the eastern shores. The fourth, Zeeberg's Elizabeth Harding hide, resembles a shipwreck and was built with part of a bequest to the WWF-South Africa for the conservation of birds in the Western Cape.

Birding for waders is most rewarding at low tide when the sand and mudflats are exposed, and among the Palaearctic waders which the birder is likely to see are grey plover, greenshank, curlew sandpiper, little stint and curlew (*see* box, p. 29).

Each year, between April and August, as many as 8 000 greater flamingoes congregate on the lagoon, especially at its southern end where large numbers can usually be observed as they feed.

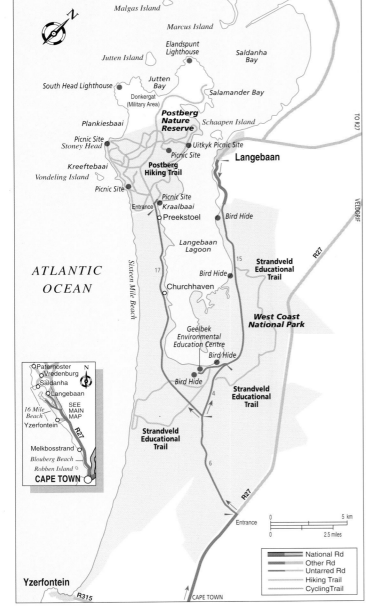

Cape gannets breed on Malgas Island between October and December.

In addition to being a bird-watcher's paradise, the lagoon is also an outstanding **watersporting venue** and has been ecologically zoned into three specific recreational areas. All forms of watersports are allowed in the multipurpose recreational area at the northern end of the lagoon, while the limited recreational area in the central part of the lagoon is out of bounds to engine-propelled boats. All water-related activities are prohibited in the wilderness area at the southern end of the lagoon.

Angling in the lagoon and at Saldanha Bay is another favourite pastime, and the sheltered beaches at Langebaan village and Kraalbaai offer safe swimming, sunbathing and snorkelling.

The park's flora largely consists of **Strandveld vegetation** – dense, low-growing scrub and thickets with peculiar local names such as klipbos, haasboegoe, traanbos and muisbos. Growing amongst these is a rich variety of succulents, bulbs and annuals – gousblomme (gazanias), bok-baaivygies (Livingstone vygies) and witbotterblomme (Cape rain daisy). Some of the bulbs flower soon after the first autumn rains and in winter, whereas the spring annuals are usually at their best between August and September.

➡ *Geelbek Environmental Education Centre lies along the southern shores of the lagoon. To reach Geelbek from the R27 entrance, follow the road for 6 km, then take the fork to the right and continue for a further 4 km; the centre is to the left. Coming from the Langebaan entrance, simply follow the road for about 10 km until you get to the Geelbek turnoff.*

MIGRANT WADERS OF LANGEBAAN LAGOON

Langebaan Lagoon is situated at the southern extremity of the East Atlantic Flyway, along which some 7 million waders migrate to wetlands south of the Arctic circle during the non-breeding season.

In midsummer the lagoon and the sandy beaches along the Atlantic coast support as many as 37 500 waders as well as other water bird species, and consequently this area is regarded by many as the most important wetland for waders in South Africa. Curlew sandpipers constitute approximately 60% of the total number of Palaearctic waders, although knot, grey plover, sanderlings and turnstone are also fairly common. In addition to these species, 11 more Arctic migrants, nine species of resident waders and 20 other water bird species are attracted to the wetlands.

The Palaearctic waders begin arriving at Langebaan in September each year – some of them having flown 15 000 km from the far-off Siberian tundra – and remain at the lagoon until the end of April when they start the long migration north.

Research has shown that the water birds at Langebaan consume about 150 tonnes of marine organisms (such as worms, shrimps and snails) a year, replenishing the system with 44 tonnes of guano.

Sheets of brightly coloured daisies spread out along the shores of Langebaan Lagoon in the West Coast National Park.

SALDANHA BAY

Sheltered by a large rocky promontory, Saldanha Bay has provided safe anchorage since 1601 when the original Portuguese name for Table Bay, *Agoada de Saldanha*, was mistakenly transferred to it.

Saldanha Bay's more recent naval history dates back to World War II when it was used as a convoy staging point and a flotilla of minesweepers was stationed in the harbour. It has a large naval base and gymnasium, known as *SAS Saldanha* since 1956, as well as the Military Academy of the South African National Defence Force.

An 850-ha **nature reserve**, 3 km from the town's centre, has been declared within the 1 800-ha military area. In addition to steenbok, grysbok, common duiker and bat-eared fox, the reserve has been stocked with ostrich, springbok, grey rhebok, mountain reedbuck, bontebok and wildcat as well as birds of prey.

A network of circular day walks, the SAS Saldanha Hiking Trail, traverse the reserve with its interesting geological, archaeological and historical features. The walks follow vehicle tracks and vary from 2 km to 14 km.

Large numbers of greater flamingo gather on the lagoon each year.

Geelbek farmhouse now serves as an Environmental Education Centre.

The small fishing village of Churchhaven is situated on the western shores of the Langebaan Lagoon.

GEELBEK ENVIRONMENTAL EDUCATION CENTRE

Geelbek has a long, interesting history which dates back to 1785 when a slate beacon was erected here to indicate the northern boundary of the Dutch settlement at the Cape. Originally known as Geelbekkefontein, in 1785 this 51-ha loan farm was allocated to Steven Verwey, who used it as a stock post.

The façade of the Cape Dutch farmhouse (which dates back to 1860) was restored as accurately as possible in 1990. The outbuildings and interior were carefully altered to serve as an environmental education centre without sacrificing the old-world atmosphere of the complex.

A variety of environmental education programmes are offered at the centre. During peak holiday season, programmes aimed at introducing visitors to the natural features of the park are offered daily. These 3-hour programmes include an illustrated lecture and a guided field excursion. For those interested in the marine environment, weekend courses in marine ecology are also offered.

➤ *Postberg Nature Reserve is situated on the peninsula, within the West Coast National Park. From the Langebaan entrance follow the road past Geelbek Environmental Education Centre. From here the road to Postberg is clearly signposted and runs along the western shores of the lagoon, passing Schrywershoek and the pretty village of Churchhaven (visit its charming little church). If you're entering the park from the R27 entrance, simply follow the Postberg signs.*

POSTBERG NATURE RESERVE

Postberg is renowned for its spectacular displays of spring flowers, its dramatic rock formations and its breathtaking views of the tranquil lagoon on one side and the ocean on the other. Covering some 1 800 ha, the area was declared a private nature reserve in 1969 and was subsequently incorporated into the West Coast National Park in 1987 as South Africa's first contractual park. In terms of the agreement, the land remains in private ownership, but is managed by the National Parks Board.

The reserve provides a habitat for more than 15 rare and endangered **plant species** and is open only in August and September, when masses of gazanias, daisies, vygies and other spring flowers create a dense floral carpet. Among the animals occurring here are eland, red hartebeest, bontebok, Burchell's zebra, springbok, gemsbok, blue wildebeest and kudu.

Of historical interest are the ruined remains of a stone fort and living quarters at Kraalbaai – the site of one of the oldest fortifications in South Africa. Built in 1669 by the Dutch to defend Saldanha against a possible French attack, the fort also served as a trading post with the Khoikhoi. Its circular shape initially led people to believe it to be the remains of a *kraal*, hence the name of the little bay.

Visitors can explore the nature reserve along several circular routes (25 km in total), and picnic sites and ablution facilities are provided at Tsaarsbank, Plankiesbaai and Uitkyk. Tsaarsbank also has a small shop which sells curios, refreshments, firewood and flower books.

For a unique experience, book your place on one of the Parks Board's **boat trips** leaving from Langebaan village. Once at Postberg you will be taken on a guided tour of the flowers.

WALKS AND TRAILS
GEELBEK ENVIRONMENTAL EDUCATION CENTRE: The **Strandveld Educational Trail** introduces the hiker to typical Strandveld vegetation and its interesting diversity of plants. This easy trail consists of two day hikes from Geelbek. There is accommodation at the Geelbek homestead; the trail fee is inclusive of delicious home-cooked meals. The first day's hike of 14,4 km leads to a granite outcrop and bird hide overlooking the lagoon, and the second day's route of 14 km covers the area southwest of Geelbek, with an optional detour along Sixteen Mile Beach. Typical Strandveld plants and other notable features are marked along the route.

POSTBERG NATURE RESERVE: In August and September visitors can explore the floral wonderland of Postberg by setting off on the **Postberg Flower Trail**, a 2-day circular route of 25 km. The first day's hike winds along the shore of the lagoon and past the Vingerklippe (Finger Rocks) before ascending to the Uitkyk viewpoint with its lagoon vista. It then crosses the peninsula to the overnight stop at Plankiesbaai, where facilities are limited to a camp site and ablution block. The second day's hike follows the rocky Atlantic coastline, with views of Vondeling Island. After a short stretch along Sixteen Mile Beach, it returns to the start.

Cytinus sanguineus spreads its bright colours on barren sands.

WEST COAST NATIONAL PARK AT A GLANCE

MAIN ATTRACTIONS
Internationally recognised wetland, sea-birds, Strandveld vegetation, spring flowers, boat trips, walks and trails, educational programmes, watersports and angling.

BEST TIMES TO VISIT
Bird-watching is best from September to April, while spring flowers are best in August and September.

WEST COAST NATIONAL PARK
Permits/bookings: Entry permits (including to Geelbek and Postberg) at main entrances to park. Book environmental courses, trails and boat trips through The Park Warden, West Coast National Park, PO Box 25, Langebaan 7357; tel. (02287) 2-2144. Note: Postberg Flower Trail bookings open on the first work day in April.
Opening times: Open all year round, from sunset to sunrise; Postberg is open only August and September 09h00–17h00 (last entry permitted at 15h00).
Accommodation: Geelbek: Dormitories with bunk beds. Postberg: Camp site with ablution facilities on Postberg Flower Trail.

Facilities: **Geelbek:** Tearoom serving light meals and refreshments (open daily 08h00–16h00). **Postberg:** Shop at Tsaarbank selling curios, refreshments, firewood and flower books.

SAS SALDANHA NATURE RESERVE
Permits/bookings: Entry and trail permits available at gate.
Opening times: Open year round, except during military activities. To confirm, contact the Officer Commanding SAS Saldanha, tel. (02281) 4-2211.

BLOMBOS FARM
Permits/bookings: For accommodation and trail bookings on Blombos Farm, contact Mrs Wightman, 14 Higgo Crescent, Higgovale, Cape Town 8001; tel. (021) 24-2755.
Accommodation: 1 self-contained bungalow and 1 rustic hut (each sleeping 6). Conveniently located just outside park; 2 circular walking trails; spring flowers.

TOURIST INFORMATION
Langebaan Publicity Association, PO Box 11, Langebaan 7357; tel. (02287) 2-2115, fax. 2-2825.

Finger Rock rises from a carpet of flowers at Postberg Nature Reserve.

6 SOUTHERN CEDARBERG

The challenge of the highest peak in the Cedarberg, Sneeuberg, and the dramatic rock formations of the Wolfberg Cracks and Maltese Cross are among the numerous scenic attractions the southern Cedarberg has to offer. Home to the beautiful snow protea, Sneeuberg rewards the hiker with some of the best views to be found anywhere. And far below, at Matjiesrivier, the Stadsaal Caves bear testimony to the San, earlier inhabitants of this rugged land, in the form of the famous rock paintings.

How to get there
The Cedarberg is situated to the northeast of Citrusdal (169 km north of Cape Town along the N7). Access to the southern Cedarberg is through Algeria, 215 km from Cape Town. From Citrusdal, follow the N7 northwards for 26 km and turn right onto the gravel road to Algeria.

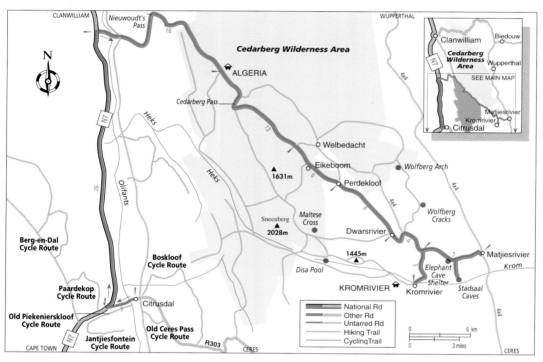

The pass, built in 1969 to replace Uitkyk Pass, was once one of the steepest in South Africa. Continue along this road until you reach Sanddrif (situated on the farm Dwarsrivier), 27 km from Algeria.

SANDDRIF AND THE WOLFBERG CRACKS

Nestled in the fertile valley between Wolfberg and Sneeuberg, Dwarsrivier farm is a convenient base from which to explore one of the Cedarberg's prime attractions – the spectacular Wolfberg Cracks (see p. 34).

The farm's camp site and guest cottages at the nearby Sanddrif, set in exquisite surroundings on the banks of the Driehoek River, are also popular retreats for those seeking the peace and tranquillity of the Cedarberg. The river and its large pool, Maalgat, provide welcome relief during the hot summer months, and visitors often spend hours on end relaxing in the river.

The farm is also known for its excellent wines, which can be sampled (and purchased) at the nearby cellar.

➡ *The turnoff to the Cedarberg Tourist Park (situated on Kromrivier farm) is approximately 3 km beyond Dwarsrivier.*

CEDARBERG TOURIST PARK

Expansive views, inviting river pools, exquisite sunsets, and its proximity to well-known natural features, such as Disa Pool and the Maltese Cross, are some of the reasons why this rest camp on the farm Kromrivier is favoured by so many outdoor enthusiasts.

The cottages at Kromrivier are set in unsurpassed surroundings.

The southern Cedarberg takes in some of the most breathtaking scenery and rock formations in the mountain range. It comprises several farms, as well as the southern block of the 71 000-ha Cedarberg Wilderness Area, which was proclaimed South Africa's third state wilderness area on 27 July 1973.

The bird and animal life is much like that of the northern and central areas, as is the vegetation (see p. 36). Additional features, however, are the dense stands of wagon trees and the rare snow protea (see box, p. 33).

➡ *From Algeria, the gravel road makes its way over the Cedarberg Pass, affording sweeping views of the rugged mountains and the broad valley of the Driehoek River.*

The rock paintings at Elephant Cave, a legacy left by the San people.

Accommodation comprises self-catering cottages (meals are available on request), set in idyllic wilderness surrounds, camp sites and a shady caravan park.

A variety of day walks and overnight hikes can be undertaken from Kromrivier (*see* p. 35), and there are also plenty of opportunities for horse-riding and mountain-biking. The river that runs through the park is a favourite retreat for tired hikers and visitors, and during the hot summer months many pleasant hours can be whiled away in its rejuvenating rock pools.

➡ *If you continue along the road to Ceres, you will reach the signposted turnoff to the Elephant and Stadsaal caves at Matjiesrivier, 4 km beyond the turnoff to the Cedarberg Tourist Park.*

MATJIESRIVIER

The rock paintings and Stadsaal Caves at Matjiesrivier are probably two of the best-known tourist drawcards in the southern Cedarberg. The rock paintings at **Elephant Cave** are easily accessible and can be seen in a shallow overhang of a rocky outcrop, about 1 km from the road. The frieze depicts six elephants and several rows of people, clad in what appear to be karosses. The figures could have been painted at fairly lengthy intervals as one of the elephants has nearly faded. Although elephants may have been inhabitants of the Matjiesrivier area, current archaeological research suggests that rock paintings were executed by *shamans*, or medicine men, and it is generally accepted that the aim of

these paintings, which depicted trance visions and experiences, was to instruct and inspire others.

The impressive **Stadsaal Caves** (meaning 'town hall'), about 1 km further on, at the end of a sandy track, consist of a conglomeration of interlinking caverns and convoluted passages supported by pillars. With time the roof of the caves has been eroded into fascinating shapes and shallow depressions which are filled with water after the winter rains. More rock paintings can be found in the overhangs along a terrace, slightly below and at the back of these caves. Matjiesrivier, a 12 800-ha property, comprising the caves and

eight farms, was acquired by the WWF–South Africa in 1994 (the Rupert family generously donated a substantial amount of money towards the purchase price) and today is managed as a nature reserve by Cape Nature Conservation.

➡ *A four-wheel-drive track runs northwards from Matjiesrivier along the eastern foothills of the Cedarberg range where it reaches the picturesque old Moravian Mission settlement of Wupperthal, approximately 35 km beyond the turnoff (see p. 37).*

SNOW PROTEA

The striking snow protea is endemic to the Cedarberg, occurring only on the very highest mountain summits between Sneeukop (where it was first collected in 1897) and Sneeuberg.

The specific name, *cryophila*, means 'fond of the cold' – an apt description as this species is often covered in snow in winter. Strangely enough, it flowers during the hottest months in the Cedarberg, between January and March, reaching its peak flowering period in February.

This sprawling shrub grows over rocks, forming clumps of about 2 m in diameter and up to 50 cm high. Flowers are borne close to the ground and plants produce no more than four flower-heads each year. The buds resemble white,

'woolly' snowballs, and the blooms, measuring about 16 cm in diameter when fully open, are red and smooth on the inside.

The snow protea grows exceptionally slowly and it has been estimated that new plants only begin flowering after about ten years.

The snow protea, endemic to the Cedarberg, in open bloom.

The Stadsaal Caves, sculpted by the erosive power of water and wind over countless millenia.

WALKS AND TRAILS

The southern Cedarberg's walks and trails present nature lovers and hikers with endless opportunities, ranging from easy rambles to demanding hikes up the high mountain peaks.

EIKEBOOM: One of the numerous access points to the southern section of the wilderness area is Eikeboom, one of the most popular starting points. From Eikeboom follow a jeep track up Sederhoutkloof to the Sneeuberg huts, conveniently situated for hikes to the **Maltese Cross** and **Sneeuberg**, at 2 026,8 m, the Cedarberg's highest peak.

From the track linking the Maltese Cross and Sneeuberg huts an ascent of Sneeuberg involves a steep climb (over 600 m is gained in altitude), followed by a short rock scramble to the summit. Those who persist will be more than amply rewarded as the view from the top of Sneeuberg must rank as one of the best in the country – you can see Cedarberg's Tafelberg to the northeast, and, if it is a clear day, even the outline of Table Mountain, 150 km away. The snow proteas (*see* box, p. 33) are at their best from January to March, so endeavour to plan your hike accordingly.

From the Sneeuberg huts hikers can either return along the jeep track to Eikeboom or hike along Noordepoort and past the rugged **Duiwelsgat** to the Cedarberg Pass.

Alternative access points into the wilderness area include Uitkyk Pass, Dwarsrivier and Kromrivier at the southern end of the wilderness area, and Boskloof on the western slopes of the range.

SANDDRIF (DWARSRIVIER FARM): The **Wolfberg Cracks** are undoubtedly one of the most spectacular features in the Cedarberg. From Sanddrif it involves a rather steep climb, during which about 400 m is gained in altitude. Just before you enter the main crack, stop to enjoy the sweeping views of the wide valley far below, framed by two sheer rock faces. To gain access to the main crack, which is about 30 m deep, you have to crawl along a narrow passage. Further along, you pass two impressive rock arches, and shortly before the end of the main crack you have to negotiate a number of obstacles. One of these, a huge boulder wedged between the walls of the cracks just above the ground, can only be negotiated by sliding underneath it. The return leg of the route is along the first crack and the round trip takes 4 to 5 hours.

From the top of the Wolfberg Cracks it is a 75-minute walk to the Wolfberg Arch, but since it lies within the wilderness area, you must obtain the necessary permit in advance. An alternative return route is to descend along Gabriel's Pass and to follow the jeep track back to Sanddrif.

Another option from Dwarsrivier is a day hike to the **Maltese Cross** in the wilderness area, provided you have the necessary permit. The hike from the car-park at the head of the

The 20-m-high Maltese Cross is one of the Cedarberg's best-known landmarks.

Dwarsrivier Valley takes about 90 minutes and the gigantic rock formation comes into view quite unexpectedly. With Sneeuberg as a backdrop, the isolated column of rock towers about 20 m above a small plain.

CEDARBERG TOURIST PARK (KROMRIVIER FARM): A highly recommended hike from Kromrivier farm is the 12-km route along the river to Kromrivier Cave and **Disa Pool**, where masses of *Disa tripetaloides* create a spectacular display in December.

Another option is to hike to the **Maltese Cross** via Sugarloaf Peak and then traverse the southern slopes of The Pup. It is advisable to set aside a full day for this walk, as it is quite demanding and takes more or less 5 hours one way.

Those looking for something less demanding could take the walk from Kromrivier to the Stadsaal Caves at Matjiesrivier (*see* p. 33).

MOUNTAIN BIKE TRAILS
At the initiative of the Goede Hoop Citrus Co-operative at Citrusdal, several mountain-bike trails have been laid out following the western slopes of the Cedarberg and in the mountains to the west of Citrusdal.

The Cedarberg is well known for its dramatic, even surrealistic, rock formations.

Trails vary from relaxing and easy 2-hour rides through orchards and farmlands to more challenging routes along the old Ceres and Piekenierskloof passes. There are also demanding technical sections for experienced riders.

Visitors at Sanddrif (Dwarsrivier farm) and the Cedarberg Tourist Park (Kromrivier farm) can also go for rides along several roads and jeep tracks in the area.

Travel by donkey cart is still a familiar sight in the Cedarberg.

SOUTHERN CEDARBERG AT A GLANCE

MAIN ATTRACTIONS
Spectacular rock formations, notably Maltese Cross and Wolfberg Cracks, breathtaking mountain scenery, rare and endemic flora, gentle day walks and challenging overnight hikes, San rock paintings, Stadsaal Caves and mountain-bike trails.

BEST TIMES TO VISIT
In winter the high peaks are often snow-capped; the fynbos is at its best in spring and summer. March to April and October to November are generally good months for extended hikes.

CEDARBERG WILDERNESS AREA
Permits/bookings: Trail permits are required; book through Cape Nature Conservation, Citrusdal District Office, Private Bag X1, Citrusdal 7340; tel. (022) 921-2289, fax. 921-3219. Reservations for March to June open on 1 February; for July to October on 1 June and for November to February on 1 October.
Opening times: Throughout the year 08h00–16h30.

Accommodation: 2 basic huts at Sneeuberg; first-come, first-served basis.

SANDDRIF (DWARSRIVIER)
Permits/bookings: Permits for trails to Wolfberg Cracks, and to pass over Dwarsrivier to Wolfberg Arch and Maltese Cross, available at Dwarsrivier.
Accommodation: Camp sites with hot/cold ablutions and 10 self-contained cottages. Book through Messrs Nieuwoudt, Dwarsrivier, PO Cedarberg 7341; tel. (027) 482-2825.

CEDARBERG TOURIST PARK (KROMRIVIER)
Accommodation: 12 self-catering cottages, caravan/camp sites with hot/cold-water ablutions; meals on request. Bookings to be made through Mrs O Nieuwoudt, PO Box 284, Clanwilliam 8135; tel. (027) 482-2807.

TOURIST INFORMATION
For more information about accommodation, attractions and mountain-bike trails, contact **Citrusdal Tourism Office,** PO Box 140, Citrusdal 7340; tel. (022) 921-2181, fax. 921-2186 or 921-3219.

7 NORTHERN & CENTRAL CEDARBERG

The northern and central Cedarberg is a region of rugged mountain peaks and crags, gnarled cedars and fascinating rock formations. These characteristics justifiably make it one of the most popular wilderness areas in the Western Cape. East of the mountain range lie the secluded Biedouw Valley, famous for its spectacular display of spring flowers, and the picturesque, historic Moravian mission village of Wupperthal.

How to get there
Clanwilliam, 223 km north of Cape Town on the N7, is the centre of the rooibos tea industry and gateway to the northern Cedarberg, Wupperthal and the Biedouw Valley. The main access point to the central Cedarberg is Algeria, which can be reached by turning off the N7 about 26 km north of Citrusdal, and continuing along this road for 17 km to the forest station.

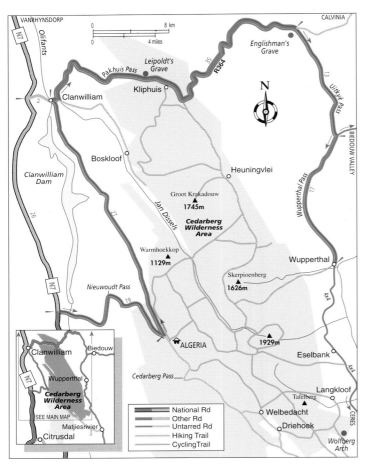

Vegetation in the Cedarberg consists largely of mountain fynbos – proteas, golden and brown Cape reeds, and ericas in shades of white and rosy pink to yellow. In late summer masses of red disas can be seen in full bloom along the clear mountain streams. Several endemic fynbos species, some of them critically rare, also occur in these mountains. Among these is the striking rocket pincushion (*Leucospermum reflexum*) with its masses of crimson-red flowers, and restricted to the Heuningvlei area in the north.

Two plants of commercial importance which are found in abundance in the Cedarberg are rooibos tea (*Aspalathus linearis*) and buchu (*Agathosma butulina*).

Mammals most likely to be seen are klipspringer, grey rhebok, baboon and rock dassie, while common duiker and grysbok are less prevalent. The Cedarberg is also one of the last leopard strongholds in the Western Cape, and was declared a leopard conservation area in 1988 – the first conservancy of its kind in the Cape.

Birdlife includes the magnificent black eagle, rock kestrel, Cape rockjumper, cinnamon-breasted warbler, Cape sugarbird and protea canary.

➡ *To get to the Pakhuis Pass from Clanwilliam, take the R364 – the same road will eventually lead you to the Biedouw Valley and Wupperthal (see p. 37).*

PAKHUIS PASS
Sculptured sandstone formations consisting of rock columns, pillars and clusters of boulders lie scattered along the Pakhuis Pass. Built in the 1870s to link

Clanwilliam and Calvinia, the pass is yet another monument to the well-known road-builder Thomas Bain.

Aproximately 15 km east of Clanwilliam the road passes an overhang with faded rock paintings of human figures, an elephant, and a plaque marking the final resting place of the ashes of **C. Louis Leipoldt**, celebrated Afrikaans poet, author and physician. Leipoldt found great inspiration and solitude in these mountains, and it was his wish that he be laid to rest here, surrounded by the mountains he so dearly loved.

A few kilometres further along you will reach the **Kliphuis camp site** (17 km from town). The camp site is the starting point of several hiking trails into the wilderness area (*see p. 38*).

From here, the pass makes a wide loop around three peaks – Faith, Hope and Charity – and about 43 km from Clanwilliam reaches the **Englishman's Grave**, a reminder of the Anglo-Boer War. The lonely grave marks the spot where 21-year-old Lieutenant Graham Clowes of the 6th Mounted Infantry was shot and killed in a skirmish with Boer forces on 30 January 1901.

➡ *The junction with the Biedouw Valley/Wupperthal road is just beyond the Englishman's Grave, and the turnoff to the Biedouw Valley just over 14 km further on (approximately 40 km from Clanwilliam).*

➡ *A slightly longer, but interesting, alternative route to the northern Cedarberg is to take the Algeria turnoff (26 km north of Citrusdal) and turn left onto the Ou Kaapse Weg just after crossing the Olifants River. The road follows the course of the river, and, further north, runs along the shores of the Clanwilliam Dam, a popular watersporting venue. Just before it reaches Clanwilliam, the road passes the Ramskop Nature Reserve (which incorporates the Clanwilliam Wild Flower Garden), renowned for its lovely spring flowers. From Clanwilliam, the route ascends the Pakhuis Pass,* which provides access to the northern Cedarberg, Wupperthal and the Biedouw Valley (see p. 37).

Dominating the scenery of the northern Cedarberg are the three Krakadouw peaks – Krakadouw (1 745 m) in the south, Middle Krakadouw (1 650 m), and Klein Krakadouw (1 621 m) – overlooking the Jan Dissels River valley. The central Cedarberg, on the other hand, boasts well-known features such as the 1 969-m-high Tafelberg, the second-highest peak in the range, and the spectacular 30-m-high Wolfberg Arch.

The Pakhuis Pass makes its way through rugged country of mountain peaks, crags and fascinating rock formations.

BIEDOUW VALLEY

This secluded valley, carved by the Biedouw River and cradled by the Tra-Tra Mountains in the south and the Biedouw Mountains to the north, lies to the east of the Cedarberg. The valley is especially attractive in spring when masses of flowers paint the usually drab veld with a dazzling mix of colours – white, orange, blue and purple. Dominating the perennial vegetation is a variety of vygies, and a rich diversity of annuals – nemesias, gazanias, mauve senecios, golden ursinias and blue heliophilas – also occurs here.

➤ *South of the turnoff to the Biedouw Valley, the road continues over the Wupperthal Pass, after which it reaches the quaint settlement of Wupperthal in the fertile Tra-Tra Valley, approximately 73 km from Clanwilliam.*

WUPPERTHAL

The green valley and the quaint village of cottages with their white-washed walls and thatched roofs contrast sharply with the arid and rocky eastern slopes of the Cedarberg. Established in 1830 by the Rhenish Mission Society, the settlement was named after the Wupper Valley in the German town of Elberfeld, where the mission society was founded. The thatch-roof church with its elegant Cape Dutch gable dates back to 1835 and is

A gnarled cedar tree stands in bold relief against a sunset sky.

CEDAR TREE

These silvery-white skeletons, which seemingly grow out of the rocks in the Cedarberg, are a mute testimony to the devastating fires which have alarmingly reduced the numbers of the Clanwilliam cedar tree. During the 1700s and 1800s gross exploitation by man also took its toll – in 1879, for instance, more than 7 000 trees were hacked down in order to provide telegraph poles between Piketberg and Calvinia.

Endemic to the Cedarberg, the Clanwilliam cedar tree (*Widdringtonia cedarbergensis*) is related to the cypress family and not to the Lebanon cedars, as is commonly believed. Occurring in patches from the Pakhuis Pass in the north to the Maltese Cross in the south, it grows at altitudes of between 1 000 m and 1 400 m above sea level, favouring rocky outcrops, crags and boulder-strewn slopes which are often covered in snow in winter.

With their gnarled trunks and twisted branches, these majestic trees reach heights of 5 m to 7 m, although those growing in protected places may reach 20 m. They grow extremely slowly and some of the enormous specimens that once covered the mountain slopes could have been almost 400 years old.

In an effort to save the cedar tree from extinction, a cedar reserve was proclaimed in 1987, and about 8 000 one-year-old trees are planted annually with the objective of re-establishing this species in the Cedarberg. Covering some 5 250 ha, the reserve is on average about 2 km wide and stretches over a distance of 21 km from just north of Skerpioensberg to Gabriel's Pass in the south.

DORING RIVER WHITE-WATER RAFTING

The Doring River, a tributary of the Olifants River, offers one of the most exhilarating white-water rafting experiences in South Africa.

Along its meandering course through the spectacular Swartruggens and the northern foothills of the Cedarberg, the river rushes through several gorges, creating ideal conditions for white-water rafting. The trip covers 30 km and, as it features both Grade 3 and Grade 4 rapids,

is not to be undertaken by the faint-hearted. However, no previous experience is needed and a safety briefing before departure will put participants in the know about paddling and river-running techniques.

There are no fewer than 32 rock paintings which can be viewed along the 'quieter' sections of the river, and, if you're lucky, you may even catch a glimpse of the magnificent African fish eagle.

Negotiating one of the exciting rapids on the Doring River.

still the focal point of the village. Although Wupperthal itself is perhaps best known for its popular *velskoene*, handmade here since 1836, its fertile valley also yields good harvests of maize, wheat and tobacco.

➡ *Wupperthal is the end of the road for sedan vehicles, but 4x4 vehicles can continue along the steep pass between Middelkop and Singkop. A rough track winds south for 35 km, passing several satellite settlements of Wupperthal, and joins the provincial road to Ceres at Matjiesrivier, providing convenient access to the southern Cedarberg (see p. 33; these routes can be treated as a circular drive, provided you have a 4x4 vehicle).*

WALKS AND TRAILS

The Cedarberg has long been one of South Africa's premier backpacking and mountaineering areas. Numerous trails criss-cross the range, providing access to the high mountain peaks, grotesquely shaped sandstone rocks and scenic spots. Trails vary from day rambles to overnight hikes and

weekend trails to week-long backpacking trips – the only limit being the amount of time trailists have at their disposal.

NORTHERN CEDARBERG: Although there are fewer footpaths in the northern Cedarberg than there are in the more popular central and southern zones of the range, the wild scenery and sheer remoteness of the area make hiking here a truly unforgettable experience.

From the **Kliphuis** camp site on the Pakhuis Pass hikers can follow Amon se Kloof to their first overnight stop, a cave near the foot of Krakadouw Pass. The trail continues up the spectacular Krakadouwpoort to **Heuning-vlei**, an ideal base for a day hike to Groot Krakadouw with its confusing jumble of boulders and labyrinth of narrow passages. The sheer eastern faces of the Krakadouws have presented an exciting challenge to rock climbers ever since the first frontal route was opened in 1936. The return leg of the route to the Pakhuis Pass is a relatively easy 12-km hike along a jeep track.

Wolfberg Arch, one of the many fascinating formations carved by wind and water into the sandstone rocks of the Cedarberg.

Wupperthal was the first Rhenish mission farm in South Africa.

Hikers rest on the banks of the Rondegat River at Algeria.

CENTRAL CEDARBERG: The main access point to the central Cedarberg is **Algeria**, on the banks of the Rondegat River. A popular weekend route winds up Helsekloof ('hellish ravine') with its impressive waterfall to **Middelberg** and then passes the crenallated spires of Cathedral Rocks. After crossing the Grootlandsvlakte, the trail ascends Groot and Klein Hartseer ('great and small heartache') to reach the delightful **Crystal Pool**, cradled in a rocky amphitheatre.

A magnificent scenic return route to Algeria winds up Engelsmanskloof ('Englishman's ravine') to Die Trap ('the step') and Sleeppad Hut. From the hut there is an expansive view of the Driehoek River Valley, sandwiched between Sneeuberg and Tafelberg. The diverse route then drops steeply down to the Grootlandsvlakte below.

An ideal weekend hike from Algeria is the 20-km **Machine Gun Ridge Circuit**. On the first day you hike 5 km to Middelberg, and on the second day you follow a wide loop around the curiously named Machine Gun Ridge.

Among other destinations are the 1 969-m-high **Tafelberg**, the second-highest peak in the range, and the **Wolfberg Arch**, an impressive 30-m-high rock arch overlooking the Tankwa Karoo and the Bokkeveld Mountains. Convenient starting points to these well-known landmarks are Driehoek and Welbedacht, the latter situated only a 2 hours' walk from Welbedacht Cave, where hikers can spend the night.

Trailists survey their surrounds from the top of Tafelberg.

NORTHERN & CENTRAL CEDARBERG AT A GLANCE

MAIN ATTRACTIONS
Spectacular rock formations, mountain scenery, endemic flora, day and overnight hikes, scenic sedan and 4x4 routes, spring flowers and white-water rafting.

BEST TIMES TO VISIT
Backpacking is rewarding all year round since each season has its own attractions. March/ April and October/ November are generally good months for extended hikes. White-water rafting is best between June and August. The flower season is between the end of July and early September.

CEDARBERG WILDERNESS AREA
Permits/bookings: Permits for trails required; contact Cape Nature Conservation (*see* below). Reservations for March to June open 1 February; for July to October, 1 June; and for November to February, 1 October.
Opening times: Throughout the year 08h00–16h30.
Accommodation: Kliphuis: 10 camp sites and farmhouse (sleeping 10; no bedding) on Pakhuis Pass. **Algeria Forest Station:** 45 caravan/ camp sites with hot/cold-water ablutions. **Uitkyk:** 2 self-contained farmhouses (sleeping 7 and 14), 5 km south of Algeria. Basic mountain huts at Boontjieskloof, Middelberg, Crystal Pool and Sleepad; on a first-come, first-served basis. Contact the Cape Nature Conservation Booking Office (*see* below).

BIEDOUW VALLEY
Permits/bookings: Can be obtained from Welbedacht farm (*see* below).
Accommodation: 2 fully-equipped, self-catering cottages (sleeping 4 and 6) at **Welbedacht farm,** PO Box 225, Clanwilliam 8135; tel. (027) 482-2832.

DORING RIVER WHITE-WATER RAFTING
Operating times: From June to August.
Operators: Felix Unite River Adventures, PO Box 96, Kenilworth 7745; tel. (021) 762-6935, fax. 761-9259. River Rafters, PO Box 14, Diep River 7856; tel. (021) 72-5094, fax. 72-5241. Which Way Adventures, PO Box 2600, Somerset West 7129, tel. (024) 852-2364, fax. 852-1584.

Cape Nature Conservation Booking Office, Citrusdal District Office, Private Bag X1, Citrusdal 7340; tel. (022) 921-2289, fax. 921-3219.

TOURIST INFORMATION Clanwilliam Tourism Association, PO Box 5, Clanwilliam 8135; tel. (027) 482-2024, fax. 482-2361.

8 DE HOOP NATURE RESERVE

De Hoop Nature Reserve lies along the southwestern Cape coast and is characterised by a rich diversity of habitats, ranging from vlei and coastal limestone plains to shifting sand-dunes and sandy beaches interspersed with rocky coves. A sanctuary to over 50 endemic plant and several rare and endangered bird species, the nature reserve also encompasses De Hoop Vlei, which is a wetland of international importance.

How to get there

De Hoop is situated about 245 km southeast of Cape Town. Follow the N2 to Caledon, take the R316 to Bredasdorp, then follow the R319 towards Swellendam for a few kilometres until you reach a fork. Turn right and after 56 km on dirt road from Bredasdorp you will reach De Hoop. Alternatively, take the Wydgeleë/Ouplaas turn-off on the N2, just west of Swellendam. If you are coming from the direction of Mossel Bay, take the Malgas/Infanta road just east of Swellendam, which will lead you to De Hoop via the Breede River pont (*see* p. 43).

Sunset on De Hoop Vlei, a 14-km wetland which offers excellent birdwatching opportunities.

➡ *There are two entry points to De Hoop Nature Reserve, one leading to the De Hoop section of the reserve and the other to Potberg (see p. 42). The turnoff to the De Hoop section is just west of Wydgeleë/Ouplaas, from where it is about 7 km along a gravel road to the main entrance gate.*

DE HOOP

One of the reserve's main attractions is the 14-km-long vlei, which affords fantastic **bird-watching** opportunities. The largest southernmost body of brackish water in Africa, the vlei is an important waterfowl

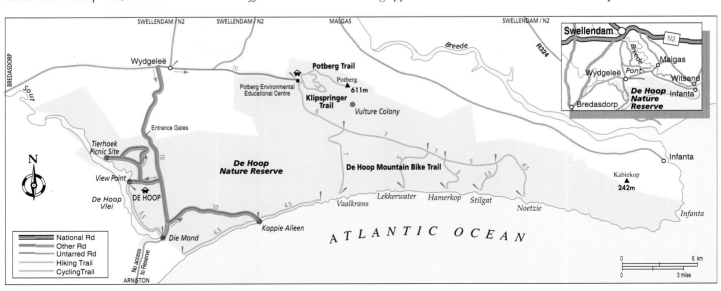

habitat, supporting 12 of the 16 species occurring in South Africa. Although bird populations fluctuate, depending on the water level of the vlei, up to 24 000 redknobbed coot and thousands of yellowbilled duck, Cape shoveller and Egyptian goose are known to congregate here.

During the summer months bird numbers swell with the arrival of large numbers of Palaearctic waders. At least 13 species have already been recorded, among them ringed plover, wood sandpiper, greenshank, curlew sandpiper and little stint.

Owing to De Hoop's diverse habitats, a total of 259 species of bird are found here, including the Cape vulture, black oystercatcher and Damara tern.

As impressive is the reserve's rich **flora** – at least 50 of the 1 500 plant species growing here occur nowhere else in the world. A number of these endemic species occur only on Potberg (*see* p. 42) and along the limestone coastal plains and hills stretching from Cape Agulhas eastwards to Potberg. Limestone

endemics of the area include the Bredasdorp sugarbush *(Protea obtusifolia)*, stinkleaf sugarbush *(Protea susannae), Stoebe muirii* and *Erica uysii*, with its light to dark pink flowers.

Game is well represented and, among others, a large bontebok population, as well as Cape mountain zebra, eland, mountain reedbuck, grey rhebok, springbok, grysbok, common duiker and steenbok are found here. Also be on the lookout for smaller mammals such as baboon, small grey mongoose, caracal and Cape fox. Along the vlei there is a possibility of chancing upon the Cape clawless otter and the water mongoose. You're almost guaranteed to see some game along the short circular drive that leads from De Hoop Rest Camp to Tierhoek.

The spectacular **coastline,** extending over about 40 km, is another notable feature. Shifting sand-dunes to the west of Koppie Alleen cover an area of about 1 000 ha, some reaching heights of up to 90 m above sea level. East of Koppie Alleen the sandy

Black oystercatchers feed on molluscs and crustaceae.

Cottages used for environmental courses at Koppie Alleen, De Hoop.

Game is plentiful in the De Hoop Nature Reserve. Among others, Cape mountain zebra (Equus zebra zebra) *can be seen.*

A southern right whale and calf along the De Hoop coastline.

THE SOUTHERN RIGHT WHALE

Each year, between April and January, hundreds of southern right whales migrate from their Arctic feeding grounds to the coast off the southwestern Cape to mate and calve. Research by Dr Peter Best, a well-known authority on whales, has shown that 72% of cow and calf pairs occur between Arniston (southwest of De Hoop) and Puntjie (east of Cape Infanta), making this stretch of coast one of the most important calving areas in the world.

It is therefore not surprising that De Hoop provides some of the best opportunities for whale-watching in the southwestern Cape. The coast east of Koppie Alleen offers several good vantage points, one of which has appropriately been named Whalewatch Point. These magnificent mammals can often be seen very close to the shore, particularly during peak calving season in August – in fact, up to 50 whales have been spotted in a single day along the De Hoop coastline.

Once endangered because they were considered the 'right' whales to hunt (they have a very high oil yield and their bodies float when harpooned), the population of southern right whales in southern African waters is now estimated at about 5 000, with an average increase of 7% a year.

beaches and rocky coves are dominated by weathered limestone cliffs. Extending 5 km out to sea is De Hoop's 23 000-ha **marine reserve**, whose rocky tidal pools provide hours of pleasure for both snorkellers and swimmers. Bathing is inadvisable elsewhere because of strong currents, and fishing is prohibited.

Visitors are well catered for: apart from the picnic sites at Tierhoek, there is a conservation office as well as picnic spots, camp sites, cottages and mountain-bike tracks at De Hoop.

➡ *The parking area at the Potberg Environmental Education Centre is approximately 10 km to the east of Wydgeleë/Ouplaas.*

POTBERG

Potberg, in the northeastern corner of the reserve, offers sanctuary to the only **Cape vulture** breeding colony in the southwestern Cape. Their population declined dramatically from over 40 breeding pairs in 1970 to less than 20 pairs in 1982, but, thanks to concerted efforts, numbers are slowly increasing, with the total population now standing at 75 – including 22 breeding pairs. The breeding sites, however, are not open to the public.

A botanist's delight, Potberg boasts no less than 12 endemic **plant species**, the most notable among them being *Protea denticulata*, a small ground protea with beautiful red flowers, and Potberg's subspecies of the long-bud sugarbush (*Protea aurea* subsp. *potbergensis*). Among other Potberg endemics are two *Roella* species, *Polygala pottebergensis* and *Adenandra gummifera*.

One of many inviting rock pools which offer safe and exciting snorkelling at De Hoop.

Cyclists rest on the cliff at Vaalkrans while on the mountain-bike trail at De Hoop.

The beautiful farm buildings at Potberg were restored in 1982 to serve as an environmental education centre, aimed primarily at educational institutions and environmentally oriented groups.

Although motor vehicles are not permitted beyond the parking area at Potberg, there are walking trails and an extensive network of cycling routes along which to explore the reserve (*see* below).

➡ *An alternative approach to De Hoop Nature Reserve or return route to Swellendam is via Malgas and the Breede River Pont. The signposted turnoff to Malgas is 4,6 km east of the turnoff to De Hoop; the pont is another 14 km further on.*

Breede River Pont

Between 1757 and 1894 several ponts were used to ferry goods, people and livestock across the Breede River. The pont at Malgas, the only one remaining in South Africa, came into operation in September 1830. Built from wood, it became waterlogged after plying the river for several years and was replaced with a steel pont which was swept away when the river came down in flood in 1906. The existing one, also made of steel, has been in use since 1914.

A novel form of transport, the pont is 'powered' by two attendants who harnass themselves to a cable and physically haul the pont across by walking forward. The only link south of Swellendam across the Breede River, the pont's maximum load is 10 tonnes.

Walks and Trails
De Hoop: The 5,5-km **Vlei Trail** along the eastern shores of the vlei to Die Mond offers excellent birding opportunities. Also worthwhile exploring is the spectacular coastline east of Koppie Alleen.
Potberg: The 8-km **Potberg Trail**, which climbs to the summit of the mountain, rewards the hiker with far-reaching views of the meandering Breede River, De Hoop Vlei and the coastal dunes. Covering 5,5 km, the **Klipspringer Trail** leads past a cave decorated with San rock paintings and with a viewpoint overlooking Vulture Kloof.

Mountain-Bike Trails
Potberg: A prime attraction and an excellent way of exploring the reserve, **De Hoop's Mountain Bike Trail** is the first overnight biking trail established by Cape Nature Conservation. Cyclists leave their vehicles at the parking area at Potberg Environmental

Centre, from where they set off on the 12-km ride to the base camp at Cupidoskraal, carrying all their provisions, clothing and bedding. Starting at the base camp are five routes to scenic

spots along the coast, ranging from 6 km to 13 km (one way). The trail requires a fair level of fitness and experience as there are several tricky sections along most of the routes.

De Hoop Nature Reserve at a Glance

Main attractions
Internationally significant wetland, Cape vulture breeding colony, endemic flora, whale-watching, day walks and mountain-bike trails.

Best times to visit
Birding is best between September and April, and whale-watching between July and October. Spring and early summer are the best seasons for flowers.

Permits/Bookings
Entry permits are obtainable at the gate.
Cottages, camp sites and mountain-bike trail: To book, contact The Manager, De Hoop Nature Reserve, Private Bag X16, Bredasdorp 7280; tel. (028) 542-1126, fax. 542-1679.
Potberg Environmental Education Centre: Contact The Officer-in-Charge,

Private Bag X18, Wydgeleë 7282; tel. (028) 542-1114, fax. 542-1317.

Opening times
Open daily 07h00–18h00 throughout the year.

Accommodation
De Hoop: 10 self-catering cottages (for 4) and 7 camp sites with hot/cold water. Cupidoskraal: 1 self-catering cottage for 12. **Potberg Environmental Education Centre:** 2 dormitories (for 60 people) with hot/cold-water ablution facilities.

Tourist Information
Suidpunt Publicity Association, PO Box 51, Bredasdorp 7280; tel. (028) 414-2584, fax. 415-1019, or **Cape Overberg Tourism Association,** PO Box 250, Caledon 7230; tel/fax. (028) 12-2090.

9 THE LANGEBERG MOUNTAINS

Stretching for 400 km from the Hex River Mountains to the Outeniqua Mountains is the Langeberg range. Its highest peak, Misty Point, towers 1 712 m above the wheatfields on the undulating coastal plains. Traversed by the Tradouw and Garcia's passes, the Langeberg is graced with important conservation areas – the Marloth and Grootvadersbosch nature reserves, Boosmansbos Wilderness Area and the Bontebok National Park.

How to get there
The quaint, historic town of Swellendam (the third oldest in the country) lies approximately 216 km east of Cape Town along the N2 and is a convenient base from which to explore the area.

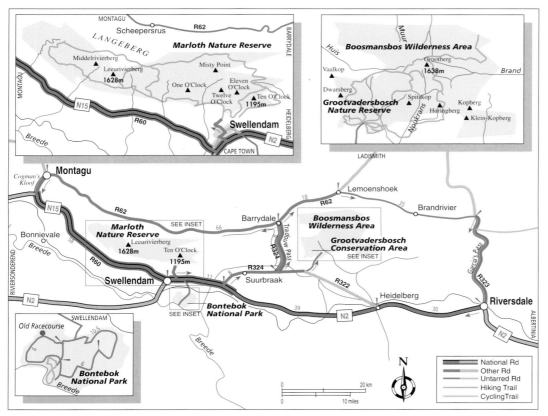

The Marloth Nature Reserve with fynbos in the foreground and the Langeberg in the background.

Although the **fynbos** vegetation of the Langeberg is not as diverse as that of the Boland mountains, over 25 erica species occur here, and in spring masses of pink ericas cover the southern slopes. At least 29 members of the protea family also grow in the Langeberg, including the rare white variation of the king protea (*Protea cynaroides*). During the summer months, those venturing into the mountains will be amply rewarded by the sight of these magnificent flowers in bloom.

Mammals inhabiting this area include rock dassie, baboon, grey rhebok, klipspringer and grysbok, while leopard and caracal are the largest predators.

Bird species likely to be seen or heard include black eagle, red-wing francolin, jackal buzzard, Cape rockjumper, Cape sugarbird, grassbird and malachite, orangebreasted, black and greater doublecollared sunbirds.

➡ *The Marloth Nature Reserve lies 2 km north of Swellendam, along a gravel road. The reserve is well signposted from the main street.*

MARLOTH NATURE RESERVE
Named after the world-renowned amateur botanist Dr Rudolph Marloth, this 11 269-ha reserve is dominated by fynbos, although patches of indigenous forest grace the kloofs on the southern slopes. Trees that are characteristic of these forests include Outeniqua and real yellowwoods, red alder, candlewood, Cape gardenia and wild peach.

The reserve's four noted peaks are the Ten O'Clock (1 195 m), Eleven O'Clock (1 399 m), Twelve O'Clock (1 428 m) and One O'Clock (1 375 m) peaks.

These owe their interesting names to the fact that the early Dutch settlers used them as natural clocks, determining the time by the position of their shadows.

Hermitage Kloof, a pleasant picnic place on the banks of the Klip River, caters for day visitors, and for hikers there are a number of trails of varying difficulty from which to choose (see p. 48).

➡ *Boosmansbos and the adjacent Grootvadersbosch are popular outdoor recreation areas about 37 km from Swellendam. To get to Grootvadersbosch (which serves as the entrance to Boosmansbos), follow the N2 eastwards, branch off onto the R324 to Suurbraak (a quaint village established as a mission station in 1812), then continue along this road to the Grootvadersbosch Nature Reserve turnoff (not to be confused with the Grootvadersbosch Homestead turnoff). The last 10 km is on gravel road.*

GROOTVADERSBOSCH NATURE RESERVE

In the southwestern corner of Boosmansbos is the 250-ha Grootvadersbosch Nature Reserve. This is the most extensive **indigenous forest** west of Mossel Bay. Large ironwoods, Outeniqua and real yellowwoods, stinkwoods, wild peach and assegai are among the 35 typical forest trees growing in the reserve. Also occurring here is the Cape chestnut with its attractive lilac flowers, a species which was first described and recorded by the Swedish botanist Charl Thunberg when he visited the forest in 1772.

Approximately a quarter of Grootvadersbosch's 196 **bird species** are forest birds, and among those likely to be of interest to birders are the martial eagle, forest buzzard and Knysna woodpecker, as well as Knysna and Victorin's warblers. A number of bird species reach the western limits of their distribution in Grootvadersbosch, notably the rednecked francolin, the Narina trogon and bluemantled flycatcher. Birders can while away many pleasant hours at the delightful canopy-level bird hide in the forest, about 500 m from the camp site.

Martial eagles (above left) are just one of the many bird species found in the Grootvadersbosch Nature Reserve (above right).

BONTEBOK NATIONAL PARK

Covering 3 000 ha, this park is regarded as one of the greatest success stories in conservation. Proclaimed in 1961 to protect the bontebok, a species that was on the brink of extinction earlier this century as a result of reckless hunting practices in the 1800s, it now boasts a thriving 200-strong herd of these magnificent antelope.

Interestingly enough, it was only after the original park, which was proclaimed in 1931 in the Bredasdorp area, proved to be unsuitable because of poor grazing and internal parasites, that the present park was established. In addition to bontebok, there are grey rhebok, red hartebeest, grysbok, steenbok, Cape mountain zebra and common duiker. Birdlife is prolific, and the 192 bird species include Stanley's bustard, fish eagle, blue crane, secretary birds, spur-winged geese and many sunbirds.

The vegetation in the park consists largely of low-growing shrub, characterised by conebushes, for example *Leucadendron salignum*, and renosterbush (*Elytropappus rhinocerotis*). Among its 470 or more plant species there are real sugarbush (*Protea repens*), two pincushion species – the common pincushion (*Leucospermum cuneiforme*) and *Leucospermum calligerum* – and a variety of ericas, pelargoniums, restios and geophytes. In winter the striking red blooms of the bitter aloes (*Aloe ferox*) growing on the appropriately named Aloe Hill provide a blaze of colour. Breede River yellowwood, sweet thorn and wild olive trees line the river's banks.

The park's road network extends over 25 km. Two 2-km walks have been laid out near the rest camp – the Aloe Hill Trail and the Acacia Walk.

Visitors may stay overnight at the pleasant rest camp on the banks of the Breede River, while day visitors have a choice of several picnic sites with braai places.

A group of red hartebeest stand guard in the Bontebok National Park.

Once almost extinct, bontebok now flourish in the park.

With its rapids and long stretches of calm waters, the Breede River offers ideal conditions for canoeing.

BOOSMANSBOS WILDERNESS AREA

Deep kloofs, amber-coloured streams and steep cliffs are some of the elements that make up this pristine wilderness area, which is accessible only to hikers (*see* p. 49). Proclaimed in 1978 and covering an area of 14 200 ha, Boosmansbos ('wicked man's forest') boasts a rich diversity of mountain fynbos, with two rare protea species, *Leucadendron radiatum* and *Spatalla nubicola*, restricted to the high slopes of Grootberg. Another notable feature of this wilderness area is the considerably large **indigenous forest** on the southern slopes of Grootberg, containing tree species such as stinkwood, white and red alders, yellowwood, Cape holly and candlewood.

Mammals which the visitor is most likely to see are baboon and dassie, but, if you're lucky, you may also spot grysbok, klipspringer and grey rhebok. Among the 170 **bird species** are black

A hikers' overnight hut in the Boosmansbos Wilderness Area.

eagle, jackal buzzard, rock pigeon, mountain chat, orange-breasted as well as lesser and doublecollared sunbirds.

➡ *The Langeberg between Swellendam and Riversdale is breached by the historic Tradouw and Garcia's passes, which can be combined into a 210-km circular drive. From Swellendam, follow the N2 eastwards, then take the R324 and continue through Suurbraak to Tradouw Pass.*

TRADOUW PASS
Designed by the genial pass-builder Thomas Bain, son of Andrew Geddes Bain, the Tradouw (Khoihkoi for 'women's path') Pass follows the winding course of the Buffeljags River – much the same route used by Khoikhoi women to cross the Langeberg. Built by 300 convict labourers, the pass was opened in 1873, but owing to incessant flooding by the Buffeljags River, it was substantially reconstructed during the 1970s.

Cascading waterfalls, rock pools, wild flowers and dramatic sandstone cliffs are only some of the features of Tradouw Pass, and a number of viewpoints along the way enables visitors to stop and admire this magnificent mountain scenery. Particularly eye-catching are the layers of lichen-encrusted sandstone which were twisted and convoluted by extreme pressures in the earth's crust some 250 million years ago.

The teak bridge over the Gats River, built by Bain in 1879 after the original bridge was washed away, can still be seen alongside its modern counterpart.

➡ *From Barrydale, continue along the R62 towards Ladismith for 18 km. Take the gravel road past Brandrivier Road for approximately*

Boosmansbos has a rich diversity of mountain fynbos and offers hikers a variety of colourful vistas.

37 km, then follow Garcia's Pass to Riversdale. Return to Swellendam via the N2.

GARCIA'S PASS
The vegetation on the northern slopes of the Langeberg, to the east of Tradouw Pass, is noticeably less lush than that growing on the southern slopes.

However, this vegetation is as attractive in its own right, and in spring the southern rocky slopes present an awesome display of flowering plants, among which are flushes of tall yellowbushes (*Leucadendron eucalyptifolium*), *Leucadendron salignum* and *Leucospermum calligerum*.

Before Garcia's Pass was completed in 1877, the Riversdale to Ladismith route was a bridle path until it was surveyed and built by the civil commissioner of Riversdale, AH Garcia, with the help of convict labour.

Approval for the construction of a new pass was granted by the Cape Parliament in 1870 and

Tradouw Pass follows the Buffeljags River, along a path used by the Khoi people in the distant past.

once again the task fell on the master road-builder of the time, Thomas Bain. Work started in 1873, and the pass was officially opened on New Year's eve, 1877.

Toll fees were collected at the toll house on the 600-m-high summit until 31 December 1918. Declared a national monument in 1968, the toll house is presently the starting point of several walking and hiking trails (*see* p. 49).

➡ *The western reaches of the Langeberg can also be explored along a 180-km circular drive. From Swellendam, follow the N2 eastwards for 9 km, then take the R324. At the northern end of Tradouw Pass, turn left onto the R62.*

MONTAGU AND COGMAN'S KLOOF CIRCULAR DRIVE

Flanked by the northern slopes of the Langeberg, the road passes through a patchwork of orchards, cultivated fields and low hills covered in Karoo scrub to reach **Montagu** 61 km beyond the turnoff. This charming Little Karoo town is renowned for its excellent muscadel wines and hot mineral springs. Some of the best dessert wines (red muscadel, white and red jerepigo) in South Africa are produced here and the region is also famous for its peaches, nectarines and apricots.

The Cogman's Kloof road sweeps through an arch on which the British built a fort in the Anglo-Boer War.

The **Montagu Springs** (2 km outside the village and well signposted), with its excellent amenities, draws scores of visitors throughout the year. Besides the hot mineral pools (43 °C), there are an additional three cold-water pools, a variety of recreational facilities, as well as a range of accommodation options, from hotel rooms to self-catering cottages (contact the local publicity

association for more details, *see* p. 49). Bordering the resort is the **Montagu Mountain Nature Reserve**, with its three trails, all of which start at the entrance gate at the top end of Montagu's Tanner Street. A popular trail is the 2,2-km Lover's Walk, which ends at the hot springs.

On leaving Montagu, the road winds along **Cogman's Kloof**, with its spectacular twisted and

folded rock strata. Although the road no longer follows the pass completed by Thomas Bain in 1877, motorists still pass through the 16-m tunnel Bain blasted through Kalkoenkrans. Perched on the crest of Kalkoenkrans is Sidney Fort, built in 1899 by the British to safeguard the pass from Boer attacks during the Anglo-Boer War. There are picnic sites along the pass and braai places and toilets at Keurkloof.

Bonnievale, with its peach and apricot orchards, vineyards and cheese factory (one of the largest in South Africa) is a worthwhile detour on the R60 return route to Swellendam. (The local publicity association will inform you of the guided tours offered by the factory, *see* p. 49.)

From Bonnievale, return to the R60, which winds for 29 km through vineyards, orchards and cultivated fields, with the southern slopes of the Langeberg prominent to the north.

WALKS AND TRAILS

MARLOTH NATURE RESERVE: There are six day walks, from the easy 2,5-km **Flower Route** to a demanding 8,5-km climb around Ten O'Clock Peak and to the summit of Twelve O'Clock Peak.

The **Swellendam Hiking Trail** offers several options, ranging from a two-day circular route

Trailing in the Marloth Nature Reserve. There are six day walks of varying distances and difficulty.

Challenging the Breede River is an exhilarating experience.

to a 74-km hike over six days. The trail traverses the southern and northern slopes of the Langeberg, rewarding hikers with spectacular mountain scenery and far-reaching views of the patchwork of wheatfields on the coastal plains and the arid Little Karoo further inland.

GROOTVADERSBOSCH NATURE RESERVE: The popular **Bushbuck Trail** consists of several loops varying from 2 km to 10 km in length. The name of the trail is rather appropriate since the bushbuck antelope was first described from a specimen collected at Grootvadersbosch by the Swedish explorer Anders Sparrman in 1775.

BOOSMANSBOS WILDERNESS AREA: Criss-crossing this area is a 64-km network of trails, with the **Helderfontein Circuit** being the most popular. The first day's hike ascends to the Helderfontein huts, situated close to the indigenous forest after which the wilderness area was named and a mere 90-minute walk from the summit of Grootberg (1 680 m) with its 360-degree view. The second day of the hike is mainly downhill, and passes through the spectacular gorge carved by the Duivenhoks River.

GARCIA'S PASS: About 40 km east of Boosmansbos is the 1 200-m-high **Sleeping Beauty**, a day's walk from the old toll house at the top of Garcia's Pass. This is also the starting point of two overnight trails – the **Kristalkloof Trail** and the **Rooiwaterspruit Trail**.

MOUNTAIN-BIKE TRAILS

The Grootvadersbosch area is criss-crossed by a 58-km network of cycling routes, most of which start at the reserve's camp site (1,5 km from Honeywood farm). One of the most popular routes traverses the foothills of the Langeberg before descending to the original Grootvadersbosch Homestead. It then returns to Honeywood farm, completing its circuit of either 20 km or 25 km. Other options include an uphill ride through indigenous forest, and two single-track routes, both of which are demanding and technically difficult.

BREEDE RIVER CANOEING

The Breede River with its long stretches of flat water and grade one and two rapids is ideal for canoeing. Trips in two-person inflatables are conducted throughout the year, starting at the Round the Bend camp, 5 km south of the Bontebok National Park. No previous experience is needed as a comprehensive safety briefing by qualified professionals is given before participants take to the water.

NAMAQUALAND, THE KALAHARI AND THE KAROO

Namaqualand, the Kalahari and the Karoo cover almost 50% of the area of South Africa. Most people associate these regions with barren landscapes plagued by periodic droughts and extreme summer temperatures. While this is true, the forces of nature have, over millions of years, fashioned spectacular waterfalls, caves with breathtaking stalagmites and stalactites, rugged mountain ranges, and deep gorges with rocky citadels; glaciers from another age have left their mark on rocks, and reptiles from a forgotten era are entombed in what were once muddy Karoo marshes.

These regions boast some of the most dramatic scenery in South Africa – from the stark granite domes of the Namaqualand Klipkoppe to the boulder-strewn mountain slopes of the Richtersveld; from the striking red sand-dunes of the Kalahari to the dolerite-capped koppies of the Karoo.

Plant and animal life have adapted to cope with the meagre and erratic rainfall in their inhospitable surroundings. After good rains though, the wind-swept plains of Namaqualand are transformed into a colourful carpet of flowers, drawing thousands of visitors to the area. Likewise, the barren dunes of the Kalahari are transformed into waving grasslands and the drab Karoo veld comes alive with colour. Few places can match the diversity of the succulents which grow in the Richtersveld – home to hundreds of species, including the strange and rare halfmens. Adding to the rich floral diversity of these regions are the geophytes of the Bokkeveld Mountains – richer in bulb, corm and tuber plants than any other area in the world.

Animal life includes the hardy gemsbok, with its rapier-sharp horns, the springbok and the sure-footed Hartmann's mountain zebra – a species with a very limited distribution in South Africa. The endangered black rhino and riverine rabbit are also found in these dry areas, as are a host of other animals, reptiles and birds. Several areas have been set aside to conserve the unique scenery, plant and animal life of these three regions. Best known among these is the Kalahari Gemsbok National Park which, together with the adjoining Gemsbok National Park in Botswana, ranks among the largest conservation areas in the world, and is one of the last true wilderness areas.

Despite the seemingly inhospitable nature of these regions, opportunities for exploration abound, ranging from easy day walks and overnight trails, to game-viewing drives and four-wheel-drive trails.

The Skilpad Wild Flower Reserve offers visitors some of the most spectacular displays of spring flowers in Namaqualand.

10 KNERSVLAKTE & OORLOGSKLOOF

Characterised by rolling hills littered with white quartz pebbles, the Knersvlakte is renowned for its spring flowers and succulents. Eastwards are striking views of the Bokkeveld Escarpment, home to the world's richest diversity of geophytes, and where fynbos and Karoo vegetation meet.

How to get there
Vanrhynsdorp, 300 km north of Cape Town on the N7, is a convenient base from which to explore both the Knersvlakte and the Sandveld.

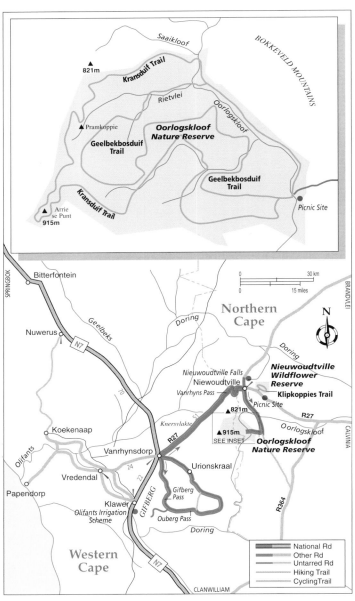

Knersvlakte has a rich diversity of succulents, dominated by vygies.

➡ *Gifberg and the Urionskraal and Koebee valleys can be combined in a scenic drive from Vanrhynsdorp, which takes in much of the Maskam – the regional name for the area.*

MASKAM
The flat-topped **Matzikama Mountain** with its sheer cliffs forms an imposing backdrop to **Vanrhynsdorp**, gateway to southern Namaqualand.

The largest nursery of indigenous succulents in South Africa is found at the eastern end of Vanrhynsdorp's Voortrekker Street. Visitors can also enjoy viewing succulents (on a 3-km walk) in their natural habitat on the local farm '**Kwaggaskop**', 29 km north of the town.

Vanrhynsdorp's barren plains belie its subterranean wealth: pearl-grey marble is quarried south of the town and one of the largest deposits of gypsum rock in South Africa occurs not far away. From here the road heads up the **Gifberg**, named after the endemic hyena poison bush which was used by early farmers to poison meat set out for these once-abundant predators.

The mountain streams, natural pools, **San rock paintings** and a profusion of proteas and other fynbos plants stand in contrast to the desolate plains below. About halfway up the Gifberg Pass the road passes a delightful **waterfall** and from the summit the route winds across the 600-m-high plateau (rooibos tea is cultivated here). Where the Matzikama and Koebee mountains meet, the road descends along the Ouberg Pass, with its interesting sandstone formations, to the fertile **Urionskraal Valley**. Lucerne, grapes and wheat are cultivated here, and the valley is covered with a floral quilt in spring.

➡ *From Nieuwoudtville the Oorlogskloof Nature Reserve is reached by travelling south along Voortrekker Road, then following a gravel road for about 16 km. Turn right at the signpost and follow the signs for about 7 km.*

OORLOGSKLOOF NATURE RESERVE
The reserve's name is derived from the scenic river of the same name which has carved a deep ravine along the eastern slopes of the Bokkeveld Mountains. This kloof is the easternmost boundary of the reserve and took its name from a nearby skirmish when a commando of colonists attacked a Khoisan kraal in 1739.

THE KNERSVLAKTE
Stretching from Vanrhynsdorp in the south to Bitterfontein in the north, the Knersvlakte borders the Sandveld to the west. The Bokkeveld Escarpment forms a natural boundary in the east.

Knersvlakte, which literally means 'gnashing plains', offers a rich diversity of **succulents**, dominated by the vygie family.

These grow on the quartz-strewn hills and sandy plains, and together with a remarkable variety of **wild flowers**, create spectacular and memorable displays during the flower season. Among the several colourful annuals are the botterblom, gousblom, the dainty yellow and white nemesia, the pale blue and white sporie as well as the beetle daisy.

Oorlogskloof is accessible only on foot, but be warned: from the Driefontein access point it is a steep walk down to the river, followed by an equally steep ascent before you are in the reserve. Deep ravines, montane fynbos and interesting sandstone formations make it a paradise for hikers, and an especially popular destination throughout the flower season. A wide diversification of watsonias, gladioli and red-hot pokers can be seen here, and the proteas are represented by the real sugarbush, laurel sugarbush, wagon tree, and the Clanwilliam sugarbush. The botterboom is a conspicuous Karoo species, while the rare elephant's foot (*Discorea elephantipes*) also occurs here.

The reserve is home to several small mammals, most notably baboon, klipspringer, common duiker, dassie and the Cape and bat-eared foxes. The area is richly endowed with birdlife, including the black eagle, gymnogene, Cape francolin, rameron pigeon and olive thrush.

There are about nine rock painting sites in the reserve, mainly on the Geelbekbosduif Trail.

➡ *Nieuwoudtville, also known as the Boland of the Karoo, is situated on the Bokkeveld Escarpment some 51 km northeast of Vanrhynsdorp. It is reached by travelling from Vanrhynsdorp on the R27, along the Vanrhyns Pass. The pass offers sweeping views of the Knersvlakte and the Sandveld further west.*

NIEUWOUDTVILLE WILD FLOWER RESERVE

This tiny reserve, situated at the northern extremity of the Cape Floral Kingdom and at the western edge of the dusty Karoo, just 2 km from the town, hosts at least 300 plant species. The area is the home of the richest concentration of geophytes (plants with bulbs, corms or tubers) in the world, and is well known for its seasonal display of spring flowers. The geophytes flower mainly during the spring and summer months, but as their

There are over 40 rock painting sites in the Gifberg.

Lichen of all shades grow on the rocks of Oorlogskloof.

Oorlogskloof is accessible on foot only. Hikers will be rewarded with deep ravines, montane fynbos and lovely sandstone formations.

The brightly coloured sparaxis make a spectacular spring display.

NIEUWOUDTVILLE'S GLACIAL PAVEMENTS

These glacial pavements are clearly signposted 7,4 km south of Nieuwoudtville on the Oorlogskloof road and date back approximately 300 million years to an Ice Age known as the Dwyka Glaciation. During this period, the southern section of the Gondwanaland supercontinent was submerged in a basin completely surrounded by snow-covered highlands.

The pavements were formed by sheets of ice which moved from the higher lying areas into the southwestern corner of the basin. Boulders and pebbles swept along by the glaciers scoured the rock surfaces, and in some places deep grooves were cut into the rock. Closer examination reveals that the ice sheets moved in a southerly and southwesterly direction.

food and water reserves are stored underground, they produce flowers even in years of poor rainfall. It is not suprising, then, that Nieuwoudtville has deservedly gained its reputation as the best flower-viewing area in South Africa. Especially conspicuous are the colourful members of the iris family, and masses of yellow bulbinellas create an unforgettable display.

➡ *Approximately 6 km to the north of Nieuwoudtville, along the Loeriesfontein Road (R357) and on the Bokkeveld Escarpment, are the Nieuwoudtville Falls. The falls are well signposted.*

NIEUWOUDTVILLE FALLS
The Doring River has its origin a short way upstream of the spectacular Nieuwoudtville Falls at the confluence of the Willems and Gras rivers. At the head

Nieuwoudtville Wild Flower Reserve is a panorama of colour in early spring as vast sheets of wild flowers cover the semi-arid veld.

of Maaierskloof the falls first cascade over a 4-m-high drop and then plunge a sheer 90 m over a sandstone amphitheatre into a large pool. During the summer months the falls are usually dry and so are best viewed between May and October; they are especially attractive after heavy rains when the Doring River thunders over the cliffs. Picnic spots are located close to the falls, and visitors can explore the montane fynbos and Karoo succulents in the area on foot.

WALKS AND TRAILS

MASKAM: Four day walks varying in length (2, 4, 7 or 20 km) can be undertaken, all of which begin at the Gifberg-Rusoord. Winding through magnificent unspoilt fynbos, past waterfalls and mountain streams, these trails offer the hiker the added attraction of San rock paintings.

OORLOGSKLOOF NATURE RESERVE: There are two circular four-day routes in the reserve: the 46-km Kransduif Trail and the 37,5-km Geelbekbosduif Trail. Visitors are also encouraged to explore the area by determining their own routes.

NIEUWOUDTVILLE WILD FLOWER RESERVE: Visitors are free to walk about the reserve. The **Klipkoppies Trail** is a 3-km, circular route crossing the dolerite koppies in the northern area.

FOUR-WHEEL-DRIVE TRAIL

MASKAM: This 20-km trail leads from Gifberg-Rusoord to the Doring River.

Yellow Bulbinella make a glorious show in late winter and early spring.

Visitors can admire the Nieuwoudtville Falls from picnic spots nearby.

KNERSVLAKTE & OORLOGSKLOOF AT A GLANCE

MAIN ATTRACTIONS
Seasonal wild flower displays, San rock paintings, waterfalls, glacial pavements, scenic views, walks and trails.

BEST TIMES TO VISIT
Up-to-date information on the flower season can be obtained from Flowerline (which can be contacted from 1 June to 31 October), tel. (021) 418-3705, fax. 21-4875.

MASKAM
Permits/bookings: Gifberg-Rusoord trails, tel. (02727) 9-1555; Nursery and Kwaggaskop farm: Mr Brink van der Merwe, tel. (02727) 9-1062.
Accommodation: Gifberg-Rusoord, PO Box 126, Vanrhynsdorp 8170; tel. (02727) 9-1555.
Enquiries: The Town Clerk, Nieuwoudtville (*see* below).

OORLOGSKLOOF NATURE RESERVE
Permits/bookings: The Manager (*see* below).
Opening times: 08h00–17h00 throughout the year.
Facilities: None.
Accommodation: None. It is advisable to carry a tent.
Enquiries: The Manager,

Oorlogskloof Nature Reserve, PO Box 142, Nieuwoudtville 8180; tel. (02726) 8-1159 or 8-1010, fax. 8-1052.

NIEUWOUDTVILLE WILD FLOWER RESERVE
Permits/bookings: At gate (no fee outside flower season).
Opening times: July to October 09h00–17h00.
Facilities: Toilets only.
Accommodation: None at reserve. **Nieuwoudtville Municipal Camp Site** and **Hotel** (*see* below).

NIEUWOUDTVILLE FALLS
Permits/bookings: At gate (no fee outside flower season).
Opening times: 08h00–17h00 throughout the year.
Facilities: Picnic sites/toilets.
Accommodation: None at falls. **Nieuwoudtville Municipal Camp Site** and **Hotel** (*see* below).

TOURIST INFORMATION
The Town Clerk, Nieuwoudtville Municipality, PO Box 52, Nieuwoudtville 8180; tel. (02726) 8-1316, fax. 8-1052. **Nieuwoudtville Hotel,** PO Box 7, Nieuwoudtville 8180; tel. (02726) 8-1046.

11 NAMAQUALAND KLIPKOPPE & SANDVELD

The name Namaqualand is synonymous with one of nature's most interesting phenomena – a dazzling display of spring flowers. For most of the year Namaqualand's plains present a picture of utter desolation, but in spring the annuals burst into flower to create one of the most spectacular kaleidoscopes of colour in the world. The region owes its name to the Nama people, a group of Khoikhoi pastoralists who settled in the arid wasteland south of the Orange River some 2 000 years ago.

How to get there
The Namaqualand Klipkoppe and the adjoining Sandveld lie in the Northern Cape. Access from Cape Town is from the north via the N7 to Springbok – a distance of 562 km. From Springbok this tour can be linked up with the Richtersveld (*see* p. 60).

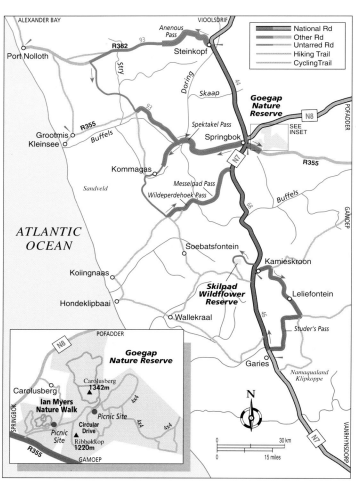

FLOWER-GAZING

The Sandveld and Klipkoppe regions are usually the first to change their seasonal garb, and as the weather warms up the floral spectacle moves southwards. Although early August to mid-September is generally considered to be the best flowering period, much depends on the rainfall in February and March and good follow-up showers two or three months later.

Because the flowers orientate themselves towards the sun, they are best viewed with the sun behind you. Viewing is most rewarding during the hottest part of the day, between 11h00 and 16h00, but on windy days the flowers don't reveal their splendour.

The names given to Namaqualand flowers by locals are as imaginative as the flowers are colourful, from descriptive Afrikaans names such as geelkopman-netjie (yellow-headed little man), the evocative vetkousie (small, fat sock) and koggel-mandervoet (lizard foot), to Nama names such as T'arra-t'kooi, t'nouroe and noerap.

In spring sterretjies even creep out of crevices.

NAMAQUALAND KLIPKOPPE

The Namaqualand Klipkoppe, a barren expanse interspersed with granite domes, forms a stark backdrop to silhouettes of the striking quiver tree, or koker-boom (*see* p. 58). Bounded by the Richtersveld to the northwest and the Knersvlakte to the southeast, this harsh but picturesque landscape is sandwiched between Bushmanland in the east and the Sandveld in the west.

Contrasting sharply with the granite outcrops are the sandy plains of the aptly named Sandveld which stretches from Port Nolloth southwards along the coast to the Olifants River.

Namaqualand's multitude of **plant species** number over 4 000 and are represented by a rich mixture of lilies, irises, oxalis, asters and succulents, including the well-known bokbaaivygie. However, it is most famous for its conglomeration of orange-yellow Namaqua daisies, gousblomme (ranging in colour from white to yellow and deep orange), gaza-nias, and beetle daisies, with their distinctive black markings.

➡ *The best approach to the Skilpad Wildflower Reserve is to go through Kamieskroon, about 495 km to the north of Cape Town and approximately 67 km to the south of Springbok along the N7. To reach this quiet reserve, follow the road past the Kamieskroon Hotel in a northerly direction and continue along the Wolwepoort Road for 17,7 km after passing underneath the N7.*

SKILPAD WILD FLOWER RESERVE

The Skilpad reserve is situated on the range of hills closest to the West Coast, and so receives a higher rainfall than the areas further inland, making it one of the best places to see **spring flowers** in Namaqualand.

The reserve was bought by WWF–South Africa in 1993 to preserve the unique plant life of the area, and is open seasonally. For many visitors the highlight of a trip to Skilpad is the fields of daisies (*Ursinia cakilefolia*) which turn the abandoned wheatfields into a sea of orange in spring, but there is a great deal to see in the surrounding undisturbed veld as well. A 5-km drive encircles the abandoned cultivated lands. Visitors are welcome to walk freely among the flowers and picnicking is permitted just outside the reserve.

➡ *At the end of the flower season a popular one-day trip from Kamieskroon follows the gravel road to Leliefontein and then joins the N7 at Garies. The round trip covers roughly 148 km. An alternative option is to return to the N7 along the Studer Pass.*

KAMIESKROON AND LELIEFONTEIN
Kamieskroon, situated in the foothills of the Kamies Mountains, takes it name from the prominent split granite 'crown' which towers above the town. The first settlement in the area was established nearby in 1864, and became known as Bowesdorp. The narrow kloof and a lack of water hampered expansion and the village was relocated to Kamieskroon in 1924. All that remains of the abandoned village are the ruins of the first church.

From Kamieskroon the road to **Gamoep** zigzags through the mountains along the Kamiesberg Pass and then swings southwards, passing through the **'Garden Route of Namaqualand'**. In addition to typical spring flowers such as gousblomme (*Ursinia*), sporie (*Heliophila*), gansogies (*Cotula*) and gazanias, there are **geophytes** which attract special attention and which include the yellow katsterte (*Bulbinella*), sterretjies (*Spiloxene*) and the aandblom (*Hesperantha*), the flowers of which open towards late afternoon only.

Leliefontein, where Wesleyan missionaries established a mission station for the Namas in 1816, lies 28 km beyond Kamieskroon. The town is named after the uil-blaar (*Androcymbium*), a member of the lily family favouring moist and sandy soil. It is a low-growing plant with a cluster of white flowers. Of primary interest in the town is the ornate sun-dial which was presented to the first missionary, the Reverend

During springtime the Klipkoppe around Kamieskroon are covered in multi-coloured carpets of flowers.

Barnabas Shaw. Also worth a visit are the old Parsonage and the neo-Gothic Church, which was completed in 1855. Many of the inhabitants of the area still live in the traditional dome-shaped Nama matjieshuise.

SPRINGBOK
The history of Springbok, the capital of Namaqualand, is closely interwoven with that of the exploitation of the rich copper deposits in the area (*see* box, right). An extensive (private) collection of over 900 rocks, minerals and gemstones, mainly from South Africa but also from abroad, can be viewed at the Springbok Lodge. Among the

Visitors can stay in traditional Nama huts in Springbok.

interesting specimens on display are unusual quartz crystals from a nearby mine, dioptase, amethyst geodes and azurite.

➡ *The Goegap Nature Reserve is situated 15 km east of Springbok on the road between Springbok and Pofadder (R355).*

GOEGAP NATURE RESERVE
The granite peaks and sandy plains of the Goegap Nature Reserve are dominated by **Carolusberg** (1 345 m), the highest point in the area. There are also several other peaks which rise more than 200 m above the surrounding plains. Goegap's **wild flower garden**

RELICS OF THE COPPER-MINING DAYS

The search for copper in Namaqualand dates back to 1685 when Governor Simon van der Stel sank three shafts on the slopes of what was known as the Koperberg. The largest of these was declared a national monument in 1959, and Van der Stel's Copper Mine can be viewed about 3 km south of Carolusberg. Although the results were promising, logistical obstacles prevented mining and thus large-scale exploitation of copper at Springbok started only in 1852 when the Blue Mine came into operation. A viewing platform overlooks the open-cast mine on the hillside west of Springbok. The historic smokestack, the only reminder of South Africa's first commercial smelting furnace, can also be seen nearby. Low-grade copper ore was smelted here between 1866 and 1871.

A visit to Nababeep's Mining Museum, 11 km west of Springbok, with its displays of equipment used by the early miners and historic photographs of the copper-mining industry, is not to be missed.

Also to be seen at the museum is the last narrow-gauge steam locomotive, named *Clara*, which transported copper ore, coal and coke between the mine and Port Nolloth. Telephone (0251) 3-8121 for information.

THE QUIVER TREE, OR KOKERBOOM

The San people hollowed out the fibrous branches of the quiver tree to use as quivers for their arrows, hence the name *kokerboom* given to it by the early Europeans.

The strange-looking quiver tree has to be one of the most characteristic sights of the Namaqualand Klipkoppe. Only three species of tree aloes occur in southern Africa, and the quiver tree (*Aloe dichotoma*) is usually found growing singly or in small clusters and favours rocky north-facing slopes.

The pearl-grey trunks of the quiver tree often flake off in diamond-shaped patterns to reveal a smooth, golden bark. The tree usually splits into several branches midway up its trunk. It has a height of 3 to 5 m, but single-stemmed trees can reach up to 10 m. The quiver tree's bright-yellow flowers are seen at their best between May and July, and contain copious supplies of nectar, attracting the exquisitely coloured malachite, lesser doublecollared and dusky sunbirds.

San people made quivers for their arrows from quiver tree branches.

sedan cars around Ribbokkop. Picnic places are available for day visitors and the information centre is well worth a visit.

➤ *A highly recommended day trip a little more than 200 km from Springbok is the circular route along the Anenous and Spektakel passes. The drive meanders through an area with a rich diversity of plants, and which has the added attraction of relics of the copper-mining days. Roughly 10 km outside of Springbok there is a turnoff to Nababeep, Namaqualand's largest mining town. Follow the N7 northwards from Springbok to Steinkopf, with its Nama matjies-huise (traditional reed huts).*

contains an excellent collection of succulents of Namaqualand. A visit is especially worthwhile during spring when many of the more than 580 **plant species** which have been recorded in the reserve cover the sandy plains in a dense carpet of flowers. In the flower season 3-hour guided tours are conducted in an open

truck. The tours follow the 4x4 routes (*see* p. 59) and give visitors the opportunity to discover more about Namaqualand's floral wealth.

Among the 45 **mammal species** visitors might see in the reserve are springbok, gemsbok, the endangered Hartmann's mountain zebra (which has been

reintroduced) and the aardwolf. Some 92 **bird species**, including ostriches, black eagles, spotted dikkops and ground woodpeckers, have been recorded in the area.

Adjacent to the reserve Simon van der Stel sank a number of shafts on the Kokerberg in search of copper (*see* box, p. 57). There is a 17-km circular drive for

ANENOUS AND SPEKTAKEL PASSES

From Steinkopf the road continues almost due west towards the diamond-mining centre of **Port Nolloth**, following the northern edge of the Namaqualand plains.

The pass, named after the Anenous Mountain (a Nama word for 'this side of the mountain'),

Over 580 plant species gather to create a medley of colours which greet the visitor to the Goegap Nature Reserve near Springbok.

follows an easy gradient from its 950-m-high summit at Klipfontein, affording travellers expansive vistas of the Sandveld's coastal plains, which are transformed into a bright tapestry of flowers in spring.

More or less 61 km west of Steinkopf the road to Spektakel turns south, reaching the Springbok/Kleinsee Road some 36 km further on. Continuing towards Springbok, the road follows the course of the Buffels River, passing the old mining settlement of **Spektakel** 26 km beyond the turnoff. Work on the copper mine here started in 1854 and by 1863 it was the largest village in

One of the many daisy species typical of Namaqualand.

Namaqualand. However, its fortunes quickly ran out and it sank into obscurity soon afterwards.

After crossing the Skaap River, the road winds through the granite mountains along the Spektakel Pass, which is renowned for its striking scenery and rich assortment of succulents. The pass is said to have taken its name after Simon Van Der Stel exclaimed 'what a spectacle' when he saw the view during his tour of Namaqualand in 1685.

➡ *Another spectacular drive from Springbok curves down the Spektakel Pass to Kommagas, returning along the Wildeperdehoek and Messelpad passes, a circuit of about 160 km. On the onward leg the road winds through a north-south trending range of Klipkoppe and there are expansive views of the Sandveld. The return route ascends the Klipkoppe range. From Springbok, follow the Kleinsee Road over the Spektakel Pass for 37 km and turn left towards the mission settlement of Kommagas.*

SPEKTAKEL AND MESSELPAD PASSES
From Kommagas the road runs along the eastern edge of the Sandveld with its seasonal display of spring flowers. About 33 km beyond Kommagas the road swings east to wind through the mountains along the **Wildeperdehoek Pass** (wild horse corner – presumably named after a herd of horses, owned by prospectors or miners, which ran wild in the area) which is renowned for its **succulents**. Among these are the yellow *Cleretum papulosum* subsp. *schlechteri*, the botterboom (*Tylecodon paniculatus*) with its distinctive yellow, flaky bark, a number of *Conophytum* species and the T'noutsiama (*Cheiridopsis denticulata*) with its lovely white flowers.

After recrossing the Buffels River the road meanders up the steep and narrow **Messelpad Pass**, built by convict labour between 1867 and 1869 for the transportation of copper between Springbok and the once busy port at Hondeklip Bay. The pass owes its name to the neat embankments of dressed stone.

WALKS AND TRAILS
FLOWER WALKS: Guided flower tours are conducted on local farms by tour guide Lita Cole. Discover the unique Namaqualand flora on one of her 1- to 3-day hikes. Hikers must form their own groups of not more than 10 people.
GOEGAP NATURE RESERVE: Two circular trails of 6 and 12 km enable visitors to explore the reserve on foot. Overnight hikes 'off the beaten track' can be undertaken. No facilities are provided on these wilderness experiences and trailists must be totally self-sufficient.

FOUR-WHEEL-DRIVE TRAILS
GOEGAP NATURE RESERVE: A 40-km four-wheel-drive day route in the eastern section of the reserve puts the skills of drivers to the test on both the sandy plains and in rocky terrain. One loop encircles the 1 224-m-high Rooiberg, a route which gains approximately 140 m in altitude.

Lapeirousia silenoides is often found in the crevices of granite oucrops.

MOUNTAIN-BIKE ROUTES
GOEGAP NATURE RESERVE: In this reserve you can do either a 2- or a 3- to 3½-hour trail. Both are over fairly demanding terrain of loose sand and rock.

PHOTOGRAPHIC WORKSHOPS
Kamieskroon Hotel offers inspiring 6-day workshops and useful tips which focus on flower photography.

KLIPKOPPE & SANDVELD AT A GLANCE

MAIN ATTRACTIONS
Unique spring flowers and succulents, the spectacular Klipkoppe, scenic drives, walks and trails.

BEST TIMES TO VISIT
Information on the flower season can be obtained from Flowerline between 1 June and 31 October; tel. (021) 418-3705, fax. 21-4875.

SPRINGBOK
Accommodation: At Namastat, 2 km outside Springbok, in traditional Nama huts (matjieshuise), PO Box 999, Springbok 8240; tel. (0251) 2-2435, fax. 2-1926.
Enquiries: **The Town Clerk,** PO Box 17, Springbok 8240; tel. (0251) 2-2071, fax. 2-1635. **Namaqualand Regional Services Council,** PO Box 5, Springbok 8240; tel. (0251) 2-2011, fax. 8-1333.

SKILPAD WILD FLOWER RESERVE
Permits/bookings: Obtainable at the gate.
Opening times: From July to October 08h00–17h00. Enquire at the Kamieskroon Hotel (*see below*).
Facilities: Ablution blocks.

Enquiries: **Skilpad Wild Flower Reserve,** tel. (0257) 948. **Kamieskroon Hotel,** PO Box 19, Kamieskroon 8241; tel.(0257) 614; fax. 675.

FLOWER WALKS
Permits/bookings: Contact Lita Cole (*see below*).
Accommodation: Simple huts, barns or tents.
Enquiries: **Lita Cole,** PO Box 30, Kamieskroon 8241; tel. (0257) 762; fax. 675.

GOEGAP NATURE RESERVE
Permits/bookings: At gate.
Guided flower tours: A minimum of 10 and a maximum of 16 are accommodated on the 3-hour flower tours, making it necessary to book through the Reserve Manager (*see below*). One trip is conducted per day during the flower season (*see also* p. 58).
Opening times: 08h00–16h30 all year round. Guided flower tours: usually at 11h00.
Facilities: Picnic sites, tourist information office, curio shop, kiosk.
Accommodation: None.
Enquiries: **The Reserve Manager, Goegap Nature Reserve,** Private Bag X1, Springbok 8240; tel. (0251) 2-1880.

12 THE RICHTERSVELD

A barren and desolate yet spectacularly beautiful region, the Richtersveld is the only mountainous desert area in the country. Boulder-strewn valleys and deep ravines formed by tributaries of the Orange River interrupt rugged mountainscape and miles and miles of flat plains that stretch westwards to the diamond-rich Atlantic coast. Home to a wealth of succulents, the Richtersveld is a delight for outdoor enthusiasts seeking a solitary getaway, with only the magical scenery to keep you company.

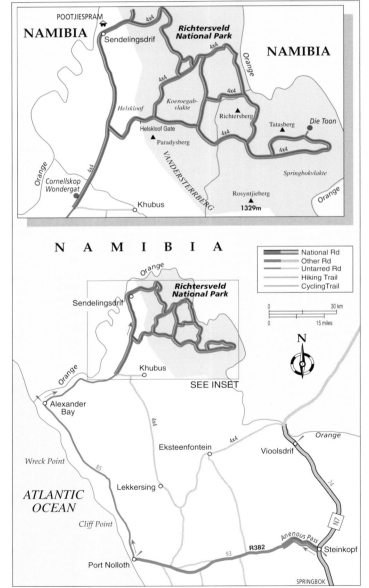

How to get there
The Richtersveld lies on the N7 about 230 km north-west of Springbok and can be approached through Steinkopf (see p. 58), Port Nolloth and along the Diamond Coast through Alexander Bay (the route is not numbered). Alternative entrance and exit routes are along the N7 from Steinkopf to Vioolsdrif, along the Namibian border, and then towards Rosyntjieberg. **Note: The roads in the Richtersveld National Park are accessible to 4x4 and high clearance vehicles only. Because the area is extremely remote, careful preplanning is required.**

long and complex geological history, the Richtersveld region has for years attracted the attention of prospectors. Evidence of this can be found in the abandoned prospecting shafts and copper mines in the area.

➡ *Port Nolloth is situated 94 km from Steinkopf on the R382, and marks the beginning of the Diamond Coast route.*

THE DIAMOND COAST ROUTE

Copper ore was once exported from the harbour at **Port Nolloth**, which today provides safe anchorage to a fishing and crayfishing fleet. In 1926 the first diamonds were discovered on the beach roughly 10 km south of Port Nolloth, and the town has been an important centre of the lucrative diamond-mining industry ever since. Diamond-bearing gravels were carried downstream by the Orange River from exposed kimberlite pipes in the interior of South Africa millions of years ago before being deposited along this coastline.

The remote mining town of **Alexander Bay** is reached after travelling north from Port Nolloth along the desolate and windswept Diamond Coast for about 83 km. Photographs and implements dating back to the early days of diamond mining at Alexander Bay are displayed at the mine museum in the town and a tour of the mine is conducted once a week. During the 3½-hour tour visitors are shown various operations of the mine, the company's oyster farm, the harbour and a colony of about 6 000 Cape fur seals.

East of Alexander Bay and on the road to Sendelingsdrif is **Cornellskop**, with its fine stands of bastard quiver trees (*Aloe pillansii*) etched against the skyline.

At the foot of Cornellskop is the **Wondergat**, a sinkhole in limestone which the Nama people believe is both home of their deity, Heitsi Eibib, and the lair of a snake guarding a treasure of diamonds. Although legend has it that the hole is bottomless, its depth has been established at about 40 m and it has been suggested that a strong spring must have existed here in the past.

➡ *The mining settlement of Reuning at Sendelingsdrif (also the headquarters of the Richtersveld National Park) is roughly 91 km from Alexander Bay. An alternative entrance and exit route to and from the national park is along the N7 from Steinkopf to Vioolsdrif, following the Namibian border from there to Eksteenfontein, Khubus and Sendelingsdrif.*

RICHTERSVELD NATIONAL PARK

By far the most striking part of the Richtersveld lies within the loop of the Orange River between Klipneus Island and

One outstanding feature of this wilderness area is its unique **vegetation**: in fact, the Richtersveld is regarded by many as home of the richest assortment of succulents in the world. Despite the seemingly inhospitable terrain various factors have combined to create perfect conditions for a variety of mesems – flowering stones (*Lithops*), vygies, plakkies, noorsdoring and the squat botterboom. Several endemic aloes are also found here. Because of its

Sendelingsdrif. The Richtersveld National Park was set aside in 1991 to preserve a tract of this land. The park is unique in that it is the first contractual park which has not been incorporated into an existing national park.

In terms of the agreement with the northern Richtersveld community, the **Nama** people, the land remains their property and they are allowed to continue livestock farming in the park. From the mountain tops their herds are often seen as specks on the dusty, dry horizon. The Nama people are descendants of the Khoikhoi – pastoralists who migrated southwards from northern Botswana towards the Orange River some 3 000 years ago. As they migrated further west the increasing aridity forced them to split into two; one group settled north of the Orange River and the other group south of it, an area which became known as Little Namaqualand (Namaqua is plural for Nama).

Although the Nama people have largely been absorbed by other cultural groups, they have retained their language with its four plosive click sounds and

their traditional dome-shaped matjieshuise can still be seen at Steinkopf and Khubus.

To preserve the wilderness atmosphere of the Richtersveld the number of visitors to the park is restricted, with groups being limited to a maximum of three vehicles and 12 people.

Some 185 **bird species** have been recorded in the park, including the swallow-tailed bee-eater, Goliath heron, spurwinged goose, pied kingfisher, Namaqua sandgrouse, Ludwig's bustard and mountain chat, as well as the fish eagle, particularly along the Orange River. The river is also home to some nine freshwater **fish species**, including angling species such as largemouth and smallmouth yellowfish, Orange River mudfish and sharptooth catfish. Angling is permitted provided the necessary permit has been obtained from the Parks Board office at Sendelingsdrif.

Although a variety of **mammals**, including klipspringer, grey rhebok, steenbok and baboon, is found in the Richtersveld, the area does not support many of the larger species. The park also

Halfmens (elephant's trunk) always point to the north.

In the early mornings the clouds hang low in the valleys of the Richtersveld, providing some respite from the heat to follow.

The quiver tree, well adapted to grow in desert conditions, adds an extra dimension to the stark beauty of the landscape.

offers sanctuary to springbok and a small population of Hartmann's mountain zebra.

Over 60 reptile and 25 snake species are known to occur in the area, including several rare and uncommon species, and eight frog species have been recorded.

WALKS AND TRAILS

An excellent way of experiencing the wilderness atmosphere, spectacular scenery and botanical wealth of the Richtersveld National Park is on foot, and certain areas are thus specially zoned for hiking. Guided hikes are conducted between April and October for groups consisting of a minimum of five and a maximum of 12 people.

The first hiking trail was opened in April 1996. It is the **Vensterval route** in the southwestern corner of the park where the western outline of the Rosyntjieberg, the Oemsberg, merges with the Vandersterberg (at 1 366 m the park's highest mountain) and the Tswaies. Here the Ganakouriep River has carved a deep canyon and those venturing up the chasm will be met with the awesome sight of a waterfall plunging more than 100 m over sheer cliff faces. The four-day route is suitable for fit and experienced hikers.

A 5-day trail for rugged hikers along the **Vandersterberg**, a 3-day route at **Leliehoek** for hikers of average fitness and experience, and an easy 2-day trail at **Kodas Peak** are all planned for the near future.

FOUR-WHEEL-DRIVE TRAILS

The Richtersveld National Park is traversed by a network of rough tracks which were created by the early prospectors and farmers who were allocated land here in the 1920s. Driving is permitted only along clearly demarcated routes which have been numbered at all major intersections to assist visitors in finding their way about. The desert ecology is extremely fragile, being easily damaged. It is thus a serious offence to wander off these demarcated roads.

Situated just short of 12 km north of the park's headquarters is the **Pootjiespram camp site** on the banks of the Orange River, an ideal stop-over for a brief or overnight visit. The sunsets here are impressive and in the late afternoon the Lorelei Mountains north of the Orange River are painted with rich pastel shades.

From Sendelingsdrif it is a drive of about three hours to **De Hoop**, another riverside camp site. With its sandy banks and expansive views across the Orange River it is one of the most popular camp sites in the park. There are several inviting swimming places here and you might see canoeists leisurely drifting past on their way to the Fish River confluence in Namibia.

THE HALFMENS

The halfmens is also known as the elephant's trunk and the Noordpool (the Afrikaans name meaning 'North Pole' refers to the crown of the halfmens, *Pachypodium namaquanum*, which always points north). According to local legend the ancestors of the Nama people retreated south of the Orange River long ago after a clash with a more powerful tribe. Those who hankered to return to their motherland after they crossed the Orange River and looked back became petrified, with their heads pointing northwards.

A more scientific explanation is that because its leaves only grow in the winter when the area receives most of its rain, they are orientated towards the sun to maximise photosynthesis.

The halfmens, one of five southern African *Pachypodium* species, is endemic to the Richtersveld and southwestern Namibia and often grows in small groups, favouring rocky, south- and east-facing slopes. This stem succulent, with a rosette of deciduous leaves at the end of its spiny trunk, reaches a height of between 2 and 3 m.

Although they occur throughout the park, large concentrations of these strange-looking trees can be seen in the Halfmens Forest in the mountains just east of Sendelingsdrif (*see* p. 64).

The tracks in the Richtersveld wind through rugged, barren countryside which can be negotiated only in a 4x4 or high clearance vehicle.

The mighty Orange River, with its popular riverside camp sites, forms the northern boundary of the Richtersveld.

The route to De Hoop takes visitors along the **Halfmens Pass**, a rocky mountain pass renowned for its dense concentration of the interesting halfmens trees (*see* box, p. 62).

After good rains the desert comes alive with wild flowers.

It then continues along plains which are covered in a talcum of red dust, and finally winds down the narrow valley, carved over time by the Kook River through the reddish-brown mountains.

Although the **Richtersberg camp site** lies a mere 11 km upstream of De Hoop, the thick sand along the Orange River makes it inadvisable to follow this route. An easier route of about 45 km leads back up the Kook River valley and then swings southwards, passing through Maerpoort where it joins the road to Springbokvlakte before winding along the Tatas River to the Orange River.

The **Springbokvlakte** is one highlight of the Richtersveld. Mostly dry and barren, the vast plain becomes a lush grassland after good rains, and livestock and their herders are often encountered here. The southern border of the Springbokvlakte is a mountain range of saw-edged peaks with fearful names such as Devil's Tooth and Mount Terror. One of these mountains, the Rosyntjieberg, is the habitat of Meyer's

aloe (*Aloe meyeri*), endemic to the area and otherwise restricted to southwestern Namibia.

From Springbokvlakte there is a choice of two routes to the camp site at **Kokerboomkloof**. Tucked away in a valley of the Tatasberg, the camp site is named after the dense concentration of quiver trees (*Aloe dichotoma*) growing here. The scenery of the Tatasberg is dominated by huge granite boulders and unusual rock formations with descriptive names such as Moon Rock, the Sphinx and the Drumstick. Die Toon, also known as Eierkop, is a familiar landmark. In the heat of the day the landscape is austere, but in the late afternoon the rocks take on an orange hue which slowly fades into pinkish tones.

Helskloof, the western exit of the park, is 60 km west of Kokerboomkloof. Having retraced your tracks along a fairly smooth road to the split to Maerpoort (about 28 km), you now follow the road across numerous dry courses of the Dabbie River (a rather bumpy ride) and, after crossing a ridge between Paradysberg (south) and Kodas Peak (north), reach the turnoff to the camp site at **De Koei**. From here the road continues along Helskloof, a rough track which follows a torturous route down a kloof which certainly lives up to its reputation. Masses of Pearson's aloe (*Aloe pearsonii*) with their dull-red leaves and the dwarf quiver tree (*Aloe ramosissima*), which flowers in May and June, are two conspicuous aloes in this part of the park.

The rugged terrain outside the park is ideally suited to four-wheel-drive travelling and there are numerous tracks which can be followed. A highly recommended route away from the park is to exit via Helskloof and travel through the Nama settlements of **Khubus**, **Lekkersing** and **Eksteenfontein** in the southern Richtersveld, joining the R328 between the towns of Steinkopf and Port Nolloth.

CANOEING TRIPS ON THE ORANGE RIVER

Another perspective of the Richtersveld's spectacular scenery and interesting geology is from a canoe trip along the Orange River, the northern boundary of the Richtersveld.

The water from Viooolsdrif to Aussenkehr is mainly placid, with only one major rapid, Shambok.

The waters of the Orange provide relief from the desert's heat, as well as splendid canoeing opportunities.

Further on downstream the river engraves a torturous course through the weathered landscape and several exciting rapids have to be negotiated. First of these is the Gamkab Rapid, followed by Roller Coaster, Surprise, Boat Crusher and Crunch Rapid. Despite these fearful names, no previous experience is necessary and participants are given a comprehensive briefing by professionals before setting off.

The section of the river from just downstream of Aussenkehr to Sendelingsdrif offers some spectacular scenery and exhilarating white-water rapids. With these named Terminator and Eliminator, this trip is definitely not for the faint-hearted.

Sunset on the Orange River and the mountains of the Richtersveld.

13 AUGRABIES FALLS NATIONAL PARK

The Khoikhoi people appropriately referred to the thundering falls in the lower reaches of the Orange River as Aukoerebis – 'place of great noise'. Here the Orange River has engraved a deep cleft through the resistant granite, creating one of southern Africa's most impressive gorges, over which the Augrabies Falls tumble in a series of spectacular cataracts. Surrounded by a moonscape of rocks and quiver trees, the gorge provides an oasis in the hot and dusty Northern Cape.

How to get there
From Johannesburg the park is approached through the towns of Upington, which links up with a Kalahari tour (*see p. 70*), Keimoes and Kakamas along the N14. The Augrabies Falls National Park is 120 km west of Upington. From Cape Town, follow the N7 to Springbok, turn onto the N14 to Pofadder and then left, about 8 km before reaching Kakamas. The park is 29 km further on. The route from Cape Town can be linked up with a Namaqualand tour (*see pp. 52 and 56*).

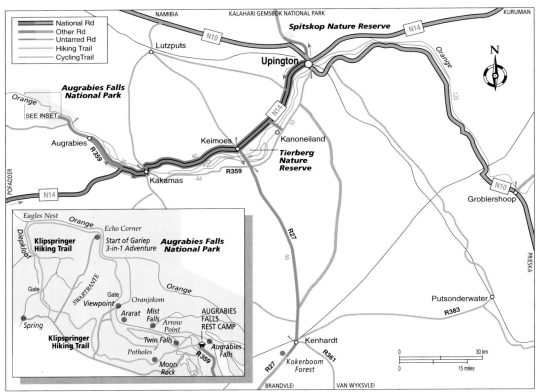

The focal point of the park is the magnificent **Augrabies Falls**. It is not the height of the falls, but rather the awesome mass of water that thunders through the narrow gorge, that is most impressive. The main falls tumble noisily 56 m over a granite cliff into the pool below, which is estimated to be at least 130 m deep. The pool is reputedly a treasure chest for diamonds transported downstream by the river over countless millenia. In total the river drops 191 m, placing it amongst the largest cataract-type waterfalls in the world. There are several viewpoints along the southern edge of the 18-km-long

Black rhino (Diceros bicornis bicornis) *were reintroduced in 1985.*

BLACK RHINO ADVENTURE

This exciting Black Rhino Adventure begins with a short trip down the Orange River, which starts at Echo Corner, approximately 10 km downstream of the main falls, in an inflatable boat.

Visitors are met downstream by Parks Board staff and taken into the rugged northern section of the park in an open four-wheel-drive vehicle. The highlight of this roughly 7-hour excursion is, of course, catching sight of one of the endangered black rhinos (*Diceros bicornis bicornis*) which inhabit the area.

The rhino were successfully reintroduced into the northern section of the Augrabies Falls National Park in 1985, almost 150 years after the last black rhino was shot in the region. These rhino, which were taken from Namibia's Etosha Pan, adapted well, and considerable excitement was caused when the first calf was born in the park in October 1987.

Visitors can gain access to the northern section of the park only by joining one of the official tours conducted by Parks Board staff.

gorge from where visitors can view the main falls, the 75-m-high, aptly named Bridal Veil Falls, the Devil's Key – a huge rock eroded in the shape of a key – and the Angel Falls. Although most of the viewpoints have safety barriers, it is very dangerous to stand too close to an unprotected edge.

Below the falls the river flows through a deep canyon, losing about 35 m in height as it rushes down several rapids, before journeying to the Atlantic Ocean, some 500 km further west.

Although 47 **game species** occur in the park, including the endangered black rhino, they are not very visible. The rocky plains are an ideal habitat for klipspringer and rock dassies. Other species occurring include springbok, chacma baboon, vervet monkeys and the aardwolf, a termite-eating hyena species which is occasionally seen in the vicinity of the Swartrante.

Among the 195 **bird species** which visitors are likely to see in the park are the black eagle, kori bustard, Namaqua sandgrouse and rosyfaced lovebird. African fish eagle and three species of kingfishers are also attracted to the perennial waters of the Orange River.

The rocky terrain is an ideal habitat for **reptiles**, and 29 gecko, agama, skink and lizard species, as well as rock and water monitors, have been recorded in the park. Especially conspicuous among the rocks on the edge of the Orange River gorge is the red-tailed rock lizard. As is often the case in nature the females are a dull grey-green, and the males have striking red tails. Nineteen snake and 12 amphibian species also reside here.

The road network in the southern section of the park covers 30 km and leads to several viewpoints, including **Moon Rock**, a huge dome-shaped rock. The pink-coloured domes are characteristic of the area and, although the rock resembles granite, it is actually a closely related metamorphic rock known as gneiss. The two viewpoints at **Ararat** and **Oranjekom** (sometimes referred to as Afdak on account of the covered picnic place)

At Augrabies the Orange River is forced through a narrow cleft and down a series of cataracts into a gorge.

Over countless millenia the Orange River has incised this dramatic gorge into the surrounding moonscape.

Lizards bring colour and life to the rocks of Augrabies.

offer visitors a commanding view over the gorge, which has an average depth of 240 m.

The road then crosses the **Swartrante**, a low ridge which is littered with black rocks that superficially resemble dolerite. They are, in fact, quartz-rich granulite, the surface of which is white when it has not been exposed by the elements, but which turns black when it is exposed. One track leads to **Fonteintjie**, a natural spring in the southwestern corner of the park, and the other leads to **Echo Corner**, where your voice will echo back to you after four seconds if you call out. Here the river virtually makes a turn of 90°.

➡ *From Augrabies a scenic drive can be taken along the Orange River (the Green Kalahari) to the towns of Kakamas (32 km), Keimoes (41 km east of Kakamas), and Upington (a further 39 km).*

KAKAMAS TO UPINGTON
In the fertile valley along the southern banks of the Orange River lies the town of **Kakamas**, synonymous with the famous yellow cling peaches of the same name. The old Transformer Building, which resembles an ancient Egyptian temple, supplied hydro-electric power to the town between 1912 and 1914, and nine bakkiespompe, or water wheels (the first one in the Lower Orange River was manufactured here towards the end of the last century), are still in use. They can be seen by following the Kenhardt road for about 2,5 km from Kakamas.

After Kakamas the road crosses the Orange River and passes through the arid northern plains. Watch for the turnoff to the historic water tunnels 8 km outside the town. The two tunnels were excavated by hand between 1898 and 1901 to divert water from the Orange River's northern

canal to irrigate crops. Further along the road returns to the river – a linear oasis. Straddling the banks of the Lower Orange River are vineyards, orchards, cotton fields and wheatlands, criss-crossed by an intricate network of water canals.

Keimoes lies on the northern banks of the river, at its widest point. Main Street houses a water wheel used to irrigate the farmlands along the Orange River. From Keimoes the R27 turns off to Kenhardt and its famous Kokerboom Forest (*see* below), but if you continue towards Upington you will reach the **Tierberg Nature Reserve** after some 5 km. A botanical paradise, this reserve provides visitors with a glimpse of the area's indigenous vegetation. Centred around a small hillock, a rich diversity of succulents is protected here, and masses of red Orange River aloes (*Aloe gariepinus*) are in full flower in July and August. From Tierkop visitors can enjoy expansive views of the lattice work of farmlands along the banks of the Orange River. From the reserve, return to the N14 and then turn right towards Upington. Along the way you will pass the turnoff to Kanoneiland (*see* below). From Kanoneiland the road continues past vineyards and fields of

lucerne, groundnuts, cotton, wheat and vegetables, to the town of Upington.

Renowned for its Palm Tree Avenue (planted in 1934/35), which stretches for over 1 km and is the longest in the southern hemisphere – **Upington** lies on the northern banks of the Orange River. Located in South Africa's northernmost wine-producing area, the town is also a major centre for processing sultanas, grapes and other produce.

At **Spitskop Nature Reserve** (signposted 13 km north of Upington on the R360), visitors can view gemsbok, springbok, eland, blue wildebeest and steenbok in their natural surroundings. The sandy plains of the reserve are traversed by game-viewing roads, and many delightful picnic spots are situated at the base of the granite koppie after which the reserve was named. Mountain-biking is permitted along the game-viewing roads.

➡ *Time permitting, make a trip to Kenhardt's Kokerboom Forest. From Keimoes follow the R27 for 75 km to Kenhardt, and then continue for a further 8 km along the R27 (towards Brandvlei) to the forest.*

KENHARDT KOKERBOOM FOREST
The small Northern Cape town of Kenhardt is best known for its Kokerboom (quiver tree) Forest, about 8 km southwest of the town. These tree aloes usually grow singly or in small, scattered groups, but several hundred trees occur here to form one of the densest concentrations of quiver trees in South Africa. This scenic drive is especially worthwhile in mid-winter when the trees are in full bloom (*see* box, p. 58).

➡ *The turnoff to Kanoneiland, the largest inhabited inland island in South Africa, is 14 km beyond Keimoes on the N14. Access to the island is gained from the river's northern bank along a double-lane bridge and from the south along a single-lane bridge.*

KANONEILAND
Approximately 14 km long and 3 km wide, Kanoneiland lies surrounded by the waters of the

The rocky plains in Augrabies provides the ideal habitat for klipspringer.

Vineyards flourish along the Orange River.

Orange River. It received its name after being bombarded by cannon fire for six days during a punitive expedition against the Korana tribe in 1878. Grapes, lucerne and cotton are all successfully cultivated on the island with its intricate meshwork of irrigation canals.

WALKS AND TRAILS

AUGRABIES FALLS NATIONAL PARK: Visitors can explore the Augrabies Falls National Park on foot and three short walks can be undertaken from the rest camp. None of these walks are overly strenuous, but sturdy footwear is essential, and walks are best taken during the early-morning hours or in the late afternoon. The **Arrow Point Trail** snakes through the rocky landscape to the V-shaped rock mass created when a side channel of the Orange River carved a deep gorge. The walk takes an hour and offers fine views of the Orange River gorge and the Twin Falls. By continuing to the fascinating Potholes, or Maalgate, the Arrow Point Walk can be extended by about 30 minutes. These potholes were scoured into the hard granite by swirling water and boulders when the river followed a much wider course.

Moon Rock Trail can be reached by car, but the 1-hour walk to the rock and back is most rewarding. The outcrop is an excellent example of exfoliation, or the flaking of sheets of rock as a result of the outer shell cooling off quicker than the underlying rock. Those keen to experience even more of the park can tackle the 40-km **Klipspringer Hiking Trail**, which includes a 5-km section along the Orange River (in

sharp contrast to the barren plains) on the second day.

KENHARDT: The **Kokerboom Forest** affords visitors close-up views of these alien-looking tree aloes along an approximately 4-km walk following the rocky dolerite ridges of the forest.

SPITSKOP: The reserve's three trails are 7, 12 and 18 km long.

GARIEP 3-IN-1 ADVENTURE

The Gariep 3-in-1 Adventure starts off at Echo Corner, from where participants canoe down the Orange River for 3 km (canoes supplied). At Diepkloof oars are exchanged for boots. After a 4-km hike, mountain bikes are provided for the last leg of the adventure – an 11-km ride back to the rest camp. The excursion is self-guided (the route is clearly marked and maps are provided) and is limited to a minimum of 2 and a maximum of 6 people. Participants must take their own food and drinks, and comfortable boots or walking shoes.

CAMEL AND CANOE ADVENTURES

Camel safaris are conducted from the Adventure Runners base camp, about 20 km downstream of Augrabies. A 51-km circular route is followed on the 5-day safari with one or two overnight stops along the Orange River. Four- and 5-day canoe trails with two easy-grade rapids are also conducted on the Lower Augrabies section of the Orange River. Another option is a 2½-day canoeing trip along a 35-km stretch of the river, followed by a 2½-day camel safari accompanied by experienced guides.

14 THE KALAHARI

An endless sea of red sand-dunes, age-old camel thorns lining dry riverbeds, huge sociable weavers' nests, springs, dolomite caves and the sounds of roaring dunes – these are all characteristic of the Kalahari. This desert area, which stretches to the furthest reaches of the Northern Cape and into Botswana, is home to the black-maned lion, elegant gemsbok, herds of springbok, the brown hyena and inquisitive surricates.

How to get there
Upington is a convenient base from which to explore the Kalahari. Situated 780 km west of Johannesburg, the town is approached along the N14 through Vryburg, Kuruman (see p. 71) and Olifantshoek. A visit can be linked to Augrabies Falls National Park (see p. 60). From Cape Town take the N7 to Springbok (see pp. 52 and 56). Turn onto the N14, continue through Pofadder and pass the Augrabies Falls turnoff about 289 km further on. Upington is 88 km from the turnoff (939 km from Cape Town).

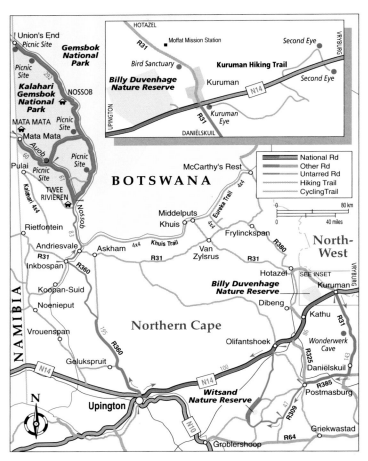

The Orange River lies at the southern edge of the Kalahari, a vast sand-filled basin covering most of Botswana and extending into Zimbabwe and Zambia in the east, Namibia in the west and to Angola. Formed 65 million years ago, this basin was filled with clay, sand and gravel. The Kalahari desert was created by sand, blown into the basin two to three million years ago.

This arid area is known for its summer heat; years can go by with little or no rainfall. Its **vegetation** varies from tree savanna to grass-covered dunes. The shepherd's tree, with its distinctive

white stem, is often seen on dune crests, and camel and grey camel thorns, white pomegranates and raisin bushes grow along the river courses. Conspicuous after good summer rains is the devil's thorn, which forms dense canopies of bright yellow flowers. Also emerging after the summer rains are the wild cucumber and the tsamma melon, plants which supplement the water needs of a wide range of animals.

➡ *From Upington explore the eastern reaches of the Kalahari along a 660-km circular drive passing Kuruman, Wonderwerk Cave and Witsand. Take the N14 to Olifantshoek (165 km); 48 km further, 2 km before Kuruman, the Billy Duvenhage Nature Reserve is signposted to the left.*

BILLY DUVENHAGE NATURE RESERVE
The **vegetation** here is typical Kalahari thornveld characterised by large camel thorn trees. The reserve can be explored along **game-viewing roads**, and white rhino, eland, kudu, gemsbok, red hartebeest, blesbok, impala, steenbok and springbok may be seen. **Birdlife** includes the pale chanting goshawk, pygmy falcon, kori bustard, clapper, fawn-coloured and spikeheeled larks, and the Kalahari robin.

SOCIABLE WEAVERS

Sociable weavers' enormous nests are characteristic of the Kalahari. Built from twigs, sticks and grass, they consist of numerous tunnels ending in nest chambers, and large nests are inhabited by up to 500 birds. Camel thorn and quiver trees, and even telephone poles, are used as sites.

The nests act as effective insulators against cold and heat; research has shown that temperatures in the chambers are 2–3 °C lower than outside temperatures during the day, but up to 8 °C warmer at night. To keep warm during cold winter nights four or five birds often roost together in a chamber, but in summer chambers are occupied by only two birds.

The main predators of the sociable weaver are the Cape cobra, which weaves its way through the nest, and the honey badger, which breaks open the nest from the top in search of eggs and chicks.

The sociable weaver, a common bird of dry areas, builds remarkably large communal nests.

➡ The Eye is situated in the centre of Kuruman, on the corner of Main and Voortrekker streets.

KURUMAN: THE EYE

Named the Oasis of the Kalahari, lush Kuruman contrasts starkly with the surrounding plains. The town owes its existence to **The Eye**, the biggest natural fountain in the southern hemisphere. Early Tswana inhabitants named the spring, which yields 20 to 30 million litres a day, Gasegonyane, or the 'little water calabash'.

Subterranean water, forced to the surface by a dyke of altered dolerite (diabase) is home to many **fish species**, including the southern mouthbrooder, carp, catfish and Mozambique tilapia.

Another spring, the **Second Eye**, is 6 km from the centre of Kuruman on the N14 to Vryburg.

To reach the **Moffat Mission Station**, 4 km north of The Eye, turn north into Tsening Road and continue for 4 km to Moffat Avenue. Turn right, then left into Thompson Street. The Mission Station was established by Scottish missionary Dr Robert Moffat in 1824. Here he translated the New Testament into Setswana, and the 1838 dressed stone church is still in use. Reminders of the mission work conducted for almost 50 years in the Northern Cape by Moffat makes a visit worthwhile.

En route you will pass the **Kalahari Raptor Rehabilitation Centre** (see box, top right) and **Kuruman's Bird Sanctuary**. Water birds represent a large percentage of the 115 bird species attracted to the park's wetland.

➡ To reach Wonderwerk Cave from Kuruman, take the R31 south towards Daniëlskuil and Kimberley. The turnoff is 43 km from Kuruman.

WONDERWERK CAVE

The oldest examples of mobiliary **rock art** in South Africa, dating back 10 000 years, were excavated in this huge dolomite cave with its 13-m-high, dome-shaped roof. Archaeologically fascinating engraved stone slabs and Later Stone Age artefacts, including pieces of decorated ostrich egg shell, have been found.

Monochrome rock paintings in black, ochre, yellow and white are near the entrance and along the walls. Beautiful stalagtites hang from the ceiling, while stalagmites are restricted to rock seams and are generally small, so are fairly inconspicuous.

The artefacts cannot be viewed in the cave as they are in Kimberley's McGregor Museum, but there is an interesting exhibition on the geology and archaeology of the area nearby.

➡ From the Wonderwerk Cave take the R31 south. Nine kilometres after Daniëlskuil turn right onto the R385 to reach Postmasburg 49 km later. From here follow the R309 and after 47 km turn right at a T-junction, and go through Matsap and Padkloof. Pass the turnoff to Groblershoop by travelling 12 km towards Olifantshoek until Witsand's turnoff. From there take the Olifantshoek road for 72 km to the N14, 6 km west of the town. To return to Upington, turn left and continue for 159 km along the N14.

WITSAND NATURE RESERVE

The stark whiteness of Witsand's dunes stands out sharply against the surrounding red sands. This contrast in colour is likely a result of the oxides having been bleached out of the dunes by subterranean water. The isolated system lies west of the Langeberg, where the dunes reach heights of 20 to 30 m, and its beauty is enhanced by natural vleis between the dunes. These are fed by seepage from two underground reservoirs, one of which has an estimated volume of 1 200 million m³ of water.

THE RAPTOR ROUTE

This self-drive tour starts at Kuruman's Kalahari Raptor Rehabilitation Centre. It covers about 1 900 km (630 km of which is in the Kalahari Gemsbok National Park), through one of the best areas in South Africa for viewing birds of prey. It is advisable to arrange to visit the centre in advance.

From Kuruman the 720-km onward route follows a tar road to Hotazel, and then a gravel road through Aansluit, Van Zylsrus, Askham and Andriesvale to the Kalahari Gemsbok National Park. The return leg is about 550 km through Upington, Prieska, Griquastad and Daniëlskuil. Shorter options are possible.

Among the many raptors to be seen are the secretarybird, bateleur, lappetfaced and whitebacked vultures, martial eagle, pygmy and rednecked falcons, and the blackbreasted snake eagle. Owls recorded in the area include the spotted, giant eagle and scops owls. Birding is especially rewarding during the rainy season when migrants such as the steppe eagle and buzzard, Montagu's harrier and hobby falcon supplement the numbers of resident species.

A bateleur, one of the many birds to be seen on the Raptor Route.

Gemsbok, migratory inhabitants of desert and semi-desert country, can go without water for long periods.

Lion, king of the beasts, spend much time surveying their kingdom.

The brown hyena is the most common large predator in the Kalahari Gemsbok National Park, but is seldom encountered because of its largely nocturnal behaviour.

With an average shoulder height of 80 cm, it is easily recognizable by its shaggy hair, varying from brown to almost black. Males weigh approximately 40 kg and females about 2 kg less.

Research by Dr Gus Mills, a world authority on hyenas, has shown that 4 to 14 usually closely related brown hyenas live in a fixed territory 230 to 480 km² in size. Their diet is more diverse than the spotted hyena's and varies from carrion to termites to fruit. A solitary animal, it usually forages alone and can cover up to as much as 55 km a night in search of food.

At the southern edge of Witsand, white sand is blown over the denser red sand, and the well-known **Roaring Sands** become animated and produce eerie, moaning sounds. Great mystery surrounds the cause of this weird phenomenon, but it is thought to be caused by friction when evenly-sized, clean particles of sand move over each other. These sounds can be heard only when the sand is bone dry.

KALAHARI PANS

A feature north of Upington is several pans that were formed thousands of years ago in depressions between the dunes. During the heat of the day these shimmering pans offer the viewer a picture of utter desolation, but in the late afternoons and at full-moon the pans transform into a surrealistic world. The Kalahari Molopo Lodge offers a romantic three-course candle-lit dinner on a salt pan and conducts day tours to the Hakskeen and Oxford pans. For enquiries contact the Kalahari Molopo Lodge, PO Box 32, Askham 8814; tel. (054902) ask for Askam 2.

➡ *The Kalahari Gemsbok National Park is 270 km from Upington. Take the R360 to Inkbospan and then the R31 to Andriesvale. Bear north to Twee Rivieren on the R360. From Johannesburg take the N14 to Kuruman, the R31 to Van Zylsrus and Andriesvale, then follow the R360 to Twee Rivieren. The 320-km road between Hotazel and Twee Rivieren is a gravel road.*

KALAHARI GEMSBOK NATIONAL PARK

Between the Namibian and Botswanan borders, in the remote northwestern corner of South Africa, is the Kalahari Gemsbok National Park. It is home to springbok, gemsbok, red hartebeest, blue wildebeest, Burchell's zebra, eland, steenbok, common duiker and aardwolf that range freely throughout the 953 103-ha park and the adjacent Gemsbok National Park in Botswana. Giraffe were reintroduced here in 1990, 87 years after the last one was shot at Kameelsleep in the course of the Nossob River.

The **game** attracts many predators – the black-maned male lions of the Kalahari, which are well known, are sometimes seen in the lower branches of camel thorn trees. Other predators that may be seen include cheetah, leopard and spotted and brown hyena.

Some 278 **bird species** have been recorded in the park, but only about 82 species are resident. Yet the Kalahari Gemsbok is a birder's paradise as more than two-thirds of southern Africa's raptors have been seen here. It is one of the best places to observe rednecked falcon and during summer acrobatic bateleurs are also prominent.

A distinctive feature of the Kalahari landscape is the **red dunes** between the Auob River in the west and the Nossob River in the east. The dunes are orientated in an east-west direction and are separated by wide 'streets'. Mostly sparsely covered by grass, good summer rains transform them into waving grasslands.

Visitors can gain excellent views of the interesting landscape from the two connecting roads across the dunes between the Nossob and Auob rivers. The southern connecting route winds for 27 km through the dunes between Kij Kij and Kielie Krankie and is an ideal circular game-viewing drive for visitors

Cheetah are sleek animals which can run at speeds of up to 112 km per hour in open grasslands.

based at **Twee Rivieren**. Further north is a 55-km connecting route between Kamqua and Dikbaardskolk – a shortcut for those travelling between **Mata Mata** and **Nossob camps**. Other than these two routes, the park's road network is restricted to the usually dry beds of the Nossob and Auob rivers.

Game-viewing here is ideal as species, such as blue wildebeest, concentrate in the riverbeds, where most of the artificial waterpoints are located during the dry season. Large concentrations of game can also be seen here when the grass begins to sprout after the first summer rains. During the rainy season there is an abundance of palatable grasses on the dunes and water in the seasonal pans, so the animals disperse.

From **Twee Rivieren** visitors can travel for 3½ hours along the Nossob River to Nossob Rest Camp, or follow the Auob River

The bat-eared fox is a shy and secretive dweller of arid areas.

for 2½ hours to Mata Mata Rest Camp, near the Namibian border (no access to Namibia here).

Tracing the Nossob River's course, the connecting route to the Auob River is 117 km off. A delightful picnic place provides a welcome break from the long drive. The road continues north for a further 45 km to **Nossob Rest Camp**, with Union's End on the Namibian border 134 km on.

Travelling along the Auob River, the Nossob River turnoff is 58 km, and the **Mata Mata Rest Camp** approximately 60 km, further on.

The picnic spots at Melkvlei, Dikbaardskolk, near Lijersdraai and Union's End on the Nossob River, and at Kamqua on the Auob River are not fenced, so beware of dangerous animals.

WALKS AND TRAILS

The **Kuruman Hiking Trail**, from the resort at the Second Eye to The Eye, passes several points of interest on its 11-km route, including two forts from the Second Anglo-Boer War, a sinkhole and dolomite caves.

FOUR-WHEEL-DRIVE TRAILS

Four-wheel-drive enthusiasts can explore the Kalahari on many easy to demanding trails.

VAN ZYLSRUS: The **Eureka Trail** (for novices) is from 'Eureka' farm, northeast of Van Zylsrus on the R31. It has an 86-km route to McCarthy's Rest, or a 39-km trip to Khuis along the Molopo River. **KHUIS:** The easy 165-km **Khuis Trail** is from Van Zylsrus or Middelputs along the Molopo River to Gemsbok border post. The R31 returns to Van Zylsrus. **MIER:** The tough 200-km **Kalahari 4x4 Trail** begins at the Kalahari Molopo Lodge. It takes

a good gravel road to Mier and continues north through thick sand, requiring a four-wheel-drive, to the overnight stop at Pulai. The second day's route follows sandy tracks along the park's border to the R360 between Andriesvale and Twee Rivieren. **PELLA:** The **Pella Trail** is in three sections: from the historic mission settlement of Pella to Viooldsrif, Viooldsrif to the Richtersveld (see p. 60), and from Lekkersing to the coast.

THE KALAHARI AT A GLANCE

MAIN ATTRACTIONS
Evocative scenery, birding (raptors), game-viewing Witsand's dunes, The Eye, four-wheel-drive trails.

BEST TIMES TO VISIT
March to October for game-viewing; summer for birders who can bear the heat.

BILLY DUVENHAGE NATURE RESERVE
Permits/bookings: Permits at gate on weekends and public holidays; on weekdays from Kuruman Municipality, tel. (05373) 2-1095.
Opening times: 1 May to 31 August 14h00–18h00 (Saturdays and Sundays); 1 September to 30 April 15h00–19h00 (Saturdays); 15h00–18h00 (Sundays and all public holidays).
Accommodation: None.

KURUMAN
Permits/bookings: Kuruman Hiking Trail: No permit required. **Kuruman Moffat Mission:** No advance booking required. **Kuruman Bird Sanctuary:** Free entry; key from municipal waterworks next to park.
Opening times: **Kuruman Eye:** Daily 06h00–20h00. **Kuruman Hiking Trail:** Daily, sunrise to sunset. **Kuruman Moffat Mission:** Daily 08h00–17h00 (except Christmas and Good Friday). **Kuruman Bird Sanctuary:** Daily, sunrise to sunset.
Accommodation: (see Tourist Information below).

Enquiries: Raptor Route Information Office:
PO Box 1667, Kuruman 8460; tel. (05373) 3-0464.

WONDERWERK CAVE
Permits/bookings: None for daytime, pay fee at cave.
Opening times: Monday to Saturday 08h30–17h00; Sunday 08h30–13h00 and 14h30–17h00.
Accommodation: Mr and Mrs G Niewoudt, PO Box 863, Kuruman 8460; tel. (0598) 30680. Equipped chalet for 6; 10 camp sites with hot/cold-water ablutions; farmstall.

WITSAND NATURE RESERVE
Permits/bookings: At office.
Opening times: Daily, sunrise to sunset.
Accommodation: Ten luxury self-contained chalets, 10 camp sites with hot/cold-water ablutions, swimming pool scheduled for completion end 1996/early 1997. Contact the Officer-in-Charge (see below).
Enquiries: Officer-in-Charge, Witsand Nature Reserve, Private Bag X3006, Postmasburg 8420; tel. (0591) 7-2373.

KALAHARI GEMSBOK NATIONAL PARK
Permits/bookings: At gate.
Opening times: All year; variable: 05h30–19h30 November/ December, 07h00–18h00 May.
Accommodation: Camp sites at all camps; contact National Parks Board Reservations (see below). **Twee Rivieren:** 3- and 4-bed air-conditioned chalets.
Mata-Mata: 6-bed cottages,

3-bed huts. **Nossob:** One 6-bed house (main room air conditioned), 6-bed cottages, 3-bed huts, all with fully equipped kitchens, 3-bed huts. Sites with braai places, scullery and ablution blocks at all camps.
Facilities: Petrol and diesel, shops, curios and drinks in all camps. Fresh meat, bread and eggs, restaurant and swimming pool at Twee Rivieren.
Enquiries: National Parks Board Reservations, PO Box 787, Pretoria 0001; tel. (012) 343-1991, fax. 343-0905, or PO Box 7400, Roggebaai 8012; tel. (021) 22-2810, fax 24-6211. Regional Marketing Officer, **Kalahari Regional Services Council**, PO Box 1480, Kuruman 8460; tel. (05373) 2-1001, fax. 2-2502. Marketing Officer, **Namaqualand Regional Services Council**, PO Box 5, Springbok 8240; tel. (0251) 2-2011, fax. 8-1333.

FOUR-WHEEL-DRIVE TRAILS
Eureka: Mr and Mrs R van Tonder, c/o Grootdors, Van Zylsrus 8467; tel. (05378) 305.
Khuis: Marketing Officer, Kalahari Regional Services Council (see above).
Kalahari 4x4 Trail: Joppie Botes, Molopo Kalahari Lodge, PO Box 32, Askham 8814; tel. (054902) Askham 2.
Pella: Marketing Officer, Namaqualand Regional Services Council (see above).

TOURIST INFORMATION
The Green Kalahari, PO Box 2856, Upington 8800; tel. (054) 2-6911, fax. 2-7064.

15 THE SWARTBERG

Stretching between Ladismith and Willowmore, where the range merges with the Baviaanskloof Mountains, the Swartberg forms a 200-km-long barrier between the Little Karoo and the Great Karoo. The Swartberg Pass, with its orange sandstone cliffs that have been weathered into fascinating shapes by the forces of nature, affords the visitor panoramic views. At its foothills lie Oudtshoorn and the nearby underground fairyland of the Cango Caves, as well as the quaint hamlet of Prince Albert.

How to get there
Oudtshoorn, gateway to the world-famous Cango Caves and a convenient base from which to explore the Swartberg, is situated some 430 km from Cape Town and 410 km from Port Elizabeth. From Cape Town follow the R62 through Montagu, Ladismith and Calitzdorp, or travel along the N2 to Mossel Bay and over the Robinson Pass on the R328. From Port Elizabeth follow either the scenic Langkloof route along the R62/N12, or the N2 to George and then over the Outeniqua Pass. The most direct approach from Johannesburg, 1 140 km away, is via Beaufort West on the N1 and the N12.

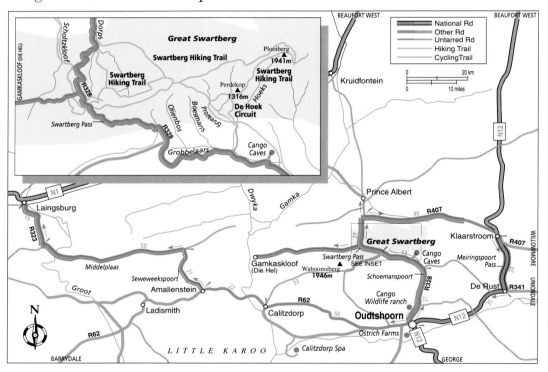

The **vegetation** of this rugged mountain range is dominated by montane fynbos comprising a diversity of ericas, restios and members of the protea family, among them the striking Ladismith protea, a species with brilliant crimson flowers which is restricted to the Little or Klein Swartberg, north of Ladismith.

Along the foothills and on the northern slopes the vegetation is dominated by Karoo veld types, including a variety of succulents of which aloes are the most prominent. Common shrubs and trees include the porkbush, rock candlewood and the yellow pomegranate.

➡ *The labyrinthine complex of fantastic limestone formations inside cavernous passages, known as the Cango Caves, is just 25 km north of Oudtshoorn, once the world's ostrich feather capital, and can be reached along the scenic Schoemanspoort (R328). Follow the directions from town. A visit to an ostrich farm and the Cango Wildlife ranch are highly recommended.*

CANGO CAVES
The Cango Caves in the southern foothills of the Swartberg are most exquisite masterpieces of

The Cango Caves are a masterpiece of nature, a world of caverns, narrow passages, columns and crystals.

Aloes grow abundantly on the steep footslopes of the Swartberg.

nature: a wonderous world of caverns, narrow passages, fluted columns and glittering crystals.

Stretching for over 3 km into the bowels of the earth, Cango is widely considered to be one of the most spectacular examples of a dripstone cave in the world. It consists of several chambers, the largest of which is Van Zyl's Hall – 107 m long, up to 54 m wide and 17 m high. Linking the caverns and chambers is a series of passages and tunnels, some of which, such as the appropriately named Lumbago Tunnel, are so narrow that one is forced to crawl on all fours.

A striking feature of the caves is the bewildering variety of stalagmites, stalagtites and helictites which have been formed over

aeons by calcium carbonate-rich water percolating through the cave roof. Among the many breathtaking formations are the 10-m-high Cleopatra's Needle in the Van Zyl's Hall, the delicate Ballerina, the Frozen Waterfall and the Curtains – a natural screen made of stalagtites.

Visitors can explore this underground maze only by joining an hour-long **guided tour**. During the tour interesting information about the caves is provided. At Jacob's Ladder visitors can either make their way back to the entrance or continue on to the Devil's Workshop, the Chimney and the Postbox, extending the tour by another hour. To many visitors this extension of the tour is the highlight of their visit to the caves, but as it involves the negotiation of several narrow passages, this section is best left to the lean and the fit.

It is advisable for all visitors to wear comfortable shoes with a good grip, and light casual clothing as the humidity in the caves averages 95%.

➤ *From the Cango Caves you could go on a 150-km round trip incorporating the spectacular Swartberg and Meiringspoort passes, returning to Oudtshoorn.*

At its northern entrance the Swartberg Pass squeezes through a gorge.

SWARTBERG PASS

Opened in 1888, the Swartberg Pass, one of the most scenic mountain passes in South Africa, is yet another example of the engineering skills of Thomas Bain, whose labourers fought foul weather on a steep incline to complete the arduous task.

Winding up the Swartberg's southern slopes the 24-km pass leads to the 1 585-m-high summit, with spectacular views of rugged mountains and the lattice-work of farmlands in the Little Karoo, 24 km past the Cango Caves. About 1 km beyond the summit the road passes the site of the old toll house (Ou Tol), marked by a clump of pine trees.

You'll soon pass the turnoff to Gamkaskloof (*see* below) and reach the most dramatic section of the pass about 6 km further on. The road twists and turns along the slopes of the valley carved by the Dorps River, revealing the dry-packed retaining walls used by Bain in the construction of the pass. At the last sharp bend the Droëwaterval, which is usually dry and hence

the name, can be seen to the left of the road, and a short way on the ruins of an old jail are passed. Some 220 convicts built the Swartberg Pass and at night the prisoners were kept here in the stone and clay building, known as the Blikstasie (tin station).

A journey along the pass takes visitors back in time millions of years, for there are few places where the results of the forces which created the **Cape Folded Mountains** can be seen more clearly than in the Swartberg. The mountains were formed when sandstone sediments were deposited in a basin 400 to 500 million years ago. However, due to the immense weight of the sediments and the unleashing of titanic forces in the earth's crust, some of the near horizontal layers were thrust up into an almost vertical position, while others were warped into bizarre arcs.

Several picnic places and viewpoints along the pass enable visitors not only to enjoy the spectacular scenery, but also to obtain a close-up view of the fynbos vegetation growing along the pass.

Swartberg was the last major pass built last century in South Africa.

The falls at Watervaldrif in Meiringspoort.

CANGO WILDLIFE RANCH

Situated about 3 km outside Oudtshoorn on the way to the Cango Caves, this ranch has over 400 Nile crocodiles and seven American aligators, as well as a unique complex where Africa's largest cats can be observed in their natural environment. An elevated walkway through natural vegetation allows visitors to watch and photograph cheetah, lion and exotic jaguar and puma. The walkway leads to a train which takes you through a deer park to a restaurant.

➡ The start of the Meiringspoort Pass is 50 km east from the Swartberg Pass along the R407.

MEIRINGSPOORT

Unlike the Swartberg Pass, which winds its way over the mountain, the 23-km Meiringspoort route follows a spectacular gorge carved through the heart of the Swartberg by the Groot River.

The magnificent 10,5-km-long gorge is hemmed in by sheer, brilliantly coloured cliff faces. Adding to the vivid orange and red tones of the contorted sandstone cliffs are bright splashes of yellow lichens. Along its winding course, the pass crosses the river 25 times, the longest straight section being only 2,5 km.

An interesting variety of birds are attracted to the river, which supports a wealth of trees: among them are Cape holly, cabbage tree, red alder and wild peach.

An unexpected surprise for many travellers is the beautiful waterfall at **Watervaldrif**, about halfway through the gorge. Here a stream of water cascades 60 m down the cliffs into a round rock pool, offering a welcome opportunity to swim. There is an information centre at the start of the short walk to the falls. The small farming settlement of **De Rust** at the southern entrance to Meiringspoort is reached about 21 km beyond the waterfall. From De Rust the road winds along the Olifants River Valley with its numerous ostrich farms and fields of lucerne, to reach Oudtshoorn 35 km further on.

➡ *If you'd prefer not to combine the two passes described above, take the R328 from the Meiringspoort turnoff (R407) for 4 km to the historic hamlet of Prince Albert.*

PRINCE ALBERT

This delightful town with its old-world atmosphere lies in the northern foothills of the Swartberg range. Named after the Prince Consort, the town has a rich 19th-century architectural heritage with numerous well-preserved buildings in Cape Dutch, Victorian and Karoo styles.

Interesting **architectural features** are the Prince Albert gables, which were built between 1840 and 1860. The old water-driven mill on the outskirts of the town dates back to 1850, and although the wheel is no longer turning, the mill is an excellent example of the methods used by the early settlers to grind wheat.

Prince Albert is a pleasant and convenient base from which to explore Gamkaskloof.

➡ *Tucked away in a secluded valley, carved by the Gamka River into the folds of the Swartberg, is the abandoned settlement of Gamkaskloof. From Oudtshoorn take the R328 to Schoemanspoort past the turnoff to the Cango Caves, and then to the summit of the Swartberg Pass. The turnoff is signposted 2,7 km beyond the summit. From Prince Albert, drive up the Swartberg Pass until you see the signpost to Gamkaskloof. From there it is a further 45 km, along a gravel road of variable condition, until you reach the settlement.*

GAMKASKLOOF

Many people simply know it as **Die Hel**, a name that this 17-km-long valley justifiably earned because of its extremely hot temperatures. Farmers of European descent first settled here in the 1830s, and in time the fertile valley was to become a home to fewer than 100 people.

Until 1963, when Gamkaskloof was linked to the Swartberg Pass by road, the valley was accessible only on foot and the inhabitants were neccessarily self-sufficient, producing their own fruit and vegetables and farming with goats. However, hardships slowly forced the small community at Die Hel to abandon the valley and the last family vacated the settlement in 1991.

In 1992 Cape Nature Conservation set aside an area of 1 500 ha in an attempt to preserve the natural beauty and cultural history of Gamkaskloof. Some of the old buildings have been restored with funds provided by the Simon van der Stel Foundation, and it is hoped to restore the entire settlement, and so to create a living museum.

➡ *Leave Oudtshoorn on the R62, travelling towards Calitzdorp. Some 28 km further on at the picturesque village of Amalienstein, turn right onto the road signposted Laingsburg and Seweweekspoort. The start of the spectacular drive through the gorge is some 5,6 km further on.*

For years ostrich farming has been a mainstay of the region's economy.

SEWEWEEKSPOORT

The suitability of the corridor between the Little Karoo and Laingsburg in the Karoo as a road was realised as early as 1862, when a throughway was built on the 15-km defile between the Swartberg and the Little Swartberg. Hemmed in by rugged mountains, the road was forced to follow the course of the Seweweekspoort River and was frequently washed away by floods – a factor which contributed to the decision by Thomas Bain to build the Swartberg Pass.

The scenic Seweweekspoort road meanders between dome-shaped mountains characterised by asymmetrical folded layers of sandstone. Guarding the northern end of the gorge is the 2 325-m-high Seweweekspoort Peak, the highest in the Swartberg.

WALKS AND TRAILS

SWARTBERG: The **De Hoek Circuit** is a pleasant day walk traversing the southern slopes of the Swartberg above the De Hoek Resort. Covering 12 km, the first 3,8 km is a steady uphill climb and the trail then crosses the slopes above the Perdepoort River valley for just over 4 km. The final 4,1 km is an easy descent along Protearug, which is, as the name suggests, covered with a profusion of proteas.

The **Swartberg Hiking Trail** leads past spectacular rock formations, through deep kloofs and along high mountain ridges, covering a total distance of 102 km. There are several starting points, enabling trailists to plan hikes from 2 to 5 days.

Summit Route: A particularly scenic option is the 2-day circular trail from Ou Tol to Bothashoek Hut. It winds for several kilometres along the crest of the Swartberg, rewarding hikers with alternating views of the Little Karoo and northwards to the Karoo. The first day covers 12.6 km, and the return leg is an easy 13,6 km along a jeep track.

GAMKASKLOOF (DIE HEL): This 41-km 3-day trail has been laid out in Gamkaskloof. From the camp site at the eastern end of the valley, the first day follows a U-shape route of 12 km initially meandering south along a kloof and then winding to Lemoen-kloof. The second day's hike also covers 12 km and traverses the north-facing valley slopes to the overnight stop near Die Hoogte. The 17-km third day returns to the starting point along the valley with its numerous historic buildings and other places of interest.

MOUNTAIN-BIKE TRAIL

THE SWARTBERG: A few kilometres after the Swartberg Pass summit, the road passes the turn-off to Gamkaskloof. The road to this secluded valley is suited to mountain-biking, but fitness is a prerequisite. Forty kilometres beyond the turnoff is a viewpoint with a magnificent vista of Gamkaskloof. From here the road twists for 5 km down into the valley; negotiation of these steep sections requires immense concentration. Enjoyable as the descent might be, the climb out of the kloof is strenuous and it is best to have a back-up vehicle to get back to the top of the pass.

The Seweweekspoort road connects the Little and the Great Karoo.

The scenic Seweweekspoort follows the course of the river.

THE SWARTBERG AT A GLANCE

MAIN ATTRACTIONS
Spectacular mountain scenery, views of the Karoo, Swartberg Pass, Cango Caves, Meirings-poort and Seweweekspoort drives, Gamkaskloof, walks and trails, mountain biking.

BEST TIMES TO VISIT
April to October are generally best, but minimum temperatures are about 5 °C from June to August. From September to November the fynbos is in full bloom. The Swartberg lies in an all-year rainfall area (bring rain gear) and snow and mist can be expected throughout the year. In mid-summer day-time temperatures can be unbearably hot.

CANGO CAVES
Permits/bookings: Advance bookings not required.
Opening times: Guided tours daily 09h00–16h00 all year.
Accommodation: Ranges from camp sites to self-catering chalets; hotels in Oudtshoorn. Contact Klein Karoo Marketing (*see* below).
Enquiries: Tel. (0443) 22-7410, fax. 22-8001.

CANGO WILDLIFE RANCH (formerly Cango Crocodile Ranch & Cheetahland)
Permits/bookings: Tel. (0443) 22-5593.

Opening times: Daily all year round from 08h00.

THE SWARTBERG
Permits/bookings: Contact Cape Nature Conservation (*see* below).
Opening times: Gamkaskloof is open throughout the year 07h30–16h15.
Accommodation: **Gamkaskloof:** Ten camp sites, cold-water shower and flush toilet. Accommodation is also available in some of the restored buildings, one of which (Cordier House) serves as overnight accommodation for hikers on the Gamkaskloof Hiking Trail. **Swartberg Hiking Trail:** Three semi-equipped overnight huts.
Prince Albert: Swartberg Hotel, PO Box 6, Prince Albert 6930; tel. (04436) 332, fax. 383.
Enquiries: **Cape Nature Conservation**, Private Bag X658, Oudtshoorn 6620; tel. (0443) 29-1739 or 29-1829.

TOURIST INFORMATION
Klein Karoo Marketing (Regional Tourism Office), PO Box 1234, Oudtshoorn 6620; tel. (0443) 22-6643, fax. 22-5007. **Prince Albert Publicity Association**, PO Box 109, Prince Albert, 6930; tel. (04436) 366.

16 THE KAROO NATIONAL PARK

The Karoo plains once supported vast herds of game and in June 1823 the British traveller George Thompson reported seeing '... prodigious flocks of springboks spread over the plains as far as the eye could see ...' near Beaufort West. The legendary springbok 'treks' have, unfortunately, long since ceased, but the Karoo still has much to offer – the distinct fragrance of the veld after a thunderstorm, its wide and beautiful open expanses and the clear, starlit skies illuminating the dolerite koppies and ridges.

How to get there
The park is 480 km from Cape Town and 920 km from Johannesburg. From Cape Town take the N1 through Laingsburg, to the signposted turnoff 2,5 km south of Beaufort West. Stop at the historic Matjiesfontein Hotel before Laingsburg. From Johannesburg follow the N1 through Kimberley (or the N12 through Bloemfontein) and Three Sisters to the signposted entrance gate 2,5 km south of Beaufort West. A visit could be combined with Tour 15 or 17 (pp. 74 and 81).

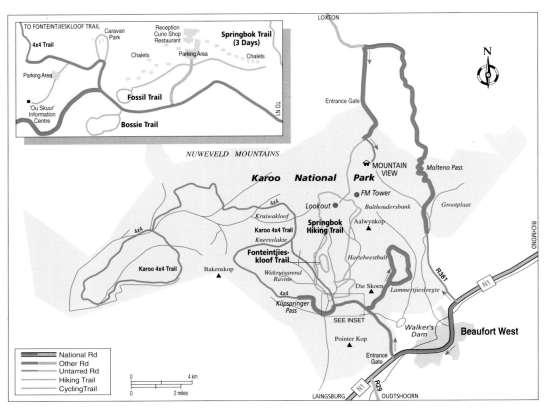

Spectacular and diverse scenery and vegetation are the greatest attractions of the Karoo National Park. Some 7 000 **plant species** have been recorded in the arid Karoo, and the mixed grass and shrub vegetation is characterised by a wealth of Karoo bushes. Known as 'bossies', many plants have captivating names such as biltongbos, koggelmandervoetkaroo, daggapit and ganna. Among the shrubs are the driedoring, kriedoring, wolwedoring, crossberry, and the wild pomegranate, with its conspicuous yellow flowers which appear soon after rains.

Animal life in the park was, until recently, scant, and only the mountain reedbuck, grey rhebok,

The black-backed jackal is protected in the Karoo National Park.

The fossils in the park can be seen in the course of the Fossil Trail.

Looking from the summit of the Nuweveld Mountains towards Beaufort West. Geological evolution has formed a starkly beautiful landscape.

kudu and klipspringer were found here. However, two years before the national park was proclaimed in 1979, a reintroduction programme began; 26 springbok and eight black wildebeest were translocated from the Mountain Zebra National Park near Cradock. Red hartebeest, gemsbok and Cape mountain zebra were reintroduced the next year.

In 1993, three black rhino were released into an 8 000-ha camp with a rhino-proof fence, as part of a programme to establish as many populations as possible. So far this has proved positive as the first calf was born in August 1995.

Today the Karoo National Park boasts 64 mammal species, and 59 reptile and eight frog species have been recorded.

KAROO FOSSILS

An estimated 240 million years ago, giant reptiles roamed freely around the flat, marshy floodplains which surrounded an inland lake, at that time covering large areas of the present-day Karoo. Most of the skeletons of these huge dinosaurs soon disintegrated, but the remains of those who died in the marshes became entombed in mud. The calcium in their bones dissolved over aeons and was slowly replaced by silica from the surrounding sediments to form perfect replicas. These

are the dinosaur fossils that were exposed millions of years later by modern rivers.

Since the discovery of the first fossil near Beaufort West in 1827, the Karoo has gained a reputation as one of the richest areas in the world for fossils of reptiles. Four of the five main groups of mammal-like reptiles are known to have occurred in this area. The small herbivorous dicynodonts were the most common, and remains of several of these can be seen along the popular Fossil Trail.

Among the smaller animals which occur are bat-eared and Cape foxes, black-backed jackal, chacma baboon and vervet monkey. The Cape clawless otter, too, is found here, usually in dams, but as it is a secretive creature it is unlikely to be seen by visitors.

A surprising number of **birds** are present in the park – a list of over 194 species has been compiled, including endemics such as the Karoo korhaan, Karoo and Namaqua prinias, rufouseared and cinnamonbreasted warblers, fairy flycatchers and rock pipits. The cliffs are ideal for black eagles – with 20 breeding pairs the park has one of their highest concentrations in South Africa.

The rugged terrain rules out an extensive road network, but there are two short game drives suitable for sedan vehicles.

A dawn or dusk game drive through **Lammertjiesleegte** in the southeastern corner of the park might be rewarded with sightings of game typical to the Karoo, including springbok, gemsbok, red hartebeest and Cape mountain zebra, along the

13-km route. The drive up the **Klipspringer Pass** links the lower plains with the middle plateau. The beautiful 3,2-km pass was constructed using the dry-wall technique, perfected by Andrew Geddes Bain. Some 7 800 m³ of rock was used for the retaining walls. Also worthwhile is a drive to **Mountain View**, a self-catering rest camp perched on the edge of the Nuweveld Mountains' plateau with its far-reaching vistas over Beaufort West, the rest camp nestling in the valley below and the surrounding mountain landscape. It is reached by taking the turnoff onto the Loxton road (R381) about 3 km north of Beaufort West. Turn left at the signposted turnoff, about 24 km along this road, to reach the entrance gate, 3,5 km on and the Mountain View Rest Camp 4 km further.

WALKS AND TRAILS
Three short walks have been laid close to the rest camp. Trail brochures are available from the reception office. **The Fossil Trail** takes visitors back in time

After rains the Karoo comes alive with colour.

some 240 million years to an era during which the Karoo was inhabited by dinosaurs. Points of interest are numbered along the 400-m route and explained in the comprehensive brochure. The route is also suitable for the blind, having been marked with a guide rope and with information provided on Braille plaques.

The **Bossie Trail** is an easy 800-m ramble for all which starts just south of the access road to the caravan park and which provides an ideal introduction to Karoo vegetation. Some 65 plants are identified along the route and facts about each plant can be found in the brochure. The

Fonteintjieskloof Trail (11 km) takes 4 to 5 hours to complete and affords visitors the opportunity to experience the essence of the Karoo – tranquillity and solitude. The trail is best hiked early in the morning – it is advisable to take a day pack with a water-bottle and a picnic lunch.

The 26,5-km-long circular **Springbok Hiking Trail** rewards hikers with breathtaking views. The 3-day trail winds from the flat plains to the summit of the Nuweberg.

KAROO FOUR-WHEEL-DRIVE TRAIL

Visitors can undertake this trail (the first of its kind in a South African national park), either on their own or by joining a guided day or overnight trip. The route climbs from the lower plains up to the middle plateau covering terrain which varies from steep passes clinging to the mountain slopes to undulating sandy plains and desolate stretches of rock. A painstakingly restored shepherd's cottage, dating back just over a century, serves as overnight accommodation for trailists. Several sites of interest have been marked along the route and are explained in a trail brochure.

From the hide near the camp birders can observe the park's birdlife.

A 4x4 trail takes visitors to some of the park's remotest corners.

THE RIVERINE RABBIT

A small group of six riverine rabbits, one of southern Africa's most endangered mammals, was released in the Karoo National Park in August 1994. This nocturnal animal had been feared extinct until one was found in 1979 near Victoria West, 32 years after the last specimen

was collected. The species had declined in the Karoo as a result of the destruction of nearly two-thirds of their riverine habitat, mainly by overgrazing. Happily, they appear to have adapted very well and the first rabbit born in the park was spotted in late November 1994.

THE KAROO NATIONAL PARK AT A GLANCE

MAIN ATTRACTIONS
Typical Karoo scenery and vegetation, fossils, Braille trail, overnight and four-wheel-drive trails, walks and hiking trail.

BEST TIMES TO VISIT
March to October are best but sub-zero temperatures are not uncommon in mid-winter.

KAROO NATIONAL PARK REST CAMP
Permits/bookings: Permits at gate. **Springbok Hiking Trail:** National Parks Board Reservations (*see* below). **Mountain View Rest Camp:** Permits available at Karoo National Park Rest Camp (*see* below).
Opening times: Gates open daily 05h00–22h00 all year.
Accommodation: Hutted accommodation, camp sites: National Parks Board Reservations (*see* below).
Springbok Hiking Trail: Two overnight huts (for 12), semi-equipped. Water, ablutions, braai facilities at second hut. **Mountain View Rest Camp:** Semi-equipped.
Facilities: **Karoo National Park:** Shop, restaurant, swimming pool, information centre and conference facilities.
Mountain View Rest Camp: Very basic facilities.

KAROO FOUR-WHEEL-DRIVE TRAIL
Permits/bookings: Contact The Park Warden, Karoo National Park (*see* below).
Opening times: Open throughout the year. While flexible, the recommended departure time for the self-guided trail is 14h30.
Accommodation: A self-catering cottage, semi-equipped; **Mountain View Rest Camp:** Self-catering, semi-equipped. **Doringhoek Guest House:** fully equipped restored farmhouse.
Facilities: Firewood and limited water are all that is provided. **Mountain View Rest Camp:** Only very basic facilities are provided.

Enquiries: **National Parks Board Reservations,** PO Box 787, Pretoria 0001; tel. (012) 343-1991, fax 343-0905, or PO Box 7400, Roggebaai 8012; tel. (021) 22-2810, fax 24-621.
The Park Warden, Karoo National Park, PO Box 316, Beaufort West 6970; tel. (0201) 5-2828, fax 5-1671.

TOURIST INFORMATION Beaufort West Tourism Office, PO Box 56, Beaufort West 6970; tel. (0201) 3001, fax. 3675.

17 THE KAROO NATURE RESERVE

This nature reserve encompasses a massive 16 000 ha of land with vegetation ranging from Karoo bushes to succulent montane veld characterised by the conspicuous spekboom or porkbush. It is constituted by four distinct sections: the west, with its awe-inspiring Valley of Desolation, the specially designated game-viewing area, Vanryneveld's Pass Dam, home to an assortment of water birds, and the mountainous eastern section.

How to get there
The reserve is outside Graaff-Reinet, 675 km from Cape Town and 210 km from Beaufort West (a visit could be linked with Tours 16 and 23, pp. 78 and 104). From Port Elizabeth the town is approached through Uitenhage and Jansenville along the R75 (260 km). From Johannesburg (880 km) follow the N1 to Colesberg, take the N9 through Noupoort and the N10 to Middelburg. About 3 km south of Middelburg rejoin the N9 to reach Graaff-Reinet after 105 km.

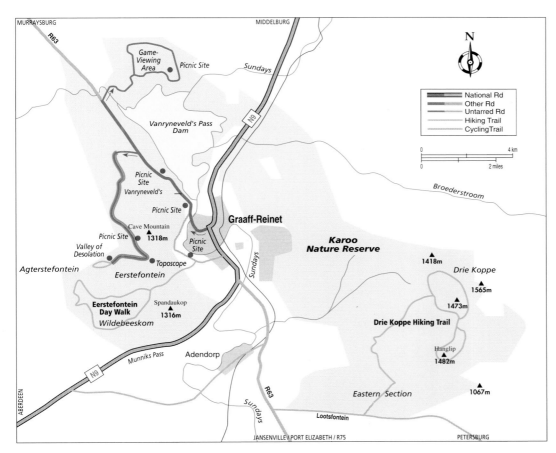

the reserve, among them the whitebrowed robin and rock bunting. Typical Karoo species include the Karoo korhaan, spike-heeled lark and larklike bunting. Ostrich have been reintroduced, and secretarybird, black eagle, kori bustard, rock pigeon, blue crane, and redwinged and pale-winged starlings also occur.

The **vegetation** of the reserve ranges from low Karoo shrubs such as gannabos (*Salsola* sp.) interspersed with thorny succulents and grasses on the lowland plains to short grasses and Karoo bushes on the mountain summits.

➤ Undoubtedly the focal point of the Karoo Nature Reserve, the Valley of Desolation is situated in the western section of the reserve. The turnoff to the Valley is sign-posted approximatley 5 km from Graaff-Reinet on the Murraysburg road. The parking area is about 9 km further on.

THE VALLEY OF DESOLATION

A jumble of rock pillars, isolated pinnacles, clusters of precariously balanced rocks and sheer cliffs – this is the epitome of desolation.

The drive to the Valley is a scenic delight, with each bend in the road providing yet another spectacular view. From the view-point on the U-bend, 1 km before the parking area, visitors can take in the whole of Graaff-Reinet and

Blesbok have been reintroduced into the Karoo Nature Reserve.

Situated in the southern foothills of the Sneeuberg, the Karoo Nature Reserve is dominated by typical Karoo koppies with their dolerite caps and steep slopes. Large **mammals**, such as the Cape mountain zebra, black wildebeest, gemsbok and blesbok, have been reintroduced into the reserve. Other mammals recorded include klipspringer, mountain reedbuck, baboon and vervet monkey, as well as smaller mammals and several rodents.

Because Graaff-Reinet marks the western limit of distribution of **birds** occurring along the east coast of South Africa, an interesting variety has been recorded in its surrounding environment. On a clear day both the Compass Mountain in the Sneeuberg range to the north and the Cockscomb Mountains to the south are seen.

An unexacting short ramble from the parking area leads the visitor to viewpoints, on the edge of precipices, overlooking magnificent dolerite buttresses and pillars. The origin of these weird formations that reach heights of up to 120 m can be traced back some 160 to 180 million years ago, when molten matter intruded along horizontal sills and vertical fissures in the overlying sandstone and shale. The magma subsequently cooled down and solidified into dolerite, causing vertical and horizontal cracks along which erosion took place. Over millions of years the overlying Karoo sedimentary rocks have eroded and have

thus exposed the underlying dolerite, which is far more resistant to erosion.

Further afield the conical Spandaukop and the Plains of Camdeboo can be seen. There is a picnic site at Ribbokberg, en route to the Valley of Desolation.

➡ *The Vanryneveld's Pass Dam north of Graaff-Reinet is a popular venue for watersports. Access for canoes and sailboards is from Piekniekbos (about 4 km from the centre of Graaff-Reinet on the R63 to Murraysburg) and for boats and yachts from the yacht club on the southern banks of the dam.*

VANRYNEVELD'S PASS DAM

Most of the dam is open for watersports, but boats are not permitted in the area where the Sundays River flows into it as this is an important bird habitat.

The dam attracts a variety of water birds, among which are great crested grebe, Egyptian and spurwinged geese, South African shellduck and yellowbilled duck. Large numbers of flamingos can usually be seen when the water level of the dam is low.

The dam has been stocked with large-mouth bass, tilapia (kurper), sharptooth catfish and carp. Light tackle-boat **angling**, as well as shore angling, is permitted with the necessary licence. The area from Piekniekbos along the southern edge of the dam to Broederstroom has been zoned for shore angling.

Picnic places are provided at Barbergat, which overlooks the dam (about 2,2 km from the centre of town), and at Piekniekbos

Rock pillars, isolated pinnacles, clusters of balanced rocks and sheer cliffs of the Valley of Desolation. A distant plain stretches to Graaff-Reinet.

Spandaukop is an excellent example of a typical Karoo koppie.

It serves as an ideal habitat for the Cape mountain zebra, klipspringer, mountain reedbuck, red hartebeest, kudu, common duiker and steenbok.

Day walks can be undertaken along routes determined by trailists themselves. Arrangements can also be made to drive along the four-wheel-drive tracks which traverse the mountainous terrain. Plans are afoot to establish a proper trail.

WALKS AND TRAILS

VALLEY OF DESOLATION: A conspicuous reptile of the park's rocky areas, the Eastern Cape crag lizard is the emblem of the **Valley of Desolation Nature Walk**, a 1,5-km ramble which takes more or less 45 minutes to complete. From the main viewpoints the walk continues in a westerly direction along the edge of the cliffs to a beacon before winding back to the car-park. In the basin below the Valley of Desolation and Spandaukop the **Eerstefontein Day Walk** offers hikers a choice between a 5-, 11- or 14-km walk. The route is fairly easy and among the animals trailists might spot are black wildebeest, springbok, kudu, common duiker and steenbok.

THE EASTERN SECTION: The **Drie Koppe Hiking Trail** covers about 26 km and can either be hiked as a 2- or a 3-day trail. Visitors are allowed to undertake self-guided day walks.

(toilets are provided) on the western shores of the dam (about 1,7 km further along the R63 to Murraysburg).

➤ The game-viewing area lies to the north of the Vanryneveld's Pass Dam. From Graaff-Reinet follow the R63 towards Murraysburg over the Vanryneveld's Dam Pass until reaching the signposted turnoff to the game-viewing area approximately 8 km northwest of the town. Visitors are required to complete the register at the Empangele gate, where a pamphlet/map of the area can be obtained.

GAME-VIEWING AREA

Characterised by riverine thickets and grassland interspersed with Karoo bushes and scrub, the game-viewing area is stocked with several antelope species, including gemsbok, springbok, blesbok, kudu, steenbok and common duiker. Red hartebeest, buffalo and black wildebeest also occur. A network of gravel roads covering 19 km winds through this section of the park, and visitors must stick to the roads and, for their own safety, may not alight from their vehicles other than at the Impunzi picnic site (toilets are provided).

➤ Access to the eastern section of the reserve is by prior arrangement only and directions on how to get there are provided when the keys to the gates are collected from the reserve authorities.

THE EASTERN SECTION

Dominated by the unmistakable Drie Koppe, a trio of Karoo koppies, the eastern section of the reserve is a mountainous area with several peaks reaching heights of over 1 400 m and towering over the low-lying plains.

THE KAROO NATURE RESERVE AT A GLANCE

MAIN ATTRACTIONS
Geological formations, scenic views, walks and trails, game-viewing, bird-watching, watersports, angling.

BEST TIMES TO VISIT
April to September are best; sub-zero temperatures are not uncommon at night and in the early morning in mid-winter.

PERMITS/BOOKINGS
Valley of Desolation: Unrestricted access. **Vanryneveld's Pass Dam:** Fishing permits must be obtained from the Magistrate's Office, 26 Church Street, Graaff-Reinet 6280; Private Bag X691, Graaff-Reinet 6280; tel. (0491) 2-2263. **Game-viewing area:** Self-access entry – visitors must complete a register at the gate. **Eastern section:** Drie Koppe Hiking Trail, Officer-in-Charge, Karoo Nature Reserve (*see* below).

OPENING TIMES
Valley of Desolation: Unrestricted access. **Vanryneveld's Pass Dam:** 07h30–18h00 (winter) and 07h30–19h00 (summer). **Game-viewing area:** 07h00–18h00 (winter) and 07h00–19h00 (summer). **Eastern section:** 07h30–18h00 (winter) and 07h30–19h00 (summer).

ACCOMMODATION
Eastern section: Drie Koppe Hiking Trail: One overnight hut for hikers only (sleeps 10), semi-equipped. Cold water only, outside shower and toilet, braai facilities. Hikers must carry their own water during the day as water is only available at the hut. Bookings to be made in advance through Eastern Cape Nature Conservation office, Graaff-Reinet (*see* below).

FACILITIES
Valley of Desolation: Ribbokberg picnic site. **Vanryneveld's Pass Dam:** Piekniekbos, Barbergat picnic sites. **Game-viewing area:** Impunzi picnic site. **Eastern section:** None on Drie Koppe Hiking Trail.

ENQUIRIES
Eastern Cape Nature Conservation office, Petrus de Klerk Building, Bourke Street, Graaff-Reinet 6280; tel. (0491) 2-3453. **Officer-in-Charge, Karoo Nature Reserve,** PO Box 349, Graaff-Reinet 6280; tel. (0491) 2-3453.

TOURIST INFORMATION
Graaff-Reinet Publicity Association, PO Box 153, Graaff-Reinet 6280; tel. and fax. (0491) 2-4248.

SOUTHERN AND EASTERN CAPE

In the southern Cape, tranquil lakes, unspoilt estuaries and lagoons merge to create one of South Africa's most scenic areas. Fringing this coastal patchwork on the landward side are indigenous forests of towering yellowwood, stinkwood, assegai and candlewood – a refuge for the last few free-roaming elephants in the country.

Along the coast, miles and miles of golden beaches are interspersed with rugged cliffs, plunging almost vertically down to boulder-strewn beaches. Separating the well-watered coastal plains from the arid Little Karoo is a natural barrier of peaks, cliffs and deep valleys. Proteas, ericas and other fynbos plants grow in profusion on the mountain slopes of the Outeniqua and Tsitsikamma mountains, and in the secluded valleys patches of indigenous forest can still be found. To the east lies the Baviaanskloof, a rugged mountain wilderness, and the Amatola range, renowned for its magnificent indigenous forests and breathtakingly beautiful waterfalls.

Although wildlife is not as abundant and diverse as that of the Lowveld, game-viewing can be rewarding. The dense Addo bush is a sanctuary to the southernmost viable elephant population of the African continent, as well as the East African subspecies of the black rhino and the flightless dung beetle. In the mountains near Cradock, Cape mountain zebra – a species which was once on the brink of extinction – abound.

Secluded bays fringed by wild banana trees, untouched beaches, waterfalls tumbling directly into the sea and undulating hills dotted with traditional Xhosa huts await visitors to the Wild Coast. It is without doubt among the most beautiful stretches of coastline in the world.

Inland, the mighty Drakensberg range, one of the last strongholds of the rare bearded vulture, towers high above the grassy slopes. In winter the peaks are often covered in a blanket of snow, creating ideal skiing conditions.

Opportunities to explore the area, or simply to relax, are virtually endless. Spectacular passes traverse the mountains and hiking trails lead to remote corners. The numerous options for watersports range from scuba diving and paddling on the waterways in a canoe to deep-sea angling.

The popular 60-km Tsitsikamma Hiking Trail leads through indigenous forests and along the southern Cape coast, rewarding hikers with spectacular views.

18 WILDERNESS LAKES AREA

Stretching through the Garden Route in a unique series of both fresh- and saltwater lakes is South Africa's Lake District. The majestic Outeniqua Mountains form the northern boundary of this tranquil paradise of lakes, estuaries, rivers and indigenous forests, while rocky cliffs and white beaches washed by the Indian Ocean form its southern borders. The holiday resort of Wilderness, with its sweeping vistas of sandy beaches, is an attractive base from which to explore the area.

How to get there
Wilderness is situated about 450 km east of Cape Town and 300 km west of Port Elizabeth along the N2. George is the nearest town (15 km west), with Knysna 46 km to the east.

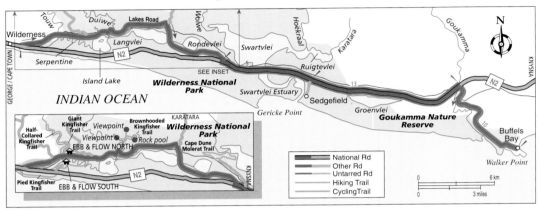

THE LAKES SCENIC DRIVE

This scenic drive, which snakes along and through the Wilderness National Park (*see* p. 87), starts at the Wilderness Hotel. At the traffic circle just beyond the hotel, turn right into Waterside Road, which initially runs along the northern edge of the Touw River estuary, and continue for 3,2 km. Above the confluence of the Serpentine with the estuary, a bridge which is also used by trains (they have right of way) crosses the Touw River. About 100 m further is the turnoff to the **Ebb and Flow Rest Camp North** (*see* p. 89).

The road then skirts the northern banks of the **Serpentine**, a natural water channel which meanders for about 5,5 km through a marshy area and links the three western lakes (Island Lake, Langvlei and Rondevlei) with the Touw River.

Continuing on this picturesque route, the road hugs the northern banks of the 150-ha Island Lake (also known as Eilandvlei), which owes its name to the prominent Drommedaris Island in its centre. After crossing the Duiwe River, the road continues to the north of the tranquil 3-km-long **Langvlei**. It then heads south through pine forests and skirts the 143-ha **Rondevlei** before joining the N2. The whole area has abundant birdlife, with bird hides at both Langvlei and Rondevlei (*see* p. 87).

Not long after joining the N2, a road bridge crosses the northern end of the Swartvlei estuary,

linking the largest and deepest of the five lakes, **Swartvlei**, to the sea. Covering 1 085 ha, Swartvlei is not permanently connected to the sea as its mouth is blocked by a sand bar for more than six months of the year.

The town of **Sedgefield** on the eastern shores of the Swartvlei estuary is a short way beyond the bridge. Flanking the estuary mouth, its vast and unspoilt sandy beaches are favoured by anglers and sunbathers. **Gericke Point**, a rocky headland west of the mouth, is ideal for **rock angling**.

Further east along the N2, travellers can enjoy good views of **Groenvlei**, which lies 3 m above sea level. It is the least brackish of the five lakes and, since it has no outlet to the sea and is not fed by a river, it relies on rainwater seeping through the dunes and freshwater springs for its water.

The seaside resort of **Buffels Bay**, with its magnificent beach, is at the end of the road that passes through the **Goukamma Nature Reserve** (*see* p. 88). **Walker Point**, a rocky promontory at Buffels Bay, has created a bay which sweeps eastwards to Brenton-on-Sea near Knysna. The sheltered bay offers a variety of **watersports**, such as swimming, surfing, paddle-skiing, and rock and surf angling.

To retrace your steps back to Wilderness, simply continue along the N2.

➡ *A highly recommended scenic drive winds eastwards from Wilderness, along the Lakes Road (which runs parallel to the railway line until after Langvlei), affording visitors superb panoramic vistas of the surrounding lakes. The route links up with the N2 immediately before crossing over Swartvlei. It continues past Groenvlei and the Goukamma Nature Reserve and then on to Buffels Bay.*

➡ *The Ebb and Flow Rest Camp South, run by the National Parks Board, is situated just 4 km from Wilderness. From George, the road crosses over the Kaaimans River mouth and leads on to Wilderness village; the rest camp is signposted 2,4 km on. From Knysna, travel past*

The beach at Wilderness, one of South Africa's premier holiday resorts.

The giant kingfisher is one of five kingfisher species in the area.

Groenvlei Nature Reserve and Sedgefield; the rest camp is sign-posted to the right, about 800 m after the Island Lake turnoff.

WILDERNESS NATIONAL PARK

The Wilderness National Park covers 2 612 ha stretching between Wilderness and the Goukamma Nature Reserve (*see* p. 88). It comprises the Touw River and its estuary, the Serpentine, Island Lake, Langvlei, Rondevlei, Swartvlei and its estuary, the Kaaimans, Duiwe and Goukamma rivers; and 28 km of coastline. A 10 000-ha National Lake Area surrounds the park.

The lakes between Wilderness and Buffels Bay comprise three independent systems – the Wilderness Lakes (Island Lake, Langvlei and Rondevlei, all connected to the Touw River by the Serpentine), Swartvlei north of Sedgefield, and Groenvlei to its east, which is outside the park.

The area does not support large numbers of **mammals**, but visitors may spot grysbok in the dune scrub and bushbuck, blue duiker, bushpig, vervet monkey and baboon in the forests.

With its lakes and forests, Wilderness is a bird-watcher's paradise; **water bird** numbers fluctuate from 5 000 to 24 500. About 230 species have been recorded here, including 79 of the 95 water bird species found in South Africa. Among the most common water birds are black-necked grebe, dabchick, reed cormorant, yellowbilled duck, redknobbed coot and darter. Five of South Africa's ten kingfisher species have been recorded (pied, giant, half-collared, brown-hooded and malachite) and walks in the park have been named

Trailing in the tranquil and beautiful surroundings of the natural forests is a popular activity.

after four of the species in the area (*see* p. 89). The Wilderness Lakes system also has one of the country's largest populations of the African marsh harrier and is a refuge to a relict population of the grass owl. Two **bird hides** are the Malachite hide at Langvlei and the Rondevlei hide; the Serpentine offers good birding from a canoe or pedal boat.

The lakes offer unparalleled opportunities for a variety of **watersports** such as sailing, boardsailing, waterskiing, pedal boating and canoeing. However,

OUTENIQUA CHOO-TJOE

For a completely different perspective of the lakes take a ride on the famous Outeniqua Choo-Tjoe, one of the few steam trains still operating in South Africa. The spectacular 2½-hour journey between George and Knysna goes over bridges (notably the Kaaimans River bridge), through tunnels, along the curving shore line (the first view of the sea is at Victoria Bay, a surfer's paradise), past tranquil lakes and through lush indigenous forests (Goukamma Valley) and plantations before reaching Knysna (*see* p. 90). Refreshments are available on the train or at the Knysna station. Visitors can either catch the train back to George after a 2-hour stop or they can make use of a shuttle service that meets every train (a separate fee is payable).

A scenic train ride can be enjoyed on the Outeniqua Choo-Tjoe between George and Knysna.

Angling and watersports are permitted on the expansive and picturesque Swartvlei.

The confluence of the Touw River and the Serpentine.

Angling is also popular along the 28-km-long coast. Rock and surf fish which can be caught include kabeljou, musselcracker, elf, yellowtail, galjoen, white steenbras and red roman.

From May to October **southern right whales** may be seen when they come to calve close inshore; humpback whales are sighted occasionally, and **dolphins** are often seen frolicking in the surf. The best vantage points are Dolphin Point, 1,5 km west of Wilderness on the N2, a viewpoint overlooking the long Wilderness beach and the railway bridge crossing the mouth of the Kaaimans River, and the Kleinkrans coastal viewpoint, signposted 6,5 km east of Wilderness on the N2.

➡ *Goukamma Nature Reserve's turnoff is 8 km east of the Lakes Road/N2 junction (at Swartvlei); the entrance gate is 6 km further.*

GOUKAMMA NATURE RESERVE

The eastern section of the Wilderness National Park is adjacent to Cape Nature Conservation's Goukamma Nature Reserve. Groenvlei along its northern boundary and the Goukamma River and estuary in the east are the focal points of this verdant 2 230-ha reserve. Its 14-km coastline, characterised by weathered sandstone cliffs, is bordered by a marine reserve extending from the high-water mark seawards for 1,8 km.

Bushbuck, grysbok, blue duiker, bushpig and the Cape clawless otter are among the **mammals** found here, but they are seldom seen, unlike the vervet monkeys in the reserve. Among the more than 150 **bird species** recorded are the secretarybird, the African fish eagle with its evocative call, martial eagle, rameron pigeon and Knysna lourie. Groenvlei provides a habitat for a wide diversity of water birds, including the dabchick, reed cormorant, yellowbilled duck, southern pochard, greenshank, curlew sandpiper and blackwinged stilt.

Two indigenous **fish species**, the Cape silverside and the estuarine roundherring, inhabit the 250-ha freshwater lake, but are not suitable for angling. The lake

due to the sensitive lake ecology, some activities are restricted to certain areas. No watersports are permitted at **Langvlei** and **Rondevlei**, and only canoes, rowing boats and pedal boats are allowed on the **Serpentine**. Powerboats and angling are permitted in demarcated areas on the **Touw River estuary**. Watersports (including waterskiing) and angling are allowed at **Island Lake** and **Swartvlei**.

Picnic places with braai places and toilets are available for day visitors at both the Ebb and Flow rest camps, except during peak periods (school holidays and December/January).

The lakes and the Swartvlei and Touw River estuaries support various **fish species** and angling is popular here. In the Touw River estuary, your chances of catching springer, harder, white stumpnose and kabeljou are generally favourable. Island Lake is another favourite spot with anglers, as is Swartvlei. However, rods and reels are not permitted along the Serpentine, at Langvlei or at Rondevlei. No permits are needed to fish at the Touw River estuary, Island Lake and Swartvlei.

MAP OF AFRICA

When viewed from the south, the winding Kaaimans River looks remarkably similar to a map of Africa. From Wilderness village, drive past the hotel and take the left turning at the T-junction, then turn right almost immediately into White's Road which climbs to Wilderness Heights. Turn right onto the tarred road, then turn left and follow the visible 'Map of Africa' signs (for approximately 2,5 km).

The pied kingfisher often hovers over the water searching for prey.

is rated as one of the best spots in South Africa to catch largemouth bass and is also stocked with Mozambique tilapia.

Delightful picnic, braai and toilet facilities are along the banks of the Goukamma River for day visitors. Recreational activities include walking and horse-riding (*see below*), swimming, walking, boardsailing and angling (an inland water angling licence is obtainable from the Receiver of Revenue). Canoeing is permitted on the lake (only one double canoe is available for visitors to the bush camp) and the Goukamma River but powerboats are not allowed on either the lake or river (boats with electric engines are permitted).

WALKS AND TRAILS
WILDERNESS NATIONAL PARK:
A 1-km **boardwalk**, ideal for bird-watching, curves along the banks of the Touw River. It is also the starting point of the

circular 10-km-long **Pied Kingfisher Trail** which has its return route along the beach. The **Giant Kingfisher Trail** is a 7-km round trip from Ebb and Flow Rest Camp North, rising through dense forests of indigenous trees along the eastern bank of the Touw River and ending high above the river at a waterfall. Look out for the lovely Knysna lourie on this walk. The **Half-collared Kingfisher Trail** is a 3-km ramble along the western bank and follows the Touw River more closely. A continuation of this walk is the 1-km Bosduif Loop. Further east, the easy 7-km **Brownhooded Kingfisher Trail** follows the course of Duiwe River which feeds into Island Lake. The **Cape Dune Molerat Trail**, a moderately easy 6-km circular route, begins at the Rondevlei office and leads across the dunes between Rondevlei and Swartvlei. A variety of flowers are seen at their best in spring and summer, among them the bright red *Erica speciosa*, krantz aloe, the green woodorchid, the pale pink to deep purple carpet geranium, sour figs, watsonias and the attractive *Conicosia bijlii* with its lemon-yellow flowers.

GOUKAMMA NATURE RESERVE:
The starting leg of the **Goukamma Nature Reserve Circuit** heads across the dunes, and then returns to the starting point through milkwood forests. Approximately 3½ hours should be set aside to hike the 8-km route. The one way **Goukamma-Groenvlei Trail** is slightly

longer, following a 13,5-km route across the dunes to the shores of Groenvlei; hikers will need to organise their return transport at the end at Groenvlei Conservation Station in advance. The 14-km-long **Beach Walk** offers splendid coastal scenery.

HORSE-RIDING
A day-long horse trail has recently been laid out along the beach and through the Goukamma Nature Reserve. Bring your own horses or hire them from the nearby Rivendell Equestrian Centre (book a week in advance).

WILDERNESS LAKES AREA AT A GLANCE

MAIN ATTRACTIONS
Pristine lake scenery, The Lakes Scenic Drive, a variety of watersports, bird-watching, walks, Outeniqua Choo-Tjoe train ride, angling, whale-watching, 'Map of Africa'.

BEST TIMES TO VISIT
Throughout the year, but remember to bring your rain gear as this is an all-year rainfall region. The angling seasons are variable, depending on the species. Spring is best for wild flowers.

WILDERNESS NATIONAL PARK
Permits/bookings: Entry permits are not required. Bookings for accommodation through National Parks Board Reservations (*see below*).
Opening times: Open daily 07h30–17h00 most of year; 07h30–20h00 in summer.
Accommodation: Ebb and Flow Rest Camp North: Ten 2-bed huts with shower and toilet facilities, five 2-bed huts with communal ablution facilities. Ebb and Flow Rest Camp South: (formerly Wilderness Rest Camp) Eight fully-equipped 4-bed log cabins and five 6-bed cottages. Ten 6-berth chalavans (caravan under roof with separate anteroom). A hundred caravan and camp sites with hot/cold-water facilities.
Facilities: There is a shop in the park which sells basic provisions only; the nearest restaurants and garage/petrol station are at Wilderness.
Enquiries: National Parks Board Reservations, PO Box 787, Pretoria 0001; tel. (012) 343-1991, fax. 343-0905; or PO Box 7400, Roggebaai 8012; tel. (021) 22-2810, fax. 24-6211.

GOUKAMMA NATURE RESERVE
Permits/bookings: Entry permits at gate.
Opening times: Daily 08h00–18h00.
Accommodation: Goukamma thatched rondavel: Self-contained 6-bed rondavel.
Groenvlei Bush Camp: Two 4-bed huts with a boardwalk to a cooking lapa.
Facilities: The nearest garage/petrol station is at Wilderness. There are picnic sites at the estuary.
Horse rides: Hire horses at the Rivendell Equestrian Centre (*see below*).
Enquiries: The Park Warden, Goukamma Nature Reserve, PO Box 331, Knysna 6570; tel./fax. (0445) 83-0042.
Rivendell Equestrian Centre, tel. (0445) 83-0138.

OUTENIQUA CHOO-TJOE
Bookings: Transnet Heritage Foundation, PO Box 850, George 6530; tel. Knysna (0445) 2-1361 or George (0441) 73-8288.
Shuttle Service: tel. 082 569 8997/(0445) 82-5878/2-3522.
Running times: Daily, except Sundays and certain holidays. Departs George 09h30, arrives Knysna 12h00; departs Knysna 14h15; arrives George 17h00. Or departs Knysna 09h45, arrives George 12h30; departs George 13h00, arrives Knysna 15h33.

TOURIST INFORMATION
Wilderness Eco-Tourism Association, PO Box 188, Wilderness 6560; tel. (0441) 877-0045, fax. 877-0045.
Garden Route Tourist Information, PO Box 1514, George 6530; tel. (0441) 73-6314/55, fax. 74-6840.

Ebb and Flow Rest Camp South in its idyllic setting.

19 THE KNYSNA LAGOON

One of the jewels of the Garden Route, the Knysna Lagoon is washed twice daily by the nutrient-rich waters of the Indian Ocean and fed with fresh water from the Outeniqua Mountains. The lagoon is a remarkable eco-system, as well as a sought-after tourist playground.

How to get there
Knysna is situated in the very heart of the Garden Route, roughly 260 km west of Port Elizabeth and about 500 km east of Cape Town along the N2, which passes through the centre of the quaint town.

Don't miss
Knysna is home to South Africa's largest oyster-farming centre, and some connoisseurs claim that its oysters are the finest in the world. Pay a visit to the Knysna Oyster Company or Jetty Tapas restaurant, both on Thesen's Island, to sample these delicacies.

Over 150 artists and crafters have homes in Knysna and a wide range of their wares – from home-made jams and pies to wooden carvings and leather – is on sale in and outside town.

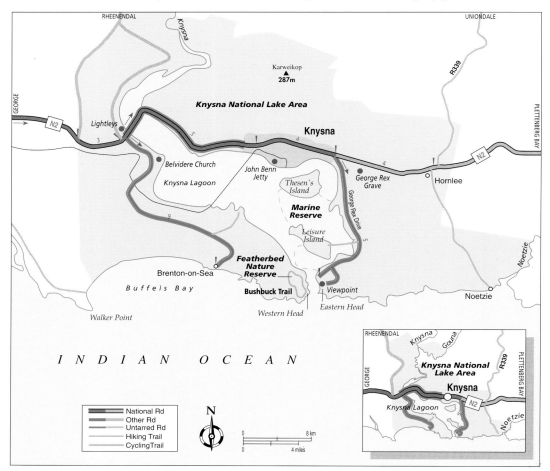

➡ The N2 highway from George crosses the lagoon and runs through Knysna. Just before the lagoon turn off to Belvidere, a small holiday village with a tiny Norman-style church, on the western bank of the lagoon. The Brenton-on-Sea resort is further along the same road.

THE LAGOON

The Knysna Lagoon, a mosaic of sandy shores, reedbeds, mudflats and salt marshes, is part of the **Knysna National Lake Area** which was proclaimed in 1985 in order to safeguard the area from increasing pressures for recreation and development. Covering about 18 000 ha, the conservation area is administered by the National Parks Board and stretches from just east of Buffels Bay to the Noetzie River. It includes the lagoon and the lower reaches of the Knysna River.

The salt marshes and mudflats of the lake are the habitat of a multitude of **invertebrates**. People can often be seen pumping the mudflats for mud prawns

Tourists have many options in Knysna – they can explore the lagoon by cruiser or visit one of its craft shops.

which are used for bait. The Knysna Marine Reserve, between Thesen's Island and Leisure Island, is a closed breeding area for invertebrates (although fishing is allowed, no bait may be collected here).

The invertebrates are a plentiful source of food for fish and for a variety of water birds. Many of the more than 230 **bird species** recorded in the Knysna area are attracted to its water habitats. Among those visitors are likely to see are the African spoonbill, osprey, avocet and several kingfisher species.

There are few **mammals** in the National Lake Area, but Cape grysbok, bushbuck and common duiker are occasionally spotted; bushpig, baboon and vervet monkey also occur.

Of the more than 200 **fish species** to be found in Knysna's lagoon, leervis, white steenbras, stumpnose and blacktail are sought-after by anglers. Out at sea **ski-boat angling** for tuna, bonito and marlin is popular.

The ideal conditions offered by the calm and sheltered lagoon for **watersports** such as swimming, yachting and boardsailing would be hard to match anywhere along the South African coast. Visitors may experience the lagoon's tranquil atmosphere by joining one of the many **pleasure cruises** on offer daily, weather permitting. Those with time on their hands who are wanting a holiday with a difference can hire a **holiday cruiser** of their own.

The Outeniqua Choo-Tjoe (*see* p. 87) runs between George and Knysna each day, giving travellers an unusual, leisurely view of the spectacular scenery of the area – lakes, beaches, forests, and finally the Knysna Lagoon. Rovos Rail offer a luxurious scenic trip between Cape Town and George, and George and Knysna.

(see p. 87)

KNYSNA SEA-HORSE

The Knysna sea-horse (*Hippocampus capensis*), one of six sea-horse species found in South Africa's waters, is known to occur in only four estuaries along the southern Cape coast. The Knysna Lagoon is the habitat of the main population, and smaller populations inhabit the Keurbooms River, Klein Brak River and Swartvlei estuaries.

This highly modified fish rarely exceeds 70 mm in length and lives in muddy, well-watered backwaters, feeding on small crustaceans. Unlike other fish, the sea-horse does not have scales. Its body and tail are encased in bony plates, rendering its head immobile. To compensate for this, its eyes can move independently.

A unique feature of the sea-horse is that several females deposit their eggs inside the breeding pouch of a male, and this is where fertilisation takes place.

Canoeing offers a strenuous but rewarding way of discovering the lake and its birdlife. For the adventurous, there are **guided canoe trips** on the Knysna River.

Diving is another popular pastime at Knysna. There are many shipwrecks (the *Paquita* and *Phantom* between the Heads, and the *Fairholme* southwest of the Western Head), spectacular coral reefs, caves and gullies. People venturing into the lagoon's underwater world from Thesen's Jetty may see the rare and endangered Knysna sea-horse (*see* box above).

A panoramic view from the Eastern Heads, where the sea creates rich feeding grounds for large shoals of fish and many species of birds.

➡ *You cannot drive to the Western Head (see Featherbed Nature Reserve, below), but the Eastern Head can be reached via the N2 on the Plettenberg Bay side of Knysna – turn down the well-signposted George Rex Drive, which follows the lagoon to Leisure Island and the Eastern Head.*

KNYSNA HEADS

Standing guard over the narrow entrance of the lagoon are the famously spectacular Knysna Heads. The best views of this promontory can be enjoyed from the end of the road skirting the eastern edge of the lagoon. A gentle footpath at the foot of the Eastern Head leads from the parking area and restaurant down to the coast, to a wooden bridge, which leads in turn to a small rocky outcrop (a favourite angling spot). Another good vantage point on these impressive sandstone cliffs is from the viewpoint at the top of the Eastern Head.

The National Sea Rescue Institute maintains a small aquarium at the Eastern Head, where visitors can see the Knysna seahorse (*see* box, p. 91).

➡ *There are no public roads to Featherbed Nature Reserve, but the Featherbed Ferry leaves from the municipal (John Benn) jetty on the northern shores of the lagoon.*

FEATHERBED NATURE RESERVE

This 70-ha private reserve on Knysna's Western Head is a World Heritage Site. On arrival, visitors are transported up the Western Head in a four-wheel-drive vehicle and trailer, and have the option of returning to the ferry either by vehicle or by joining a 2,5-km guided walk (one way) along the **Bushbuck Trail**. More than 100 bird species have been recorded in the reserve, and bushbuck, Cape grysbok and blue duiker may be spotted (the reserve is sanctuary to South Africa's largest breeding population of blue duiker).

WALKS AND TRAILS

FEATHERBED NATURE RESERVE: The 2,5-km **Bushbuck Trail** offers vistas of the lagoon, Knysna and the sea. There are plenty of walks and trails through the Knysna Forest (*see* p. 94).

The Knysna River meanders slowly through dense natural forests.

The Knysna Heads, a spectacular gateway between lagoon and sea.

20 THE KNYSNA FOREST

The Knysna Forest is part of South Africa's largest natural forest, a green belt from Mossel Bay to Harkerville with the Outeniqua Mountains forming its inland boundary. This wonderland of forest giants, bright mosses, fungi and birds is home to the few remaining Knysna elephants.

How to get there
Knysna is an ideal base from which to explore the fairy-tale forests of the southern Cape region. The charming coastal town is situated on the N2, about 500 km east of Cape Town and 280 km west of Port Elizabeth.

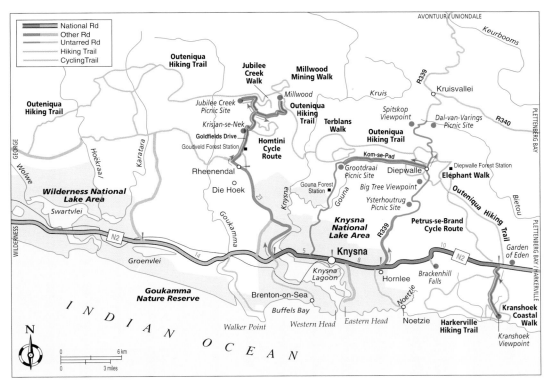

Visitors are likely to see the Knysna lourie in the forests.

➡ *A recommended scenic drive through the Knysna Forest follows the Avontuur-Uniondale road (the R339). Turn off the N2, 6 km east of Knysna and continue along Kom-se-Pad before you return to Knysna.*

KOM-SE-PAD SCENIC DRIVE

This drive follows a forestry road for 13 km through the forests of the Diepwalle and Gouna forest stations. Flanked by towering Outeniqua yellowwoods, false ironwoods and stinkwoods, the road winds through these unique forests – a magical world of ferns, monkey ropes and yellowwoods festooned with their characteristic old man's beard.

Many picnic sites along the route allow visitors to experience the atmosphere of the forest and to get acquainted with some of the 125 **tree species** found here. Among these are the stinkwood, easily identified by pale orange and white patches on its grey bark, candlewood, white els, hard pear, assegai and ironwood.

The crimson wings of a Knysna lourie are unlikely to escape attention, but many of the 35 forest **birds** are more easily identified by their call than by sight. Other species include rameron

A track through Gouna State Forest offers an easy and pleasant hike.

KNYSNA ELEPHANTS

During the previous century the Knysna Forest and surrounding areas were the stronghold of between 400 and 500 elephants. However, their numbers were drastically reduced by hunters and, by the beginning of this century, these elusive forest dwellers numbered between 40 and 50. By 1979 the population had shrunk to a mere three animals – a bull, a cow and a calf – and today only one of the original population still roams the forest.

After years of debate three young elephants from the Kruger National Park were released in the forest in 1994 to boost the numbers of these renowned elephants. Sadly one died of exhaustion and pneumonia shortly after their release, and today there is a total of three living in the forest (one of the original herd and two from the Kruger). At this stage, the success of this reintroduction remains to be seen, but it seems unlikely that more elephants will be introduced.

Although the Knysna elephants are not a distinct subspecies, they represent the southernmost population of elephants on the African continent and the only free-ranging population in South Africa. In addition, they are the only South African population that has adapted to living in a forest habitat.

pigeon, redbilled woodhoopoe, Knysna woodpecker, Cape batis and bluemantled flycatcher.

From the 1800s to the 1950s these forests were exploited for timber. A stroll from **Ysterhout-rug picnic site** (on the R339) leads to the route of the narrow gauge railway that transported timber from Diepwalle to Knysna from 1907 to 1949.

Two kilometres on is the Diep-walle **Big Tree viewpoint**. A short ramble from here leads to the monarch of the Big Trees, the King Edward Tree (*see* p. 95).

Further on, the road passes Diepwalle Forest Station, once the legendary Knysna elephants' haunt. Kom-se-Pad meets the R339 at Diepwalle. Detour north on the R339 to **Dal-van-Varings picnic site**, a most enchanting, tranquil place with tall forest tree ferns. A drive or walk to nearby **Spitskop viewpoint** affords sweeping views of the forest-clad Outeniqua Mountains, Knysna Lagoon (*see* p. 90) and southern Cape coast.

Return to Kom-se-Pad and continue to the picnic site at Grootdraai at the Gouna Forest Station, a rest spot popular with trailists on the Terblans Walk.

➡ *Another scenic drive passes through Goudveld's indigenous forest to Jubilee Creek and the historic gold-mining settlement of*

An old mineshaft of the once bustling mining settlement at Millwood.

The George lily grows in the Outeniqua Mountains.

Millwood. Take the N2 west to Rheenendal's turnoff, then the road signposted Millwood/ Goldfields before Rheenendal.

THE GOLDFIELDS DRIVE

In the 1880s miners panned for alluvial gold in Knysna Forest's streams, leading to names such as Golden Gulley, Forest Creek and Jubilee Creek.

The left fork of the Millwood-Jubilee Creek road leads to **Jubilee Creek picnic site** on the banks of the creek named in honour of Queen Victoria's Golden Jubilee celebrations. A pleasant walk from here follows the creek 2 km upstream, passing relics of the gold-mining era, and then returns the same way.

The right fork leads to the once bustling gold-mining village of **Millwood**. In its heyday it boasted 75 permanent buildings, including six hotels, a bank, post office and music hall. As well as 400 permanent residents, 600 diggers lived here in tents. But when luck ran out the miners and fortune-seekers abandoned Millwood. The only reminders of this era are disused mine shafts and machinery – Millwood House has been moved to town, and is now a museum. The miners' cemetery is near the start of the 5,6-km Millwood Mining Walk, from Materolli House. Also known as Monk's Store and now a museum, this timber and corrugated iron house is one of two buildings to have survived in their original state.

➡ *There are many charming picnic sites and viewpoints along the N2 from Harkerville to Plettenberg Bay. The Kranshoek drive has magnificent views of the rugged coastline.*

KRANSHOEK SCENIC DRIVE

Driving east along the N2 to Port Elizabeth, take a short detour (to the right) through bluegum plantations to the picnic and viewing site overlooking **Brackenhill Waterfall**. After a series of cascades, the falls plunge into a deep ravine through which the Noetzie River passes.

A few kilometres further, the N2 goes through a stretch of forest, the **Garden of Eden**, 2 km west of the turnoff to the Kranshoek scenic drive. Starting at the picnic site, a 30-minute walk meanders through a magnificent patch of indigenous forest.

Pertinent information about the forest ecology is provided on a board at the picnic site. There is also a wheelchair route.

Diverging off the N2, take the road to the right through indigenous forest to a picnic site where the Kranshoek River disappears over the sandstone cliffs into a deep, forested gorge. A viewing site with wooden safety railings overlooks the falls, which are sometimes reduced to a mere trickle, but are especially spectacular after rains. The drive ends a short way on at the

Colourful fungi grow on rotting wood or in damp places.

Kranshoek viewpoint with its unsurpassed views over the rugged coastline some 200 m below. This section of the coast is characterised by rocky promontories alternating with small coves, and is one of the southern Cape's most rugged and spectacular stretches of coast.

WALKS AND TRAILS

Several delightful day walks in the area give visitors the opportunity to experience the tranquillity of the Knysna Forest.

FOREST GIANTS

The Knysna Forest is known for its enormous Outeniqua yellowwoods, the biggest being the famous King Edward Tree in the Diepwalle State Forest. With a height of 39 m, a crown spread of 24 m and a circumference of 6 m, it is estimated to be over 600 years old.

The Outeniqua yellowwood is the tallest of the four yellowwood species occurring in South Africa and is one of the dominant species in the Knysna Forest. Locally known as the kalander (which is said to be short for 'Outeniqualander'), the Outeniqua yellowwood is not as common as the real, but smaller, yellowwood. In certain areas of the Knysna Forest, yellowwoods can comprise up to 40% of the canopy-forming tree species.

Despite the large number of Big Trees occurring in the southern Cape forests, the second largest Outeniqua yellowwood is not found here, but, surprisingly, near The Downs in the Northern Province. It is 36 m high, has an average crown spread of 33,6 m and a girth of 5,9 m.

Some of the massive Outeniqua yellowwoods are over 600 years old.

Jubilee Creek has a delightful picnic site on the banks of the river.

GOUNA STATE FOREST: Two highlights of the easy 6,5-km-long **Terblans Walk** are the fern glades and cold, but irresistible pool near the half-way mark.

DIEPWALLE STATE FOREST: One of the area's best-known walks is undoubtedly the **Elephant Walk**. Trailists can hike the long 18,2-km route or opt for a shorter version of 9 km, 7 km or 6,5 km. This is Big Tree country and there are no fewer than 10 fine specimens along the trail.

HARKERVILLE STATE FOREST: The 2-day **Harkerville Hiking Trail** is largely a forest route, but its highlight is the coastal scenery. On both days the trail follows the coastline. At several places narrow ledges have to be negotiated and chain handholds and bridges assist hikers. The trail should not be undertaken by those with a fear of heights.

KNYSNA FORESTS: Energetic hikers can explore the forests by shouldering their backpacks and setting off on the well-known **Outeniqua Hiking Trail**, a 7-day route which passes through the indigenous forests between Beervlei and Harkerville forest stations. The trail covers 105 km, but shorter routes in the Knysna Forest are possible.

CYCLING ROUTES

The numerous forestry roads and tracks are ideal for cycling and two specially designated cycle routes have been opened in the Knysna Forest.

DIEPWALLE STATE FOREST: Starting at the forest station, the **Petrus-se-Brand Cycle Route** is a 23,5-km ride to the aptly-named Garden of Eden on the N2. After descending to the Petrusbrand River, the trail climbs to Petrusbrandeiland and then continues to Kleineiland (a relict patch of fynbos surrounded by indigenous forest) where cyclists are rewarded with views of the Outeniqua and Tsitsikamma mountain ranges and the white, sandy beaches of Plettenberg Bay. The descent into the Kleineiland River Valley is followed by a fairly strenuous climb to the 18-km mark, where it levels out. The route can be completed at a leisurely pace and takes about three hours.

GOUDVELD STATE FOREST: Starting and ending at the Krisjan-se-Nek picnic site, the **Homtini Cycle Route** is a fairly easy 19-km circuit. The route meanders through spectacular high forest and, after descending to the Lawnwood River, climbs steeply up to Portland Heights with its impressive expansive views over the indigenous forests and the Knysna Heads further afield. The trail enters the forest again at the 14-km mark. One of the many highlights along the route is the exhilarating descent along a single-track section to Boer-se-Pad, an old forest track. Cyclists should allow approximately three leisurely hours in which to complete the route.

THE KNYSNA FOREST AT A GLANCE

MAIN ATTRACTIONS
Magnificent forest scenery, diverse birdlife, Big Trees, Millwood, Jubilee Creek, historic gold-mining relics, walks and trails.

BEST TIMES TO VISIT
Throughout the year, but remember to bring your rain gear as this is an all-year rainfall region.

WALKS AND TRAILS
Permits/bookings: **Day walks:** No permit required, but trailists must sign the register at starting point.
Outeniqua and Harkerville hiking trails: The Regional Director of Forestry (*see below*).
Opening times: Forestry recreation areas open all year 06h00–18h00.
Accommodation: Overnight huts with bunks and mattresses. Water, firewood, braai places and toilets provided.

Enquiries: **The Regional Director of Forestry,** Private Bag X12, Knysna 6570; tel. (0445) 82-5466, fax. 82-5461.

CYCLING ROUTES
Permits/bookings: Southern Cape Regional Forestry Office (*see below*).
Diepwalle Forest Station (Petrus-se-Brand): tel. (0445) 82-6066, fax. 82-6280.
Goudveld Forest Station (Homtini): tel. (0445) 4750, fax. 4681.
Opening times: Forestry recreation areas open all year 06h00–18h00.
Enquiries: **Southern Cape Regional Forestry Office,** Private Bag X12, Knysna 6570; tel. (0445) 82-5466, fax. 82-5461.

TOURIST INFORMATION
Knysna Publicity Association, PO Box 87, Knysna 6570; tel. (0445) 2-1610, fax. 2-1646.

21 TSITSIKAMMA

Plettenberg Bay is a holiday mecca with its 12-km sandy beach, Robberg Peninsula and tranquil Keurbooms River Lagoon. Characterised by rugged coastline, indigenous forests and patches of fynbos, the Tsitsikamma National Park has long been a most popular South African park.

How to get there
Situated 525 km east of Cape Town and 236 west of Port Elizabeth along the N2, Plettenberg Bay is a convenient base from which to explore the beauties of the Tsitsikamma area. Approaching from Knysna on the N2, make a detour (turn to the right onto the R339) to the seaside hamlet of Noetzie, famous for its modern stone 'castles', but steel yourself for a steep walk.

Keurbooms River Lagoon with Plettenberg Bay in the distance.

The rocky promontory of Robberg.

➡ *In order to reach the Robberg Nature Reserve from Plettenberg Bay, follow the road south towards Plettenberg Bay Airport, which is clearly signposted. The turnoff leading to the unspoilt reserve is marked on the left.*

ROBBERG NATURE RESERVE
Just south of Plettenberg Bay a 148-m-high rocky promontory juts out into the Indian Ocean for approximately 4 km, forming the Robberg Peninsula. To protect its spectacular coastal scenery and rich archaeological heritage, a 240-ha nature reserve has been set aside here.

Not to be missed is a visit to the archaeological interpretation site at **Nelson's Bay Cave**. The first inhabitants of this site were Middle Stone Age people who lived here from about 120 000 to 50 000 years ago. Inhabitants of the Later Stone Age and Khoi-khoi pastoralists subsequently also used the cave.

Rock angling is a popular pastime and there are no fewer than 33 angling spots dotted along the peninsula. Angling species include galjoen, red roman and yellowtail. The best months for elf are usually between June and September. Anglers must beware of freak waves at all times.

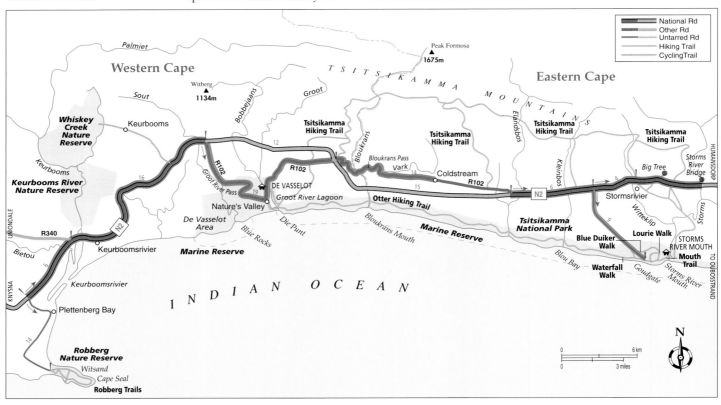

There are various **trails** in the reserve (*see* p. 98), and **picnic sites** with braai facilities are provided near the entrance gate.

➡ *For travellers heading towards the Storms River Rest Camp, the old national road (R102) over the Groot River and Bloukrans passes offers motorists a pleasantly scenic alternative to the toll road (N2).*

PASSES SCENIC DRIVE

From the **Robberg Nature Reserve** (*see* p. 97), the N2 bypasses Plettenberg Bay and 7 km further on reaches the turn-off to the **Keurbooms River Nature Reserve** (*see* box, p. 98). The turnoff to Nature's Valley follows 14 km further on. After crossing the Sout River, turn off to the right onto the R102. The road winds across the narrow coastal escarpment and soon begins its tortuous descent along the spectacular **Groot River Pass**, built by Thomas Bain in the 1880s with convict labour.

Hugging the forested slopes of the Groot River Valley for about 3 km, the pass drops 200 m. The turnoff to the secluded holiday village of Nature's Valley is at the very bottom of the pass. After skirting the edge of the **Groot River Lagoon**, the road winds

steeply upwards while passing underneath a dense canopy of indigenous trees.

Pause to enjoy the delightful viewpoint near the top of the pass overlooking the Groot River Lagoon, the De Vasselot section of the Tsitsikamma National Park and Nature's Valley.

The road continues eastwards for 6 km across the coastal plateau through fynbos, pine plantations and indigenous forest before descending along the **Bloukrans Pass**, the second of the Tsitsikamma passes built by Thomas Bain. Clinging to the wooded precipices, it twists and turns through forests of yellowwoods draped with old man's beard and ferns as it descends to the Bloukrans River. The route passes through a scenic gorge, providing a dramatic view of the 216-m-high Bloukrans Bridge to the right. It then traverses the Vark River before making a tight U-turn as it ascends to the coastal plateau with its pine and eucalyptus plantations. Picnic facilities with tables, benches, fireplaces and toilets are available at the **Rugbos picnic site** at the summit of the pass.

Rejoin the N2 just before it crosses the Elandsbos River; the turnoff to the Storms River Rest

Camp is 7 km further on, and the rest camp itself is 10 km along this road. The famous Otter Trail starts here, the Tsitsikamma Trail ends at the suspension bridge, and there are several other walks in the area (*see* p. 99). Built in the 1950s, the Storms River Bridge (*see* p. 98) over the gorge remains a remarkable feat of engineering. The nearby restaurant complex provides spectacular views of the gorge.

➡ *Approaching from Plettenberg Bay on the N2, take the signposted Nature's Valley turnoff onto the R102; the De Vasselot camp site is signposted about 1 km beyond the Nature's Valley turnoff. To reach the Storms River Rest Camp, continue along the N2 for 50 km and turn right at the Tsitsikamma National Park signpost. The park is 6 km further along this road and the rest camp another 4 km.*

TSITSIKAMMA NATIONAL PARK

Stretching from Nature's Valley in the west to Oubosstrand at the Groot River in the east (two of the rivers in the park are called Groot), the 65-km-long Tsitsikamma National Park encompasses a thin ribbon of coastline which more or less follows the 200-m contour as its inland boundary, although at De Vasselot it extends as far as 3,5 km inland, and 5,5 km out to sea. It originally comprised two separate parks, the Tsitsikamma Coastal National Park and the Tsitsikamma Forest National Park, a 478-ha tract of indigenous forest just west of the Storms River Bridge. In 1987 the De Vasselot Nature Reserve was transferred from the Department of Environment Affairs to the National Parks Board in exchange for the Forest Park, which was then deproclaimed.

There is a wealth of **flora** in the park: indigenous yellowwood, stinkwood, ironwood and milkwood forests spill down the slopes to the coast where yellow gazanias cling to the lichen-encrusted ledges. Between June and August the scarlet krantz aloe flowers provide a most colourful display amongst the rocks. On the coastal plateau the

Vervet monkeys, lively residents of the Tsitsikamma Forest.

evergreen forests are occasionally interrupted by patches of fynbos dominated by ericas, proteas, reeds and rushes.

About 40 of the park's 220 **bird species** are associated with the sea and shore. Species likely to be seen include flocks of common tern (during summer), whitebreasted cormorant and kelp gull. Forest species to watch for include the crowned eagle, forest buzzard, terrestrial bulbul, paradise flycatcher, greenspotted dove, Knysna woodpecker and the chorister robin.

Mammals include rock dassies, which are common at the Storms River Rest Camp. If trailists move quietly, they may also encounter the diminutive blue duiker, chacma baboon and vervet monkey on forest walks. Although bushbuck and bushpig occur, they are seldom seen. Similarly elusive is the Cape clawless otter (*Aonyx capensis*), which gives its name to one of the world's most famous hiking trails, the Otter Trail, which starts in the park (*see* p. 99).

The rare and delicate pansy shell, symbol of Plettenberg Bay.

The scenic Groot River Pass, built by Thomas Bain in the 1880s.

PANSY SHELL

The rare, delicate pansy shell (*Echinodiscus bisperforatus*) is the unofficial emblem of Plettenberg Bay. This purple sea urchin, whose short spines resemble fur, occurs mainly between Mossel Bay and

Plettenberg Bay. The disc-shaped shell, with its pansy pattern, is the skeleton which protects the internal organs. The shells are highly prized, but remember it is an offence to collect live animals.

The cascade on the Waterfall Walk is an ideal place to relax and swim.

KEURBOOMS RIVER NATURE RESERVE

The scenery of this 2 230-ha reserve is dominated by the Keurbooms River which originates in the Outeniqua Mountains and flows into the sea just east of the popular Plettenberg Bay.

The river derives its name from the keurboom or blossom tree, a species found along the coast from the Cape Peninsula to the southern Cape. Between October and December it is covered in masses of beautiful pinkish-mauve flowers.

The forested slopes of the Keurbooms River Valley are home to blue duiker, bush-buck, bushpig and vervet monkey. Birdlife includes the African fish eagle, the elusive Narina trogon and the Knysna lourie with its crimson wings.

There is a 1-hour trail along the banks of the river, but the true beauty of the reserve can only be discovered by canoeing upstream. For the energetic, there is a 7,5-km canoe trail with an overnight hut.

The intertidal zone of the coast is a wonder-world of colourful sponges, sea stars and algae. A snorkelling trail has been laid out in the small bay at Goudgate just west of the Storms River oceanettes, and divers with a third class SAUU or equivalent diving certificate can follow the diving route around Mooi Bay and Sand Bay at the Storms River Rest Camp restaurant complex.

Dolphins occur along the Tsitsikamma coast and large schools of Indian Ocean bottlenosed dolphins are often seen frolicking in the waves near the shore. In winter **southern right whales** may be seen along the coast in the rest camp and from the Otter Trail (*see* p. 99).

Angling is permitted along a 3-km stretch of coast west of the caravan park at Storms River Rest Camp. Among the popular angling species are kabeljou, musselcracker, elf, white steenbras and galjoen.

Sand Bay, the small sandy bay near the restaurant complex, offers safe swimming, and the swimming pool built amongst the rocks near the caravan park is very popular on hot days.

De Vasselot at the western edge of the park encompasses the breathtaking Groot River Valley, as well as a stretch of rocky coastline. Situated in an indigenous forest on the banks of the Groot River are rustic log cabins, each with its own canoe to enable visitors to explore the lagoon. The cabins are equipped with two beds (linen is provided) and braai places (no kitchen). Visitors share ablution facilities with the camp site. The vegetation is dominated by indigenous forest of Outeniqua and real yellowwoods, stinkwood, Cape beech and assegai. A rich variety of fynbos (restios, ericas and several members of the protea family) occurs on the coastal plateau. Prominent among the proteas are the tall yellowbushes and the Tsitsikamma variety of the king protea with its pink flowers.

The Groot River Lagoon is popular with the watersports fraternity, and sailing, board-sailing, canoeing and rowing are permitted. Blue Rocks along the coast offer excellent scuba diving opportunities.

➡ *From the Storms River Rest Camp, return to the N2 and turn right. Continue for about 5 km to the turnoff to the Big Tree.*

THE BIG TREE
Although it is possible to follow a short gravel road to this well-known forest giant, a far more rewarding route is to follow the **Big Tree Trail**, which begins at the parking area alongside the N2. The 15-minute walk meanders past glades of ferns and giant yellowwood, stinkwood, candlewood and assegai trees to the Big Tree, an Outeniqua yellowwood. Estimated to be about 800 years old, the tree has a height of 36,6 m, a crown spread of 32,9 m and a circumference of 8,5 m at chest height.

➡ *Continuing east along the N2, the Storms River Bridge is another 3,4 km further on.*

STORMS RIVER BRIDGE
This 192-m-long bridge (first named the Paul Sauer Bridge) spans the deep gorge formed by the Storms River through the coastal plateau and is one of the most impressive in South Africa. It was completed in 1956 to eliminate the old Storms River Pass further downstream, and was constructed by lowering two concrete arches which meet in the middle, 139 m above the river. Spectacular views of the bridge and gorge can be enjoyed from the viewpoint just below the restaurant at the bridge.

WALKS AND TRAILS
ROBBERG NATURE RESERVE: Trailists undertaking the walks in the reserve are rewarded with breathtaking coastal scenery. The

A suspension bridge crosses the Storms River on the Mouth Walk.

walks range from a 2-km circuit via **The Gap** to the 5,5-km **Witsand** circuit and a 9,2-km trail to **The Point**. The route to The Point should not be attempted by inexperienced hikers, nor by those with a fear of heights.

TSITSIKAMMA FOREST: From the **Rugbos picnic site** at the summit of the Bloukrans Pass there is a choice of a 700-m or a 1,3-km circular walk to a patch of indigenous forest with a magnificent Outeniqua yellowwood.

TSITSIKAMMA NATIONAL PARK: The 43-km **Otter Hiking Trail** is South Africa's most popular trail. It stretches between the Storms River Rest Camp and the Groot River estuary at Nature's

The Cape clawless otter, elusive dweller of the Tsitsikamma rivers.

Valley, alternating between the rocky coastline and the coastal plateau with its beautiful indigenous forests and patches of fynbos. The trail lasts for five days.

Another popular overnight trail, the **Tsitsikamma Hiking Trail**, stretches for 60 km between the De Vasselot Rest Camp and the Storms River suspension bridge, or Storms River Bridge. The route through fynbos and patches

of indigenous forests along the Tsitsikamma Mountains rewards hikers with far-reaching views and takes five days to complete. Shorter options are also available.

Several short walks have been laid out in the vicinity of the Storms River Rest Camp. One of the most popular is the **Mouth Trail**, which winds through the forest to the Storms River Mouth. The route, 1 km each way, includes many deviations to the coast's rocky bays. Shortly before the Storms River there is a turnoff to a **Strandloper Cave** where a display provides information about the early people who inhabited the cave between 5 000 and 2 000 years ago.

The Storms River is a short way on and views of the deep gorge can be enjoyed from the suspension bridge spanning the river. From the eastern bank a trail leads to a viewpoint at **Bakenkop** on the coastal plateau. Although the climb is steep in places, the magnificent view of the Storms River Rest Camp is ample reward, and dolphins may be spotted far below.

Another recommended ramble is the **Waterfall Walk** which follows the Otter Trail for about 2,5 km to a waterfall cascading into a magnificent pool – an ideal place for a swim on a hot day.

The forested slopes above the rest camp are crossed by two other popular walks, the 1-km **Lourie Walk** and the 3-km **Blue Duiker Walk**. Both offer the avid birder ideal opportunities for spotting some of the 35 species of forest birds in the park, including the Knysna lourie.

The trails in the De Vasselot section of the park, lasting between two and eight hours, vary from forest walks to routes through fynbos and a ramble along the coast. Starting at the De Vasselot Camp Site is the **Uitsig Trail**, which ascends for 2,8 km through indigenous forest and fynbos to the picnic site on the Groot River Pass. Depending on how energetic you are, you

can either continue along the **Keurpad** and the **Forest Hall Trail** for a 15-km round trip, or you can opt to descend along the **Sout River Path**. From the western end of Nature's Valley trailists can follow the 1,8-km **Rotspad** to the Sout River Mouth and the 1,9-km **Kuspad** to the Brak River (both along the coast), returning on the **Mondpad** to the Sout River Mouth.

The Storms River Rest Camp's log cabins, set between forest and sea.

22 ADDO ELEPHANT NP & BAVIAANSKLOOF

Where the Cape Folded Mountains end in the Eastern Cape, they have created a wilderness of mountain peaks, ravines and river valleys. East of the Groot Winterhoek range the almost impenetrable Addo bush is a sanctuary to the Addo elephants, buffalo and black rhino.

How to get there
Port Elizabeth is an ideal base from which to explore this part of the Eastern Cape. It is situated 763 km east of Cape Town (take the N2) and 1 054 km south of Johannesburg (take the N1 to Colesberg, the N10 to Ncanara and the N2 west).

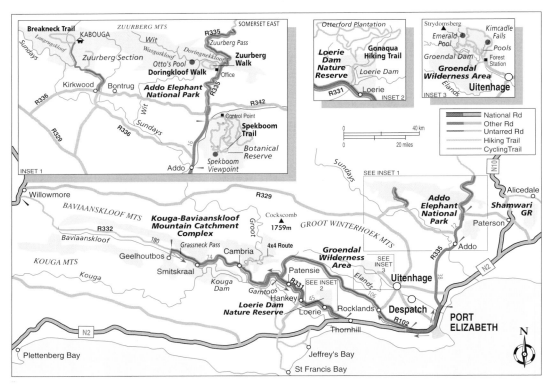

➡ The Addo Elephant National Park is 72 km northeast of Port Elizabeth. Take the N2 from Port Elizabeth for about 11 km (northeast) and turn off to the left onto the R335 (the turnoff to St George's Strand is to the right). The signposted turnoff to the park is 12 km beyond the settlement of Addo.

ADDO ELEPHANT NATIONAL PARK

The major drawcard of this 54 000-ha park is the **elephants**, which have increased from 11 when the park was proclaimed in 1931 to 212 at the time of writing.

The Addo elephants are not a sub-species of the elephants in the Kruger National Park (*see* pages 166–177), but represent an isolated gene pool with unique features. The tusks of the bulls are considerably smaller than those of the Kruger and the females are generally tuskless.

The park is home to what was originally the only foot and mouth and corridor disease-free **buffalo** population in South Africa. Founder populations have since been established in a number of conservation areas. Since only a small part of the Addo section of the park consists of grassveld, the Addo buffalo are largely browsers. Dense bush and their nocturnal habits mean that chances of seeing these buffalo are best during early morning or late afternoon.

Another rare species enjoying protection in the park is the East African **black rhino**, introduced from Kenya in 1961/62, and numbering 35 in the park. Among the **antelope** to be seen are eland, red hartebeest, kudu, bushbuck, grysbok and common duiker. Warthog may also be spotted.

One of the most conspicuous smaller creatures is the **flightless dung beetle**, usually seen rolling a ball of dung along the road. These beetles depend on the droppings of elephant, buffalo and rhino, and are restricted to the Eastern Cape, with the Addo park being the habitat of the most viable population. The ball of dung, known as the nuptial ball, is buried by the male and a single egg is laid in it by the female. When the egg hatches, the larva feeds on the dung

Dung beetles help to remove dung and control flies and parasites.

and the pupa remains within the hard outer shell, emerging during the rainy season when conditions are favourable. The beetles have a lifespan of about three years.

A network of roads covering about 70 km winds through the park, passing several waterholes where visitors may see elephant and other game. **Game-viewing** can also be rewarding from the hide at the Spekboom Viewpoint, situated close to the botanical reserve. At night nocturnal animals may be seen at the illuminated waterhole just outside the perimeter of the rest camp, near the northern boundary of the park, 3 km east of the entrance gate.

Another way of seeing nocturnal creatures is to join a guided night drive. During these visitors may see nocturnal animals such as porcupine, bat-eared fox and genet, as well as the park's buffalo, which are to a large extent nocturnal. The drives start at the reception office, where bookings must be made in advance.

Among the 185 **bird species** recorded in Addo are ostrich, secretarybird, black korhaan and cardinal woodpecker. A hide overlooking a small reed-fringed dam in the rest camp affords birders an opportunity to see some of the park's water birds.

The park's **vegetation** is dominated by dense semi-succulent thickets with the spekboom (also known as porkbush) a conspicuous species. Other common species include Karoo boer-bean, common guarri, sneezewood, Cape honeysuckle and plumbago. A botanical reserve of 300 ha has been set aside in the southern section of the park to conserve its valley bushveld vegetation.

Addo's elephants belong to an isolated gene pool; they are smaller, bulls have smaller tusks and females are generally tuskless.

➡ *From the southern section of the Addo Elephant National Park, drive for 16 km on the R335 to Zuurberg Inn. The entrance to the Zuurberg section of the Addo Park is immediately opposite the inn. The pass meanders up the southern slopes of the Zuurberg Mountains to reach its 960-m-high summit after 9 km, affording splendid vistas of the Sundays River Valley to the south.*

ZUURBERG SECTION

Approximately 50 km north of the more established part of the Addo Elephant National Park (*see* above) lies the relatively unknown Zuurberg section of the park. Situated in the Klein Winterhoek Mountains, this 35 000-ha section is a wilderness of river valleys and folded mountains, formed aeons ago when pressures inside the earth's crust forced the layers of sedimentary rock upwards. Formerly a conservation area managed by the Department of Forestry, it received national park status in 1985, but is now part of the Addo Elephant National Park.

One of the main attractions of this area is its **flora** – the valley bushveld vegetation is considered the most pristine in the Eastern Cape. Interesting plants that are found here include three cycad species, the grass-leaved aloe and the Zuurberg cushion bush.

Game occuring naturally in the area includes kudu, bushbuck, mountain reedbuck, grey rhebok, common and blue duiker, and bushpig. In an exciting development, a family group of hippo from the Kruger National Park was translocated to the Sundays River in 1992, and a breeding herd of 11 Cape mountain zebra (which used to occur here) was introduced to this area in 1993. In 1995 seven black rhino of the sub-species *Diceros bicornis bicornis* (which used to occur naturally in the area) were reintroduced to the Zuurberg section of the park.

Kabouga guest house on the western side of the area can be reached via a gravel road from Kirkwood. Guests at Kabouga

may **fish** in the Sundays River, and a self-guided **walk** starts from the guest house (*see* p. 103).

There are few tourist amenities in this section, but plans are afoot to zone it for various recreational uses – part of these zones will be declared a wilderness area, through which a five-day hike will pass. A zone will be set aside for day hikes and horse trails, and a large area for big game (elephant, buffalo and black rhino).

Various **trails** are offered in this part of the park (*see* p. 103).

➡ *From Port Elizabeth motorists can also explore in a northwesterly direction and combine the Elands River Valley and Baviaanskloof scenic routes. Take the Kraggakamma interchange on the N2 onto the R102 and then head for the settlement of Rocklands.*

BAVIAANSKLOOF SCENIC DRIVE

Continuing northwest from Rocklands, the road follows the spectacular Elands River Valley between two parallel mountain

ranges. Large tracts of these mountains are still in a pristine state. To the north the scenery is dominated by the Groot Winterhoek Mountains, with the 1 180-m-high Strydomsberg prominent at the eastern end of the range where the 30 000-ha **Groendal Wilderness Area** has been set aside. Situated at the eastern end of the Groot Winterhoek Mountains, Groendal is a rugged mountainscape of deep ravines with patches of indigenous forest, challenging cliff faces and fynbos-covered slopes. The wilderness area is accessible only on foot (*see* p. 103) and among the animals trailists might encounter are common and blue duiker, baboon, klipspringer, bushbuck and bushpig.

At the western end of the Groot Winterhoek range lies the highest peak in the mountains – the 1 759-m Cockscomb with its five crests resembling a rooster's comb.

The road then swings south, making its way up to a nek between the Cockscomb and

SHAMWARI GAME RESERVE

A close neighbour to the Addo Elephant National Park, Shamwari Game Reserve is 72 km northeast of Port Elizabeth. This 10 000-ha reserve, which was opened in 1992, is sanctuary to black and white rhino, lion, elephant, leopard (seldom seen), buffalo and 18 antelope species. Day and night drives offer visitors the opportunity to view big game from open vehicles. Walking trails allow birders to spot the more than 250 bird species recorded in the reserve. A private 'African Rail Safari' train runs between Johannesburg and a siding adjacent to the park.

Visitors at Shamwari enjoy a close-up view of a white rhino.

Baviaanskloof ('cleft of baboons') is a remarkable valley running for 150 km through scenic countryside.

Elands Mountain and joins the R331. It then follows the course of the Gamtoos River with its horseshoe bend, and after about 14 km winds past a striking cliff of Enon conglomerate, resembling Queen Victoria's profile. About 4 km after joining the R332 (the R331 becomes the R332), you pass the turnoff to the **Kouga Dam** (previously Paul Sauer), a popular canoeing and angling venue. From here you continue along a gravel road and a short way on you enter the Groot River Valley, between the Komdo and Coutomiet mountains at the eastern end of the spectacular Baviaanskloof. Named after the large numbers of baboons seen here by the early Dutch explorers, the kloof stretches westwards for 120 km and an unspoilt area of 167 000 ha has been zoned as wilderness. After 5 km you reach the Komdomo Camp Site, set to become the eastern entrance to the proposed Baviaanskloof Wilderness Area. Visitors travelling along the R332 through the wilderness area do not require a permit, but those venturing off the proclaimed road must obtain a permit in advance.

The **vegetation** is a mixture of spekboomveld (with characteristic species such as the spekboom, aloes, the valley bushveld euphorbia and jacket-plum), scrub forest and mountain fynbos. Of particular interest is the Willowmore cedar, endemic to the Baviaanskloof and Kouga mountains. One of three South African cedars, it is related to the Clanwilliam cedar, endemic to the Cedarberg (*see* box, p. 37), and the more common mountain cedar.

Although the area does not support large **game** populations, mountain reedbuck, grey rhebok, klipspringer, kudu, bushbuck and baboon might be seen. Eland and Cape mountain zebra have been reintroduced into the eastern part of the conservation area.

The wilderness atmosphere makes the area suitable for a range of recreational activities; in addition to backpacking, there is a **four-wheel-drive route** in the Sandrivier area (*see* p. 103). The public road (R332) with its magnificent scenery is ideally suited to **mountain biking**.

Continuing further, the road crosses the Groot River and, after passing the old Goede Hoop Mission Station and Cambria (a farming settlement), meanders along a narrow, winding pass to the Bergplaats plateau. Further along the road passes a massive rock in the Kouga River with the ominous name of Doodsklip (Death Rock) and the camp sites at Rooihoek and Smitskraal. After crossing the Baviaanskloof River, the road passes the restored homestead at Doornkraal and winds up the narrow Grassneck Pass, and reaches the turnoff (the planned western gateway to the Baviaanskloof Wilderness Area) to **Geelhoutbos** about 84 km beyond Komdomo. This delightful spot, 3 km south of the R332, is named after a clump of yellowwood trees growing in a kloof. Facilities here consist of five 6-bed chalets and a swimming pool in the river which flows nearby. Unless you are continuing to Willowmore, this is the recommended turn-around point.

Returning to the R331, the road follows the fertile Gamtoos Valley with its patchwork of cultivated fields. Just outside Patensie

Aloes are a characteristic feature of the Baviaanskloof area.

a road turns off to the right to the **Phillip's Tunnel**, built in 1844 to divert water from the Gamtoos River to land earmarked for cultivation by the London Missionary Society. The parking area to the **Bergvenster**, a huge hole in a conglomerate outcrop overlooking the Gamtoos Valley, is 1 km on. The short steep walk to the 'window' is well worth the effort.

About 16 km beyond Hankey (a citrus, tobacco, lucerne and potato centre), the road passes the turnoff to the 1 000-ha **Loerie Dam Nature Reserve** which is an environmental education centre. It is also the starting point of the **Gonaqua Hiking Trail** (*see* below). From Loerie the road continues in a southeasterly direction to join the N2 at the Thornhill interchange.

WALKS AND TRAILS

ADDO ELEPHANT NATIONAL PARK: Since the botanical reserve is enclosed with an elephant-proof fence, visitors can alight from their vehicles for a close-up view of the vegetation on the **Spekboom Trail**. Covering about 6 km, the trail winds up a low hill overlooking the surrounding countryside. Trees along the route have been labelled with their national tree list numbers, enabling trailists to identify them.

ZUURBERG SECTION: Two circular walks have been laid out to afford visitors an opportunity to explore the area on foot. The **Doringkloof Walk** covers 12 km and takes about 4 hours to hike, while the **Zuurberg Walk** is a 2,5-km circuit which is hiked in about one hour. It is not necessary to book for these marked, self-guided walks which start at the summit of the Zuurberg Pass, opposite the Zuurberg Inn. There are also two walks starting at the Kabouga Guest House. The **Blue Duiker Walk**, an easy 30-minute circuit, leads past fine specimens of the Zuurberg cycad and there is a good chance of seeing the small antelope after which the trail is named. The **Breakneck Trail** is a demanding seven-hour route to the summit of the Zuurberg, but the mountain scenery makes the effort worthwhile.

BAVIAANSKLOOF: This area is ideally suited to wilderness backpacking, and trailists are encouraged to determine their own routes. A day hike with shorter options has been laid out at Geelhoutbos.

OTTERFORD PLANTATION: The strenuous **Gonaqua Trail**, which covers 30 km over two days, starts in this reserve. It offers stunning views of the surrounding mountainous landscape, rivers, pools and waterfall. Swimming is permitted in the streams and at Lily Pool.

FOUR-WHEEL-DRIVE TRAIL

A 32-km-long four-wheel-drive route has been set aside in the Sandrivier region of the Baviaanskloof.

ADDO ELEPHANT & BAVIAANSKLOOF AT A GLANCE

MAIN ATTRACTIONS
Game-viewing, spectacular mountain scenery, unique vegetation.

BEST TIMES TO VISIT
Throughout the year. The Eastern Cape lies in an all-year rainfall area, where the rainfall is distributed fairly evenly throughout the year. Average temperatures are moderate although summer days can be hot.

ADDO ELEPHANT NATIONAL PARK
Permits/Bookings: Entry permits at gate. National Parks Board Reservations (*see* below).
Opening times: The park is open every day, 07h00–19h00.
Accommodation: Two 6-bed cottages; 24 chalets (sleep four); 2-bed huts; 20 camp sites with hot/cold-water ablution facilities.
Facilities: Shop with groceries and curios, à la carte restaurant, swimming pool, tennis court, petrol only.
Enquiries: **National Parks Board Reservations,** PO Box 787, Pretoria 0001; tel. (012) 343-1991, fax. 343-0905; or PO Box 7400, Roggebaai 8012; tel. (021) 22-2810, fax. 24-6211.

ZUURBERG SECTION
Permits/bookings: Day permits obtainable at park office.
Accommodation: Contact Addo Elephant National Park (*see* below).
Opening times: Open daily, 06h45–17h30.
Accommodation: One fully-equipped 6-bed cottage.
Enquiries: **Addo Elephant National Park,** PO Box 52, Addo 6105; tel. (0426) 40-0556, fax. 40-0196.

BAVIAANSKLOOF WILDERNESS AREA
Permits/bookings: Contact Cape Nature Conservation (*see* below).
Opening times: The R332 which winds through the Baviaanskloof is a public road. Entry into the conservation area is permitted between sunrise and sunset.
Accommodation: Ranges from primitive bush camps to camp sites and fully equipped cottages throughout the conservation area.
Enquiries: **Cape Nature Conservation,** PO Box 218, Patensie 6335; tel. (04232) 3-0270, fax. 3-0915.

GROENDAL WILDERNESS AREA
Enquiries: The Officer-in-Charge, Groendal Wilderness Area, PO Box 445, Uitenhage 6230; tel. (041) 992-5418, fax. 992-7570.

OTTERFORD PLANTATION
Enquiries: **Gonaqua Hiking Trail,** SAFCOL, Private Bag X537, Humansdorp 6300; tel. (0423) 91-0393, fax. 5-2745.

SHAMWARI GAME RESERVE
Bookings: **Accommodation:** Contact The Park Warden (*see* below). '**African Rail Safari' train:** Spoornet (*see* below).
Opening times: All year. Booking essential.
Accommodation: **Longlee Manor:** Accommodates 24 people. **Shamwari Lodge:** Accommodates 10 people. **Carningly and Highfield:** self-catering parties of up to 6 people.
Facilities: Curio shop, conference centre for 50 people. Swimming pools at all lodges. Airfield at Longlee Manor.
Enquiries: **The Park Warden, Shamwari Game Reserve,** PO Box 91, Paterson 6130; tel. (042) 851-1196, fax. 851-1224. **Spoornet,** PO Box 2671, Joubert Park 2044; tel. (011) 773-6978, fax. 773-7643.

TOURIST INFORMATION
Port Elizabeth Publicity Association, Donkin Reserve, Belmont Terrace, PO Box 357, Port Elizabeth 6000; tel. (041) 52-1315, fax. 55-2564.

23 MOUNTAIN ZEBRA NATIONAL PARK

Despite its comparatively small size and the absence of 'big game', the Mountain Zebra National Park offers excellent game-viewing and a wide range of game. It is the home of the Cape mountain zebra, a variety of antelope, smaller mammals, and over 200 bird species.

How to get there
The park is 280 km from Port Elizabeth along the N10 and 25 km from Cradock, off the R61. From Port Elizabeth take the N2 east for 45 km. At Ncanara (en route to Grahamstown), turn to the left onto the N10. Continue for 204 km to Cradock (Olive Schreiner House in Cradock commemorates the writer, *see* box, p. 105; the Karoo Sulphur Springs and the dolerite Egg Rock are outside Cradock), and for 6 km more towards Middelburg; take the R61 towards Graaff-Reinet. The signposted turnoff to the park is 6 km on; the entrance gate 12,5 km along a gravel road and the turn-off to the rest camp to the left, 1,1 km from the gate. From Graaff-Reinet follow the N9 towards Middelburg for 47 km and then turn right onto the R61. Continue for 80 km to the signposted turnoff to the park.

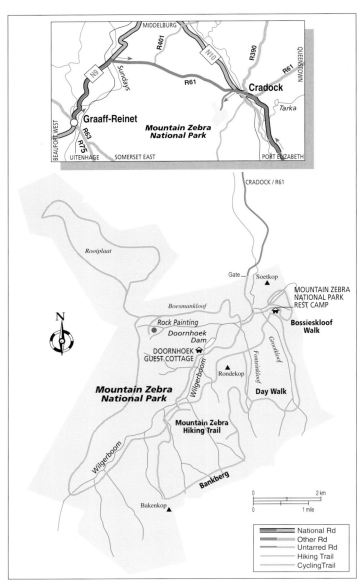

Ostriches are adapted to living in arid areas.

out for grey rhebok on the plateaux, as well as klipspringer and mountain reedbuck on the rocky mountain slopes. The park is also home to several hundred mountain reedbuck, a species which has its highest density in the Cradock district, but common duiker, steenbok and a host of smaller mammals are also present. The densely wooded Wilgerboom River Valley is the favoured habitat of kudu.

The caracal is the largest **predator** in the park. Among the more than 200 **bird species** recorded are ostrich, secretarybird, black eagle, booted eagle and black harrier. Species attracted by the water habitats (the Wilgerboom River Valley and Doornhoek Dam, the small impoundments in Fonteinkloof and Weltevredekloof along the lower slopes of Bankberg, and two dams on the Rooiplaat plateau) include yellowbilled and African black ducks, as well as the malachite and giant kingfishers. The Cape robin and the

southern boubou are found in the riverine bush of the Wilgerboom River Valley and the wooded valleys on the slopes of the Bankberg.

An interesting creature which visitors might see in the park is the giant *Microchaetus* **earthworm** (*see* box, p. 108) which reaches a length of up to 4 m and is up to 2 cm thick. It spends most of its life underground, but after rains emerges at night, returning underground in the morning. They can usually be seen at Rooiplaat and near Weltevrede Dam.

The **vegetation** in the park ranges from dense riverine bush in the valleys (sweet thorn, karree and wild olive) to sour grassveld on the plateaux and high mountain slopes. The Rooiplaat plateau in the northern section of the park, with its highly nutritious sweet grassveld, is much favoured by game; a game-viewing drive to this plateau is usually rewarding (*see* p. 105). Tree species occurring on the dolerite

MOUNTAIN ZEBRA NATIONAL PARK

Dominated by the Bankberg with its rounded dolerite outcrops and the Wilgerboom River Valley, the 6 536-ha Mountain Zebra National Park, west of Cradock in the Cape Midlands, is a place of scenic beauty and tranquillity.

The park lies in an elongated amphitheatre bounded in the south by the Bankberg and a high

ridge merging into the Rooiplaat Plateau in the west. The runoff from the watershed finds its way into the Wilgerboom River Valley, running through the centre of the park. The park was established as a sanctuary for **Cape mountain zebra** in 1937, then on the brink of extinction (*see* box, p. 105).

Antelope you are likely to see include blesbok, black wildebeest, eland and springbok. Look

A panoramic view of the park with its open expanses of grassveld, which provide grazing for a variety of animals.

outcrops include the white stinkwood, mountain cabbage tree and the coral aloe.

In spring the veld is brightened by the **flowers** of numerous Karoo bushes, including the wild aster with its yellow centre, the Karoo aster, the yellow resin bush, Michaelmas daisies, and the Karoo violet.

To enable visitors to enjoy the scenery and view the game, a 42-km **circular drive** traverses the park. It leads up from the

OLIVE SCHREINER

Doornhoek, a typical Eastern Cape farm complex of the 1830s.

Olive Schreiner is one of South Africa's foremost authors. She is best remembered for her novel *The Story of an African Farm*, which was filmed at Doornhoek Guest Cottage in the Mountain Zebra National Park. Not only was she an ardent feminist, but she was also a social campaigner and pamphleteer for human rights. She worked as governess on farms around Cradock for six years in the 1870s. In 1894 she revisited the area, and met and married Samuel Cronwright, a local farmer. In deference to her wishes, he called himself Cronwright-Schreiner until her death in 1920.

Cape mountain zebra came within a hair's breadth of extinction.

CAPE MOUNTAIN ZEBRA

In the mid-1930s the entire world population of Cape mountain zebra was probably under 100. Six of these, an old mare and five stallions, were on Babylon's Toren, a farm that was proclaimed the Mountain Zebra National Park in 1937. The mare died the next year after giving birth to a filly. After the stallions died, a neighbouring farmer, J H Lombard, donated 11 zebra to the park in 1950. By 1964 the population had risen to 25. In the same year the park was enlarged to its present size and the population was swelled by a further 30 from neighbouring farms. By 1980 the population in the park exceeded 200 for the first time and several hundred have since been reintroduced into other areas where they used to occur. Among these are the De Hoop and the Cape of Good Hope nature reserves (*see* pp. 40 and 16) in the Western Cape, Tsolwana Game Park and Zuurberg section of the Addo Elephant National Park (*see* p. 101) in the Eastern Cape. The second largest population (after the Mountain Zebra National Park) is in the Karoo National Park (*see* p. 78).

rest camp to the Rooiplaat plateau and then descends to the Wilgerboom River Valley, before returning to the rest camp.

The **Doornhoek** farmhouse, a typical Eastern Cape farm complex of the 1830s, was acquired by the National Parks Board in 1964 when the farm was incorporated into the park. After standing empty for a number of years, the farmhouse was used as a cultural-historical museum for a while. In 1984 it was restored to its former glory at a cost of R100 000 and converted into a guest cottage. Two years later, it was declared a national monument (see box, p. 105).

Visitors can ask at the reception office for a guide to accompany them to a rock painting site, a short way off the Rooiplaat road. The paintings depict a large antelope, three smaller antelope and four other animals in ochre, and two human figures, an antelope, three baboons and a feline, painted in black.

WALKS AND TRAILS

Two day walks have been laid out in the vicinity of the rest camp. The **Bossiekloof Walk** follows an easy route from the rest camp along a small kloof between Soetkop and a large dolerite outcrop, climbing steadily to a viewpoint where trailists enjoy stunning views of the rest camp, the Wilgerboom River Valley and the Bankberg, before

returning to the rest camp. Since the entire trail covers only 2,7 km, it can be completed in just over an hour. However, the view is especially magnificent in the early morning and late afternoons, so allow two hours at a more leisurely pace.

The longer **day walk**, which covers just under 10 km, follows the first few kilometres of the Mountain Zebra Hiking Trail and is an ideal introduction to those planning to tackle the longer route. Ascending along Grootkloof, the trail passes a 6 000-tonne rock which broke loose in 1976 and slid down the mountainside. After crossing Kwaggarif, the trail descends Fonteinkloof, passing Rondekop, one of the few sandstone outcrops in the Wilgerboom River Valley.

An attraction of the three-day **Mountain Zebra Hiking Trail** is the chance to see the sure-footed Cape mountain zebra and other game species. The trail takes hikers along ridges, through deep kloofs and past dolerite domes; on the second day it ascends to Bakenkop (1 957 m), the highest point of the Bankberg, and magnificent views are a highlight of the trail.

HORSE RIDING

Horse rides, which should be booked a day in advance at reception, are available during school holidays.

Rock paintings in the park are reminders that others were here before.

The mountain cabbage tree grows mainly on dry, stoney hills.

MOUNTAIN ZEBRA NATIONAL PARK AT A GLANCE

MAIN ATTRACTIONS
Karoo scenery, scenic/game-viewing drive, Cape mountain zebra, horse-riding, bird-watching.

BEST TIMES TO VISIT
Summer temperatures are high and most rain falls between January and April. Winter days are pleasant, but night-time temperatures are cold with sub-zero temperatures not uncommon. Snow occurs frequently on the high mountain peaks.

PERMITS/BOOKINGS
Entry permits at gate. **Accommodation and hiking trail:** National Parks Board Reservations (see below). **Horse rides:** The Park Warden (see below). Rides must be booked a day in advance.

OPENING TIMES
May to September 07h00–18h00; October to April 07h00–19h00.

ACCOMMODATION
Mountain Zebra National Park Rest Camp: Cottages with 2-bedrooms; caravan/

camp sites (hot/cold-water ablutions). **Doornhoek guest cottage:** Three bedrooms. **Mountain Zebra Hiking Trail:** Bunks with mattresses, lamps, basic cooking utensils, fireplaces, water, shower and toilet.

AMENITIES
A la carte restaurant; fuel (petrol and diesel); shop stocked with non-perishables (including liquor), meat, bread and curios; swimming pool; conference facilities for 60.

ENQUIRIES
National Parks Board Reservations, PO Box 787, Pretoria 0001; tel. (012) 343-1991, fax. 343-0905, or PO Box 7400, Roggebaai 8012; tel. (021) 22-2810, fax. 24-6211. **The Park Warden, Mountain Zebra National Park,** Private Bag X66, Cradock 5880; tel. (0481) 2427, fax. 3943.

TOURIST INFORMATION
Cradock Information Centre, PO Box 414, Cradock 5880; tel. (0481) 2383, fax. 71-1421.

24 AMATOLA MOUNTAINS

Extending east from Katberg to Stutterheim for 85 km, the Amatola range rises in places over 1 200 m above the Eastern Cape coastal plains. The range encompasses valleys, cliff faces, waterfalls, and indigenous forests of yellowwoods, Cape chestnut, knobwood and lemonwood. It comprises several subsidiary ranges, of which the Katberg, Hogsback and Amatolas are best known (Hogsback and Katberg are popular resorts). The area is steeped in history, many relics testifying to nine frontier wars, fought from 1779 to 1878 between the British colonists and the Xhosa.

How to get there
King William's Town, 60 km northwest of East London and 250 km east of Port Elizabeth on the N2, is a convenient base from which to explore the area.

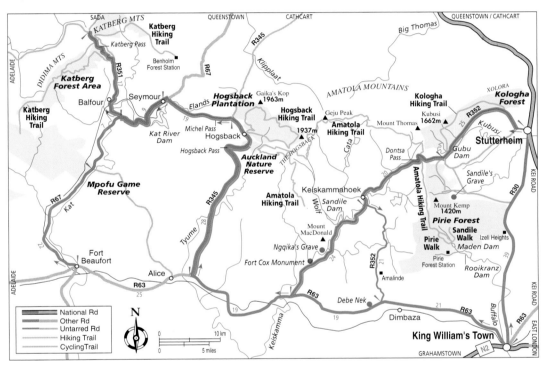

The Gubu Dam, overlooked by Mount Kubusi, a spur of the Amatolas.

➡ *The mountain scenery of the area can be enjoyed by taking an approximately 200-km scenic drive from King William's Town (itself worth visiting for the Kaffrarian and Missionary museums) starting on the R30.*

AMATOLA SCENIC DRIVE

Heading north from King William's Town on the R30 in the direction of Stutterheim (with its attractive 19th-century buildings), the turnoff to the **Rooikranz** and **Maden dams** and the **Pirie Forests** is reached after 13 km. The Amatola Hiking Trail and Sandile Walk (*see* p. 109) start at Maden Dam, and the Pirie Walk (*see* p. 109) passes through the Pirie Forests. The 85-ha Rooikranz Dam is popular

with the local sailing fraternity (the King William's Town Yacht Club is based here). The Rooikranz and the 10-ha Maden Dam, about 2 km upstream, have been stocked with trout and there are picnic places on the banks of the Maden Dam.

The road, the R30, then ascends steadily to the turnoff to **Sandile's Grave** at the top of the Izeli Heights. Sandile, a 19th-century Xhosa chief, was a leading figure in the last three frontier wars. The Seventh Frontier War (War of the Axe) was precipitated because Sandile refused to give up one of his people who had stolen an axe from a Fort Beaufort shop.

During Sandile's reign the 'national suicide' of the Xhosa occurred: the 15-year-old Nong-qawuse said the ancestral spirits had spoken through her and ordered the mass killing of cattle and destruction of crops, which would rid them of the white man. However, Sandile was reluctant to kill his cattle and started only when ordered to do so by King Sarhili, king of all the Xhosas. Sandile was injured in a skirmish in the Isidenge Forest in May 1878 and died a few days later.

About 10 km on the road joins the R352, passing **Gubu Dam**, which is overlooked by the Xolora Mountain, a spur of the Amatolas. The dam with its coves is popular with trout anglers, yachtsmen, and windsurfers, but no motorboats are allowed; to reach the dam, turn right, immediately after crossing over the dam wall turn left. Further along, the road crosses a nek between Mount Kemp and Mount Thomas along the **Dontsa Pass** (which is crossed in the course of the Amatola Hiking Trail, *see* p. 109), twisting through

Hogsback offers walks through the surrounding forests and plantations.

indigenous forests and pine plantations as it enters the scenic Keiskammahoek basin.

To the north the scenery is dominated by the Amatolas, with Geju Peak rising 1 200 m above the Keiskamma Valley. The indigenous forests on the mountain slopes are home to bushbuck, bushpig, samango monkey and the tree dassie. Among the colourful birds attracted to the forests are the Cape parrot and the Knysna lourie.

At Keiskammahoek motorists can see the ruins of **Castle Eyre**, one of several British military outposts, established after the War of the Axe to defend the eastern frontier of the Cape Colony against attacks by the Xhosa. The road then passes

Sandile Dam, at the confluence of the Wolf and Keiskamma rivers, in a magnificent setting of precipices, forests and grasslands.

After passing the 994-m-high Mount MacDonald, the turnoff to **Ngqika's Grave** is reached. Ngqika, Sandile's father, was defeated in a struggle for chieftaincy against his uncle, Ndlambe, at Amalinde in 1818 in one of the bloodiest battles in Xhosa history. About 7,5 km on is the **Fort Cox Monument**; a military outpost was established here around 1835 and in 1847 a fort was built. The fort was used as a central embarkation point for the frontier wars.

Continuing on the R63 towards Alice (the University of Fort Hare, which lists President Nelson Mandela among its illustrious former students, overlooks this town), the route heads north to Hogsback along the Tyume River Valley. Shortly before reaching **Hogsback** (*see* below), the road winds steeply up the lush mountain slopes, passing through the indigenous forest of the 218-ha **Auckland Nature Reserve**.

From Hogsback the road meanders along the Michel Pass and the Elands River Valley to Seymour on the Kat River Dam. It then ascends to the top of the Didima Mountains of the Groot Winterhoek range along the **Katberg Pass** (*see* p. 109), which offers panoramic views over hills and forests.

➡ To get to Hogsback, follow the directions to the Amatola Scenic Drive; go north from King William's Town to Stutterheim on the R30, to Dimbaza on the R352, to Alice on the R63, and to Hogsback on the R345. A shorter option is to go west from King William's Town straight onto the R63; just before Alice turn right onto the R345, which leads to Hogsback.

HOGSBACK

The charming village of Hogsback at the western end of the Amatolas is a favourite mountain retreat for those seeking peace and tranquillity. Towering above the village are the three Hogsback peaks. The southwesterly peak is The Spine and the highest peak (1 937 m) the Third Hog. Further north is the 1 963-m-high Gaika's Kop, the highest peak in the area.

Surrounded by lush indigenous forests and pine plantations, Hogsback is renowned for its gardens of rhododendrons and azaleas (these, and the other flowers of the area, are best in spring), as well as its wide variety of wild and cultivated berries.

Typical forest **mammals** include bushpig, bushbuck and blue duiker. Baboon, klipspringer and rock dassie favour the rocky mountain areas. Among the predators are leopard, caracal and African wild cat. The indigenous forests, pine plantations and mountain fynbos attract a diversity of **birds** and to date some

In the right light, the Madonna and Child can be seen near Hogsback.

220 species have been recorded in the Hogsback area. Species to keep an eye out for in the forests include the rameron pigeon, cinnamon dove, Cape parrot, Knysna woodpecker, grey cuckooshrike, brown robin and forest canary. Gurney's and Cape sugarbirds, sentinel rock thrush, bokmakierie and palewinged starling occur in the mountain fynbos.

Among the cascading waterfalls within walking distance of the village are the **Madonna and Child**, **Thirty-Nine Steps** and **Kettlespout**. Also accessible are the **Eastern Monarch**, a 34-m-high yellowwood with a circumference of 8 m, the **Oak Avenue**, dating back to 1880, and the **arboretum**. The various 'piggy trails' (*see* below), which have been laid out in the area by the Hogsback Inn, lead trailists to all of these attractions.

➡ *Follow the directions to Hogsback (see p. 108) and 3,5 km beyond Hogsback turn left onto the Seymour road, continuing over Michel's Pass to reach Seymour 17,5 km on. From Seymour follow the R67 for 8 km; turn right and after about 4 km right again onto the R351 (Balfour/Katberg road). Continue on this road for 7,5 km to the Katberg Hotel. The Katberg Forest Station is just over 1 km further. To reach Katberg from Fort Beaufort, drive north along the R67 for 34 km and then turn left onto the R351 (gravel); continue for 13 km to the Katberg Hotel.*

KATBERG

The scenic Katberg is a patchwork of verdant indigenous forest, aromatic pine plantations, fynbos and montane grasslands. Dominating the scenery are the Didima Mountains, boasting several peaks of over 1 800 m. In winter they are often covered by a dense blanket of snow. The Katberg Pass is testimony to the ingenuity of the famous road builder, Andrew Geddes Bain, who worked on the pass in 1860.

Opportunities for outdoor recreation include walks and trails (*see* below), mountain biking (*see* below) and horse riding (*see* below).

WALKS AND TRAILS

AMATOLAS: The **Amatola Hiking Trail** covers 105 km between Maden Dam and Hogsback, with two shorter circular options. Winding through indigenous forests, past spectacular waterfalls and to the summit of the Amatolas, the trail rewards hikers with breathtaking scenery along the five-day route.

Those with neither the time nor required level of fitness to do an overnight trail can set off on two day walks starting at Maden Dam. The 9-km **Pirie Walk** follows the route of a railway line, built in 1910 to transport logs from the forest. Alternatively, there is the **Sandile Walk** which leads to the cave where Sandile took refuge in 1878 when he was pursued by British troops.

Two days are required to hike the 34-km-long **Kologha Hiking Trail** (closed at the time of writing) which takes hikers through magnificent indigenous forests and then traverses the upper slopes of Kubusi Mountain before descending through the Kologha Forest.

HOGSBACK: These indigenous forests are renowned for their **'piggy trails'**, ranging from a short 3-km ramble to a 20-km day walk. Those with time on

Hogsback's well-known 'piggy' trail markers.

their hands can do the 32-km, two-day circular **Hogsback Hiking Trail** which covers indigenous forests, mountain fynbos and pine plantations.

KATBERG: There is a choice of several day walks, a two-day circular trail of 40 km and the three-day **Katberg Hiking Trail** which stretches over 51 km between the Mpofu Game Reserve and the Benholm Forest Station.

HORSE RIDING

KATBERG: Horse trails leave from the Katberg Protea Hotel and last between half an hour and a day. They pass through the Katberg Forest and some go up the Katberg Pass. Horses can be hired from the hotel.

CYCLING ROUTES

KATBERG: Cycling trails through the forest area, lasting from several hours to a day, leave from the Katberg Protea Hotel. Mountain bikes are available from the hotel. Booking is not necessary.

AMATOLA MOUNTAINS AT A GLANCE

MAIN ATTRACTIONS
Spectacular mountain scenery, waterfalls, scenic drives.

BEST TIMES TO VISIT
Each season has its own attraction, with spring being especially rewarding. In winter the mountain peaks are often covered in snow. Rain falls throughout the year, with a peak between February and April.

PERMITS/BOOKINGS
Katberg: Katberg Protea Hotel (*see* below). **Amatola and Katberg hiking trails:** Tourist Information (*see* below). **Kologha and Hogsback hiking trails:** SAFCOL (*see* below). **Pirie and Sandile walks:** No permits are required.

ACCOMMODATION
There are three hotels and several cottages and chalets in Hogsback. **Katberg Protea Hotel:** Accommodation with en suite facilities. **Hiking**

trails: Accommodation consists of overnight huts equipped with bunks and mattresses. Water, firewood, braai places and toilets. Contact Pat Shepherd (*see* below).

FACILITIES
Katberg Protea Hotel: Swimming pool, golf, tennis, squash, bowls, table tennis, snooker, horse riding.

ENQUIRIES
Pat Shepherd, PO Box 49, Hogsback 5721; tel. and fax. (045) 962-1050. **Katberg Protea Hotel,** PO Box 665, Fort Beaufort 5720; tel. and fax. (0404) 3-1151. SAFCOL, Private Bag X537, Humansdorp 6300; tel. (0423) 91-0393; fax. 5-2745.

TOURIST INFORMATION
Keiskamma Eco-tourism Network, 9 Chamberlain Street, King William's Town 5600; tel. and fax. (0433) 2-2571.

The Katberg mountains offer hiking, riding and trailing opportunities.

25 THE WILD COAST

The Wild Coast is a landscape of ever-changing vistas: rolling hills and deserted beaches, secluded bays fringed with wild banana trees and tranquil lagoons. The spectacular 280-km coastline stretches between the Mtamvuna River in the north and the Kei River in the south.

How to get there
Umtata, one of the access points to the Wild Coast, is 235 km northeast of East London (on the N2) and 447 km southwest of Durban (take the N3 to Pietermaritzburg, the R56 as far as Stafford's Post, and the N2 to Umtata). Lusikisiki, via the R61, is the access point to the northern sections of the area. Port St Johns, Coffee Bay and Hluleka Nature Reserve can all be used as bases from which to explore the area.

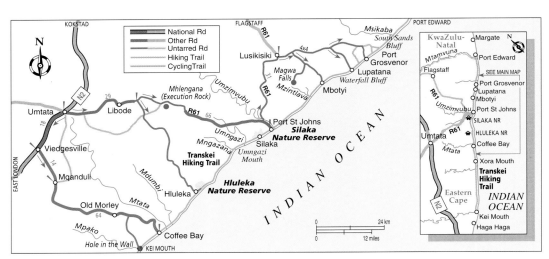

A Xhosa woman in the former homeland of Transkei.

The **vegetation** of the Wild Coast ranges from short grasslands dotted with aloes, to dune forests of coast red milkwood and patches of coastal forest of white stinkwood, water berry and sneezewood.

Among the more than 200 **bird species** recorded along the Wild Coast to date are the African fish eagle, Knysna lourie, trumpeter hornbill and the forest weaver, as well as seven of the 10 kingfisher species that are found in southern Africa.

The coast is rich in **marine life** and the diversity of shells along some sections are ranked among the richest in the world. Rock and surf anglers have long been attracted by the excellent fishing which can be enjoyed here. Sought-after species include kob, blacktail, garrick, black musselcracker and shad.

The pristine beaches are irresistible for **swimming**. **Boardsailing** is popular in sheltered lagoons and estuaries such as those at Mngazi and Mbotyi. **Surfers** are attracted by the challenging waves, particularly at Coffee Bay and Second Beach at Port St Johns. The offshore reefs are favoured by **spearfishermen** and experienced **divers**. There are diving sites at Hluleka (from the nature reserve), Presley's Bay (north of the Mdumbi River mouth) and Harrison's Gallery (north of the Mtata River Mouth). However, do not lose sight of the fact that sharks do occur along the coast.

A number of short self-guided **walks** can be taken in the area, as well as the popular **Transkei Hiking Trail** (*see* p. 113). Xhosa villages are dotted around the countryside, particularly between Coffee Bay and Port St Johns. A striking feature of the section of the Eastern Cape north of the Kei River is the traditional Xhosa huts adorning the landscape. The doors of these rondavel-shaped huts with their thatched roofs and white-washed dung and clay walls invariably face north.

Many rural Xhosa-speaking people still practise their traditions way of life, customs and traditions. While travelling through the area, you are likely to encounter women smoking long-stemmed pipes, and headdresses indicating the status, seniority and age-group of women are still commonly worn. Although traditional bead-work has largely disappeared, some women still wear beaded head, arm- and neckbands, as well as strings of beads.

You might also come across Abakwetha youths undergoing the coming-of-age ceremony of young Xhosa males, an Igqira (witchdoctor) or an Ishwele (herbalist).

➤ To reach Hole in the Wall, take a turnoff on the N2, 19 km south of Umtata, onto a tar road. About 31 km from this turnoff you pass a stone beacon on the left-hand side of the road, marking the route taken by Dick King in his historic ride from Port Natal to Grahamstown in 1842. Turn right after 57 km and follow a gravel road for 19 km to Hole in the Wall. En route you will pass through typical Bomvanaland scenery – undulating grassy hills dotted with thatched rondavels and herds of cattle.

HOLE IN THE WALL
Situated at the mouth of the Mpako River, Hole in the Wall was once part of the rocky headlands flanking it. The enormous hole through the centre of the rock formation is the result of erosion of the soft sandstone dykes within the shales of the Lower Ecca group of sedimentary rock by the huge breakers pounding against the formation.

Known as EsiKhaleni in Xhosa (meaning 'place of the sound'), the rock formation is about 200 m long and towers up to 34 m above the sea.

➤ Backtrack to the Coffee Bay road, turn right and continue through undulating countryside to reach Coffee Bay, a charming seaside village, after 22 km.

COFFEE BAY
Sheltered by two rocky headlands, the 1-km-long beach at Coffee Bay is one of the most popular Wild Coast resorts. The small bay is said to have been named when coffee beans took root along the Nenga River at the southern

A typical Wild Coast scene with undulating hills in the background. It is not uncommon to see animals grazing right down to the beach.

end of the bay, after a ship ran aground in the bay in 1863. The beach is ideal for swimming, angling is popular and the 2½-hour walk to Hole in the Wall (*see* p. 113) is well worth the effort.

➡ *To reach Hluleka Nature Reserve, follow the Port St Johns road (the R61) to the signposted turnoff 3 km east of Libode. The reserve is approximatley 90 km on along a gravel road and is accessible in a sedan car.*

HLULEKA NATURE RESERVE

Forest, grassland, lagoon and coast merge at Hluleka into one of the most exquisite spots in the area. Covering 772 ha, the reserve is rich in **birdlife**. Species to look out for include the longcrested eagle, osprey, African finfoot and the green coucal. The forests are the natural habitat of a number of **mammals**, among them bushpig and bushbuck. Eland, blue wildebeest, blesbok and Burchell's zebra have been introduced. Self-guided **walks** can be taken in the reserve (*see* p. 113). Visitors can stay in the camps' log chalets.

➡ *Port St Johns is 98 km east of Umtata along a fully tarred road, the R61, past Libode and Mhlengana (Execution Rock) with its Cape vulture colony. The Umngazi River Bungalows, south of Port St Johns, are 12 km beyond the signposted turnoff (57 km beyond Libode). From here it is possible to walk to the Mngazana mangroves.*

PORT ST JOHNS

Set on the banks of the Umzimvubu River, Port St Johns is one of the best-known coastal resorts along the Wild Coast, popular for its angling and swimming. Overlooking the river mouth are the Gates of Port St Johns, two sandstone buttresses towering more than 300 m above the river.

The **Blow Hole** and the **Gap** are both worth visiting. The latter is a deep gully which has almost detached the headland

Hole in the Wall, created by the erosion of the sea, is a popular holiday resort.

THE MANGROVES OF THE WILD COAST

Mangroves are specialist trees that grow in sheltered lagoons and estuaries along the shores of tropical areas throughout the world. They live in complex communities requiring specific conditions, including a soft, muddy substrate, tidal flushing and a constant supply of fresh water. Aerial roots enable them to breathe when their roots are submerged during high tide.

Mangrove communities are important nursery areas for several species of marine fish and also provide a habitat to a wide variety of animals, such as the mud-skipper, fiddler and mud crabs, molluscs and the mangrove kingfisher, which is found mainly in mangrove communities.

In South Africa mangrove communities occur from Kosi Bay to the Kobonqaba River, just north of the Kei River (the southernmost community in Africa), although small numbers of white mangroves occur in a few rivers further south towards East London. Two of the five species found in South Africa, the Tonga and Indian mangroves, do not occur south of Kosi Bay. Three species are found south of Kosi Bay: the white mangrove (the commonest), the red mangrove and the relatively uncommon black mangrove.

Along the Wild Coast there are 17 mangrove communities between the Mtamvuna and the Kobonqaba rivers, often with only one or two species, but at the Mngazana, Mtata and Mntafufu estuaries all three occur. The communities at Mngazana and Mtata, the most extensive of the Wild Coast (150 and 34 ha respectively), are considered the finest in South Africa.

from a rocky outcrop along the coast north of Second Beach. A cable and a wooden ladder give access down the cliffs of the Gap to the Blow Hole, through which the incoming tide sends plumes of spray into the air.

Situated in a small forested valley overlooking Third Beach, just south of Second Beach, is the **Silaka Nature Reserve**, starting point of the popular Port St Johns to Coffee Bay section of the Transkei Hiking Trail (*see* p. 113.). The reserve encompasses a magnificent tract of coastal forest, grass-covered hills dotted with aloes and a rugged stretch of coastline.

Mammals found in the Silaka forests include bushbuck and blue duiker. Both are seldom spotted due to their secretive nature. Also rarely seen is the Cape clawless otter, whose spoor can sometimes be seen on the beach. Burchell's zebra, blue wildebeest and blesbok have been introduced and roam the grassy plains.

Birdlife in the forests includes the cinnamon dove (an unobtrusive species), Knysna lourie, redbilled woodhoopoe, trumpeter hornbill, grey cuckooshrike, terrestrial bulbul, chorister robin and forest weaver.

➤ *To reach the Magwa Falls (accessible by sedan car), drive north for 43 km from Port St Johns on the R61, to Lusikisiki. Take the turnoff to the coast 1,5 km south of Lusikisiki onto a major gravel road. Turn right after 6 km and right again 8 km later. After 3 km the road splits; take the right fork and continue for 5 km to the falls.*

MAGWA FALLS

The Magwa Falls are without doubt one of the most stunning of the many scenic cascades in the area. A tributary of the Mzintlava River cascades some 125 m over a sheer cliff into a narrow forested gorge created by the Egossa Fault. During the dry winter months the falls are often reduced to a thin thread of water,

Hiking along the Wild Coast's remote beaches and rocky coastline is a very popular recreational activity.

but after good summer rains the water thunders into the gorge with a deafening roar.

➤ *Waterfall Bluff is best reached from Lupatana, which is accessible only by a vehicle with a high ground clearance or a four-wheel-drive. Take the turnoff to the coast 1,5 km south of Lusikisiki and continue for about 1,5 km past the Magwa/Mbotyi turnoff. Bear right here and continue for about 11 km before turning right for Lupatana, which is another 15 km on. From here it is a 3-km walk southwards to Waterfall Bluff.*

WATERFALL BLUFF

At high tide when huge waves crash against the flat rock shelves at Waterfall Bluff south of Lupatana, they send spectacular plumes of spray several metres into the air. The near-vertical sandstone cliffs, rising 100 m above the rocky coast, follow the direction of the Egossa Fault and were formed as a result of the resistance of the sandstone to erosion. However, the softer rock on the seaward side of the fault was eroded by the sea.

Extending for about 5 km along the coast, Waterfall Bluff is a place of exceptional beauty. Two of the few waterfalls in the world which plunge directly into the sea, the **Mlambomkulu Falls** and the 80-m-high **Mfihlelo Falls** are along Waterfall Bluff. Also of interest is **Cathedral Rock**, an enormous sea-stack with an archway carved through the rock by the never-ending onslaught of the waves.

➤ *Port Grosvenor, where the famed HMS Grosvenor ran aground on the night of 2 August 1782, is an easy 10-km walk north of Lupatana, through grassland at the edge of the rocky beaches. Alternatively, it can be reached in a vehicle with a high ground clearance, or a four-wheel-drive vehicle, by turning south, about 14 km beyond the Lupatana turnoff.*

PORT GROSVENOR

Early mariners feared the treacherous currents, huge waves and rocky coastline of the Wild Coast, regarded as one of the largest shipping graveyards in the world.

Legend has it that the *HMS Grosvenor* was laden with treasures, including the Peacock Throne of India. An abandoned tunnel (built in 1921 through the seabed in an endeavor to reach the wreck), a rusty piece of machinery and derelict buildings are reminders of numerous attempts made since 1842 to salvage the treasures. Diving in this area is difficult due to large swells and strong currents.

➤ *To reach South Sands Bluff from Port Grosvenor, backtrack to the main coast track, turn right and continue east (ignore a track further on branching off to the right) for 11 km, to the end of the road.*

SOUTH SANDS BLUFF

Situated at the mouth of the Msikaba River, South Sands Bluff is the site of yet another Wild Coast shipwreck, the *São Bento*, which ran aground here in 1554. The camp site under the canopy of a patch of coastal forest is one of the most scenic along the Wild Coast, but visitors must be self-sufficient as no facilities are provided. As with other spots along the Wild Coast, the main attraction is angling, but it is also possible to canoe upstream for 2 km. The northern banks of the river are one of only two places in the world where the rare Mkambati palm, with its feather-shaped leaves, occurs (the other place is along the Mtentu River further north). The river forms the southern boundary of the 8 000-ha Mkambati Nature Reserve, which extends to the Mtentu River. Entry to Mkambati from the coast is prohibited.

WALKS AND TRAILS

Opportunities for **self-guided day walks** from holidaying spots along the Wild Coast are virtually unlimited and there are also several delightful paths through the coastal forests in the Silaka and Hluleka nature reserves.

The famed **Transkei Hiking Trail** stretches between the Mtamvuna River in the north and the Mbashe River in the south covering a distance of over 280 km. The trail has been divided into five sections, each with its distinctive atmosphere

and attractions. On all these sections numerous large rivers have to be crossed, adding a dimension of adventure to the trail experience.

Highlights of the northernmost section covering the 100-km-long stretch of coast between the Mtamvuna River and Port St Johns include the 75 to 80-million-year-old Mzamba fossil beds (accessible at low tide) and Waterfall Bluff (*see above*).

The popular 60-km section between Port St Johns and Coffee Bay is characterised by its unspoilt beaches, secluded bays and undulating hills. In addition to the magnificent coastal scenery, trailists will also gain an insight into the culture of the

Bomvana and Mpondo people living here, as the trail occasionally passes through villages.

Hikers should be courteous to local people at all times. Bear in mind that the trails traverse tribal, not public, land. Should you wish to photograph people, ask their permission and negotiate a fee (most insist on payment). Never leave backpacks and personal effects unattended – they might not be there when you return.

The next section of the trail stretches between Coffee Bay and the Mbashe River. An attraction on this section is the impressive Hole in the Wall. The terrain is generally more gently undulating than the coast between Port St Johns and Coffee Bay.

THE WILD COAST AT A GLANCE

MAIN ATTRACTIONS
Spectacular coastal and rural scenery, unique waterfalls, rock formations, rock and surf angling, spearfishing, diving.

BEST TIMES TO VISIT
April to September are generally the best months to visit the Wild Coast. May and August are good for surfing, August to March best for boardsailing. The months between May and June are generally best for diving.

PERMITS/BOOKINGS
Hole in the Wall Hotel: Reservations (*see* below). **Silaka and Hluleka nature reserves and camp sites along the coast:** Department of Agriculture and Forestry (*see* below). **Umngazi River Bungalows:** The Manager (*see* below). **Port St Johns, Second Beach Holiday Resort:** The Manager (*see* below). **Trails:** Department of Agriculture and Forestry (*see* below) (no booking necessary).

ACCOMMODATION
Hole in the Wall Hotel: Rooms with en suite bathrooms and thatched family cottages. **Hluleka Nature Reserve:** Self-contained log chalets (sleep 6); three rustic

camps. **Silaka Nature Reserve:** Fully equipped self-catering four-bed bungalows. **Umngazi River Bungalows:** Thatched bungalows with en suite bathroom. **Second Beach Holiday Resort, Port St Johns:** Fully-equipped self-catering chalets with en suite bathrooms; camping sites with hot/cold water ablutions.

FACILITIES
Petrol can be bought at Coffee Bay, Port St Johns and Lusikisiki.

ENQUIRIES
Reservations, Hole in the Wall Hotel, PO Box 13135, Vincent 5217; tel. and fax. (0431) 31-2715. **Department of Agriculture and Forestry,** Private Bag X5002, Umtata 5100; tel. (0471) 2-4322, fax. 31-2713. **The Manager, Umngazi River Bungalows,** PO Box 391, Pinetown 3600; tel. (0471) 2-2370, fax. 2-2397. **The Manager, Second Beach Holiday Resort,** PO Box 18, Port St Johns 4830; tel. (0475) 44-1245.

TOURIST INFORMATION
Wild Coast Tourism, Private Bag X5029, Umtata 5100; tel. (0471) 31-2885, fax. 31-2887.

26 CAPE DRAKENSBERG

After extending south from the Magoebaskloof for over 1 000 km, the Drakensberg range ends in the northeastern Cape. Often snow-capped in winter, the Cape Drakensberg is characterised by dramatic views, exceptionally beautiful sandstone formations and mountain streams.

How to get there
Aliwal North, a base from which to explore the Cape Drakensberg, is on the N6, 360 km from East London via Queenstown, and 207 km from Bloemfontein.

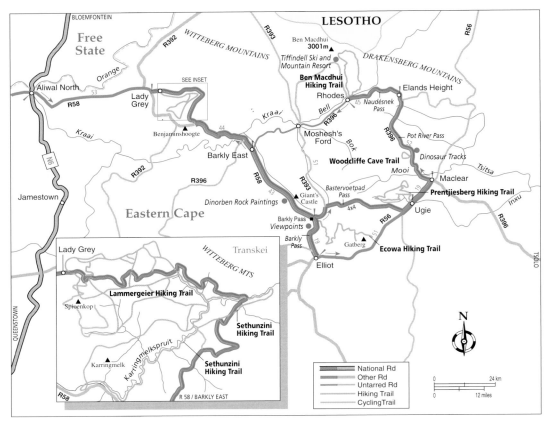

➡ *Aliwal North on the R58 is the starting point for this 570-km-long circular scenic drive, which leads to Barkly East on the R58, to Elliot down the Barkly Pass (with an optional detour onto the Bastervoet-pad Pass), to Ugie on the R56, to Maclear and Rhodes on the R396, via the Pot River and Naudésnek passes, and, still on the R396, back to Barkly East, and back to Lady Grey and Aliwal North on the R58.*

CAPE DRAKENSBERG SCENIC DRIVE

From **Aliwal North** travel eastwards on the R58 to **Lady Grey**. Continuing south, the road crosses the Karringmelkspruit and ascends the Benjaminshoogte, passing through grassland to reach **Barkly East** 77 km beyond Lady Grey.

At the 33-km road marker the R58 passes the signposted turnoff to Dinorben farm where several hundred **rock paintings** executed by San artists cover a 32-m area on the walls of an overhang. This, one of the longest galleries of rock art in southern Africa, includes paintings of eland, smaller antelope and therianthropes (humans with animal features).

To the east of Dinorben the scenery is dominated by the aptly named **Giant's Castle**, a circular conglomeration of huge rocks.

Further along the R58 is the turnoff to the Bastervoetpad Pass (*see* p. 117) to the left; to the right is the Mountain Shadows Hotel and the **Kransies Viewpoint** with its breathtaking views of the sandstone formations and the river valleys far below. Nearby are three other speactacular viewpoints: **Camel Rock**, **Vultures' Roost** and **The Castle**.

You might wish to break your journey either at this point or at the Washington Guest Farm

Naudésnek Pass, the highest pass in South Africa, presents a real challenge to cyclists.

The road over Barkly Pass traverses some of the most spectacular scenery in the Cape Drakensberg.

between Ugie and Elliot (on the R56). If you are travelling in a four-wheel-drive vehicle, a stunning diversion from the scenic drive is the **Bastervoetpad Pass** (*see* p. 117 for details), best negotiated by descending it; start at the turnoff opposite the hotel and drive to Ugie, from where you can continue to Maclear on the scenic drive (R56).

Heading further south, the summit of the **Barkly Pass** (1 994 m) is 1 km beyond the hotel, and the road then starts its 11-km descent, passing through spectacular mountain scenery.

From Elliot, at the bottom of the Barkly Pass, the road joins the R56 to Ugie. Some 20 km east of Elliot, a rocky outcrop perched on top of a grass-covered ridge can be seen to the north of the road. The formation owes its name, **Gatberg** ('hole mountain'), to the hole eroded through the rock, much in the same way as its namesake in the Mdedelelo Wilderness Area in the KwaZulu-Natal Drakensberg.

Further east another prominent feature, the picturesque **Prentjiesberg**, with its rock spires and turrets, comes into view northwest of Ugie. Named after the rock paintings adorning the overhangs, the 3 000-ha mountain is a Natural Heritage Site. From Ugie the road passes through grassveld and maizefields to reach Maclear after 21 km.

About 18 km further north of the town along the R396 is the turnoff to the **dinosaur tracks** on Oakleigh farm (*see* box, p. 116). Just over 12 km later is the summit of the 1 765-m-high **Pot River Pass**. The road continues through undulating country to reach the start of the **Naudésnek Pass** 40 km on. Winding up grass-covered mountain slopes, the road reaches the summit of the 2 500-m-high Naudésnek Pass (the highest pass in South Africa negotiable by sedan car) after 6 km. The parking area commands spectacular views of the surrounding countryside. About 2 km further, a public telephone, in a corrugated iron booth inside a sheep pen, links this remote area with the outside world.

The road descends for 19 km through the Bell River Valley. To the right of the road, at the foot of the pass, is a **picnic site** and a monument to the Naudé brothers, who surveyed the route of a pass over the mountain in 1896.

Continue along the Bell River Valley for approximately 12 km to the picturesque old-world town of **Rhodes**, set in the shadows of the 3 001-m-high Ben Macdhui (*see* Walks and Trails, p. 117), the highest peak in the Cape Drakensberg. Rhodes is particularly popular in winter when the snow-covered slopes of Ben Macdhui attract large numbers of skiers.

At the **Tiffindell Ski and Mountain Resort**, 25 km north of Rhodes, snow-farming techniques are used to supplement the winter snow falls. Instructors are on hand to teach novices, and skiers are taken about two-thirds of the way up the ski run with a ski lift. Equipment is available for hire.

The scenery west of Rhodes on the R396 is dominated by the high peaks of the Cape Drakensberg, with white sandstone outcrops prominent in the valleys of the foothills. About

7 km after crossing the Bell and Kraai rivers (on single-lane bridges), the road passes **The Caves**, one of the largest overhangs in South Africa, said to be big enough to accommodate 2 000 dancing couples. Barkly East is about 27 km on.

An interesting detour to Lady Grey is the 47-km-long scenic route over **Joubert's Pass** (the turnoff is 47 km northwest of Barkly East). The road winds steeply (a 1:6 gradient) to the 2 349-m-high summit in the Witteberg Mountains.

The sandstone rock has been eroded into fascinating formations.

SOUTH AFRICA'S EARLIEST DINOSAUR TRACKS

Although large numbers of dinosaur fossils have been found in the rocks of the Stormberg Group, the dinosaur tracks on the farm Oakleigh are preserved in Stormberg's lowest rocks, the Molteno Formation. Dating back 200 million years, these tracks provide the earliest evidence of dinosaurs in southern Africa. The tracks of at least seven carnivorous two-legged dinosaurs with three toes, and a four-footed herbivorous dinosaur and its tail drag are preserved in the rock. The mud patterns of the 10-m tail drag clearly show the direction in which the animal walked.

Dinosaur tracks have also been discovered on a farm in the Ugie district 40 km southwest of Oakleigh, at Clarens in the northeastern Free State, at Leribe and Quthing in Lesotho, and at Mount Etjo and Waterberg in Namibia.

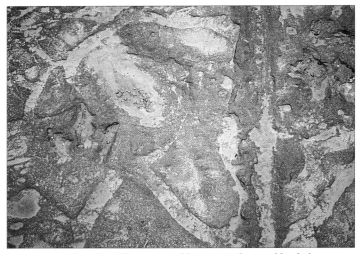

Dinosaur tracks, 200 million years old, preserved on Oakleigh farm.

➤ An alternative route from the summit of Barkly Pass (see directions, p. 114) to Ugie is to leave the R58 and take the Bastervoetpad Pass to Ugie (a four-wheel-drive vehicle is recommended).

BASTERVOETPAD PASS

Few passes in South Africa can exceed the scenic grandeur of Bastervoetpad, with its sheer rock faces, grass-covered slopes and a seemingly endless succession of deep valleys.

The turnoff to the pass, which follows an old livestock trek road, is at the summit of Barkly Pass on the R58. A four-wheel-drive vehicle or a vehicle with a high ground clearance is recommended, but depending on the condition of the road sedan cars can negotiate this scenic pass, provided care is exercised (check the condition of the road first with the Elliot Municipality or the Drakensberg Regional Services Council, *see* At a Glance right). Some 22 km beyond the turnoff, the pass descends steeply over the Drakensberg escarpment in a series of tight bends, losing 740 m over 10 km.

About 20 km from the summit of the pass the road reaches the B78, where you have the choice of bearing left, continuing for 7 km to the junction with the R56, 5 km west of Ugie, or alternatively you can turn right, passing close to Gatberg, and join the R56, 23 km west of Ugie.

WALKS AND TRAILS

Numerous overnight trails in the northeastern Cape provide opportunities to explore this scenic area on foot.

The three-day **Lammergeier Hiking Trail** at Lady Grey is a 60-km circular route through spectacular mountain scenery in the Witteberg Mountains. Among the many highlights of the **Sethunzini Hiking Trail**, a 60-km guided trail, are the impressive Karringmelk Canyon, rock paintings and waterfalls. One of the most scenic trails in South Africa, the **Ecowa Hiking Trail** near Elliot should be attempted only by fit hikers (it was being re-routed at the time of writing, so distances were not available). The trail leads past Gatberg, a well-known landmark in the northeastern Cape mountains. Imposing sandstone cliffs, rock paintings and patches of cool indigenous forests are the ingredients of the **Prentjiesberg Hiking Trail** northwest of Ugie. This three-day trail stretches over 50 km, but there is also a two-day option. The **Woodcliffe Cave Trail** north of Maclear meanders across grass-covered slopes from the foothills of the Drakensberg

The Woodcliffe Cave Trail meanders across grass-covered slopes of the Drakensberg foothills.

to the escarpment, covering 62 km over five days. There is also a circular one-day trail. Breathtaking mountain scenery and views are the rewards for hikers setting off on the **Ben Macdhui Hiking Trail**, a demanding three-day route over 51 km in the mountains north of Rhodes. An optional excursion from the first overnight hut is an ascent of the 3 001-m-high Ben Macdhui, the highest peak in the Cape Drakensberg.

CAPE DRAKENSBERG AT A GLANCE

MAIN ATTRACTIONS
Spectacular mountain scenery, scenic drives, cycling and four-wheel-drive trails, dinosaur tracks, San paintings.

BEST TIMES TO VISIT
Tiffindell's snow-skiing season stretches between 25 May and 10 September, the peak period being from 15 June to 20 August. Autumn and spring are the best seasons for hiking, but trailists must be well prepared for snow and mist. Summer days are hot and dry, but pleasant, with the chance of violent thunderstorms.

PERMITS/BOOKINGS
Mountain Shadows Hotel: The Manager (*see* below). **Washington Guest Farm:** The Manager (*see* below). **Rhodes Hotel:** The Manager (*see* below). **Tiffindell Ski and Mountain Resort:** Reservations (*see* below). **Dinosaur tracks:** No permits are required to visit the dinosaur tracks on Oakleigh farm and the rock paintings on the farm Dinorben. **Lammergeier Hiking Trail:** Lady Grey Muncipality (*see* below). **Sethunzini Hiking Trail:** Sethunzini Trails (see below). **Ecowa Hiking Trail:** Elliot Muncipality (*see* below). **Prentjiesberg Hiking Trail:** Northeast Cape Forests (*see* below). **Woodcliffe Cave Trail:** Woodcliffe Cave Trail (*see* below). **Ben Macdhui Hiking Trail:** Mr G van Zyl (*see* below).

OPENING TIMES
Dinorben rock paintings: Daily 08h00–16h00.
Dinosaur tracks: Daily sunrise to sunset.

ACCOMMODATION
Mountain Shadows Hotel: 17 rooms with private bathrooms. A la carte restaurant. **Washington Guest Farm:** Cottages with private bathrooms. **Rhodes Hotel:** 12 rooms, 8 with en suite bathrooms; self-catering cottages.

ENQUIRIES
The Manager, Mountain Shadows Hotel, PO Box 98, Barkly East 5580; tel. (045) 313-2233, fax. (04542) ask for 66. **The Manager, Washington Guest Farm,** PO Box 251, Indwe 5445; tel. (045) 855-0011. **The Manager, Rhodes Hotel,** PO Box 21, Rhodes 5582; tel. (04542) ask for Rhodes 21, fax. ask for 31. **Reservations, Tiffindell Ski and Mountain Resort,** 14 Fairway Avenue, Linksfield North 2192; tel. (011) 640-7416, fax. 485-2915. **Lady Grey Muncipality,** PO Box 18, Lady Grey 5540; tel. (05552) 19. **Sethunzini Trails:** PO Box 64 Lady Grey 5540; tel. (05552) 272. **Elliot Muncipality,** PO Box 21, Elliot 5460; tel. (045) 313-1011. **Drakensberg Regional Services Council,** Private Bag X102, Barkly East 5580; (04542) ask for 158. **Northeast Cape Forests,** Regional Office, Private Bag, Ugie 5470; tel. (045) 333-1044. **Woodcliffe Cave Trails,** PO Box 65, Maclear 5480; tel. (045) 323-1550. **Mr G van Zyl,** PO Box 299, Barkly East 5580; tel. (04542) 71021.

TOURIST INFORMATION
Northeastern Cape Tourism Association, Private Bag X1011, Aliwal North 5530; tel. (0551) 4-1362, fax. 3008.

KWAZULU-NATAL AND NORTHEASTERN FREE STATE

While KwaZulu-Natal covers only a small part of the total land area of South Africa, it is rich in flora and fauna, with an incredible diversity of landscapes. Here the Mzimkhulwana River has gouged out a fantastic 24-km-long ravine into the Oribi Plains.

The mighty Drakensberg range forms a formidable barrier of more than 200 km along the western border of KwaZulu-Natal. Often snow-capped in winter, the distinctive band of sandstone cliffs of the 'Berg, as it is known, are the domain of the bearded vulture, or lammergeier. The grasslands and valleys of the Little 'Berg, characterised by grass-covered spurs and ridges and river valleys with patches of indigenous forest, extend westwards from the foothills of the Drakensberg and play host to herds of eland.

Lake St Lucia is one of Africa's largest estuaries and the focal point of the country's fourth largest reserve – the Greater St Lucia Wetland Park – a wonderland of lily-covered pans, papyrus swamps and high forested dunes. Lake St Lucia and the Hluhluwe-Umfolozi Park share the status of the oldest protected areas in Africa. Only recently joined with Hluhluwe to form one park, Umfolozi is world-renowned for its efforts in saving the white rhino from extinction. It was here that Africa's first wilderness area was set aside, and here that the first wilderness trails were conducted.

Eastwards of the Drakensberg lie the KwaZulu-Natal Midlands – a series of undulating plains and thickly forested escarpment reaching towards the Lebombo Mountains, western boundary of Maputaland. A mosaic of lakes, pans lined with fever trees, palm veld and coastal dune forests, Maputaland is the meeting place of tropical and subtropical plants and animals. Many plants are unique to Maputaland, which is home to two-thirds of the total bird species found in South Africa. The area's uniqueness extends offshore to the southernmost coral reefs in the world – an underwater fantasy of colourful tropical fishes and cauliflower, staghorn and honeycomb corals.

And inland, nestled between the KwaZulu-Natal and Lesotho borders, just inside the Free State and in the foothills of the Maluti Mountains, is a place of singular beauty – the Golden Gate Highlands National Park. Here the forces of nature have sculptured sandstone to create gigantic mushrooms, cathedral-like caves and rock formations standing sentinel over the valley of the Little Caledon River.

Meander Hut enjoys one of the loveliest views in the Drakensberg, looking across a broken valley to Giant's Castle hewn out of solid rock.

27 ORIBI GORGE NATURE RESERVE

At the head of the Mzimkhulwana Gorge and covering about 1 837 ha of wild canyon scenery – which consists of towering cliffs, unspoilt evergreen coastal scarp forests and valley bushveld – is the Oribi Gorge Nature Reserve. The Mzimkhulwana River, in its meanderings across the Oribi Flats, has carved a spectacular 24-km-long gorge into the heart of the reserve, to create one of South Africa's least-known natural wonders. The Oribi Gorge, a massive 5 km wide and 500 m deep, has exposed magnificent sandstone cliffs, dappled with bright yellow lichens.

How to get there

Oribi Gorge Nature Reserve lies inland from the KwaZulu-Natal South Coast, 138 km south of Durban. From Durban, head south towards Port Shepstone on the N2, passing such well-known resorts as Amanzimtoti, Kingsburgh, Scottburgh and Hibberdene. The turnoff is 21 km on along the Harding/Kokstad road.

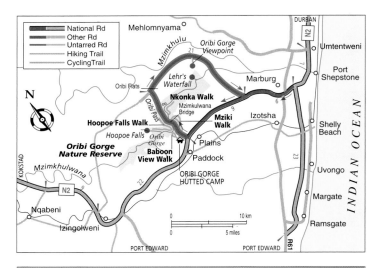

The slopes below the cliffs in the reserve are covered by dense forests of twin-berry trees, red beech, forest bushwillow, tree fuchsia and thorny gardenia. Large-leaved dragon trees and cycads provide ground cover. These forests are home to blue and common duiker, samango monkey and bushbuck. Oribi, after which the gorge has been named, inhabit the grassy plains. Among the more than 220 bird species recorded in the reserve are cinnamon dove, Knysna lourie, Narina trogon and the trumpeter hornbill with its raucous call. Raptors include crowned eagle, jackal buzzard and African goshawk. The

THE BANANA EXPRESS

A novel, fun way of visiting the Oribi Gorge Nature Reserve is on board the Banana Express, one of the few narrow-gauge (610 mm) railway lines still in operation in the world. The line between Port Shepstone and Paddock was completed in 1911 and was subsequently extended to Harding. In 1986 it was closed, not being economically viable any more. The line was re-opened in December the following year and is now run by the Port Shepstone and Alfred County Railway Company. It is primarily used to transport timber, sugar cane, cement and fertiliser between Port Shepstone and Harding, but regular passenger trips are also offered. The passenger coaches are pulled by a Narrow Gauge Garrat 16 locomotive, and number 155 and 156, which are owned by the Alfred County Railway Company, are the last Garrat class locomotives built in the world. The 60-ton engines are capable of hauling a load of 150 tonnes on 14 trucks.

Passenger excursions depart from the Beach Terminus at Port Shepstone. Chugging along the narrow-gauge railway line to Paddock Station, the Banana Express winds its way though sugarcane and tropical fruit plantations, and grasslands decorated with traditional Zulu huts. At Paddock Station, a historical monument, visitors are treated to a braai in the grounds of the Station Master's house. From here passengers can take a steam train trip to Plains Station, drive from there to the Oribi Gorge Reserve with a ranger, and hike along the Baboon View Trail, or go by motorcoach to some of the Oribi viewsites. From Paddock Station visitors can either return to Port Shepstone by train or by coach.

The Banana Express runs all year round on Wednesdays and Saturdays at 10h00.

For bookings contact: Banana Express, PO Box 572, Port Shepstone 4240; tel. (03931) 7-6443.

The spectacular Mzimkhulwana River gorge winds through the reserve.

Mzimkhulwana River attracts African black duck, several species of kingfisher and longtailed wagtail.

There are two pleasant picnic sites on the Oribi Pass – 2 km below the rest camp, and sites with braai facilities and ablutions a further 2 km on where the Gorge road crosses the Mzimkhulwana River.

➡ *From the Oribi Gorge hutted camp the road hugs the forested slopes of the Oribi Pass, crossing the Mzimkhulwana River after 4,3 km. It then ascends the northern slopes of the gorge, reaching the top of the pass 5,3 km further on. Turn right here and continue for 7,3 km to the turnoff to the Oribi Gorge Viewpoint.*

ORIBI GORGE VIEWPOINT

Nowhere are the vistas of the gorge more dramatic and spectacular than from the **Fairacres Estate**, situated on the plains above the gorge. A 5-km road network on the estate provides access to several viewpoints where sheer cliffs drop hundreds of metres to the valley below.

Especially stunning is the view of the wide meanders of the Mzimkhulwana River, known as Horseshoe Bend. Other nearby vantage points overlook the appropriately named Pulpit, Leaning Tower, Camel and Rock Chimney. About 1 km on is the Baboons' Castle Viewpoint, an isolated rocky citadel rising from the forested slopes, and Lehr's Waterfall. Even more spectacular

views of these two features can be enjoyed further along. Another well-known viewsite is the Overhanging Rock which projects over the edge of the gorge – a favourite subject of photographers.

The more adventurous can scramble down a rocky side gorge to the magnificent pool at the base of Lehr's Waterfall. The descent is steep in places (wear shoes with a good grip) and takes 15 to 20 minutes. The return journey takes a little longer.

Return to the tar road and turn right. Travel along another scenic pass through the gorge to the Harding/Kokstad road 14 km on.

WALKS AND TRAILS

MZIMKHULWANA BRIDGE: The bridge over the Mzimkhulwana River on the Oribi Gorge Pass is the starting point of three well-maintained walks to scenic spots in the reserve.

Hoopoe Falls Walk, 7 km long, follows an easy course along the Mzimkhulwana River for an hour-and-a-half and then meanders along the Mbabala Stream to where the Hoopoe Falls plunge into a deep pool.

Nkonka Walk is also an easy route along the forested slopes above the river and then runs along the base of the drier west- and north-facing slopes with their valley bushveld vegetation. The 5-km round trip takes about two-and-a-half hours.

A delightful walk leads to the **Samango Falls,** a round trip of 45 minutes. Starting at the bridge near the picnic site, there is a

An oribi, a small antelope, after which the reserve is named.

short but steep climb. For the next 10 minutes the route follows a contour path before climbing steeply to the base of the falls.

ORIBI HUTTED CAMP: Visitors can also set off on two walks from the Oribi Gorge hutted camp.

The **Baboon View Walk** is an easy 30-minute walk through the forests just below the rest camp,

to a viewpoint overlooking the junction of the Baboonspruit and Mzimkhulwana River. This walk is particularly rewarding at sunset.

The **Mziki Walk** runs along the edge of the cliffs from the camp before dropping down steeply to the picnic site on the Gorge Road. Covering 9 km, the return route follows the pass back to the camp.

The Banana Express, a fun way of visiting the reserve.

ORIBI GORGE NATURE RESERVE AT A GLANCE

MAIN ATTRACTIONS
Dramatic scenery, walks, bird-watching, picnic sites, the Banana Express.

BEST TIMES TO VISIT
Throughout the year.

PERMITS/BOOKINGS
Obtainable at reserve office and at Oribi Gorge Hotel.

OPENING TIMES
Oribi Gorge Pass is a public road. **Camp Manager's Office:** 08h00–12h30 and 14h00–16h30. **Oribi Gorge Viewpoint (Fairacres Estate):** Sunrise to sunset.

ACCOMMODATION
Natal Parks Board accommodation: 7-bed self-contained cottage; three 1-roomed huts; three 2-bed huts; all fully equipped. Meals

prepared by cook. Contact Natal Parks Board (*see* below). **Oribi Gorge Hotel:** 12 double rooms: Contact The Manager, PO Box 575, Port Shepstone 4240; tel. and fax. (0397) 9-1753.

FACILITIES
Oribi Gorge hutted camp: Curio shop only. Visitors must be self-sufficient.

ENQUIRIES
Natal Parks Board Reservations, PO Box 1750, Pietermaritzburg 3200; tel. (0331) 47-1981, fax 47-1980; **general enquiries,** tel. (0331) 47-1891, fax. 47-1037.

TOURIST INFORMATION
South Coast Publicity Association, PO Box 1253, Margate 4275; tel. (03931) 2-2322, fax. 2-1886.

28 SOUTHERN DRAKENSBERG

Stretching from the Giant's Castle Game Reserve to Bushman's Nek, the southern Drakensberg is a wild, unspoilt region of waterfalls, trout-streams, and caves with magnificent rock paintings. Pastoral scenes in the rambling foothills of the 'Berg roll into imposing sandstone cliffs and high mountain peaks to form an ever-changing picture of tranquillity and beauty. This region comprises several nature reserves and wilderness areas.

How to get there
Underberg, the main access point to the southern Drakensberg area, is 187 km from Durban and 535 km from Johannesburg. From Johannesburg take the N3 past Harrismith and Estcourt to Mooi River. From here take the R103 south to Nottingham Road through Rosetta, and the Lower Loteni road to Underberg. From Durban take the N3 north to Pietermaritzburg. From here take the R617 to Underberg (111 km).

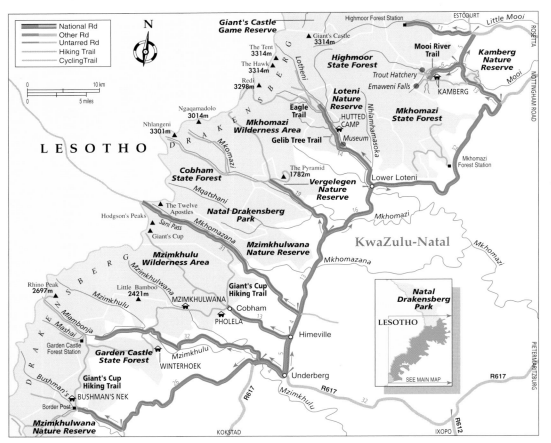

and bushbuck. Other animals occurring in the southern 'Berg include baboon, black-backed jackal and smaller predators such as genet and mongoose.

➡ *Bushman's Nek is 38 km from Underberg. Follow the R626 towards Kokstad for 5 km and then turn right, continuing for 25 km on a gravel road and turn right again. The South African border post is 8 km on at Bushman's Nek, where the road ends.*

BUSHMAN'S NEK

Situated in the foothills of the Drakensberg, Bushman's Nek is the southernmost access point into the **Mkhomazi Wilderness Area** and, with the exception of the Sani Pass, it is the only official border post between KwaZulu-Natal and Lesotho. The South African border post lies 10 km from Lesotho, which is accessible along the Bushman's Nek Pass, a route that is only negotiable on foot or horseback. Backpacking and horse-riding trails lead from here to Lesotho's **Sehlabathebe National Park**, an area renowned for its scenic splendour. The scenery in Sehlabathebe is dominated by the Devil's Knuckles. Other features include fascinating sandstone formations (the highest altitude at which sandstone formations have been exposed in southern Africa), waterfalls and rock paintings (there are over 60 sites

The lovely crowned crane.

➡ *The Mzimkhulu Wilderness Area and the adjoining Mzimkhulwana Nature Reserve can be accessed through Underberg. From here they can be approached via Bushman's Nek, Garden Castle or Cobham. Both conservation areas can be explored on foot.*

MZIMKHULU WILDERNESS AREA

Bordering on the Sehlabathebe National Park in Lesotho in the south, the Mzimkhulu Wilderness Area and the adjoining **Mzimkhulwana Nature Reserve** together cover over 57 000 ha. The escarpment is dominated by the twin Hodgson's Peaks and the

appropriately named Rhino Peak, while the Little 'Berg is characterised by spectacular sandstone formations. Although this area is not as popular as the 'Berg further north there is much to see and do. It is second only to Cathedral Peak (*see* p. 132) for its excellent **birding**, and among the interesting species to be seen are crowned cranes, the orange-breasted rockjumper and the Drakensberg siskin.

The southern Drakensberg is home to large numbers of eland and, although the other species of **antelope** are not abundant, you might encounter reedbuck, mountain reedbuck, grey rhebok in the park). The Tsoelikane River is the habitat of the endangered Drakensberg minnow and the sandstone rock pools are the habitat of the rare aquatic plant, *Aponogeton ranunculiflorus*, which is endemic to the park.

➡ *Garden Castle is 36 km from Underberg. From here follow the R626 towards Kokstad for 4 km and then turn right onto a gravel road. The forest station, in the Mzimkhulu Wilderness Area, is 32 km further on.*

GARDEN CASTLE STATE FOREST

The Garden Castle area is named after a prominent sandstone outcrop which towers more than 650 m above the Mlambonja River Valley. Originally known as Giant's Castle, it was later renamed Garden Castle; the original name has been used for another area in the central Drakensberg (*see* p. 128).

There are numerous rock paintings in the Garden Castle area. The sculptured sandstone formations known as the Monk and Sleeping Beauty form a striking backdrop to the forest station. Rhino Peak juts out from the main escarpment, standing sentinel over the sandstone formations of the Little 'Berg. The grasslands are home to grey rhebok, mountain reedbuck and eland.

➡ *From Underberg travel along the Loteni road to Himeville, which is 13 km from the Cobham Forest Station.*

COBHAM STATE FOREST

Cobham is a convenient base from which to explore the northern section of the nature reserve and the wilderness area. A catchment area for the Mzimkhulu River and its tributaries, the wilderness area is dotted with many crystal-clear natural pools created by small waterfalls, a welcome sight in the summer.

➡ *The Mkhomazi Wilderness Area can be accessed through Vergelegen, Loteni and Kamberg nature reserves, as well as the Highmoor and Mkhomazi forest stations (see directions, p. 125). The wilderness area can only be explored on foot.*

Eland migrate to the Little 'Berg valleys in winter.

Rhino Peak looms above Navarone Dam, one of several resorts in the southern Drakensberg.

Jacob's Ladder Falls, just one of several spectacular falls that hikers can visit in the Loteni Nature Reserve.

➡ From Underberg go northwards along the Underberg/Nottingham Road road for 9 km and continue for another 13 km on a gravel road to the signposted turnoff to the left. The Vergelegen Nature Reserve is 19 km further on.

VERGELEGEN NATURE RESERVE

Covering 1 159 ha of grassy hillsides and deep river valleys formed by the Mkhomazi River and its tributaries, the Y-shaped Vergelegen Nature Reserve is secluded and peaceful. Antelope found in the reserve include eland, reedbuck, mountain reedbuck, grey rhebok and oribi. The reserve is open to day visitors and provides access to the adjoining Mkhomazi Wilderness Area. Further off, in Lesotho, lies the 3 482-m-high Thaba Ntlenyana, the highest peak south of Kilimanjaro. An expedition to this peak should not be taken lightly, as the 25-km (one-way) trip gains over 2 000 m in altitude.

➡ Access to Loteni Nature Reserve is through Lower Loteni. Follow the Underberg/Nottingham Road road from Underberg in a northerly direction for 38 km and turn left at the Loteni Store. The entrance gate to the reserve is 10 km further on.

LOTENI NATURE RESERVE

Also situated in the foothills of the Drakensberg, Loteni is renowned for its spectacular mountain scenery. Dominant peaks on the escarpment are the conspicuous Tent, the Hawk and Redi. The forces of nature have combined efforts to sculpture an incredible eagle likeness into the sandstone outcrop. Adding to the scenic mountain splendour are numerous waterfalls cascading down the mountain slopes in thin white ribbons.

Loteni is home to reedbuck, mountain reedbuck, eland, common duiker, oribi and bushbuck. Spring heralds a show of exquisite wild flowers. The montane environment lends itself well to habitation by raptors such as the black eagle and the bearded vulture.

Well worth visiting in the reserve is the old homestead of the Root family who settled here in the 1890s. It has been converted

Carrying water through grasslands sprinkled with cosmos, near Loteni.

MKHOMAZI WILDERNESS AREA

Inhabiting this wilderness of waving grassland, protea veld and sheer rock faces are common duiker, oribi, mountain reedbuck, grey rhebok and klipspringer. Birdlife is prolific and includes the largest breeding colony of the bald ibis within a protected area in KwaZulu-Natal, and the only breeding site of wattled cranes in the Drakensberg.

The 60 000-ha Mkhomazi Wilderness Area can be reached on foot through the Highmoor and Mkhomazi forest stations, as well as the Kamberg, Loteni and Vergelegen nature reserves.

into the **Loteni Settlers' Homestead Museum** and reflects the Victorian lifestyle of the early settlers, including the wattle and daub shearing shed. Among the items on display are old farming implements, wagons and household utensils.

➤ *From Underberg follow the Underberg/Nottingham Road road through Lower Loteni, continuing for 20 km to the turnoff at the iNzinga River. The Mkhomazi Forest Station is 1 km further on.*

MKHOMAZI STATE FOREST

Named after the Mkhomazi River which flows further south, the state forest provides access to the adjoining wilderness area. The Little 'Berg is characterised by grassy ridges interspersed with wide valleys and extends further east here than elsewhere in the Drakensberg. This, combined with a lack of facilities at the forest station, has resulted in the area not being utilised as heavily as the central and northern 'Berg; the advantage is that you are unlikely to meet large groups.

➤ *From Lower Loteni go towards Nottingham Road for 32 km, turn left and after 13 km left again. The reserve is 6 km on.*

KAMBERG NATURE RESERVE

This scenic reserve nestles in a valley in the foothills of the Little 'Berg along the Mooi River. Its well-stocked trout waters are one of Kamberg's main attractions.

Flanked by outliers of the Little 'Berg, the nature reserve is home to herds of eland, blesbok, black wildebeest and red hartebeest. Mountain reedbuck, common duiker and oribi also occur.

Those interested in rock art should not miss a visit to **Game Pass Shelter** which is considered one of the best preserved rock-art sites in the Drakensberg (*see* p. 127). The central feature of the site is a 1,5-m-long frieze of eland paintings, superimposed on humans. Figures wearing karosses, elegant blue cranes and a small red elephant are other noteworthy paintings.

➤ *From the turnoff to Kamberg Nature Reserve, continue north for 5 km and turn left and, a short way on, left again, continuing for 11 km to the Highmoor State Forest.*

HIGHMOOR STATE FOREST

On a plateau of the Little 'Berg, only a few kilometres east of the Giant's Castle Game Reserve (*see* p. 128), is the Highmoor State

Visitors to Kamberg admire the rock art at Game Pass Shelter.

SANI PASS

A journey up Sani Pass, the highest in South Africa, is an unforgettable experience. To get there, travel northwards from Underberg through Himeville. Four kilometres further on, turn left onto the Sani Pass Road. From the South African border post (25 km on) the pass follows a tortuous route through spectacular hair-pin bends up the V-shaped Mkhomazana River Valley, twisting and turning vigorously to gain 1 000 m in altitude over the final 6 km. Sedan cars are not permitted beyond the border post, but regular four-wheel-drive tours are conducted to the top of the pass, where the highest pub in southern Africa is situated. Contact Sani Pass Tours for all bookings (*see* p. 127).

This route is not only the easiest way to ascend the escarpment, which is 2 874 m above sea level, it also offers stunning views and an opportunity for twitchers to tick off some of the Drakensberg birds which occur only at high altitudes. Until its completion in 1955, the pass was nothing more than a bridle path. Today it is the only road link between KwaZulu-Natal and the remote areas of eastern Lesotho.

Sani Pass, the only road link between KwaZulu-Natal and eastern Lesotho, follows a tortuous, spectacular route up the Mkhomazana River Valley.

Forest. Popular with trout-anglers (there are two dams), the natural wetlands also offer good birding opportunities and Egyptian geese, African marsh harrier, osprey and the endangered wattled crane can all be seen here. Animals recorded in the area include eland, red hartebeest, mountain reedbuck, reedbuck, grey rhebok and oribi, as well as baboon, black-backed jackal and caracal.

WALKS AND TRAILS

While the southern Drakensberg is not as well known as the areas further north, a variety of trails ranges from short walks to overnight hikes. There are also many opportunities for overnight trails into the wilderness areas, but backpackers must be fit, experienced and properly equipped.

SANI PASS AND BUSHMAN'S NEK: The five-day **Giant's Cup Hiking Trail** is an ideal opportunity to explore the area, with the added attraction of comfortable overnight huts at the end of each day's hike. Covering just less than 70 km, the trail winds between Sani Pass and Bushman's Nek, generally following an easy route through the Little 'Berg.

GARDEN CASTLE: Hiking is the main attraction of the Garden Castle area. **Three Pools** is a walk which should not be missed – a rewarding 5-hour round trip, to the exquisite pools.

Walking trails start at Garden Castle Forest Station and include excursions to **Sleeping Beauty** and **The Monk**, an impressive sandstone outcrop which dominates the Little 'Berg scenery. Also popular is an ascent of **Rhino Peak** (3 051 m) along the Mashai Pass. This demands a high degree of fitness as some 1 200 m in altitude is gained.

COBHAM: Day walks can be taken to the inviting **Ngenwa Pool** (8,5 km/2 hours one way) and **Siphongweni Shelter** (20 km circular route/7–8 hours) with its interesting rock paintings of men spearing fish. Both walks set out from Cobham Forest Station.

LOTENI NATURE RESERVE: Except for a few steep gradients, the **Gelib Tree Trail** is an easy 5,5-km circular route which meanders past the Gelib Tree, an acacia which grew from seed collected in North Africa during World War II by the owner of the farm (now part of the reserve). Twelve points of interest are marked along the 12,5-km interpretative **Eagle Trail** which starts 500 m from the hutted camp and

The chalets at Loteni enjoy an expansive view of the Drakensberg.

Trout fishing is a popular form of recreation in the Drakensberg. This dam in the Kamberg Nature Reserve is one of many attractive venues.

takes about six hours to complete. Information is provided in a trail brochure, obtainable from the reserve office. Day walks can also be taken from the hutted camp to **Ash and Yellowwood caves**, **Jacob's Ladder**, a stunning series of waterfalls a mere 1,8 km from the hutted camp, and the **Canyon**, a deep ravine formed by the Bhodla River.

KAMBERG: The Mooi River Trail is a 2,5-km-long self-guided walk (part is suitable for the blind and disabled). **Gladstone's Nose Trail** is a 7,5-km circular trail around this prominent rock formation just west of the hutted camp. At 09h30 on Sundays Kamberg Rest Camp offers a guided 1½- to 2-hour walk (each way) to the **Game Pass Shelter**.

TROUT-FISHING

The southern Drakensberg is renowned for its trout-fishing: local records boast catches of 4,9 kg and 3,3 kg from dam- and

A young male bushbuck at close quarters.

river-fishing respectively. As well as 13 km of brown trout waters in Kamberg's **Mooi River**, several dams in the reserve are stocked with brown and rainbow trout.

Trout-fishing is one of the chief attractions of the **Loteni Nature Reserve**, in which 8 km of the Lotheni River are stocked with trout (the dam at Simes rustic cottage is reserved for residents).

Anglers can also try their hand in the rivers at **Garden Castle**, **Cobham** and the **Bushman's River**; the nearby Sehlabathebe National Park in Lesotho is known for excellent trout catches.

The **Highmoor State Forest** in Mkhomazi offers trout-fishing in two dams, high on the escarpment, surrounded by fantastic views. Book in advance at Natal Parks Board offices.

SOUTHERN DRAKENSBERG AT A GLANCE

MAIN ATTRACTIONS
Spectacular mountain scenery, wilderness areas, walks and overnight trails, rock paintings, trout-fishing, horse-riding, Sani Pass.

BEST TIMES TO VISIT
Each season has its own attractions. Snow frequently falls in winter, and thunderstorms are common in the afternoons in summer. Spring and summer are generally the best seasons for flowers. The trout season for rivers stretches from September to June, while dam angling is open throughout the year.

MZIMKHULU WILDERNESS AREA
Permits/bookings:
Bushman's Nek and **Garden Castle overnight hiking:** The Warden, Garden Castle, PO Box 378, Underberg 4590; tel. (033) 701-1823. **Cobham camping and overnight hiking:** Officer-in-Charge.
Opening times: **Sani and Bushman's Nek passes:** Daily 08h00–16h00.
Garden Castle and Cobham entrance gates: 1 October to 31 March 05h00–19h00 and 1 April to 30 September 06h00–18h00.
Accommodation:
Mzimkhulu: Trailists sleep in the open or in caves and need to be self-sufficient. **Cathedral Peak Hotel:** PO Winterton 3340; tel. and fax. (036) 488-1888. **Sani Top Chalet:** PO Box 232, Himeville 4585, tel. (033) 702-1069. **Giant's Cup Hiking Trail:** Five huts (accommodating 30 people), semi-equipped. **Cobham:** Open camp sites for 60 people with cold water ablutions.
Angling: Provincial licence and daily angling permits required. Contact the Officer-in-Charge.
Enquiries: Sani Pass Tours: Mokhotlong Mountain Transport, PO Box 12,

Himeville 4585; tel. (033) 702-1615, fax. 701-1347.
Cobham Officer-in-Charge: PO Box 168, Himeville 4585; tel. and fax. (033) 702-0831.

MKHOMAZI WILDERNESS AREA
Permits/bookings:
Mkhomazi overnight hiking: Officer-in-Charge, Mkhomazi, PO Box 105, Nottingham Road 3280; tel. and fax. (0333) 3-6444.
Highmoor camping and overnight hiking: Officer-in-Charge, Highmoor, PO Box 51, Rosetta; tel. (0333) 3-7240.
Opening times: **Mkhomazi:** 06h00–16h00. **Highmoor:** 07h00–17h00.
Accommodation:
Mkhomazi: Trailists sleep in the open or in caves and need to be self-sufficient.
Highmoor: Open camp sites for 20 people, cold-water ablutions. Trailists can sleep in caves.
Angling: Provincial licence and daily angling permits required. Contact the Officer-in-Charge.
Facilities: Visitors to Kamberg, Loteni, Cobham, Garden Castle and Bushman's Nek must be self-sufficient. Maps and curios obtainable at Loteni and Cobham.

VERGELEGEN
Permits/bookings:
Overnight hiking: Contact the Officer-in-Charge, Vergelegen, PO Box 53, Himeville 4585; tel. (033) 702-0712.
Opening times: Daily sunrise to sunset.
Accommodation: None.
Facilities: None. Visitors need to be fully self-sufficient.

LOTENI
Permits/bookings:
Overnight hiking: Contact the Officer-in-Charge.
Opening times: Entrance gates: 1 October to 31 March 05h00–19h00 and 1 April to 30 September 06h00–18h00.

Accommodation: **Hutted accommodation:** Eight 2-bed and four 3-bed self-contained chalets, two 6-bed cottages and one 10-bed cottage, fully-equipped. Twelve camp sites with hot/cold-water ablutions. Contact Natal Parks Board Reservations (*see* below).
Angling: Provincial licence and daily angling permits required. Obtainable from the Officer-in-Charge.
Facilities: Visitors must be self-sufficient. Maps and curios available.
Enquiries: Officer-in-Charge, Loteni, PO Box 14, Himeville 4585; tel. (033) 702-0530.

KAMBERG
Permits/bookings:
Overnight hiking: Officer-in-Charge, PO Box 72, Rosetta 3301; tel. (0333) 3-7312.
Opening times: **Entrance gates:** Daily sunrise to sunset.
Game Pass Shelter: Guided walk on Sundays only at 09h30.
Accommodation: Five 3-bed huts and 5-bed self-contained cottages with cook.
Stillerus farm house: Six-bed self-contained cottage and 4-bed rondavel. Visitors must supply own bedding and towels and do own cooking. **Hutted accommodation:** Natal Parks Board Reservations (*see* below).
Angling: Provincial licence and daily angling permits required. Contact the Officer-in-Charge (*see* above).
Facilities: Visitors must be self-sufficient.

ENQUIRIES
Natal Parks Board Reservations, PO Box 1750, Pietermaritzburg 3200; tel. (0331) 47-1981, fax 47-1980.
General enquiries, tel. (0331) 47-1891, fax. 47-1037.

TOURIST INFORMATION
Drakensberg Publicity Association, PO Box 325, Bergville 3350; tel. (036) 448-1557.

29 CENTRAL DRAKENSBERG

The Injasuti Triplets, Mafadi, Trojan Wall, Bannerman Face, Long Wall and Giant's Castle, affectionately referred to as The Giant, are some of the intriguing and familiar names of peaks, rock walls and domes found in the central 'Berg. Refuge to huge herds of eland, the largest antelope species, and the rare and majestic bearded vulture, or lammergeier, Giant's Castle offers a seemingly endless list of outdoor activities and is regarded by many as the prime area of the Drakensberg.

How to get there
The central Drakensberg is about 200 km from Durban and 460 km from Johannesburg. From Durban take the N3 westwards to Pinetown and continue along the R613 through the Valley of a Thousand Hills and along the N3 to Pietermaritzburg and Howick, where a short detour leads to the magnificent Howick Falls. Continue on to Mooi River, entering the town at the toll plaza. Approaching from Johannesburg, follow the N3 through Harrismith and take the Central 'Berg Resorts interchange into Estcourt.

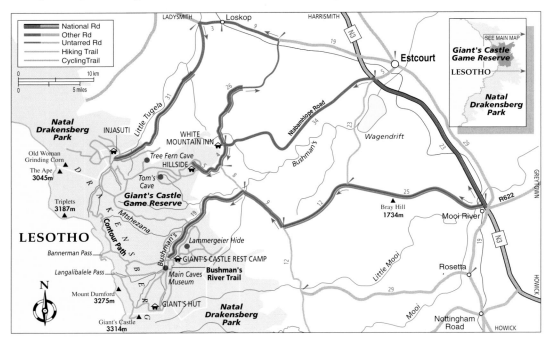

➡ From Mooi River go westwards for about 3 km and then turn right onto the scenic route which winds past Bray Hill. After about 37 km turn right and after 9 km turn left to reach the rest camp at Giant's Castle some 19 km on. From Estcourt join the Ntabamhlope road at the traffic light intersection of Conner and Lorne Street, continuing for 34 km to the White Mountain Inn junction. Turn left here. The turnoff to Giant's Castle Rest Camp is signposted 12 km on.

GIANTS'S CASTLE GAME RESERVE

Proclaimed in 1903 to protect the dwindling number of eland in the Drakensberg, Giant's Castle Game Reserve is today a sanctuary for several hundred of them. These large **antelope** feature prominently in San paintings. In addition to eland, visitors to the reserve might also see grey rhebok, mountain reedbuck and oribi.

Much of the reserve is dominated by grass-covered hills and ridges, extending to the cliffs of the High 'Berg.

The major attraction among the 160 **bird species** recorded in the reserve is the bearded vulture. Malachite and greater doublecollared sunbirds, ground woodpecker, yellowbreasted pipit, and the orangethroated longclaw – recognisable not only by its bright orange 'bib' but also by its cat-like mew when alarmed – also occur.

A large spotted genet, seen at Giant's Castle Game Reserve.

The Drakensberg is renowned for its well-preserved San paintings.

Giant's Castle is located in a picturesque valley, overlooked in winter by snow-covered mountains.

Within walking distance of the hutted camp are the **Main Caves**, one of the most easily accessible major rock-art sites in the 'Berg. Perched on top of a ridge, it consists of two large overhangs, and contains nearly 550 rock paintings. Therianthropes (human figures with antelope features), harte-beest, eland, lion and snakes are among the interesting paintings to be found in the Northern Cave. More paintings can be seen in the Southern Cave which also contains a realistic display of the

lifestyle of the San people and a stratagraphical reconstruction of an excavated hearth. A guided tour with a tape-recorded commentary on the San and some of the paintings is conducted hourly by a game guard. It starts at the Main Caves and visitors have to walk 2 km there (one way).

The **Vulture hide** is extremely popular with birders and photographers in winter when meat and bones are 'served' at the 'restaurant'. Although the thrill of a close-up view of the

bearded vulture (*see* box, below) is obviously the highlight, other raptors, including Cape vulture, black eagle, jackal buzzard, lanner falcon and rock kestrel, also drop in for a meal. Groups are transported to the hide in a Natal Parks Board vehicle from the Giant's Castle hutted camp.

Several kilometres of the Bushman's River, where day visitors can enjoy a picnic, have been stocked with brown trout.

➤ *Follow the N3 from Mooi River to Estcourt, and turn onto the Ntabamhlope road towards the White Mountain Inn. Turn left at*

The bearded vulture, or lammergeier, occurs in isolated populations.

BEARDED VULTURE (LAMMERGEIER)

With a wingspan of up to 2,6 m and its distinctive diamond-shaped tail, the bearded vulture is one of the most impressive raptors in flight, capable of reaching speeds of up to 230 km/h. It is confined to high altitudes of the KwaZulu-Natal and Cape Drakensberg, the Malutis in Lesotho and the northeastern Free State, and the total southern African population is estimated at a mere 200 breeding pairs.

About 40 pairs breed in the Drakensberg and three nesting sites have been located in the Giant's Castle area. This magnificent bird owes its

common name to the tuft of black facial feathers resembling a beard. Another interesting feature is that the striking orange or rufous-coloured underbody feathers are the result of iron oxides which the birds accumulate when they sand bathe or while they are sitting on cliffs.

The use of its earlier name, lammergeier, is no longer encouraged as it wrongly suggests that it preys on lambs. Its diet consists largely of bones which are either swallowed whole or shattered into smaller pieces by dropping them from a height of about 50 m onto a rock slab.

Towering above Injasuti Camp is Champagne Castle on the left, Monk's Cowl in the centre and Cathkin on the right.

Guided horse trails are a pleasant way of enjoying the Drakensberg.

the White Mountain Inn junction. Continue for 4 km and turn right to reach Hillside 5 km further on.

HILLSIDE

Situated in the northeastern corner of the Giant's Castle area, Hillside is best known for its **guided horse trails** into the foothills of the 'Berg. These trails last for either two or three days, and caves or a hut are used as overnight accommodation. Morning, afternoon and day rides are also available. There are a number of pleasant day walks to nearby scenic spots (*see* Walks and Trails, p. 131).

➡ At the White Mountain Inn junction continue north for 26 km to the Loskop road. Turn left and after 12 km left again to reach Injasuti camp 31 km further on. Alternatively, take the Loskop/ Central 'Berg offramp north of Estcourt on the N3, and follow the Loskop road for 27 km to the signposted turnoff to Injasuti.

INJASUTI

Tucked away at the head of the Injasuti Valley in the northern section of the Giant's Castle area is the Injasuti Hutted Camp. This remote camp is set in spectacular surroundings, with

Cathkin Peak, Monk's Cowl and Champagne Castle dominating the scenery. The rocky terrain of Injasuti is ideally suited to the agile klipspringer, and blesbok, oribi and common duiker also occur in the area.

One of the most interesting rock painting sites in the Drakensberg, **Battle Cave**, may only be visited by those joining a guided walk from the camp. The site contains some 750 paintings and, in addition to the battle scene between two rival San clans, lion, eland, rhebok, elongated animal-headed figures (therianthropes) and people are also depicted. The walk covers 12 km and takes four to five hours.

WALKS AND TRAILS
(*See* box, p. 123.)
GIANT'S CASTLE GAME RESERVE: From the Giant's Castle hutted camp visitors have a choice of nine short day walks. **Bushman's River Trail**, the most popular of these, is a 3-km interpretative walk which winds along the river of that name to the Main Caves and back.

Many hikers are attracted to Giant's Castle by the prospect of sleeping in one of the reserve's comfortable thatched-roof stone mountain huts. Hikers and backpackers have a choice of 15 routes from the hutted camp to the Contour Path, the four mountain huts and the summit.

Just below the 3 314-m-high **Giant's Castle**, Giant's Hut is a convenient base from which to ascend to this well-known landmark – a demanding 8-hour

round trip from the hut. Another popular route is the **Contour Path** which provides access to the summit and links Giant's Castle and Injasuti. Other routes to the summit include **Bannerman Pass** and **Langalibalele Pass** where the graves of three Carbineers and two local Zulus, who died on 4 November 1873 in the Langalibalele 'Rebellion', can be seen. Both passes require a high degree of fitness and an ascent should not be attempted by the unfit.

HILLSIDE: The Forest Walk is an easy 4,5-km ramble through four small patches of forest, while the more energetic can explore **Tom's Cave** and **Tree Fern Cave** further afield.

INJASUTI: As in other areas in the 'Berg, the Injasuti area is criss-crossed by a network of trails. Especially rewarding is the 8-km circular walk to the **Van Heyningen's Pass Viewpoint**; from here visitors can enjoy an uninterrupted view of the solid rock wall stretching all the way from Cathkin Peak to Giant's Castle.

From Injasuti it is possible to undertake extended overnight trails into the adjoining Mdedelelo Wilderness Area and the summit, or hikers can follow the contour path to Giant's Castle, a 40-km traverse with three mountain huts.

For those keen to find out more about the fascinating diversity of plant and animal life of the area, **guided three-day wilderness trails** are conducted between October and May.

Walks are conducted from Injasuti Camp to Battle Cave.

CENTRAL DRAKENSBERG AT A GLANCE

MAIN ATTRACTIONS
Spectacular mountain scenery, rock paintings, Vulture Hide, day walks and overnight trails with huts, game-viewing, horse-riding and trout-fishing.

BEST TIMES TO VISIT
Each season has its own attractions. Snow frequently falls in winter and violent thunderstorms are common in the afternoons in summer. Spring and summer are the best seasons for wild flowers, and the Vulture Hide is open in the autumn months. The trout season for rivers stretches from September to June, and dam angling is open throughout the year.

GIANT'S CASTLE GAME RESERVE
Permits/bookings: At gate.
Vulture Hide: Officer-in-Charge, Giant's Castle, Private Bag X7055, Estcourt 3310; tel. (0363) 2-4616.
Opening times: Entrance gates: 1 October to 31 March 05h00–19h00 and 1 April to 30 September 06h00–18h00.
Main Caves: Open daily 09h00–15h00, guided tour hourly. **Vulture hide:** Weekends May to September. Depart 07h30. Advance reservation essential.
Accommodation: Four 6-bed cottages; two 2-bed and seven 3-bed bungalows; four 5-bed bungalows.
Mountain huts (hiking trails): Three huts with 8 bunk beds, one hut accommodating 4 people. **Giant's Lodge:** Three bedrooms (accommodating 7 people), bathrooms, meals prepared by cook. **Hutted accommodation, lodge and mountain huts:** Book through Natal Parks Board Reservations (*see* below).
Angling: A provincial licence and daily angling permits, obtainable from the camp manager, are required.
Facilities: Limited groceries, petrol and curio shop.

HILLSIDE
Permits/bookings: At gate.
Camp site, hutted accommodation, horse trails: Officer-in-Charge, PO Box 88, Estcourt 3310; tel. (0363) 2-4435 (08h00–13h00 daily).
Opening times: Entrance gate: 08h00–18h00 (unless otherwise arranged). **Horse trails:** September to May, weather permitting, from 2 to 5 days. Morning, afternoon and day rides also offered. Advance booking essential.
Accommodation: 8-bed rustic hut, semi-equipped. 32 camp sites with hot/cold-water ablutions. **Horse trails:** Caves or huts used as overnight stops.
Facilities: Small shop, limited range of groceries, curios.

INJASUTI
Permits/bookings: At gate.
Camp site and caves: Camp Manager, Private Bag X7010, Estcourt 3310; tel. (036) 488-1050. **Wilderness trails:** Natal Parks Board Reservations (*see* below).
Opening times: Entrance gates: 1 October to 31 March 05h00–19h00 and 1 April to 30 September 06h00–18h00.
Battle Cave: Guided walk daily at 08h30 (advance booking essential).
Accommodation: 16 6-bed self-contained cabins, own cooking. Two 8-bed cabins, braai facilities. Open camp site for 80 with hot/cold-water ablutions. **Hutted accommodation:** Natal Parks Board Reservations (*see* below).
Facilities: Limited range of groceries, curios.

ENQUIRIES
Natal Parks Board Reservations, PO Box 1750, Pietermaritzburg 3200; tel. (0331) 47-1981, fax 47-1980. **General enquiries,** tel. (0331) 47-1891, fax 47-1037.

TOURIST INFORMATION
Drakensberg Publicity Association, PO Box 325, Bergville 3350; tel. and fax (036) 448-1557.

The High 'Berg is a conglomeration of majestic peaks and overhangs, deep valleys and dramatic scenery. The Tugela River, rising near Mont-aux-Sources, plunges dramatically into the Amphitheatre, which towers over the Royal Natal National Park, and galleries of historic rock art decorate the Ndedema Gorge. Dwarfed by the majesty of Cathedral Peak, Champagne Castle and Monk's Cowl, hikers, mountaineers and nature-lovers alike can enjoy the splendour of the mecca of the northern Drakensberg.

How to get there
The southern reaches of the northern Drakensberg can be accessed along the N3 from Durban and Johannesburg. From Durban go through Mooi River, bypass Estcourt (*see* Tour 29, p. 128) and turn off the N3 to Winterton. From Johannesburg take the N3 past Ladysmith, and then the R600 to Winterton (a small farming town among the grass-covered foothills of the Drakensberg and an important dairy-producing centre).

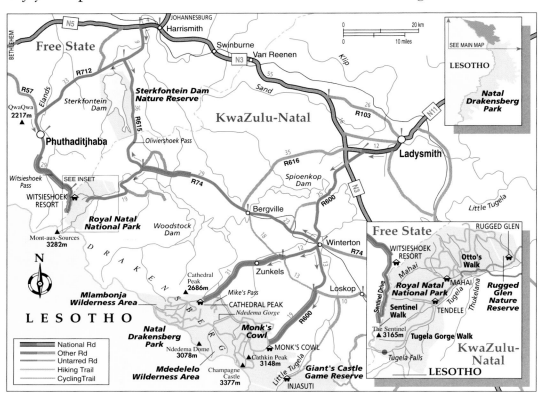

Monk's Cowl is obtained only after a steep 14-km walk from the forestry station. Its sheer cliffs make it one of the most difficult peaks to climb in the Drakensberg, and the first successful ascent was accomplished only in 1942. Other well-known peaks in the area include the 3 377-m-high Champagne Castle, the fourth highest peak in southern Africa, Gatberg, which owes its name to the enormous hole which has been eroded through the basalt rock, and the Dragon's Back. Several pleasant and scenic walking and backpacking trails are available (*see* Walks and Trails p. 134).

➡ From Winterton take the Cathedral Peak road at the southern end of the town and travel for about 43 km to Mike's Pass entrance gate.

CATHEDRAL PEAK
The combination of jagged mountain peaks, towering spires, crisp mountain streams and fascinating rock paintings of the Cathedral Peak area has made this one of the most popular backpacking and mountaineering destinations in the 'Berg. Cathedral Peak falls in the **Mlambonja** and the **Mdedelelo wilderness areas**, encompassing the Mlambonja River, the Bell and Cleft Peak.

The area is home to more than **210 bird species**. Raptors breeding in the area include crowned and martial eagles. Rednecked

The Tugela River plunges down the rock-face of the Amphitheatre.

➡ From the Estcourt offramp on the N3 travel west along the Loskop road for 31 km and then turn left onto the R600, continuing for a further 19 km to Monk's Cowl Forest Station. Approaching from Winterton, take the R600 south for 32 km, Monk's Cowl is 215 km from Durban and 410 km from Johannesburg.

MONK'S COWL
Monk's Cowl falls within the **Mdedelelo Wilderness Area**, which lies between Cathedral Peak and the Giant's Castle Game Reserve. The 3 243-m-high peak after which the forestry station has been name is obscured by Cathkin Peak, known in Zulu as Mdedelelo, and Sterkhorn. The first uninterrupted view of

francolin, groundscraper thrush, blue crane and Gurney's sugarbird are also found here.

The **mammals** which might be seen in the Cathedral Peak area include baboon, rock dassie, mountain and common reebuck, grey rhebok, bushbuck and common duiker.

Another attraction of the area is **Ndedema Gorge** which shelters the largest indigenous forest in the Drakensberg. The gorge is world-renowned for its fine rock paintings and is considered one of the richest rock art areas in the world (*see* box, right).

Mike's Pass provides the only road access in the Drakensberg to the top of the Little 'Berg, affording motorists splendid views of the surrounding mountain scenery. The 10,5-km-long road starts at Mike's Pass Gate near the Cathedral Peak camp site, and gains approximately 500 m in altitude, ending at the Arendsig Gate.

➡ *To access the Royal Natal National Park from the south take the Winterton/Berg Resorts turnoff north of Estcourt on the N3 and travel through Winterton and Bergville. From here continue along the R74 for 29 km and turn left to reach the entrance gate 16 km further on. From Johannesburg take the N3 to Harrismith and follow the R615 past the Sterkfontein Dam Nature Reserve (see Tour 37 p. 162) and the Oliviershoek Pass for 49 km and then turn right, continuing for 16 km.*

ROYAL NATAL NATIONAL PARK

Dominating the scenery of the Royal Natal National Park is the Amphitheatre – a 500-m-high sheer rock wall stretching for 5 km between the Sentinel and Eastern Buttress. Here the Tugela River plunges hundreds of metres in five leaps to the valleys below before continuing its 330-km journey to the Indian Ocean.

ROCK ART GALLERIES

The caves and overhangs of the Drakensberg are incredibly rich in rock art and some 20 000 individual paintings have been recorded at 500 different sites between the Royal Natal National Park and Bushman's Nek (*see* p. 122).

While some sites contain only a single painting, the walls of the major sites are decorated by hundreds of illustrations. Portrayed on the cave walls are animals (most often the eland), human figures, therianthropes (humans with animal heads or hoofs) and geometric figures. Other paintings depict ox-wagons and mounted men with rifles.

It is now widely accepted that these paintings were not merely an expression of artistic flair or a visual narrative of the everyday life of the San. Instead, meticulous research of San beliefs has suggested that the paintings were executed by shamans, or medicine men, to depict trance visions.

Among the most celebrated sites is Ndedema Gorge, where 3 900 paintings have been recorded in 17 sites, one of which, Sebaayeni Cave, contains no fewer than 1 146 individual paintings.

A further 130 sites with over 8 800 individual paintings are known to occur in Cathedral Peak and the adjoining Mdedelelo Wilderness Area. Other richly endowed sites include the Main Caves in Giant's Castle Game Reserve, Battle Cave in the Injasuti Valley and Game Pass Shelter in the Kamberg Nature Reserve.

Flanked by the Sentinel (right) and Eastern Buttress (left), the Amphitheatre provides a dramatic backdrop to the Royal Natal National Park.

Looking across the face of the Amphitheatre at Eastern Buttress, Devil's Tooth and Inner Tower.

Much of the park is covered by **grasslands** which change their colour with the seasons – golden in autumn and emerald in summer. In spring the brown winter grasslands are transformed into a blaze of colour when a variety of bulbs burst into flower – pale pink dieramas, blue aristeas and yellow hypoxis. Proteas are common on the slopes below the sandstone cliffs, and enchanting patches of forest occur in the sheltered valleys.

Among the **mammals** which trailists might happen upon while exploring the park are mountain reedbuck, blesbok, bushbuck

and baboons. **Birding** is usually best between August and December. Common birds found in the park include black eagle, rock kestrel, blackcollared barbet and bokmakierie.

However, unlike many other parks, the chief attraction of Royal Natal is not herds of big game, but its breathtaking mountain scenery and the peace and tranquillity which visitors to the park can enjoy.

Trout-fishing is a popular pastime and anglers trying their hand in the dams at Royal Natal are a familiar sight. Daily horse rides are conducted from the

stables at Rugged Glen. There are also delightful picnic sites along the Mahai River.

➤ *One of the highlights of a visit to the northern 'Berg is a drive along the Sentinel Route – a round trip of 260 km from the Royal Natal National Park. The route meanders over the Oliviershoek Pass, through Phuthaditjhaba and then along the Witsieshoek Pass and Mountain Road, ending at the car-park below the Sentinel, in the Free State.*

THE SENTINEL ROUTE

Winding along the watershed between the Free State and KwaZulu-Natal, the Sentinel Route follows the Witsieshoek Pass (2 270 m) and then continues along the Mountain Road, one of the highest roads in South Africa negotiable in a sedan car. About 20 km from the information centre in Phuthaditjhaba is the Mountain Road toll gate, and about 2 km further on the road passes underneath an enormous overhang. A few kilometres further on is the turnoff to the Witsieshoek Mountain Resort. At an altitude of 2 200 m, this is one of the highest resorts in southern

Africa and over the final 5,5 km the Mountain Road gains nearly 300 m in altitude, with stunning views of the Maluti Mountains.

The road ends approximately 2 540 m above sea level at a car-park below the Sentinel, starting point of the popular Sentinel Walk (*see* p. 135). Nearby are a number of viewpoints which afford visitors awe-inspiring vistas over the Royal Natal National Park, more than 1 500 m below, with the Eastern Buttress, the Devil's Tooth and the Inner Tower prominent in the southeast.

WALKS AND TRAILS
(*See* box p. 123.)
MONK'S COWL: Like other areas of the Drakensberg, walking and backpacking are the most popular activities in Monk's Cowl and the Mdedelelo Wilderness Area. Pleasant day walks can be undertaken from Cathkin Park to the **Fern Forest**, **Jacob's Ladder** and **Stable Cave**; Monk's Cowl is an ideal base for rambles to the **Sphinx** and **Sterkspruit Falls**. It is also the main access point to the **Contour Path** and **Ndedema Gorge**, and overnight trails to the higher areas of the 'Berg. Routes to the escarpment include the **Organ Pipes** and **Mlambonja** passes.
CATHEDRAL PEAK: Walks range from short rambles to extended overnight backpacking trails. For those seeking exercise without having to exert themselves too much, there are numerous short walks from Cathedral Peak Hotel to scenic spots such as **Rainbow Gorge**, **Mushroom Rocks**, **Neptune's Pool** and the **Oqalweni Forest**. For many visitors, however, the ultimate challenge is an ascent of the 3 004-m-high **Cathedral Peak**, a 20-km full-day round trip which demands a high degree of fitness.
ROYAL NATAL NATIONAL PARK: No fewer than 25 walks, ranging from 3 km to a demanding 45-km route to Mont-aux-Sources, lead to scenic spots such as **Fairy Glen**, **Sunday Falls**, the rock paintings in the **Sigubudu Valley** (all three starting at the Royal Natal National Park Hotel) and the **Crack and Mudslide** (both starting at Tendele Camp).

A black eagle in flight high above the mountains.

Otto's Walk, which is a 3-km interpretive walk, serves as a good introduction to the geology, vegetation, birdlife and ecology of the park. Starting at the carpark next to the Visitor Centre, it is an easy walk with several points of interest which are explained in an informative trail booklet (available from the reception office in the Visitor Centre). It takes about an hour to complete at a leisurely pace.

The **Gorge Walk**, despite being a 22,5-km round trip, is one of the most popular routes in Royal Natal. The trail starts at the parking area just below Tendele Camp and winds along the Tugela River, passing the conspicuous Policeman's Helmet, and near the end trailists can either scramble through the 60-m Tunnel or scale a chain ladder and then boulder-hop further up the Tugela River. The rewards are great with awe-inspiring views of the Amphitheatre, the sinister Devil's Tooth and the Eastern Buttress.

The **Sentinel Walk**, the easiest route onto the High 'Berg, initially winds steeply to the base of the Sentinel before easing off to reach the well-known chain ladders 3 km from the start. Two 30-m-high chain ladders have to be negotiated to gain access to the summit of the Amphitheatre, but, alternatively, trailists can scramble up The Gulley, about 1 km before you reach the chain

A chain ladder gives access to the plateau above the Amphitheatre.

ladders. From the summit it is a short, easy walk to the edge of the Amphitheatre with its awesome views of the Tugela Falls (it plunges over 600 m in five leaps), the Eastern Buttress and the Devil's Tooth.

The 3 282-m-high Mont-aux-Sources, the largest of the domes in the area, lies about 3,5 km southwest of the Amphitheatre on the border with Lesotho. Named in 1836 by two French missionaries, it is the source of five rivers – the Tugela, the Western and Eastern Khudebu (tributaries of the Orange River), the Elands and the Bilanjil. It is an easy walk, which follows the Tugela River upstream to its source and then continues to the stone beacon at the summit.

At the Royal Natal National Park, visitors can go on Otto's Walk.

NORTHERN DRAKENSBERG AT A GLANCE

MAIN ATTRACTIONS
Spectacular mountain scenery, rock paintings, Sentinel Drive (one of the highest passes accessible to sedan cars in South Africa), wilderness areas, day walks, overnight trails, trout fishing.

BEST TIMES TO VISIT
Each season has its own attraction. Snow frequently falls in winter, and thunderstorms are common in the afternoons in summer. Spring and summer are the best seasons for flowers. The trout season for rivers stretches from September to June, while dam fishing is open throughout the year.

MDEDELELO WILDERNESS AREA AND MONK'S COWL
Permits/bookings: Officer-in-Charge (*see* below).
Opening times: Entrance gates: 1 October to 31 March 05h00–19h00 and 1 April to 30 September 06h00–18h00.
Accommodation: **Monk's Cowl Forest Station:** Camping facilities for up to 100 people, with hot/cold-water ablutions. **Reservations:** The Officer-in-Charge.
Enquiries: **Officer-in-Charge**, Monk's Cowl, Private Bag X2, Winterton 3340; tel. (036) 468-1103.

MLAMBONJA WILDERNESS AREA AND CATHEDRAL PEAK
Permits/bookings: Officer-in-Charge. An entrance fee is payable at the gate, which is open 24 hours a day.
Opening times: **Cathedral Peak camp site:** Daily 24 hours. **Office:** 08h00–16h00.
Accommodation: 21 camp sites with hot/cold-water ablutions. Contact the Officer-in-Charge.
Facilities: Curio shop at booking office. Petrol at Cathedral Peak Hotel.
Enquiries: **Officer-in-Charge**, Cathedral Peak, Private Bag X1, Winterton 3340; tel. and fax. (036) 488-1880.

ROYAL NATAL NATIONAL PARK
Permits/bookings: Available at gate.
Opening times: **Royal Natal National Park** and **Rugged Glen** entrance gates: 1 October to 31 March 05h00–19h00 and 1 April to 30 September 06h00–8h00.
Accommodation: **Tendele Hutted Camp:** Eight 3-bed and five 5-bed bungalows, six 2-bed and seven 4-bed chalets, two 6-bed cottages. Meals prepared by cooks, except self-catering chalets. **Tendele Lodge:** Three bedrooms, private bathrooms, braai facilities. Meals prepared by cook. Contact Natal Parks Board Reservations for hutted camp and lodge (*see* below). **Royal Natal National Park Hotel:** Accommodation in thatched cottages, luxury rooms and rondavels. Reservations: Private Bag X4, Mont-aux-Sources 3353; tel. (036) 438-6200. **Mahai Camp Site:** Open camp site for 400, with hot/cold-water ablutions.
Rugged Glen Camp Site: Open camp site for 45 people with hot/cold-water ablutions. Reservations for camp sites, contact the Officer-in-Charge.
Facilities: Basic food supplies are available from the shop at Visitor Centre and hotel, petrol, curio shop at Visitor Centre and Tendele.
Angling: Provincial licence and daily angling permit. Contact the Officer-in-Charge.
Enquiries: **Officer-in-Charge, Royal Natal National Park,** Private Bag X1669, Bergville 3350; tel. (036) 438-6303, fax. 438-6310. **Natal Parks Board Reservations,** PO Box 1750, Pietermaritzburg 3200; tel. (0331) 47-1981, fax 47-1980; **general enquiries,** tel. (0331) 47-1891, fax. 47-1037.

TOURIST INFORMATION
Drakensberg Publicity Association, PO Box 325, Bergville 3350; tel. and fax. (036) 448-1557.

31 ITALA GAME RESERVE

One of South Africa's best-kept secrets, Itala covers nearly 30 000 ha of steep valleys, grasslands and open bushveld. In the extreme north of KwaZulu-Natal and renowned for its striking scenery, it has a rich diversity of plants, birdlife is prolific and four of the Big Five occur in the reserve.

How to get there
Itala is situated in northern KwaZulu-Natal, 435 km from Durban and 460 km from Johannesburg. From Durban take the N2 north past Umhlanga Rocks, Tongaat Beach, Shaka's Rock and Zinkwazi Beach. Take the R68 to Eshowe, continue towards Melmoth to the Shakaland turnoff (the cultural village is 4 km from the road); at Vryheid turn onto the R69 for 60 km through grassy hills to Louwsburg, where the reserve is signposted. The entrance gate is 7 km on and the rest camp 7 km further. From Johannesburg, take the R23 through Standerton and Volksrust, continuing to Vryheid on the R34 through Utrecht.

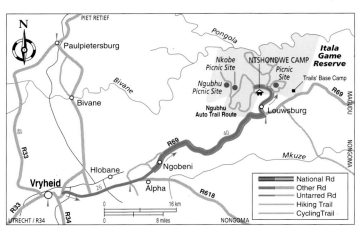

In 20-odd years Itala has grown from over-grazed farmland to one of South Africa's top conservation areas. Bordering on the Pongola River in the north, Itala is dissected by many rivers. A difference of over 1 000 m between the highest and lowest points makes for a rugged but beautiful landscape.

Often overlooked is Itala's fascinating **geological history**. Much of the area is underlain by alternate layers of shale and quartzite of the Mozaan Group, accumulated in the Pongola Basin 3 000 million years ago. In places these rocks are overlain by Karoo formations dating back only 250 million years, an inexplicable break in the geological history.

KwaZulu-Natal's only Tsessebe Population

Tsessebe reach the southernmost limit of their distribution at Itala in KwaZulu-Natal. Elsewhere in South Africa this rare antelope also occurs in the Pilanesberg and Kruger national parks and a few provincial and private reserves in the Northern Province.

They have reddish-brown bodies marked with purple sheen, are inquisitive and do not take flight easily – but when they do their reputation as the fastest antelope over short distances (they reach speeds of up to 100 km/h) certainly comes to the fore.

These grazers are closely related to the bontebok and the blesbok, and have an average shoulder height of 1,3 m. Males weigh about 140 kg, and females average 126 kg.

Females live in small herds with a resident bull. Males join bachelor herds at about eight to 16 months.

Tsessebe are frequently seen on visits to Itala.

The Karoo formations can be seen on the Ngubhu Loop Auto Trail (*see* p. 137).

Over 900 **plant species** have been recorded in Itala, and some 320 of KwaZulu-Natal's 780 tree species are known to occur here.

As four of the Big Five (barring lion) are found in the reserve, game-viewing is one of its main attractions. Of the 80 **mammal species** recorded, you are most likely to see blue wildebeest, impala, giraffe, red hartebeest, kudu, eland, tsessebe (*see* box, left), Burchell's zebra and warthog. Chances of seeing some of the 160-odd rhino are also good. Although Itala supports a healthy black rhino population, they and elephant are seen only occasionally. Other less commonly seen mammals include nyala, mountain reedbuck, waterbuck, klipspringer, red duiker and cheetah.

Itala has several camps, Ntshondwe being the main one; the luxurious Ntshondwe Lodge is situated on its perimeter. Thalu and Mbizo bush camps and Mhlangeni Bush Lodge are small and secluded, situated away from the main camp. The reserve's three picnic sites are set in delightful settings and visitors should not miss the opportunity

White rhino, rolling grasslands, acacia thickets and distant mountains – attractions that make Itala popular.

to enjoy a picnic brunch after an early morning game drive. Braai places and toilets are provided, and, as the rivers running past the picnic sites are free of crocodiles and bilharzia, visitors can cool down in the rivers in summer.

Itala is traversed by a 70-km road network and visitors can explore the park on five loop roads. Particularly worthwhile is the **Ngubhu Loop Auto Trail**, a 30-km circuit with 24 points of interest – from trees and their uses to animals, and geological features (explained in the *Visitor's Guide to Itala Game Reserve*, on sale in the Ntshondwe Camp shop) – marked along the route.

Many visitors opt for **morning and afternoon game drives**, conducted by guides who know the best game-viewing areas and the behaviour of the animals.

During a **night drive** from Ntshondwe visitors might see some nocturnal inhabitants such as porcupine, honey badger, white-tailed mongoose, large-spotted genet and spotted hyena.

With a **bird list** of over 320 species, Itala is popular with birders. Interesting species include the bald ibis (which breeds in the park), the brownheaded parrot, fantailed flycatcher, yellowspotted nicator, the yellowthroated long-claw, and Heuglin's and white-throated robins. The possibility of ticking raptors is good; among the 28 recorded species are white-backed vulture, black, martial and crowned eagles, bateleur and gymnogene. A **hide** and the deck of the restaurant in Ntshondwe Camp overlook a waterhole which attracts a variety of birds and game and is always worth a visit.

Many visitors come to Itala simply to relax in the peaceful surrounds of the rest camp, nestling in a valley between the cliffs of the Ngotshe plateau and the twin-peaked Ntshondwe. A swimming pool is tucked among trees and large boulders in a delightful setting; the camp blends in extremely well with its surroundings. Few South African camps can match the environmental sensitivity with which Ntshondwe was built.

WALKS AND TRAILS

NTSHONDWE CAMP: Four **self-guided nature trails** near the camp range from one to four hours. Winding below the magnificent cliffs overlooking the rest camp, the trails pass several points of interest. Trees along the way include the common tree euphorbia, rock alder, common cabbage tree, green-stem corkwood, weeping boer bean and broad-leaved coral tree. Also of interest are relics of the earlier Zulu inhabitants of the area – a grinding stone, a grain storage site, graves and an old donkey path.

A rewarding way of exploring Itala is a **guided early morning or afternoon walk**, usually lasting two to three hours. Since potentially dangerous animals such as rhino and buffalo can be encountered, groups are accompanied by an armed game guard.

During the cooler months three-day guided **Bushveld Trails** are conducted from a tented base camp in the remote wilderness area of the reserve. This area is only open to those fortunate few joining a Bushveld Trail and game such as rhino and elephant are often encountered in addition to the more common species. Trailists also gain an insight into the complexities of nature, as well as the flora, fauna, geology and history of the area.

Ntshondwe, a flagship of Natal Parks Board, blends into the background.

ITALA GAME RESERVE AT A GLANCE

MAIN ATTRACTIONS
Scenery, game-viewing, Bushveld Trails, game walks, self-guided walks, morning, afternoon and night drives, bird-watching, picnicking.

BEST TIMES TO VISIT
The dry winter months (June to October) are generally the best for game-viewing, while birding is best between September and March.

PERMITS/BOOKINGS
At gate. **Ntshondwe Camp and Lodge, Thalu, Mbizo and bush camps, Mhlangeni bush lodge, Bushveld Trails:** Natal Parks Board Reservations (*see below*). **Doornkraal Camp Sites:** Officer-in-Charge (*see below*). **Guided walks with game guard:** Book at Ntshondwe Camp; arrangements for a game guard for Thalu and Mbizo bush camps must be made with the nearby field staff office; a game guard is assigned to Mhlangeni Bush Lodge. **Night drives:** Book at Ntshondwe Camp reception.

OPENING TIMES
Entrance gate: 1 October to 31 March 05h00–19h00; 1 April to 30 September 06h00–18h00. **Wilderness trails:** March to October.

ACCOMMODATION
Book through Natal Parks Board Reservations (*see below*). Meals prepared by cook at Ntshondwe Lodge and Mhlangeni Bush Lodge. **Ntshondwe Camp:** Four 2-bed (bachelor), twenty-one 2-bed, twelve 4-bed and two 6-bed self-contained chalets, twenty-eight 2-bed chalets, no kitchen. **Ntshondwe Lodge:** Three rooms (sleeping 6) all with en suite facilities, small pool. **Mhlangeni Bush Lodge:** Five 2-bed units, three hot/cold-water ablution facilities, communal lounge and kitchen. **Mbizo Bush Camp:** Two 2-roomed units (one double bed and two single beds in each unit), separate hot/cold-water ablutions, communal braai area. **Thalu Bush Camp:** One 2-roomed unit (one double bed and two single beds), hot/cold-water shower, flush toilet. **Doornkraal camp sites:** Three sites with kitchen, thatched lounge/dining shelter, cold-water shower and toilet.

FACILITIES
Ntshondwe Camp: Coffee shop, restaurant, bar, curios, groceries, swimming pool, excellent conference facilities. The conference centre can seat up to 90 (56 can be accommodated in the camp's 28 non self-catering chalets). Petrol at entrance gate.

ENQUIRIES
Natal Parks Board Reservations, PO Box 1750, Pietermaritzburg 3200; tel. (0331) 47-1981, fax. 47-1980; **general enquiries,** tel. (0331) 47-1891 fax. 47-1037. **Officer-in-Charge, Itala Game Reserve,** PO Box 42, Louwsburg 3150; tel. (0388) 7-5239.

TOURIST INFORMATION
Zululand Joint Services Board, Private Bag X1025, Richards Bay 3900; tel. (0351) 4-1404, fax. 4-1409. **Energy Demoina Publicity,** PO Box 2149, Vryheid 3100; tel. (0381) 81-2133, fax. 80-9637.

32 HLUHLUWE-UMFOLOZI PARK

Set aside for game protection in 1895, at the same time as Lake St Lucia, the Hluhluwe and Umfolozi reserves (as they were then known) form one of Africa's oldest conservation areas. The two reserves were originally separated by the Corridor, a stock-free zone created to prevent the spread of nagana to the cattle of the tribespeople living in the area. The Corridor was proclaimed a game reserve in 1989, facilitating the consolidation of Hluhluwe and Umfolozi into a single unit. Today the Hluhluwe-Umfolozi Park, with its wooded savanna, floodplains and valleys, provides a sanctuary to southern Africa's largest populations of white and black rhino. Steeped in the history of the Zulu nation and rich in wildlife, it epitomises the true spirit of Africa.

How to get there
To reach the park from Durban, travel along the N2 to the signposted turnoff north of Mtubatuba, entering the park via the Mambeni Gate. A worthwhile detour from Mtubatuba is to Dumazulu Traditional Village, which is an authentic kraal where visitors can gain insight into the culture of the Zulu people. Approaching from Johannesburg along the N2, take the R66 to Nongoma at Pongola and continue along the R618 to the Mambeni Gate through Hlabisa. If travelling from the Itala Game Reserve (*see* Tour 31, p. 136), travel eastwards from Louwsburg on the R69 to its junction with the R66 and continue as above.

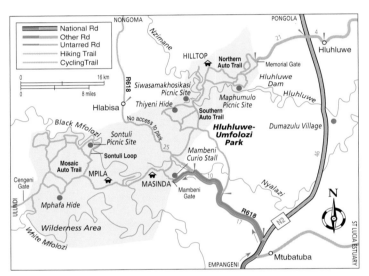

➡ *The Umfolozi section of the park is 270 km north of Durban and 625 km from Johannesburg. Access is along the R618, which is joined 3 km north of Mtubatuba on the N2. The turnoff to the park is signposted 22,5 km further on and the Mambeni Gate is reached after another 5 km.*

UMFOLOZI SECTION
On entering the park, stop at the **Mambeni curio stall** where a wide variety of traditional handicrafts and household implements, ranging from grass mats and wood carvings to delicate beadwork, are sold at very reasonable prices. The stall was built by the Natal Parks Board as a neighbour-relations project, enabling the adjacent enziMambeni communities to benefit directly from tourism, and is run by the communities themselves.

The Umfolozi section of the park is characterised by gently undulating hills interspersed with broad plains, and lies largely between the meandering White and Black Mfolozi rivers.

Umfolozi's 25 000-ha wilderness area was the first such area to be set aside in Africa, and it was here too that the first wilderness trails were pioneered by Dr Ian Player in the 1950s (*see* Emonyeni Trail, p. 141).

In addition to seeing game on foot, the experiences of wilderness trailists are enriched by the insight they gain into the Zulu history and culture, ecology and archaeology of the area.

Rainfall is lower than that of the Hluhluwe section, with the result that this section of the park is less densely vegetated. **Vegetation** varies from open acacia savanna to broadleaf woodlands, thickets and grasslands. Common trees include the marula, buffalo thorn, knob thorn

The Black Mfolozi River, steeped in Zulu history and legend, and an integral component of the park.

The sickle bush has pink sterile and yellow fertile flowers.

and tamboti. Magnificent sycamore fig and weeping boer-bean forests used to fringe the Black and White Mfolozi rivers, but were destroyed by cyclone Demoina in 1984. Fortunately, though, the trees are slowly recovering. Animals and birds in the Umfolozi section of the park are similar to those in the Hluhluwe section (*see* below), and game-viewing is the chief activity here too.

There are 115 km of game-viewing roads. The **Sontuli Loop**, a 14,3-km loop winding largely along a wide section of the Black Mfolozi River, is favoured by white rhino, lion, cheetah, waterbuck and impala. Visitors can alight from their vehicles at the Sontuli picnic site (5,2 km from the start of the loop road) on the banks of the river.

There are also two viewpoints which overlook the river. The **Mphafa hide,** overlooking a waterhole in the Mphafa Stream, is most rewarding during the dry winter months.

The **Mosaic Auto Trail** covers 67 km and takes about five hours to complete. Seventeen points of interest along the route are explained in the trail pamphlet (obtainable from the shops in Mpila and Masinda camps) which provides an excellent introduction to the plant and animal life of the area.

Picnic places are provided at **Umbondwe** on the banks of the Black Mfolozi River, at **Mpila Camp** and along the **Sontuli Loop Road**, and at several viewpoints visitors may alight from their vehicles at their own risk.

Many of the park's mammals are nocturnal, and the **guided night drives** conducted from Mpila offer an opportunity to see some of these animals. As is the case with game-viewing in general, much depends on luck.

Early morning drives in the Umfolozi section are conducted from Mpila by qualified trail officers and focus on the interpretation of Umfolozi's history, flora and fauna. Drives last about three hours and follow normal tourist roads and off-the-beaten track routes in the Gqoyeni Basin

Waterbuck are gregarious antelope that form small herds.

– a low-lying area along the Black Mfolozi River, north of Mpila Camp – and the Corridor.

➡ *From Umfolozi the Hluhluwe section of the park can be reached by following the Link Road, a 16,8-km stretch of tar linking the two sections of the park. An alternative entrance is via Memorial Gate, which is approached from the Hluhluwe village offramp.*

HLUHLUWE SECTION

The scenery of the Hluhluwe section of the park is spectacular – a succession of deep valleys, rivers

fringed with palm trees, and rolling hills. Vegetation ranges from lush semi-deciduous forests to woodlands and grasslands.

The area is renowned for its herds of big game and in addition to the Big Five – lion, leopard, elephant, rhino and buffalo – no fewer than 79 other mammal species have been recorded.

Visitors can be assured of good sightings of the once-endangered white rhino. Black rhino are present but less frequently spotted because of their preference for wooded areas. Buffalo are also plentiful in Hluhluwe.

Among the animals most likely to be seen are impala, nyala, kudu, blue wildebeest, Burchell's zebra and warthog, as well as giraffe; common duiker and a host of smaller mammals also occur. Two mammal species which can only be seen in the Hluhluwe section of the park are samango monkey and hippo. The samango monkey is restricted to the forests in the north of Hluhluwe, while hippo inhabit the Nzimane and Hluhluwe rivers.

Over 370 bird species have been recorded in Hluhluwe-Umfolozi to date including the whitebacked vulture, bateleur, greenspotted dove and lilac-breasted roller, as well as trumpeter and ground hornbills. Of special interest to birders is the

White rhino are grazers and hence their lips are square.

OPERATION RHINO

The white rhino was once considered one of the most endangered animal species in the world, and its conservation in Umfolozi is considered as one of South Africa's greatest environmental success stories.

When Umfolozi was proclaimed a 'Reserved Area for Game' in 1895, the white rhino was on the brink of extinction, with an estimated world population of probably no more than 50 animals.

However, as a result of the protection they enjoyed in Umfolozi, the numbers of white rhino increased to 120 by 1929, when the first official survey was conducted. By 1960 the population stood at just over 700 and it became

necessary to translocate some of the animals elsewhere, to prevent over-population.

Operation Rhino was launched in 1961 when the first white rhino was translocated to Mkuzi Game Reserve (*see* p. 151), but unfortunately the animal died.

Undeterred by early setbacks, capture techniques have been refined and more than 4 000 rhino have since been translocated successfully to conservation areas throughout southern and east Africa (10 rhino were translocated to Kenya in September 1994), and several overseas countries, including the USA, Spain, Portugal, the UK, India, Japan and Taiwan.

Hilltop Camp commands magnificent views across the Hluhluwe section of the park.

yellowbilled oxpecker, a species which was reintroduced into the park in 1986.

A road network of 93 km traverses the hills and valleys and there are numerous viewpoints where visitors are permitted to alight from their vehicles (at their own risk) to enjoy the scenery and to scan the bush for game. There is an abundance of perennial waterholes in the Hluhluwe section, so game is generally widely dispersed. **Thiyeni hide**, which overlooks a waterhole, can be rewarding, especially during the dry winter months, but be prepared to spend a few hours in wait.

A most enjoyable way of exploring the park is to set off on the two self-guided auto trails. The **Northern Auto Trail** provides fascinating insight into the management of the park, covering aspects such as bush encroachment, wetland reclamation and the reintroduction of elephants into Hluhluwe. The **Southern Auto Trail** focuses on the delicate interrelationships between plant and animal life. Both trails cover 43 km and take about three hours to complete. Several points of interest along the trails are explained in the trail brochures which can be bought at the Hilltop camp shop.

One of the most attractive features of Hluhluwe is its delightful picnic spots. **Maphumulo picnic site** overlooks the backwaters of the Hluhluwe Dam and hippo and crocodile might be spotted here, while a variety of waterbirds are also attracted to the dam. Shaded by a grove of tall tamboti trees, **Siwasamakhosikasi picnic site** is situated 11,5 km south of Hilltop above the palm-fringed Nzimane River. There are also picnic sites just below **Hilltop Camp** and in an enclosure at **Thiyeni hide**, 17,5 km south of Hilltop.

Guided night drives and early morning game drives are conducted from Hilltop.

WALKS AND TRAILS

UMFOLOZI SECTION: Three short, self-guided trails in the Umfolozi section of the park afford visitors an opportunity to experience the feeling of walking in the African bush. The **Masinda Trail** is about a 5-minute walk near the camp of the same name and offers a bird's-eye view over the Black Mfolozi River and the undulating hills of the Corridor, while some of the finest views of Umfolozi can be enjoyed on the **Mpila Hill Trail**. The trail covers 1,5 km and overlooks the White Mfolozi River, with the wilderness area to the south and the Black Mfolozi, the Corridor and Hluhluwe to the north.

Usually shy, buffalo become ferocious when threatened or provoked.

Bald ibis nest in crevices and ledges on cliff faces high above the ground.

Another expansive view of the wilderness area can be enjoyed by trailists on the **Emonyeni Trail**. The route, which takes approximately 30 minutes, winds uphill, through white milkwood, tamboti, common crow-berry and red ivory trees, to a toposcope which indicates the positions of the trail camps and other features. This pristine area is only accessible to those undertaking a guided wilderness trail.

Weekend Wilderness Trails covering between 12 and 15 km each day are conducted throughout the year and are ideally suited to those with limited time on their hands. Two nights are spent in a tented camp in the wilderness area from where day walks are conducted.

During the cooler months the **Traditional Wilderness Trails** are conducted. Trailists spend the first night at a base camp, while the second and third nights are spent at a trails camp in the wilderness.

The more adventurous can join one of the **Primitive Trails** which combine backpacking and conventional wilderness trails. Trailists carry all their equipment and food in backpacks and sleeping is in the open around a camp fire or in tents provided by trailists themselves.

Early morning and afternoon walks lasting from two to three hours are conducted from Hilltop and Mpila (Masinda visitors must drive to Mpila), offering trailists the excitement of encountering game on foot. Impala, Burchell's zebra, blue wildebeest and zebra are frequently seen at close range, but rhino, elephant and buffalo could also be encountered.

HLUHLUWE SECTION: The **Umbhombe Trail** in Hilltop Camp is a 30-minute self-guided route which meanders through semi-deciduous forests of feverberry, Natal fig, common cabbage and marula trees. Also to be seen here is the species after which both the park and the Hluhluwe River have been named, the thorny rope or *um-Hluhluwe*. Birders might spot the cinnamon dove, purplecrested lourie, white-eared barbet and the yellowspotted nicator.

Giraffe are inquisitive, keeping a watchful eye on all intruders.

HLUHLUWE-UMFOLOZI PARK AT A GLANCE

MAIN ATTRACTIONS
Big game, self-guided auto trails and walks, guided walks, wilderness trails, game hides, night drives, charming picnic sites, Mambeni craft market, Dumazulu Village.

BEST TIMES TO VISIT
The dry winter months (June to October) are generally best for game-viewing, but early mornings and evenings are usually cold. Summer temperatures are high, with thunderstorms in the afternoon.

UMFOLOZI SECTION
Permits/bookings: Entry permits at gate. Natal Parks Board Reservations (*see* below).
Guided walks, early morning and night drives: Camp offices. **Gqoyeni Bush Lodge** and **Sontuli and Nselweni Bush Camps:** Game guard available for walks.
Opening times: Nyalazi **Gate:** (on road between Hluhluwe and Umfolozi) Sunrise to sunset. **Mambeni** and **Cengweni Gates:** October to March 05h00–19h00; April to September 06h00–18h00.
Trails: Weekend Wilderness Trails: Throughout the year. Traditional Wilderness Trail: March to November.
Accommodation: Meals prepared by cooks at all the following accommodation:
Mpila: Two 7-bed and six 5-bed self-contained cottages; twelve 4-bed rest huts with refrigerator, cold-water hand basin and communal ablutions. **Masinda:** Six 4-bed rest huts with refrigerator, cold-water hand basin, communal ablutions. **Masinda Lodge:** Three bedrooms (one with en suite bathroom) sleeping six. **Gqoyeni Bush Lodge:** Four 2-bed units with shower and toilet. **Sontuli and Nselweni**

Bush Camps: Four 2-bed units, communal ablutions.
Facilities: Mpila: Petrol for sale and curio shop.

HLUHLUWE SECTION
Permits/bookings: Entry permits at gate. Natal Parks Board Reservations (*see* below).
Guided walks, early morning and night drives: Hilltop. **Mtwazi Lodge** and **Muntulu and Munyawaneni Bush Lodges:** Game guard available for guided walks.
Opening times: **Memorial gate:** October to March 05h00–19h00; April to September 06h00–18h00.
Accommodation: Meals prepared by cooks except at Hilltop. **Hilltop:** Twenty 2-bed rondavels with communal kitchens and ablutions. Seven 2-bed and twenty-two 4-bed self-contained chalets. Twenty chalets (no kitchen) with fridge and kettle. **Mtwazi Lodge:** Three 2-bed rooms with en suite bathrooms, 3-bed annex with en suite bathroom. **Muntulu Bush Lodge:** Two 2-bed units and two 3-bed units with en suite ablutions and game-viewing decks. **Munyawaneni Bush Lodge:** Four 2-bed units with en suite shower and toilet.
Facilities: **Hilltop:** Restaurant, bar, curio shop, groceries, petrol.

ENQUIRIES
Natal Parks Board Reservations, PO Box 1750, Pietermaritzburg 3200; tel. (0331) 47-1981, fax. 47-1980; **general enquiries,** tel. (0331) 47-1891, fax. 47-1037.

TOURIST INFORMATION
Zululand Joint Services Board, Private Bag X1025, Richards Bay 3900; tel. (0351) 4-1404, fax. 4-1409.

33 GREATER ST LUCIA WETLAND PARK

Covering a massive 250 000 ha, the Greater St Lucia Wetland Park lies in the south of Maputaland, a vast coastal plain stretching from St Lucia Estuary north to Mozambique and westwards to the Ubombo and the Lebombo ranges. The park, the third largest in South Africa, comprises a patchwork of conservation areas proclaimed over the last century. Angling, snorkelling and diving are a major attraction of the area, as are guided wilderness trails conducted on foot through wilderness areas.

How to get there
Mtubatuba, 220 km north of Durban and 590 km from Johannesburg, is the main access point to the Greater St Lucia Wetland Park's Western Shores. From Durban travel north along the N2 past Stanger and Empangeni. From Johannesburg follow the N2 via Piet Retief, Pongola and Hluhluwe Village (access point at False Bay Park). All the rest camps are well signposted.

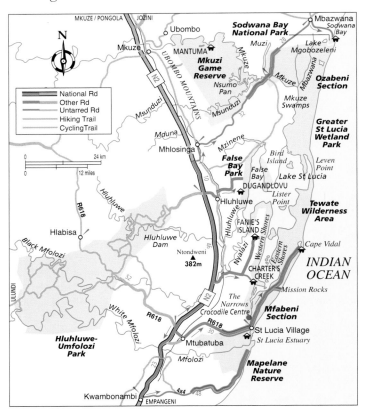

The Greater St Lucia Wetland Park is a mosaic of water, reed-covered islands, forested dunes, woodlands and papyrus swamps. The focal point of the park is the large expanse of water of Lake St Lucia which is connected to the sea by an estuary lined with mangrove swamps. In the west the lake is bounded by the savanna, thornveld and sand forest vegetation of the Western Shores.

The Eastern Shores section of the park is characterised by towering dunes which form a barrier between the lake and the ocean. These dunes, said to be among the tallest vegetated dunes in the world, are covered by forests of Natal wild banana, Natal fig, white milkwood, coastal red milkwood and coast silver oak, attracting a rich diversity of birds.

On the seaward side, the dunes slope down to miles and miles of unspoilt beaches, secluded bays and off-shore reefs; renowned for their excellent snorkelling and diving opportunities. To protect the rich marine life off-shore, two marine reserves have been set aside, stretching from Cape Vidal northwards to Mozambique and extending 5 km into the sea.

At the northern end of Lake St Lucia, the Mkuze River has created a vast wetland of papyrus swamps and reeds, pans, riverine and swamp forests. The Mkuze Swamps play an important ecological role by retarding the flow of the river, feeding water into the system during the dry season.

To the northwest of the Mkuze Swamps lies the Mkuzi Game Reserve (see Tour 34, p. 151), with its herds of game, fig forests and excellent birding, which became part of the Greater St Lucia Wetland Park when the various conservation areas were amalgamated into a single park.

LAKE ST LUCIA AND THE WESTERN SHORES

The 36 826-ha St Lucia Game Reserve, proclaimed in 1895, covers the water area and islands of Lake St Lucia and together with Hluhluwe and Umfolozi is the oldest conservation area in Africa. The main lake, which is about 40 km long and between 3 and 8 km wide, is linked to the sea by way of the Narrows, a 21-km-long winding channel.

The lake is one of the most important habitats of hippos and crocodiles in South Africa. Numbering about 800, the hippos mainly favour the eastern edge

Hippos tend to favour those parts of the lake where they feel secure and have access to grazing at night.

St Lucia estuary opens to the sea across white beaches lined by casuarina plantations. In the distance are the steep forested dunes at Mapelane.

of the lake and the Narrows, while the population of about 1 200 crocodiles occur throughout the lake.

The 300-km² lake is also an important habitat for fish and to date over 120 species have been recorded. Among the more common species are springer, flathead mullet, spotted grunter and river bream. Fishing is allowed without a permit.

With an area of 12 545 ha, the St Lucia Park encloses a 1-km-wide strip of land from the Mfolozi River northwards along the Western Shores of the lake to the Nyalazi River and along the Eastern Shores to the Mkuze River.

➡ *Charter's Creek is situated in the St Lucia Park, 259 km from Durban and 590 km from Johannesburg. Turn off the N2 to Charter's Creek about 20 km north of Mtubatuba and continue for 12.5 km on a tar road. At the Fanie's Island junction continue*

straight on gravel for 4,2 km to the entrance gate and 1 km further to the office. Approaching from the north, the turnoff is signposted about 26 km south of the Hluhluwe village offramp.

CHARTER'S CREEK

Anglers, birding enthusiasts and those seeking solitude have long been attracted to this charming rest camp overlooking the lake. Although best known for its light tackle boat **angling**, there is much to see and do in and around this rest camp. With some 385 **bird species** recorded along the Western Shores of the lake to date, bird-watching is rewarding.

A first-hand impression of the lake can be gained by joining a two-hour lake cruise on board the *Flamingo Tourer*. Visitors usually have good views of hippo, African fish eagle and occasionally crocodile, while reedbuck are frequently sighted on the Eastern Shores of the lake.

There are several inviting picnic places with braai facilities, and the swimming pool provides welcome relief on summer days.

➡ *Fanie's Island camp is 48 km north of Mtubatuba. Follow the directions towards Charter's*

Creek (as above), until you reach the Fanie's Island Junction. Turn left here and follow the signposted road for 14,8 km to the entrance gate and the office 700 m on. Fanie's Island is about 54 km south of the Hluhluwe village offramp.

Charter's Creek hutted camp provides comfortable accommodation.

Red duiker are mainly solitary, living in secluded bush habitats.

FANIE'S ISLAND

A more delightful setting than that of Fanie's Island would be hard to find. As with nearby Charter's Creek, the rest camp at Fanie's Island is a long-standing favourite light tackle boat angling destination. The forests of the Western Shores are home to the trumpeter hornbill, purple-crested lourie and the elusive Narina trogon, as well as animals such as red duiker, bushbuck or reedbuck.

➡ *Lister Point, also on the Western Shores of Lake St Lucia, is situated in False Bay Park, 285 km from Durban and 565 km from Johannesburg. The park can be reached via Hluhluwe Village from where the old Hluhluwe main road is followed in a northerly direction for 1,5 km. Turn right and after 7,2 km right again, continuing for just over 4 km to the park's entrance gate. Lister Point, where the key to the entrance gate to Dugandlovu must be collected, is about 4 km on.*

FALSE BAY PARK

This section of the park lies between the Hluhluwe and Mzinene rivers along the Western Shores of the lake.

Light tackle boat and shore angling is one of False Bay's chief attractions, and among the many species of fish that can be caught are yellowfin bream, springer, mullet and spotted grunter.

Another of the park's many attractions is that it is the only place where visitors are allowed to explore the area in canoes. Canoeing is, however, restricted to the Western Shores between the Hluhluwe and Mzinene rivers and canoeists must remain within 50 m of the shore.

FOSSILS OF ST LUCIA

False Bay Park is unique in its abundance of ammonites and other marine fossils, and a walk along the Western Shores takes visitors back in time millions of years.

The ammonites became extinct about 65 million years ago as a result of increasing competition from newly evolved predators, including modern bony fishes. Some of the shells sank to the ocean floor where they were filled with mud and silt and preserved in their muddy grave.

At around this time, the end of the Cretaceous Period, there was a considerable drop in the level of the sea, which exposed the Zululand coastal plain with the result that many marine reptiles, snails and clams became extinct.

Also of interest are the fossil corals at Lister Point, Rocky Point and Picnic Point. These hard limestone promontories were deposited some 50 000 years ago when the sea level was about 5 m higher than its present level.

Some of the fossils found along the Western Shores are displayed in the small Fossil Museum at the Lister Point office. The museum provides insight into these marine fossils and the origin of the lake and should not be missed.

Ammonites can be seen along the western shore of False Bay Park.

The magical hour of sunrise at Fanie's Island, situated on the Western Shores of Lake St Lucia.

Trailists on Dugandlovu Hiking Trail stay in the camp of the same name.

The yellowbilled stork is seen mainly in summer.

There is much of interest for those keen on **bird watching**. False Bay is one of the best places to see the African broadbill. Other noteworthy species include crested guineafowl, Narina trogon, yellowspotted nicator, Neergaard's sunbird and pinkthroated twinspot.

From the picnic places at **Rocky Point** (700 m south of Lister Point) and **Sandy Point** (3,5 km south of Lister Point) uninterrupted views can be enjoyed of the lake, with **Hell's Gate**, the 2-km-wide channel between Nibela Peninsula and Nolozi Peninsula, a prominent landmark in the background.

There is also a swimming pool in the camp. The platform at the Dugandlovu rustic camp has a spectacular view over the lake and the Hluhluwe River floodplain, which is much favoured by nyala, reedbuck, eland and Burchell's zebra.

WALKS AND TRAILS: WESTERN SHORES

CHARTER'S CREEK: An ideal way to get to know the trees and birds found at Charter's Creek is to set off on the two self-guided trails in the rest camp.

The 5-km **Umkhumbe Nature Trail** winds through coastal forests of white stinkwood, wild plum and small knobwood to the shore of Lake St Lucia and then meanders back to the starting point. Umkhumbe is the Zulu name for the red duiker and chances of seeing these small antelope are usually good.

The **Isikhova Nature Trail** follows a 7-km route through the coastal forest and some excellent examples of the powder puff tree can be seen along the way.

FANIE'S ISLAND: Visitors can explore their surroundings at Fanie's Island by setting off on the two self-guided walks which are also ideal for bird watching. The 5-km **Umkhiwane Trail** meanders through coastal bush, coastal forest, grasslands and along the banks of the reed-lined Fanie's Channel, and the 2-km **Umboma Trail** winds along the edge of Lake St Lucia.

FALSE BAY PARK: Three self-guided trails have been laid out in False Bay Park.

The **Dugandlovu Hiking Trail** winds for 8 km from the entrance gate to the park to the rustic Dugandlovu camp just north of the Hluhluwe River. The route passes through acacia and silver cluster-leaf veld, where trailists can expect to see red and common duiker, impala, nyala and warthog, then swings to Lake St Lucia, passing a small pan where crocodiles are often seen and then follows the lake shore for an hour before turning inland to the camp.

The **Mpophomeni Trail** is an interpretative trail which offers visitors the option of a 10-km route and a shorter route of 7 km through woodland, thickets and sand forest. The 6-km-long **Ingwe Trail** winds along the lake shore before passing through woodland and a patch of sand forest.

WESTERN SHORES AT A GLANCE

MAIN ATTRACTIONS
Angling, bird-watching, walks, launch trips, marine fossils.

BEST TIMES TO VISIT
Throughout the year, depending on interest. December and January are the most popular months. Angling for yellowfin bream, springer, mullet and spotted grunter generally best during winter. Dugandlovu Hiking Trail is best hiked in the cooler winter months.

PERMITS/BOOKINGS
Obtainable at entrance gate.

CHARTER'S CREEK
Opening times: Entrance gates: 1 October to 31 March 05h00–20h00 and 1 April to 30 September 06h00–20h00.
Charter's Creek launch tours: Daily throughout the year, weather permitting – winter 09h30 and 14h30; summer 09h00, 12h00 and 15h00. Contact Natal Parks Board Reservations (*see* below).
Accommodation: Seven-bed cottage, ten 4-bed, four 3-bed and one 2-bed fully furnished huts with communal lounge. Communal hot/cold-water ablutions. Meals prepared by cook. Contact Natal Parks Board Reservations (*see* below).
Facilities: Limited non-perishables, petrol, curios. Swimming pool.

FANIE'S ISLAND
Opening times: Entrance gate: 1 October to 31 March 05h00–20h00 and 1 April to 30 September 06h00–20h00.

Accommodation: One cottage with seven beds, twelve 2-bed huts with refrigerator. Communal hot/cold-water ablution facilities. Meals are prepared by a cook. Contact Natal Parks Board Reservations (*see* below). Twenty camp sites with hot/cold-water ablutions.
Facilities: Limited non-perishables, petrol, curios.

FALSE BAY PARK
Opening times: Entrance gates: From 1 October to 31 March 05h00–20h00 and from 1 April to 30 September 06h00–20h00.
Accommodation:
Dugandlovu Rustic Camp: Four 4-bed huts, cold-water showers, two gas stoves, paraffin lamps, braai places and flush toilets (bring your own bedding). **Lister Point:** 38 camp sites with hot/cold-water ablution facilities. Contact the Camp Manager, False Bay Park, PO Box 222, Hluhluwe 3960, tel. and fax. (035) 562-0425.
Facilities: Curios, limited non-perishables, pool.

ENQUIRIES
Natal Parks Board Reservations, PO Box 1750, Pietermaritzburg 3200; tel. (0331) 47-1981, fax. 47-1980; **general enquiries,** tel. (0331) 47-1891, fax. 47-1037.

TOURIST INFORMATION
Zululand Joint Services Board, Private Bag X1025, Richards Bay 3900; tel. (0351) 4-1404, fax. 4-1409.

Fishing is one of the main attractions at Cape Vidal.

How to get there
There are several points of
entry to the Eastern Shores
of Lake St Lucia, all of which
are approached from the N2.
Mapelane Nature Reserve is
reached from the Empangeni/
Mtubatuba road. St Lucia
village can be approached
through Mtubatuba. Sodwana
Bay is accessed through
Jozini and the Ozabeni
Section is approached from
the Lower Mkuze Road. Specific, individual directions
are given below.

LAKE ST LUCIA'S EASTERN SHORES, WILDERNESS AREAS & MARINE RESERVE

With its ever-changing landscapes – unspoilt beaches, lily-
covered pans and forested dunes
– the Eastern Shores and the
coastline of the Greater St Lucia
Wetland Park encompasses one
of South Africa's most scenic
areas. Offshore divers can
explore the underwater world
of Africa's southernmost coral
reefs at Raggie Reef, also renowned for its excellent game-
fishing. The Eastern Shores of
Lake St Lucia comprise the
Mfabeni Section, Cape Vidal
and the Tewate Wilderness Area,
and can be approached through
St Lucia village.

➤ *Mapelane Nature Reserve is
to the south of St Lucia Estuary,
245 km from Durban and 640 km
from Johannesburg. The Mapelane
Rest Camp is 50 km along a gravel
and sand road after taking the
signposted turnoff to Cape St Lucia
lighthouse at Kwambonambi on
the Empangeni/Mtubatuba road
(N2). A four-wheel-drive vehicle or
a vehicle with a high ground clearance is essential from the turnoff.*

MAPELANE NATURE RESERVE

Situated on the southern bank of
the Mfolozi River, the remote
Mapelane rest camp is sheltered

Barrier dunes have been formed along the Maputaland coastline, but at Cape Vidal the beach widens to form this low-lying, undulating dune system.

by a sweeping bay created by an offshore reef. Mapelane's reputation for its excellent fishing stretches back over 50 years and it is extremely popular with skiboat, as well as rock and surf anglers.

At low tide visitors can spend several rewarding hours exploring the inter-tidal rock pools with their interesting marine life, while crayfishing and mussel collecting are also permitted, provided the necessary licence has been obtained.

The coastal dune forests in the 900-ha reserve provide a habitat for vervet monkeys, bushbuck, the diminutive blue duiker, bush-pig and red squirrel, as well as a wealth of birds.

Bird-watching is particularly rewarding in the Mapelane Rest Camp and from the tracks in the reserve. Among the more than 200 species recorded to date are Knysna and purple-crested louries, white-eared barbet, yellowbellied bulbul and green twinspot.

➡ *St Lucia village, 250 km north of Durban and 620 km from Johannesburg, is approached through Mtabutuba, just off the N2. From Mtubatuba, travel east for about 30 km to St Lucia village from where the Crocodile Centre, St Lucia Game Park, the Mfabeni Section (including Mission Rocks) and Cape Vidal are accessed. The Crocodile Centre and St Lucia Game Park can be reached by turning left as you enter St Lucia village, continuing for 2 km. The Crocodile Centre is situated just before the control gate of the Mfabeni Section and the game park can be accessed on foot from here.*

ST LUCIA ESTUARY

St Lucia Estuary is a mecca for light tackle boat and surf anglers and during the peak holiday season the beaches are packed with anglers, while a never-ending stream of boats can be seen cruising up and down the estuary.

One of the highlights of a visit to St Lucia is a cruise on board the 80-seater *Santa Lucia* launch, which departs from the bridge over the estuary just before entering the village. Trips last about two hours and from the viewing deck visitors enjoy uninterrupted views of the estuary and close-up views of hippos and crocodiles. Birds likely to be seen include Goliath and blackheaded herons, African fish eagles and pied kingfishers.

Not to be missed is a visit to the **St Lucia Crocodile Centre** where Nile crocodiles of varying ages can be seen at close range. The centre is also home to two other crocodile species, the long-snouted and the dwarf crocodile, as well as their American relative, the alligator. The weekly feeding of the crocodiles is accompanied by an interesting talk on the activities of the centre.

The **St Lucia Game Park** is criss-crossed by a 12-km network of trails alternating between grassland and Umdoni parkland, marshes, swamp forests and the dune forest.

Be sure to set an hour and a half aside for the **Imvubu Trail** which winds down to the mangrove-lined banks of the estuary where hippos can usually be seen. Other animals you might

About 1 200 crocodiles occur in the St Lucia Lake System.

happen to spot include impala, reedbuck, waterbuck and blue wildebeest.

➡ *From St Lucia village (see the directions above) head north along the Cape Vidal road to reach the control gate of the Mfabeni Section. Pass through the gate and continue for 12 km to the signposted turnoff to Mission Rocks and then for another 3 km to the parking area at Mission Rocks.*

THE MFABENI SECTION

This section of the park stretches from just north of the St Lucia Game Park to Cape Vidal and the Tewate Wilderness Area. A striking feature of the area is the forested dunes, up to 150 m high and said to be the second highest forested dunes in the world. It is a sanctuary to the highest concentration of reedbuck in Africa, and black rhino, buffalo, impala and red duiker also occur.

A bird's-eye view of the intricate network of pans, vleis, swamp forests and forested dunes of the Eastern Shores awaits visitors from the viewpoint near the Mission Rocks outpost. Visitors can enjoy the view while they are having a picnic and with the help of a toposcope well-known places such as Catalina Bay, Fanie's Island, Charter's Creek and False Bay can be pin-pointed. The rocky shores at Mission Rocks are a popular rock angling spot and during spring low tide the rock pools are well worth exploring. Several delightful picnic spots with braai places are tucked away under the dune forest.

➡ *Follow the directions for Mission Rocks (as above), but pass the Mission Rocks turnoff and continue north for another 26 km to Cape Vidal.*

The Santa Lucia *provides a relaxing way of seeing St Lucia.*

An aerial view of Cape Vidal illustrates its narrow ribbon beaches and the forested dunes (among the highest in the world) of the Maputaland coast.

CAPE VIDAL

Cape Vidal is a much sought-after coastal destination, offering a spectrum of activities, including surf and skiboat angling, scuba diving and snorkelling.

Although most of the outdoor activities are centered on the marine environment, Cape Vidal is an attractive bird-watching destination as several interesting species, such as Narina trogon, green coucal, brown robin and Woodward's batis, can be ticked here. Birding can be enjoyed along the access road to the rest camp, as well as on Cape Vidal's two self-guided trails (*see* p. 150).

➡ *Access to the Tewate Wilderness Area is on foot only from Cape Vidal.*

TEWATE WILDERNESS AREA

Covering about 10 000 ha, the Tewate Wilderness Area stretches northwards from Cape Vidal to Leven Point where it adjoins the Ozabeni Section of the Greater St Lucia Wetland Park. This area is only accessible to those intrepid visitors undertaking a wilderness trail (*see* p. 150).

The vegetation of the wilderness area ranges from dune forests to grassveld interspersed with reed and sedge swamps. The animals inhabiting the area include crocodile, hippo, black rhino, reedbuck and red duiker. Among the more than 250 bird species recorded to date are crested guineafowl, purplecrested lourie, green coucal, Narina trogon, yellowspotted nicator, Rudd's apalis and Woodward's batis.

➡ *Take the Southern Maputaland turnoff from the N2, approximately 14 km north of Hluhluwe village. Turn left at the T-junction a short way on, following the road signposted to Sodwana Bay. Travel north for 3,6 km and, immediately after crossing over the railway line, turn right, continuing towards Sodwana Bay. About 37,6 km after turning off the N2, turn left onto a road signposted Lower Mkuzi*

Section. After about 1 km you will pass through a gate to reach the Warden's office a short way on.

OZABENI SECTION

Bordering on the Tewate Wilderness Area in the south, the Ozabeni Section, previously the Sodwana State Forest, is characterised by papyrus swamps, reed-lined channels, pans, grasslands and fig tree forests. The central feature of the area is the Mkuze Swamps, the largest swamp area in South Africa.

Small numbers of nyala, waterbuck, impala, bushbuck, oribi and warthog occur here, but it is the spectacular scenery which is the chief attraction. With 363 bird species recorded to date in Ozabeni and the adjoining Sodwana Bay National Park (*see* below) and another 20 species awaiting confirmation, bird-watching is another attraction. One of the best ways of discovering the area's birdlife is to join a guided canoeing trip on the pans of the Mkuze Swamps.

Currently only the area west of the Mbazwana River is open to tourists. The area is criss-crossed by a 50-km network of sandy (and muddy) tracks and is accessible only by four-wheel-drive vehicles. It is also ideally suited to hiking.

➡ *Sodwana Bay is 346 km from Durban and 575 km from Johannesburg. Access is through Jozini and Mbazwana from the north or, from the south, along the Southern Maputaland turnoff on the N2, north of Hluhluwe village. From Mbazwana follow the signposted road to the park, to reach the entrance gate after 14,3 km. The rest camp is 2 km on. Approaching from the south, take the N2 to the Southern Maputaland turnoff, 10 km north of the Hluhluwe village offramp, continuing for 60 km to Mbazwana, from where you continue as above.*

SODWANA BAY NATIONAL PARK

Sodwana is one of South Africa's top holiday destinations and during peak holiday periods

THE SEA TURTLES OF MAPUTALAND

The beaches of Maputaland are the main breeding ground of the leatherback turtle in the southern Indian Ocean. These large sea turtles can reach a length of up to 2 m and weigh up to 646 kg. The nesting season stretches between October and February and females can lay over 1 000 eggs in a season, the average number of eggs per clutch being just over 100. The eggs hatch after about two months, but only about two out of every thousand hatchlings reach adulthood. Also nesting along the Maputaland coast is the orange-brown to reddish-brown loggerhead turtle which reaches a length of up to 1,2 m and a mass of 140 kg. Four to five batches of 100 to 120 eggs are laid at intervals of 13 to 20 days.

Other sea turtles occurring in the waters off southern Africa include the hawksbill, green and olive ridley turtles.

Offshore coral reefs are home to fish of tropical and temperate waters.

A leatherback turtle covers her eggs before returning to the sea.

thousands of visitors are attracted to pursue game fishing, scuba diving and snorkelling.

Kingfish, pompano, king mackerel and barracuda are much sought after, while the months between October and May are generally good for billfish. Rock and surf angling is also popular.

The southernmost coral reefs in Africa occur along the Maputaland coast and Sodwana Bay is considered the prime scuba-diving spot along the South African coast. Unlike the true coral reefs, the coral along the Maputaland coast live on sandstone outcrops, but the marine life is no less spectacular than Australia's famous Great Barrier Reef.

The corals occur in infinitely varied shapes and sizes to create an underwater garden of exquisite beauty. Among the incredible array of colourful fishes are the flute-mouthed butterflyfish, the blue-spotted rock cod, honeycomb moray eels, sea goldies, wrasses and clownfish.

Among the many popular offshore diving spots are Two Mile, Five Mile, Seven Mile and Nine Mile reefs. Closer inshore, the rock pools and coves provide ideal opportunities for snorkelling.

During January and February visitors to Sodwana have the opportunity to witness one of the most incredible natural phenomena when loggerhead and leatherback turtles come ashore to nest on the beaches at night. **Guided Turtle Tours** lasting between two and three hours are conducted for camp residents during these months, weather and tides permitting.

Some 47 mammal species are known to occur in the area, but visitors are unlikely to see more than a handful, as most of them are either small and thus easily overlooked or nocturnal. Animals most likely to be seen are vervet and samango monkeys, red duiker and reedbuck, and hippos and crocodiles inhabit Mngobozeleni Lake.

WALKS AND TRAILS: EASTERN SHORES

MAPELANE NATURE RESERVE: Mapelane's **Lookout Trail** is a short 1-km ramble to a viewpoint on the coastal dunes, from where visitors can enjoy sweeping views of their surroundings.

MFABENI SECTION: In the Mfabeni Section day visitors can undertake walks along sections of the Mziki Hiking Trail to places such as the **Mfazazana Pan hides** or walk from Mission Rocks to **Bats' Cave**, home to thousands of Egyptian fruit bats.

The **Mziki Trail** consists of three day routes which are hiked from the base camp at Mount Tabor. Covering 38 km in total, the trails alternate between open grassveld, coastal dunes and the unspoilt coastline.

Deep-sea fishing is popular, as the waters off Maputaland offer some of the best game fishing in the world.

CAPE VIDAL: The 7-km-long **Mvubu Trail** at Cape Vidal meanders through the coastal forest and then winds down to the shores of Lake Bhangazi where trailists chance spotting hippo and crocodile.

Also at Cape Vidal is the **Imboma Wetlands Trail** – an easy one-hour ramble past several seasonally inundated pans fringed with clumps of umdoni trees south of Lake Bhangazi. Visitors need to be cautious, though, as buffalo, hippos and crocodiles could be encountered. This trail is especially rewarding during the wet summer months when a variety of water birds is attracted to the pans and vleis.

TEWATE WILDERNESS AREA: The unspoilt Tewate Wilderness Area is out of bounds to all but those joining one of the **guided wilderness trails** which are conducted between April and October. The first and last nights of the trail are spent at the base camp on the shores of Lake Bhangazi, while accommodation is provided in tented camps in the Tewate Wilderness Area. The trails are led by a qualified trails officer and alternate between the lake shore and across the dunes to the magnificent beach at Cape

A honeycomb moray eel peers out of his hole.

Vidal. In addition to exploring the area on foot, trailists also venture onto Lake St Lucia in canoes, while snorkelling opens up the underwater world of the Maputaland coast.

SODWANA BAY NATIONAL PARK: Visitors wishing to explore the Sodwana Bay National Park on foot can set off on the **Mngobozeleni Trail**, a 5-km interpretative trail focusing on some of the trees and their uses, as well as the ecology of the area.

EASTERN SHORES AT A GLANCE

MAIN ATTRACTIONS
Coral reefs, game-fishing, rock, surf and light tackle boat angling, snorkelling, turtle tours, bird-watching, walks, trail, and guided wilderness trails.

BEST TIMES TO VISIT
Conditions for scuba diving and snorkelling are best between May and July, while November and December are good months for bill fishing. Turtle tours are conducted in January and February.

MAPELANE NATURE RESERVE
Permits/bookings: Obtainable at the gate.
Opening times: Entrance gate: 1 October to 31 March 05h00–19h00 and 1 April to 30 September 06h00–18h00.
Accommodation: Ten 5-bed log cabins, fully equipped kitchenette; 45 camp sites with hot/cold-water ablutions.
Camp sites: Camp Manager, Private Bag, St Lucia Estuary 3936; tel. and fax. (035) 590-1407. **Hutted accommodation:** Natal Parks Board Reservations (*see* below).
Facilities: Limited non-perishables, curios and petrol.

ST LUCIA ESTUARY, MFABENI AND CAPE VIDAL
Permits/bookings: **Mziki Hiking Trail:** Natal Parks Board Reservations (*see* below). **Day visits to Mfabeni and Cape Vidal:** Permits at entrance gate to St Lucia Game Park (maximum 100 per day).
Opening times: **St Lucia Crocodile Centre:** 08h00–12h30 and 14h00–16h30 (weekdays); 08h30–12h30 and 14h00–17h00 (Saturdays); 09h30–12h00 and 14h00–16h00 (Sundays). Croc feeding on Saturday at 15h00. **St Lucia Game Park, Mfabeni and Cape Vidal:** 05h00–19h00 (1 October to 31 March), 06h00–18h00 (1 April to 30 September). **St Lucia Estuary:** Sugarloaf camp site open throughout the

year; Iphiva and Eden Park camp sites only open during peak holiday season.
Accommodation: **St Lucia Estuary:** Camp sites at Sugarloaf, Iphiva and Eden Park with hot/cold-water ablutions. Contact the Officer-in-Charge, Private Bag, St Lucia Estuary 3936; tel. (035) 590-1340, fax. 590-1343. **Cape Vidal:** 18 fully equipped 5-bed and twelve 8-bed log cabins; five fully equipped fishing cabins sleeping 8, 12, 14 and 20; 4 self-contained two-bed huts at Bhangazi Bush Camp; 50 camp sites with hot/cold-water ablutions. **Camp sites:** The Officer-in-Charge, Cape Vidal, Private Bag, St Lucia Estuary 3936; tel. (035) 590-1404, fax. 590-1300.
Hutted accommodation: Natal Parks Board Reservations (*see* below). **Mfabeni (Mziki Trail):** Mount Tabor Hikers' Hut: Eight semi-equipped bunks, shower and toilet.
Facilities: **Cape Vidal:** Limited range of non-perishables, curios and petrol. **Mfabeni:** Picnic spots with ablutions at Mission Rocks.

TEWATE WILDERNESS AREA
Permits/bookings: **St Lucia Wilderness Trails:** Natal Parks Board Reservations (*see* below).
Accommodation: Rustic tented camps, communal ablutions at Bhangazi Lake (base camp has hot/cold water) and in the wilderness area (bucket shower with hot water). Book through Natal Parks Board Reservations (*see* below).
Opening times: April to September.
Facilities: Meals provided, but bring your own alcohol.

OZABENI SECTION
Permits/bookings: Officer-in-Charge (*see* below). Canoe trips: Ntini Safaris, PO Box 50, Balgowan 3275; tel. (033) 234-4551.
Accommodation: Small camp site at Manzimbomvu with basic ablution facilities. Officer-in-Charge (*see* below).

Opening times: Throughout the year, 08h00–16h00.
Enquiries: Officer-in-Charge, PO Box 457, Hluhluwe 3960; tel. (035) 571-0011.

SODWANA BAY NATIONAL PARK
Permits/bookings: At gate.
Beach permits for travelling between White Sands and Mabibi: Sodwana beach entrance, 16h00 the day before the journey (only 20 per day).
Opening times: 24 hours.
Accommodation: Ten 5-bed and ten 8-bed fully-equipped chalets; 413 camp sites with hot/cold-water ablutions; 33 luxury camp sites with electricity, running water and hot/cold-water ablutions. **Camp sites:** Contact the Camp Manager Sodwana Bay National Park, Private Bag 310, Mbazwana 3974; tel. and fax. (035) 571-0051. **Hutted accommodation:** Natal Parks Board Reservations (*see* below).
Facilities: Shop with groceries, curios, petrol, freezer space and diving shop.
Charter and Diving Companies: **Sodwana Bay Fishing Charters,** Sodwana Bay Lodge, Private Bag 317, Mbazwana 3974; tel. (035) 571-0095, fax. 571-0144. **Blue Print Diving,** PO Box 72, Glenvista 2058; tel. (011) 432-2292, fax. 432-2293. **Sodwana Dive Retreats,** Private Bag 317, Mbazwana 3974; tel. (035) 571-0055. **Santa Lucia Launch Tours:** Natal Parks Board, Private Bag X01, St Lucia Estuary 3936; tel. (035) 590-1340, fax. 590-1343.

ENQUIRIES
Natal Parks Board Reservations, PO Box 1750, Pietermaritzburg 3200; tel. (0331) 47-1981, fax. 47-1980; **general enquiries,** tel. (0331) 47-1891, fax. 47-1037.

TOURIST INFORMATION
Zululand Joint Services Board, Private Bag X1025, Richards Bay 3900; tel. (0351) 4-1404, fax. 4-1409.

34 MKUZI GAME RESERVE

Nestled against the Ubombo Mountains in northern Zululand, Mkuzi is 36 000 ha of pristine bushveld wilderness. Majestic sycamore figs dominate the riverine forests along the Mkuze River, and the fever tree forests of the lower Mkuze floodplain and Nsumo Pan form a hauntingly beautiful picture. Excellent game-viewing and birding opportunities add to the reserve's scenic attractions. Mkuzi is part of the Greater St Lucia Wetland Park and is linked to this conservation area by means of the Mkuze Swamps.

How to get there
Mkuzi, in northern Zululand, is 335 km from Durban and 450 km from Johannesburg. From Durban take the N2 via Empangeni to Mtubatuba and continue to the turnoff 28 km north of the Hluhluwe village offramp. Turn onto the old Hluhluwe Main Road (gravel) and continue north for 12 km to the reserve turnoff. The Emshopi gate is 7,7 km on, the rest camp 9 km further. From Johannesburg drive on the N2 to Ermelo; continue through Piet Retief and Pongola to Mkuze village. Follow the old Hluhluwe Main Road south for 9 km to the signposted turnoff to the reserve. This tour can be linked with Tour 33 (*see* p. 142), to cover the entire Greater St Lucia Wetland Park.

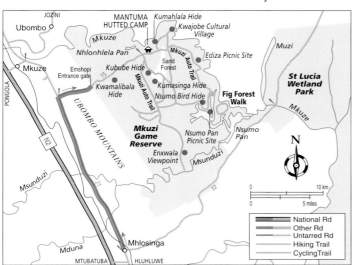

the park, and giraffe are also often seen. Other antelope species include kudu, common reedbuck, and red and common duiker. The shy suni are confined to the sand forest east of the rest camp.

Both white and black rhino occur, and elephant were released in the Msunduzi River area in 1994. Hippo and crocodile are easily seen from the hides and the picnic site at the edge of Nsumo Pan. The two most prominent **predators** are leopard and spotted hyena, and there is a small cheetah population.

To experience Mkuzi's African atmosphere visitors can stay at the Nhlonhlela Bush Lodge overlooking Nhlonhlela Pan or the Umkumbi Bush Camp, in the

controlled hunting area south of the Msunduzi River. Gameviewing is facilitated by the reserve's 87-km road network, but is especially rewarding from the hides – Kumasinga and Kubube

The **birdlife** of Mkuzi is surpassed only by that of Ndumo Game Reserve in northern Maputaland (*see* p. 157), and an amazing 418 bird species have been recorded in the reserve, including the rare Pel's fishing owl. Other species to look out for are crested guineafowl, African broadbill, Heughlin's and bearded robins, Neergaardt's sunbird and pinkthroated twinspot. Two hides overlook Nsumo Pan, which attracts a wide variety of water

birds. Birding here is generally most rewarding when the water level is low, and among the water birds that might be seen here are white and pinkbacked pelicans, whitebreasted cormorant, pygmy and spurwinged geese, knobbilled duck and the unmistakable African fish eagle.

Game is abundant and easy to spot. Impala, nyala, warthog, Burchell's zebra, blue wildebeest, chacma baboon and vervet monkeys are most frequently seen in

NSUMO'S PINKBACKED PELICANS

Nsumo Pan is the habitat of the only breeding population of pinkbacked pelicans in South Africa. For many years these pelicans bred in the trees on the Hluhluwe River floodplains along the Western Shores of Lake St Lucia. In 1975 some of the birds moved to Richard's Bay and Jozini Dam where they bred before returning to their St Lucia breeding site the following year. However, in early 1987 the birds migrated to Nsumo.

Although the pinkbacked pelican is widespread in tropical Africa, it is classified as rare in South Africa and the total breeding population is estimated at 110 pairs. They have also been recorded as summer visitors to Barberspan in the North-West (*see*

p. 200) and as vagrants in Mpumalanga and the Western Cape. Elsewhere in southern Africa they occur as vagrants along the coast at Walvis Bay and the Caprivi in Namibia, the Okavango Delta in Botswana, and in Zimbabwe.

The pinkbacked pelican differs from the white pelican in that it is smaller, and is greyish in colour, with pink feathers on its back.

The pinkbacked pelican is rare in South Africa.

A raised walkway leads to the first bird hide at Nsumo Pan.

Kudu ewes are wary and dissolve into the bush when alarmed.

on the edge of the sand forest, and Kumahlala and Kwamalibaba in the drier western part.

After sunset, experience the sights and sounds of the African bush on a two-hour **night drive** from Mantuma hutted camp, during which you may see species unlikely to be spotted by day.

The easiest and most rewarding way to become familiar with the reserve's flora, fauna and geology is to follow the 41-km self-guided **Mkuzi Auto Trail** from Mantuma camp. Winding through a variety of landscapes and habitats, the drive takes about three hours to complete and 14 information points along the route are described in a pamphlet obtainable at the curio shop in the camp.

In addition to the delightful **Nsumo Pan picnic site** at the edge of the pan, picnic facilities are provided at **Kumasinga hide** (4,5 km south of Mantuma camp),

the **Enxwala Viewpoint** (near the controlled hunting area in the south), **Ediza** (near the eastern edge of the park), and at the reception area in Mantuma camp.

A variety of handicrafts such as mats, woodcarvings and carved household items can be bought at the **Kwajobe cultural village** close to Mantuma camp.

The Kwajobe people, descendants of the Amatonga, lived in the area until 1947 when they were resettled outside the reserve. In 1992 a cultural zone including the sacred burial site of the Jobe chiefs was set aside in the northeastern part of the reserve. The village, comprising several beehive huts and a kraal, commemorates the burial site.

WALKS AND TRAILS

NSUMO PAN: A highlight of a visit to Mkuzi is the **Fig Forest Walk** of just over 3 km in the southeastern corner of the park. This easy ramble starts at the picnic site east of Nsumo Pan and, after crossing the Mkuze River via a suspension bridge, meanders through the forest dominated by fever trees and sycamore figs. Birds likely to be spotted include green coucal, broadbilled roller, white-eared barbet, fantailed and paradise flycatchers, and forest weavers.

MANTUMA CAMP: An early morning birding walk from Mantuma can be rewarding. The 8-km walk first winds through the riverine

forests of the Mkuze River and then meanders to a viewpoint overlooking the Nhlonhlela Pan before returning to the rest camp.

Guided early morning and afternoon walks are conducted for those who are primarily interested in viewing game on foot.

ENXWALA WILDERNESS ZONE: Visitors with time could join a **Bushveld Trail.** Guided game walks and drives are undertaken from the camp where trailists are accommodated for three nights.

The yellowbilled hornbill is a raucous bird.

MKUZI GAME RESERVE AT A GLANCE

MAIN ATTRACTIONS
Game- and bird-viewing hides, bird-watching, self-guided auto trail, Fig Forest Walk, guided walks and wilderness trails, night drives.

BEST TIMES TO VISIT
The dry winter (June to October) is generally best for game-viewing and water birds on Nsumo Pan. Summer temperatures are high with thunderstorms in the afternoon.

PERMITS/BOOKINGS
Entry permits obtainable at gate. **Mkuzi Bushveld Trails:** Natal Parks Board Reservations, PO Box 1750, Pietermaritzburg 3200; tel. (0331) 47-1981, fax. 47-1980. **Game and birding walks, night drives:** Book at Mantuma camp office.

OPENING TIMES
Emshopi entrance gate: 1 October to 31 March 05h00–19h00; 1 April to 30 September 06h00–18h00. **Mkuzi Bushveld Trails:** March to November.

ACCOMMODATION
Mantuma Hutted Camp: Six 3-bed rest huts with communal ablutions; five 5-bed and four 3-bed bungalows with own bathroom. Two 7-bed self-contained cottages with refrigerator. Meals prepared by cook. **Tented Camp (adjacent to Mantuma):** Six 2-bed and two 4-bed tents with en suite shower, hand basin and toilet, fridge, crockery and

linen. Contact Natal Parks Board Reservations (*see* below). **Nhlonhlela Bush Lodge:** Four 2-bed rustic huts with en suite facilities, communal lounge and kitchen. Meals prepared by cook. Game guard available for guided walks. Contact Natal Parks Board Reservations (*see* below). **Umkumbi Bush Camp:** Four 2-bed safari tents with en suite shower, hand basin and toilet. Meals prepared by cook. Game guard available for guided walks. Contact Natal Parks Board Reservations (*see* below). Umkumbi is a hunting camp and is only available for general accommodation from October to March. **Open camp sites** (for a maximum of 60 people) with hot/cold-water ablutions at entrance gate. Reservations for camp sites to be addressed to the Camp Superintendent, Private Bag X550, Mkuze 3965; tel. (035) 573-0003; fax. 57-0080.

FACILITIES
Mantuma Camp: Limited groceries, curios, swimming pool. Petrol at entrance gate. Picnic sites throughout the reserve with braai facilities; toilets at Nsumo Pan and Mantuma Camp.

ENQUIRIES
Natal Parks Board Reservations, PO Box 1750, Pietermaritzburg 3200; tel. (0331) 47-1981, fax 47-1980; **general enquiries,** tel. (0331) 47-1891, fax. 47-1037.

Blue wildebeest and Burchell's zebra around a water hole.

35 COASTAL MAPUTALAND

The combination of lakes, marshes, secluded beaches and coral reefs in South Africa's northeastern corner is an incomparable tropical paradise. Coastal Maputaland is a region of breathtaking scenery, and the habitat of the rare palmnut vulture, the Kosi palm, unique mangrove swamps and a myriad water birds. The fascinating Maputaland region encompasses the vast coastal plain stretching from just south of the Mfolozi River northwards to Mozambique and inland to the Ubombo and Lebombo Mountains.

➡ How to get there
Access to the region is via Jozini, a frontier town which is perched on the summit of the Ubombo Mountains. From Johannesburg and Durban follow the N2 to the signposted turnoff, about 11 km north of the Mkuze village turnoff. From here the road winds east, ascending the western slopes of the Ubombo Mountains, to reach the top of the spectacular pass 10 km beyond the turn-off. Jozini is 9 km further on.

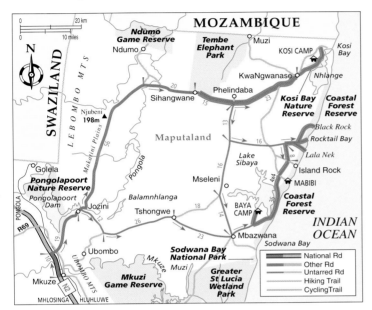

➡ *En route to Jozini from the N2, 11 km north of Mkuze village the road winds east and the Pongolapoort Nature Reserve is signposted to the left.*

PONGOLAPOORT NATURE RESERVE

Covering 11 693 ha, this nature reserve encompasses the Pongolapoort Dam and surroundings. **Angling** is one of the main attractions of this scenic nature reserve, which is overlooked by the Lebombo Mountains to the north and the Ubombo Mountains to the south. The dam is the habitat of several species of fish, including sharptooth catfish, Mozambique tilapia and tigerfish.

The grassland savanna, acacia scrub and the dam attract a large variety of **birds**. Among the more than 225 species recorded to date are several species of duck, pink-backed pelican, osprey, secretary-bird, lilacbreasted roller, African fish eagle and Rudd's apalis.

The reserve is open to day visitors and there are no facilities.

➡ *Lake Sibaya is just inland, north of Sodwana Bay. From Jozini follow the Sodwana Bay signs to Mbazwana for 59 km. Bear left onto the signposted road to Baya Camp on the eastern outskirts of Mbazwana; continue for 19 km and turn left to reach Baya Camp after 7 km.*

LAKE SIBAYA

Covering 7 750 ha, Sibaya is the country's largest freshwater lake. It is home to a healthy **hippo** population, an estimated 150 **crocodiles**, 18 **fish species** and a wide variety of **birds**. The surrounding lush coastal dune forests harbour vervet and samango monkeys, thicktailed bushbaby, common and red duiker, bushpig and red squirrels.

With a birding checklist approaching the 300 mark, bird-watching is certainly rewarding.

Beautiful and pristine Kosi Bay, a unique wetland system, affords fishermen ample opportunities to catch a variety of fish.

The two hides near Baya Camp provide excellent opportunities for the keen birder.

Among the many water birds to be seen are whitebreasted and reed cormorants, Goliath, squacco and greenbacked herons, whitefaced duck, pygmy goose, African fish eagle, terns and kingfishers. The forests and forest fringes support crested guineafowl, purplecrested lourie and broadbilled roller, as well as trumpeter and crowned hornbills.

Not to be missed is a boat trip on the lake. These trips not only afford close-up views of hippo,

The cry of the trumpeter hornbill is common in coastal dune forests.

but are also extremely rewarding for birders. The lake is out of bounds to private boats, but anglers can hire boats with a coxswain. Although sizeable catfish are caught, the tilapia rarely exceed 1,5 kg in weight as a result of the low nutrient levels in the lake, so angling has a limited appeal.

Baya Camp is an ideal base for day visits to **Nine Mile Beach**, a well-known angling and picnicking spot on the coast. The sandy track can only be negotiated in four-wheel-drive vehicles or vehicles with a high ground clearance.

➡ *Rocktail Bay is 480 km from Durban and 630 km from Johannesburg. From Jozini drive across the Pongolapoort Dam wall and continue north for 40,6 km. Turn right and continue eastwards for 46 km (passing the turnoff to Ndumo Game Reserve and Tembe Elephant Park – see p. 157) to Phelindaba. Turn right and travel south for 16 km and then turn left, continuing for 18,8 km. For Mabibi Coastal Camp continue straight for another 13 km, but, if you are headed for Rocktail Bay, Lala Nek or Black Rock, turn left and immediately right to reach the Manzengwenya gate 7,5 km on. A 4x4 is essential from here, but guests of Rocktail Bay Lodge travelling in*

The malachite kingfisher, one of Maputaland's many kingfishers.

sedan cars are transferred from here by the lodge. The turnoff to Lala Nek is signposted 6,2 km beyond the gate and the Black Rock turnoff just before Rocktail Bay Lodge, 12 km from the gate.

COASTAL FOREST RESERVE

Stretching north from Sodwana Bay to the Mozambican border, the Coastal Forest Reserve lies parallel to the Maputaland Marine Reserve. The reserve covers over 32 700 ha of grass-covered dunes interspersed with water berry trees and graceful lala palms, and magnificent dune forests of coastal red milkwood, Natal wild banana, Lowveld mangosteen and Natal mahogany. Wildlife is not abundant, but includes thicktailed bushbaby, vervet and samango monkeys, bushpig, blue and red duiker, oribi and reedbuck. Well over 200 bird species have been recorded in the reserve. Among them are crested guineafowl, purplecrested lourie, trumpeter and crowned hornbills, yellowspotted nicator and Woodward's batis. There are several scenic coastal spots such as Rocktail Bay and Black Rock (see below) in the reserve, which is open only to day visitors, except to guests of Rocktail Bay Lodge and those camping at Mabibi. Tucked away in dense coastal dune forests, the **Mabibi Camp** is a few minutes' walk from the beach. Although Mabibi is out of bounds for ski boats it is popular with rock and surf anglers (no permits are

necessary); the rock pools with their bewildering array of marine life are ideal for snorkelling.

➡ See *directions to the Coastal Forest Reserve above.*

ROCKTAIL BAY

Midway between Kosi Bay and Sodwana Bay lies the coastal paradise of Rocktail Bay. Flanked on either side by miles and miles of unspoilt beaches, it is not only a haven of peace and tranquillity, but also one of South Africa's top angling spots. Sought-after species include kingfish, shad and barracuda. The reefs at Rocktail Bay and nearby Lala Nek are ideal for snorkelling.

Rocktail Bay Lodge nestles behind the dunes at Rocktail Bay and blends in extremely well with the coastal dune forests. Rock and surf angling, salt-water flyfishing and snorkelling are offered to guests, and tours for day visitors can be arranged to Black Rock (*see* below), Lala Nek, Lake Sibaya and Hippo Pools. Lala Nek owes its name to the profusion of lala palms growing in the area. It is a popular angling spot and the reef which comes close inshore offers excellent snorkelling opportunities. Between November and the end of February turtle tours are conducted at night from the lodge (*see* box, p. 149). The lodge was one of the first joint venture projects between the KwaZulu conservation authorities and a private company, and a percentage of the income is channelled to the local tribal authorities.

➡ *Another popular spot along this section of the coast is Black Rock. Follow the directions for Rocktail Bay (above) and turn north about 500 m before reaching the lodge, continuing for 8 km. A four-wheel-drive vehicle is essential.*

BLACK ROCK

Snorkelling and rock angling are the main attractions of this prominent landmark which also offers the chance of catching deep-water species such as wahoo and sailfish from the shore.

Black Rock is also home to the endemic Bouton's skink (*Cryptoblepharus boutonii*). Although widespread along the

---

KOSI PALMS AND PALMNUT VULTURES

The Kosi palms found at Lake Amanzimnyama and the scattered groups near Manguzi are the only populations occurring naturally in South Africa. Another grove occurring further south at Mtunzini near Richards Bay was established at the turn of the century from seed obtained at Kosi Bay. Elsewhere in southern Africa they occur naturally only along the coast of southern Mozambique.

Known by names such as the giant, raphia and raffia palm, it is one of seven species of the palm family occurring naturally in southern Africa. It grows to a height of 10 m, but its most impressive feature is its enormous leaves which, at up to 10 m in length, are the largest in the

plant kingdom. An interesting feature of these palms is that they reach maturity after 20 to 30 years, set fruit and then begin to die slowly. The reddish-brown fruit is about 9 cm long and as many as 10 000 fruits are produced.

The palms provide nesting sites to one of South Africa's rarest breeding birds, the palmnut vulture. Since the breeding and feeding habits of these birds are closely associated with oil palms, the only breeding sites in South Africa are at Kosi Bay and Mtunzini.

While the fleshy outer covering of the fruit forms an important part of the palmnut vulture's diet, much of its time is spent foraging for fish, while crabs, molluscs and carrion are also eaten.

To the left high dunes separate Kosi Bay from the sea. To the right the 18-km Kosi Lake system extends to form a chain of lakes and waterways.

East African coast and Indian Ocean islands, the skinks at Black Rock represent an isolated population which is separated from the nearest population on the Mozambican coast by 550 km. The Black Rock population numbers only about 130 and is considered vulnerable.

➡ *Kosi Bay lies a mere 2 km from the Mozambique border and can be accessed through Jozini, Sihangwane and KwaNgwanase. From here follow the signposted road to Kosi Bay for 6,5 km and then turn right, continuing for about 4,8 km where the track splits off to the left to Kosi Mouth. Do not take the left turn but continue straight ahead for 1 km to the entrance gate of Kosi Bay Nature Reserve. Kosi Camp, on the shores of Lake Nhlange, is a short way on.*

KOSI BAY NATURE RESERVE

To protect the unique tract of land in the northeastern corner of KwaZulu-Natal, an area of 10 961 ha has been set aside as the Kosi Bay Nature Reserve. The 8 000-ha Kosi System (mouth, estuary and lakes) is a mosaic of swamp forests, unique mangroves, lakes and marshes. Home to several rare and endangered animals and plants, it is considered South Africa's best-preserved large estuary system.

Despite its name, Kosi is not a bay, but an estuary at the northern end of a series of four interconnected lakes stretching south from the Mozambican border for 18 km. The lakes are, from north to south, Makhawulani, Mpungwini, Nhlange, and Amanzimnyama.

The mangrove swamp near the estuary mouth is unique – it is the only community in South Africa with five mangrove species. Two of these, the Indian and Tonga mangroves, reach the southern limit of their distribution here.

The lakes and the estuary provide an ideal habitat to a variety of fish and nine freshwater species are known to occur, while over 160 marine species have been recorded in the Kosi Bay estuary. Light tackle angling is, therefore, not surprisingly one of the main attractions of this scenic region and common catches include spotted grunter, stumpnose and various kingfishes.

Boat trips lasting about two hours can be arranged from Kosi Camp, providing visitors with an opportunity to discover the many facets of the lake system.

The white mangrove's roots protude from the mud flats at low tide.

Fish traps have been used in the Kosi lake system for over 500 years.

Kosi Mouth is a pleasant day trip from Kosi Camp but, because of the sandy nature of the track, the 35-km round trip can be undertaken by four-wheel-drive vehicles only. No more than five vehicles are allowed at the mouth per day, and, due to the remoteness of the camp, it is not possible to make advance reservations. Surf angling is popular, and the mouth is considered one of the best snorkelling spots along the South African coastline.

A camp site has been established at the entrance gate to Kosi Mouth by the local community. Guides can be hired to take visitors to the mouth and the fishing kraals on foot.

WALKS AND TRAILS

LAKE SIBAYA: To enable visitors to explore their enchanting surroundings at Lake Sibaya, the 3,4-km-long **Baya Camp** **Trail** has been laid out in the coastal forests behind the camp. The trail winds up to a viewing tower which overlooks the lake and then meanders through the forest, passing the bird-watching hides, before winding its way back to the camp.

KOSI BAY: One of the best ways of exploring the many fascinating features of Kosi Bay's unique environment is to undertake the four-day **Kosi Bay Hiking Trail**. This trail covers 34 km and encircles the four lakes comprising the system. Guided day walks can be undertaken to Lake Amanzimnyama, Kosi Mouth, the Mtando Channel between Mpungwini and Nhlange lakes and Lake Makhawulani with its traditional fish traps. These ingenious traps consist of wooden and reed fences designed to guide the fish towards funnel-shaped baskets.

COASTAL MAPUTALAND AT A GLANCE

MAIN ATTRACTIONS
Unique lake system, rare and endangered plant and animal species, coral reefs, guided walks, bird-watching, angling, turtle nesting tours.

BEST TIMES TO VISIT
The summer months are best for angling for kingfish, while the winter is the main season for shad and barracuda fishing. The conditions for snorkelling are generally most favourable during the months of April and May.

LAKE SIBAYA
Permits/bookings: Baya Camp boat trips and permits for Nine Mile Beach: Book at camp office.
Opening times: **Entrance gates:** 1 October to 31 March 05h00–19h00 and 1 April to 30 September 06h00–18h00.
Accommodation: **Baya Camp (Lake Sibaya):** Three 4-bed and four 2-bed reed huts with cold-water hand basin. Meals prepared by cook. Communal ablutions with hot/cold water. Contact Central Reservations, Department of Nature Conservation (*see* below).
Facilities: Visitors must be self-sufficient.

COASTAL FOREST RESERVE (MABIBI, ROCKTAIL BAY, BLACK ROCK)
Permits/bookings: **Permits to drive from Sodwana to Mabibi along the coast:** Visitors must obtain permits at the entrance gate to the beach at Sodwana at 16h00 on the day prior to the journey. Only 20 permits are issued per day. **Permits for Rocktail Bay, Black Rock and Lala Nek:** Obtainable at Manzengwenya entrance gate. Only 10 permits are issued for each area per day.
Opening times: **Entrance gates:** 1 October to 31 March 05h00–19h00 and 1 April to 30 September 06h00–18h00.
Rocktail Bay Lodge turtle

tours: Conducted between November and February, weather and tides permitting.
Accommodation: **Mabibi:** Ten camp sites with communal hot/cold water ablutions. Contact Central Reservations, Department of Nature Conservation (*see* below). **Rocktail Bay Lodge:** Ten 2-bed wooden chalets with private bathroom, dining area for camp, swimming pool. Contact Wilderness Safaris, PO Box 651171, Benmore 2010; tel. (011) 884-1458, fax. 883-6255.
Facilities: Visitors to Mabibi must be self-sufficient.

KOSI BAY
Permits/bookings: **Kosi Bay Hiking Trail:** Central Reservations, Department of Nature Conservation (*see* below). **Kosi Bay guided walks and boat trips:** Book at the camp office. **Kosi Mouth:** Permits obtainable at Kosi Bay office. Only five permits are issued per day.
Opening times: **Entrance gates:** 1 October to 31 March 05h00–19h00; 1 April to 30 September 06h00–18h00.
Accommodation: **Kosi Bay:** Three thatched lodges accommodating two, five and six people respectively; 15 camp sites with communal hot/cold-water ablutions, electric points. Contact Central Reservations, Department of Nature Conservation KwaZulu-Natal (*see* below).
Facilities: Visitors must be self-sufficient.

Enquiries: **Central Reservations, Department of Nature Conservation KwaZulu-Natal,** Private Bag X9024, Pietermaritzburg 3200; tel. (0331) 94-6696, fax. 42-1948.

TOURIST INFORMATION Zululand Joint Services Board, Private Bag X1025, Richards Bay 3900; tel. (0351) 4-1404, fax. 4-1409.

36 NORTHERN MAPUTALAND

The vast coastal plains of northern Maputaland are a mosaic of dense thickets, floodplains and sand forests. Rising up to 550 m above these plains, the Lebombo Mountains form a natural boundary to the west; in the Ndumo Game Reserve the Usutu and the Pongolo rivers seasonally spill over into a series of spectacular pans. The variety of habitats supports a rich diversity of animals, birds and plants, among them several subtropical species which reach the southern limit of their distribution here.

How to get there
Mkuze village, 350 km north of Durban and 505 km from Johannesburg on the N2, is a convenient starting point for this tour. Access is through Jozini (*see* Tour 35, p. 153).

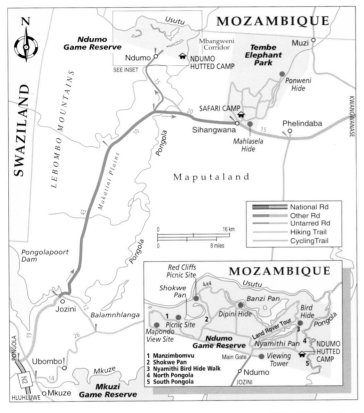

➡ *Ndumo Game Reserve is in northern Maputaland, 420 km from Durban and 575 km from Johannesburg. From Jozini, cross the dam wall; continue north for 40,5 km and turn right at the T-junction, continuing for 11 km to a veterinary control gate. Turn right just under 1 km further on and left again after 5 km. Continue for almost 11 km to Ndumo village, where you bear left to reach the park's entrance gate 800 m on.*

NDUMO GAME RESERVE

Bounded by the foothills of the Lebombo Mountains in the west and the Usutu River in the north, the 10 100-ha Ndumo Game Reserve is situated on a low-lying, flat coastal plain which extends southwards from Mozambique.

The park is characterised by richly diverse **vegetation** types, from the dense Mahemane bush to floodplain grasslands and riverine forests dominated by enormous sycamore fig trees.

Especially striking are the fever trees lining the pans – a favourite subject of photographers.

The park was established as a sanctuary for the dwindling **hippo** population. With numbers in excess of 300, Ndumo is now one of the few areas in South Africa with a large hippo population. Ndumo also boasts a large population of crocodiles; about 700 with a body length of more than 2 m inhabit the pans and rivers.

The park probably has South Africa's highest density of the pretty nyala antelope. Large numbers of red duiker also occur. Other **game** include black and white rhino, giraffe, Burchell's zebra, reedbuck, impala, suni and common duiker. Although buffalo occur, they are seen only occasionally, since they tend to favour the floodplains.

There are no lions in Ndumo and only a few leopard (the only records are from spoor), so the spotted hyena is the most prominent predator in the park.

There are about 47 km of roads in the western section of the park for game-viewing drives. The road network also provides access to the **Mapondo viewpoint**, on one of the few hills in the park, and the **Dipini hide** which overlooks a waterhole near the western end of Banzi Pan.

Picnicking is permitted at the site of the old Native Recruitment Centre in the west of the park and at Red Cliffs (magnificent views over the Usutu River and Mozambique). Facilities include braai places, cement tables and toilets.

Access to the eastern section is strictly controlled– it can be visited only in the company of a game guard. A **Land Rover tour** follows the road along the unspoilt southern edge of Nyamithi Pan, renowned for its breathtaking

Nyala ewe and foals. These beautiful antelope are common in Northern Maputaland.

Nyamithi Pan, fringed by distinctive green-barked fever trees, abounds in hippo, crocodile and birdlife.

Nile crocodile occur naturally in the east and northeast of South Africa.

scenery. The fever trees along the edge of the pan are especially striking in the winter months. Guided tours to Banzi and Shokwe pans can also be arranged.

Visitors can also explore the park from the luxurious, but environmentally aware **Ndumo Wilderness Camp**, situated in a section of the park which is closed to the public. Guests are met at the park's entrance gate. Situated on the banks of Banzi Pan, Ndumo Wilderness Camp is a haven of peace and tranquillity. The entire camp is elevated and from the deck of the lounge overlooking

the lily-covered pan visitors can see a wide variety of birds and crocodiles basking on the banks.

Like its sister camp, Rocktail Bay Lodge, a percentage of the lease fee is channelled to the local Thonga community.

The lodge offers one of the finest wilderness experiences in South Africa and among the activities offered are bird-watching, game-viewing drives, scenic drives to Nyamithi Pan and bush walks. All these activities are conducted by well-informed guides.

➡ *Tembe is 416 km from Durban and 570 km from Johannesburg. From Jozini follow the directions to the Ndumo Game Reserve turnoff, but continue on the tar road towards Sihangwana for 19 km and turn left into the park. The safari camp is 2 km from the gate.*

TEMBE ELEPHANT PARK

A 5,5-km-wide strip of land, the Mbangweni Corridor, separates the 30 000-ha Tembe Elephant Park from the Ndumo Game Reserve; its northern boundary follows the border between South Africa and Mozambique. The two parks have been administered as a unit since 1989 with a view to eventual consolidation.

Tembe's major drawcard is its elephants which, with the exception of the small relic population of Knysna elephants in the southern Cape (*see* p. 94), were as recently as 1989 the last free-ranging elephants in South Africa. These were originally part of a much larger population of about 400 which used to migrate periodically into the area from southern Mozambique. When the park was proclaimed in 1983, the western, eastern and southern boundaries were fenced to stop them roaming onto the adjoining tribal lands, but the northern boundary was left unfenced to keep open their century-old migration route. As a result of poaching during the civil war in Mozambique, their numbers declined to an estimated 120 by 1989, when it was decided that the northern boundary should be fenced off as well.

The visibility of the elephants is, of course, hampered by the dense vegetation, and any sightings should be regarded as a

---

NDUMO: BIRDER'S PARADISE

Notwithstanding its small size, Ndumo is a bird-watcher's paradise. With an impressive bird list of some 420 species the park is undeniably one of the country's top birding spots, and is home to 85% of the birds of Maputaland. At least 17 of the 21 bird species which reach the southern limit of their distribution in Maputaland have been recorded in Ndumo. Among these are greyhooded kingfisher, yellowspotted nicator, Stierling's

barred warbler, Woodward's batis and the purplebanded sunbird. Ndumo is also one of only two breeding sites of the openbilled stork in South Africa. Birders will find a visit to the Natal Bird Club hide near the northeastern corner of Nyamithi Pan rewarding. The hide is alongside a small reed-fringed pan which does not form part of Nyamithi and is only accessible to participants on the Nyamithi Bird Hide Walk.

The openbilled stork, one of 420 bird species at Ndumo.

bonus. Because these elephants are unpredictable, visitors are not allowed to explore the park unaccompanied or to alight from their vehicles except at the safari camp, the hides and the picnic site. Each party is accompanied, in their own vehicle, by a guide who is well acquainted with the behaviour of the elephants and whose instructions should be heeded at all times.

Tembe's vast sand forests provide sanctuary for the elusive suni antelope, which is restricted to this habitat. White and black rhino, giraffe, waterbuck, blue wildebeest, reedbuck, nyala, impala, common and red duiker, and warthog also occur here.

Tembe lies within the transitional zone between tropical and sub-tropical species; many visitors are totally unaware of the variety of plants occurring in Maputaland and nowhere else in South Africa. Among these are the pod mahogany with its distinctive large dark-brown pods, the Zulu milkberry and the sand onionwood.

Tembe also provides protection to South Africa's largest tract of **sand forest**. Characteristic species which grow on the slopes and crests of old sand-dunes include the Lebombo wattle, Zulu podberry and false tamboti.

The northern section of the park is administered as a wilderness area. Game-viewing is limited to the southern half which is criss-crossed by an 80-km network of sandy tracks. The tracks wind through various vegetation types, past seasonally inundated pans and to two **game-viewing hides – Mahlasela** which overlooks the Mahlasela Pan and **Ponweni** overlooking the Muzi Swamp. There is also a picnic site with braai facilities at the southern edge of the wilderness area, about 14 km north of the camp.

Birding can be rewarding and Tembe is one of the best places to spot Rudd's apalis, Woodward's batis, Neergaard's sunbird, pink-throated twinspot and lemon-breasted canary.

WALKS AND TRAILS

NDUMO: One of the best ways of experiencing Ndumo's bushveld atmosphere is on an **early morning or afternoon walk**, accompanied by a game guard. Three are conducted in the eastern section of the park, and two in the western section. Walks last about two hours and, depending on their interests, visitors can choose a walk which offers good opportunities for birding, game-viewing or tree identification.

TEMBE: To enable visitors to explore Tembe's unique sand forests on foot, 2 km² of the Ngobozana area near the gate has been enclosed with an elephant-proof fence. Two **self-guided sand forest trails** wind through the forest and visitors can either do a 2,2-km route, or extend it to a 3,5-km walk. In addition to tree identification, a suni or red duiker could also be spotted.

The tiny and secretive suni antelope.

Until 1989 Tembe's elephants migrated into the park from Mozambique.

37 GOLDEN GATE HIGHLANDS NP

Nestled in the foothills of the Maluti Mountains, Golden Gate is renowned for its towering sandstone cliffs, waving grasslands dotted with colourful flowers in summer, herds of game typical of the highlands, and inviting walks. It is a photographer's paradise and a favourite subject for artists.

How to get there
The Golden Gate Highlands National Park is situated in the northeastern Free State, about 300 km from Bloemfontein and 320 km from Johannesburg. Access via the western entrance is through Bethlehem, and from the east from Harrismith. At Bethlehem take the N5 towards Kestell for 8 km and turn right onto the R711 to reach Clarens after 30 km. From Clarens follow the signposted road eastwards for 20 km to Brandwag Rest Camp and continue 1 km further to Glen Reenen Rest Camp. From Harrismith, follow the N5 towards Kestell for 6,5 km and then turn left onto the R74/R712, continuing along the R712 for 30 km. Glen Reenen Rest Camp is 29 km further along the road to Clarens and Brandwag is 1 km on.

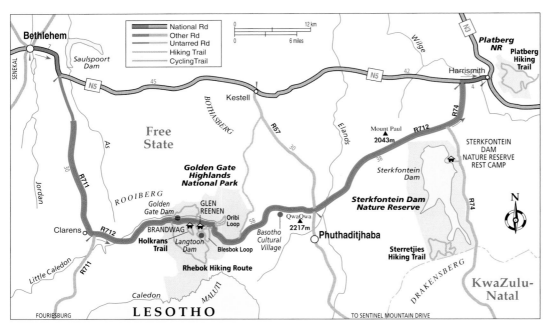

Golden Gate is best known for its dramatic sandstone rock formations with descriptive names such as the Sentinel, Mushroom Rocks, Echo Ravine and the two portals after which the park was named.

The **geological history** of the park dates back some 200 million years when alternating layers of course sandstone, shale and mudstone were laid down. Overlying these sedimentary layers, known as the Molteno Formation, are layers of red and purple mudstone, shale, sandstone and silt, comprising the 180-million-year-old Elliot Formation.

About 170 million years ago the climate became increasingly drier, and fine, wind-blown sand accumulated over the Elliot Formation to form the Clarens Sandstone Formation which is so characteristic of the northeastern Free State, the Little 'Berg and the Eastern Cape.

The next chapter in Golden Gate's long geological history started about 160 million years ago when pressures within the earth's crust caused molten magma to intrude sills and dykes in the sedimentary layers and the lavas of the overlying Drakensberg Formation. Vast flows of lava spread over much of southern Africa, in some places up to 1 300 m high, and subsequently cooled down to form basalt, capping the high mountain peaks. This is clearly visible on the Platberg (see p. 162).

Over the last 130 million years the forces of nature – wind, water and extremes of temperature – have formed the spectacular Drakensberg and Malutis.

Herds of blesbok, black wildebeest, Burchell's zebra and eland graze on the mountain slopes, and springbok occur on the more level areas. The high mountain plateaux are the favoured habitat of family groups of grey rhebok, and in the short grassland areas look out for oribi, a species classified as vulnerable.

In common with other high mountain areas, **birdlife** is not abundant. However, some 150 species have been recorded, two of them noteworthy: the bald ibis and the bearded vulture (see p. 129). There are four breeding colonies of the rare bald ibis in the park, as well as a resident pair of bearded vultures. These spectacular birds of prey may be seen in the eastern part of the park, as well as Cape vulture, black eagle, jackal buzzard and lanner falcon at the vulture restaurant.

The two dams in the park, Langtoon and Golden Gate, attract a variety of water birds and the hide at the Golden Gate Dam is well positioned for ticking species such as whitebreasted cormorant, blackheaded heron, Egyptian goose, moorhen and redknobbed coot.

FOSSILS OF GOLDEN GATE

Within the upper part of the Elliot Formation and the lower part of the Clarens Formation in Golden Gate the remains of several prehistoric animals have been encased. One of the most exciting discoveries was made in 1978 when a clutch of six dinosaur eggs was discovered during road building operations in the Rooidraai area – the first such discovery of the Upper Triassic Age (220 to 195 million years ago).

Further discoveries of fossil eggs were made in 1984 and 1988 and research has shown that the eggs of the Massospondylus dinosaur represent a transition between reptiles and birds.

Other fossils discovered in the park include parts of a crocodile-like dinosaur, two specimens of a small thecodont (animals with their teeth set firmly in their jaw) and advanced cynodonts (dog-toothed animals).

Typical montane species to be seen include the sentinel rock thrush, orangebreasted rockjumper and rock pipit, while yellowthroated longclaw occur in the short grasslands.

Picnicking is popular with day visitors passing through the park, and the 10-m-long rock slab over which the water from Langtoon Dam cascades into a natural rock pool at Glen Reenen is irresistible in summer.

There are two game-viewing drives – the 4,5-km **Oribi Loop** in the eastern part of the park and the 7-km **Blesbok Route** which winds along the lower slopes of Generaalskop. **Guided night drives** are conducted in the game-viewing areas from Brandwag Rest Camp, and participants may well see some of the nocturnal animals which occur in the park.

➡ From the Golden Gate Highlands National Park a scenic drive can be undertaken by following the R712 to Harrismith, where you can link up with Tour 30 to the Royal Natal National Park (see p. 132) and the Sentinel Route (see p. 134).

GOLDEN MOUNTAIN SCENIC DRIVE

From the Golden Gate Highlands National Park, the R712 meanders eastwards along a route which reveals the full splendour of the northeastern Free State – towering yellow sandstone cliffs, valleys and grass-covered mountain slopes and hills.

Twenty kilometres from Brandwag Rest Camp is the **Basotho Cultural Village**, which portrays the history, culture and lifestyle

Sentinel Rock with its impressive sandstone cliffs is one of the best-known formations in the park.

The Basotho Cultural Village near Brandwag Rest Camp.

of the South Sotho people of the area. Visitors are taken on a guided tour of the complex which consists of traditional huts in the different building styles used from the 16th century onwards.

The scenery to the south is dominated by **Mount Qwa-Qwa** (meaning 'white white'), an isolated table-top sandstone mountain rising above the grasslands, with the majestic Maluti Mountains forming an impressive backdrop. The steep cliffs capping the massif are home to one of the Free State's few breeding colonies

of the Cape vulture. Over the years the cliffs have been 'painted' white by their droppings.

The turnoff to Phuthaditjhaba (also to the Sentinel Mountain Drive, a spectacular diversion) is 30 km beyond Brandwag Rest Camp. After a further 26,5 km you pass the earth wall of the 6 900-ha **Sterkfontein Dam** (part of the Tugela-Vaal Water Scheme). The dam is popular for watersports and fresh-water angling. The more adventurous can set off on a two-day hiking trail (*see* Walks and Trails, p. 162) in

the **Sterkfontein Dam Nature Reserve** around the dam. To reach the camp on the eastern shores of the dam, turn right onto the R74 and continue for nearly 8 km to the signposted turnoff.

The **vegetation** of the almost 18 000-ha reserve is dominated by mountain grassveld interspersed with patches of proteas. In spring the grassveld is transformed into a blaze of colour by the scarlet flowers of the Natal bottlebrush, a species growing among the sandstone cliffs, and by many other flowering plants.

Mammals in the reserve are typical of the mountain grassveld and include mountain reedbuck, grey rhebok, common duiker, steenbok and baboon.

From the junction of the R74 with the R712, continue north for 9 km and turn right onto the N5 to reach Harrismith after a further 6,5 km. Towering approximately 660 m above the town is the conspicuous Platberg which has been proclaimed a nature reserve. The 7 000-ha **Platberg Nature Reserve** generally has no fewer than 1 500 head of game, including Burchell's zebra, black and blue wildebeest, red hartebeest, fallow deer, springbok, eland, waterbuck, blesbok, duiker, mountain rhebok, grey rhebok, ostrich, baboon, caracal and white-backed jackal.

Among the 120-odd **bird species** recorded in the reserve are black and longcrested eagles, black sparrowhawk, jackal buzzard, secretarybird, forktailed drongo and the Cape robin. The reserve is traversed by a circular hiking trail, renowned for its magnificent views (*see* Walks and Trails below). There is also is a trout dam in the reserve.

Also worth a visit is the **Platberg Wild Flower Reserve**, adjacent to the reserve at the foot of the sandstone massif. Over 1 000 plants and tree species typical of the Drakensberg can be viewed in their natural surroundings and in cultivated sections of the 114-ha garden. Two water storage dams, dating back to the turn of the century, form a focal feature of the garden. Nearby is a blockhouse (now a National Monument) built by the British troops to protect the town's water supply during the Anglo-Boer War of 1899-1902.

WALKS AND TRAILS
GOLDEN GATE HIGHLANDS NATIONAL PARK: Several short walks have been laid out in the vicinity of Glen Reenen and Brandwag rest camps. An overnight trail is available for the more energetic.

One of the most popular walks is the **Holkrans Trail**, a 45-minute circular route along the base of the sandstone cliffs behind Brandwag Rest Camp. The route is characterised by several almost circular caves eroded into the sandstone and, at some of these, wooden ladders have been placed, enabling visitors to potter around the caves.

The footbridge over the Little Caledon River at Glen Reenen Rest Camp is the starting point of several walks ranging from 45 minutes to four hours. A particularly popular walk is to the top of the **Sentinel** with its expansive view over the Little Caledon Valley, while other routes wind to **Boskloof**, **Echo Ravine**, the **Glen Reenen Viewpoint** and the spectacular **Mushroom Rocks**. Trailists on the walk to **Wodehouse Peak** are rewarded with a bird's-eye view of the surrounding countryside, but be warned – it is an exhausting climb, of four to five hours!

Not to be missed is a guided walk to the **Cathedral Cave**, considered one of the best examples of sandstone erosion in South Africa. Here a tributary of the Little Caledon River plunges 60 m over the lip of a dome-shaped roof and then flows through a narrow gorge carved through the sandstone rocks. Since a colony of bald ibis breeds here, walks are not conducted between April and September.

Trailists setting off on the **Rhebok Hiking Trail** follow a 30-km route past spectacular rock formations, along grassy mountain slopes, a delightful waterfall and high mountain peaks. About 13 km are covered on the first day, while more than 700 m is gained in altitude to Generaalskop on the second day's hike of 17 km.

STERKFONTEIN DAM NATURE RESERVE: The **Sterretjies Hiking Trail** (southwestern corner of the reserve) takes its name from the sterretjie (*Hypoxis*), which produces yellow star-like flowers in spring and summer. Covering 25,5 km, the circular trail winds across grassveld, past waterfalls and sandstone cliffs, through forested kloofs and along the shores of the dam.

PLATBERG NATURE RESERVE: The circular **Platberg Hiking Trail** covers 20 km over two

The northeastern Free State is a panorama of colour and beauty, a combination of sandstone cliffs, valleys, grassy plains and distant mountains.

days. The hike ascends Platberg, rewarding hikers with splendid views of Sterkfontein Dam, the Drakensberg and the Malutis. Hikers pass spectacular sandstone cliffs on the slopes of Platberg, go through natural forests, along mountain streams and past Anglo-Boer War historical sites.

HORSE-RIDING

Another way of exploring the Golden Gate Highlands National Park is to join one of the horse trails conducted from the Gladstone stables near the western entrance to the park. Rides last for about

The Sterretjies Hiking Trail is named after this yellow flower.

an hour and leave the stables each morning and afternoon. Two-hour rides can be arranged.

ENVIRO COURSES

The park is renowned for its environmental education courses for youth groups and up to 60 groups are accommodated at Wilgenhof Hostel each year.

Courses last from one to five days and are aimed at creating an awareness of the importance of environmental conservation. Subjects covered range from geomorphology to grassland ecology and in addition to talks and slide shows on the environment, a variety of outdoor activities, including abseiling, are pursued.

At the annual National Youth Symposium, held at Golden Gate since 1981, the winners of regional environmental competitions held at primary and secondary school levels countrywide and in neighbouring Namibia present their projects to see who has made the biggest contribution to environmental conservation.

GOLDEN GATE HIGHLANDS NP AT A GLANCE

MAIN ATTRACTIONS
Spectacular mountain scenery, Cathedral Cave, vulture restaurant, walks and trails, horse trails, environmental courses for young people.

BEST TIMES TO VISIT
All year, but snow can fall on the surrounding mountains; thunderstorms are common in summer. The wild flowers are spectacular in spring and summer. The vulture restaurant is most rewarding in winter.

GOLDEN GATE HIGHLANDS
Permits/bookings: Obtainable on arrival. **Environmental courses:** Park Warden, Golden Gate Highlands National Park, Private Bag X3, Clarens 9797; tel. and fax. (058) 256-1471. **Vulture hide, night drives, walks to Cathedral Cave:** Book at Brandwag Rest Camp. **Horse-riding:** Book at Gladstone stables in the park. *Opening times:* Access road open 24 hours. *Accommodation:* If the park is full, there is a range of accommodation in nearby towns (see Tourist Information below). **Brandwag Rest Camp:** National Parks Board Reservations (see below). **Main building:** Seven single rooms with shower; 27 double rooms with 2 single beds or double beds, shower and toilet; one suite with double bed, bathroom, separate shower and toilet. All rooms with telephone and television. **Brandwag chalets:** Thirty-four 1-bedroom chalets with double bed, living room with two single beds, bathroom (with bath), kitchenette semi-equipped, braai places, telephone and television.

Wilgenhof Hostel: Four dormitories for groups accommodating up to 90. **Glen Reenen Rest Camp:** National Parks Board Reservations (see below). One house with 1 double and 4 single beds, fully equipped, telephone and television. Six rondavels with 1 double and 2 single beds, shower, semi-equipped. Seven 1-room rondavels with 2 single beds and a bunk bed, shower, semi-equipped. Camp sites with hot/cold-water ablutions, scullery and braai places. *Facilities:* **Brandwag:** Licenced restaurant, curio shop, coffee shop, ladies' bar, conference facilities, laundromat. **Glen Reenen:** Shop with groceries, perishables, firewood and liquor. Petrol is available. *Enquiries:* **National Parks Board Reservations,** PO Box 787, Pretoria 0001; tel. (012) 343-1991, fax. 343-0905; or PO Box 7400, Roggebaai 8012; tel. (021) 22-2810, fax. 24-6211.

BASOTHO CULTURAL VILLAGE
Permits/bookings: No advance bookings required. *Opening times:* Monday to Friday 09h00–16h00; weekends 09h00–17h00. *Accommodation:* None. *Facilities:* Tea room and curio shop. *Enquiries:* Private Bag X826, Witsieshoek 9870; tel. (058) 721-0300, fax. 721-0304.

STERKFONTEIN DAM NATURE RESERVE
Permits/bookings: Entry permits obtainable at gate. *Opening times:* **Office:** 07h30–16h00 all year. **Gates:** 06h00–22h00 all year.

Accommodation: **Rest camp:** Self-contained chalets sleeping 4, 6 and 8; camp/caravan sites with hot/cold-water ablutions in caravan park and along the dam shore. **Sterretjies Hiking Trail:** Camp site with water and toilet at start. Chief Conservator (see below). *Facilities:* Picnic sites with braai places and toilets. *Enquiries:* **Chief Nature Conservator,** PO Box 24, Harrismith 9880; tel. (05861) 2-3520, fax. 2-1772.

PLATBERG NATURE RESERVE & WILD FLOWER RESERVE
Permits/bookings: Entry permits at the gate. For trout fishing and to book for the trail, contact Harrismith Tourist Information (see below). *Opening times:* 07h00–18h00 in summer; 08h00–16h00 in winter (May–Sept). Nature reserve is closed during the week in hunting season (April–Sept). *Accommodation:* **Platberg Hiking Trail:** Overnight huts with bunks, mattresses, water, and gas stove **Wild Flower Reserve:** None. *Facilities:* **Nature Reserve:** Picnic lapa with braai places and toilets; other braai places. **Wild Flower Reserve:** Picnic sites with braai places and toilets. *Enquiries:* Harrismith Tourist Information (see below).

TOURIST INFORMATION
Highlands Tourism Association, PO Box 927, Ficksburg 9730; tel. (05192) 5447, fax. 5449. **Harrismith Tourist Information,** PO Box 43, Harrismith 9880; tel. (05861) 2-3525, fax. 3-0923.

LOWVELD AND ESCARPMENT

Covering nearly 2 000 000 ha of unspoilt bushveld typical of the Lowveld, the Kruger National Park is one of the world's most famous wildlife sanctuaries. Chief among the attractions are the Big Five – elephant, rhino, buffalo, lion and leopard – but there is much more to attract visitors. It is home to an amazing 147 mammal species, including several with a limited distribution elsewhere in South Africa – Lichtenstein's hartebeest, Sharpe's grysbok, roan and sable.

With over 500 species on record, the birdlife in the park is also prolific. More than 50 raptors, the purplecrested lourie, a variety of kingfishers, bee-eaters, rollers, hornbills, starlings and sunbirds, to name a few, occur here.

The park is criss-crossed by a network of game-viewing roads covering thousands of kilometres, and visitors have a wide choice of accommodation in the park's rest camps and bushveld camps.

To the west of the Kruger National Park the plains give way to the Drakensberg Escarpment with its sheer rock walls and grass-covered mountain slopes. Endowed with an abundance of water, it is a magical world of waterfalls, crystal-clear pools, potholes and the awe-inspiring Blyde River Canyon. Fascinating rock formations and far-reaching views of the Sudwala Caves add to the attractions of the region.

In the sheltered kloofs of the Escarpment, patches of indigenous forest still survive, but pine plantations have replaced much of the grasslands which once covered the mountain slopes. The remaining grasslands support one of South Africa's most endangered birds, the blue swallow, as well as several endemic proteas, cycads and other plants.

In addition to game-viewing and bird-watching, options for outdoor recreation abound. This region is one of South Africa's prime trailing areas: visitors to the Kruger National Park in the Lowveld can go on several guided wilderness trails, as well as numerous overnight hikes and day walks; the Escarpment is one of the country's prime holiday spots, offering unrivalled hiking opportunities.

The Escarpment is also rich in historic interest: old mining villages, some long abandoned, tunnels and rusty pieces of machinery provide evidence of the frantic search for gold in the hills and valleys, more than a century ago.

The picturesque Forest Falls near Mac-Mac are among the numerous cascading splendours of the Escarpment.

Bounded by the Crocodile and Sabie rivers in the south and north, the southern Kruger National Park comprises the historic Government Game Reserve, proclaimed in 1898. Abundant wildlife, diverse vegetation and varied landscapes make it one of the park's most popular areas.

How to get there
Nelspruit (375 km east of Johannesburg) is conveniently close to the southern Kruger. Follow the N4 through Witbank and Waterval-Boven. From Nelspruit continue on the N4 towards Komatipoort for 62 km to the turnoff to Malelane Gate. Berg-en-dal Rest Camp is 12 km beyond the gate. The southern section can also be accessed at Crocodile Bridge Gate on the N4, and through White River and Hazyview on the R538. Access to Numbi and Paul Kruger is along the R569 and R536 respectively. Directions between the rest camps are clearly indicated throughout the park.

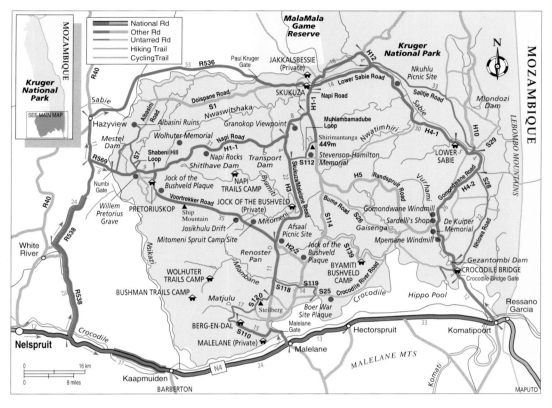

chat, lazy and croaking cisticolas, as well as redwinged starling, in the rocky habitats.

From the rest camp visitors can set off on **self-guided game drives** (*see* p. 167), undertake a **guided bush drive** or join a **night drive** (*see* p. 168). The **Rhino Walk** (*see* p. 169) provides visitors with an opportunity to engage in birding, tree identification and game-viewing within the safety of the camp. The swimming pool provides welcome relief after a summer's game-viewing drive.

PRETORIUSKOP

This lovely rest camp (the first to be opened in the park) near Numbi Gate lies on a high-lying, gently rolling plain, punctuated by rocky outcrops. This area is rich in history: nearby places of interest include the Voortrekker Road and the Albasini Ruins (*see* p. 168).

The area is densely wooded with alternating patches of silver cluster-leaf trees, sickle bush thickets and stands of tall tamboekie grassveld. Growing among the rank vegetation are two colourful species – the Barberton daisy and the Pride-of-De-Kaap.

Owing to the dense vegetation, **game-viewing** requires patience, but the area does have wildlife attractions. Visitors are drawn by

BERG-EN-DAL

Nestling among the valleys and rocky domes of the Malelane Mountains on the banks of Matjulu Dam is Berg-en-dal Rest Camp. This southwestern section, unlike the plains typical of most of the park, is characterised by low granitic mountains.

The **bush savanna** in this area is dominated by red bushwillow, silver cluster-leaf and sickle bush trees, and the mountain seringa and Lowveld chestnut grow among the rocky outcrops. Conspicuous in the **riverine scrub** in spring and summer are the brilliant red flowers of the Pride-of-De-Kaap.

Commonly seen **animals** include giraffe, kudu, waterbuck and impala. The area is also noted for its large white rhino population but elephant are less abundant than elsewhere in the park. The mountainous terrain provides the only suitable habitat in the park for the mountain reedbuck and is favoured by klipspringer.

Birding can be rewarding and species include the marabou stork, purplecrested lourie, greater blue-eared starling and a variety of raptors – vultures, martial eagle and bateleur. Look out for striped pipit (a summer visitor), mocking

White rhino were reintroduced from Zululand in the sixties.

A waterhole near the Lower Sabie Rest Camp.

outcrop, overlooking a waterhole. Continuing through undulating country, the road meanders to the top of **Steilberg** and the viewpoint here offers splendid vistas of the bushveld plains fading away to the north and east and the rugged Malelane Mountains to the southwest. On joining the H3, continue to **Renoster Pan** where you might come across white rhino, giraffe, kudu, impala, warthog and wild dog.

Backtrack to the H3, and drive north to the **Afsaal picnic site** – ideal for a mid-morning stop. Then head south along the H3 and take the S118 and then the S119, winding along the southern bank of the Mlambane River, before returning to the rest camp.

LOWER SABIE

Visitors can take several drives from Lower Sabie. Most popular is the 90-km **Gomondwane Road Drive**, linking Lower Sabie and Crocodile Bridge. Along this drive you could encounter breeding herds of elephant, giraffe, buffalo, kudu, waterbuck, blue wildebeest and impala. You might see the major predators – lion, leopard, cheetah and wild dog.

the chance of close-up views of white rhino – the first were released in a boma near the rest camp in 1961. In addition to the more common species (giraffe, kudu, blue wildebeest, impala and Burchell's zebra), you may also see sable, tsessebe and Lichtenstein's hartebeest – three species with a limited distribution in the park.

Birdlife abounds and includes rock kestrel, yellowfronted tinker barbet, yellowthroated longclaw, black sunbird, Cape white-eye and thickbilled weaver.

Visitors can also join a **night drive** or a **guided walk** (*see* pp. 168 and 169). The popular swimming pool is built in a setting of natural rock.

LOWER SABIE

This rest camp, on the banks of the Sabie River in the southeastern corner of the park, has a reputation for excellent game-viewing. Its tall shady trees contribute to the peaceful atmosphere.

The **vegetation** in this part of the park is a mosaic of tree savannas dominated by marula, red bushwillow and acacia trees. Typical of the lush riverine forest are the leadwood, sausage tree and Natal mahogany. The vegetation and the Sabie River (one of only five perennial rivers in the park) support a rich diversity of **game**, including elephant, giraffe, buffalo, kudu, impala, bushbuck, warthog, baboon and vervet

monkey. Herds of Burchell's zebra and blue wildebeest are attracted to the savanna. **Predators** include lion, cheetah (the southern section supports nearly half of the park's 170-odd cheetah) and wild dog.

Among the numerous **birds** to be seen are ostrich, a variety of herons, African finfoot (in the Crocodile River), secretarybird, kingfishers, the lilacbreasted roller, yellow- and redbilled hornbills and Burchell's starling.

Visitors can embark on **game-viewing drives** in their own vehicles, or join a guided **night drive** (*see* this page and p. 168).

SKUKUZA

Set on the southern banks of the Sabie, Skukuza is the park's largest rest camp and the administrative headquarters. It is named after the Sabie Game Reserve's first ranger, James Stevenson-Hamilton, who was called Skukuza ('sweeping clean') by the Tsonga.

The **bush savanna** consists of mixed bushwillow and acacia. Among the dominant trees are the horned thorn, knob thorn, red bushwillow, marula and tamboti.

Animal life is varied, with kudu, giraffe and impala. Chances of spotting elephant and lion are good, and leopard and wild dog are also seen from time to time.

Birds that might be ticked include African finfoot (in the Sabie River), openbilled stork, crowned

and yellowbilled hornbills, purple-crested lourie, Burchell's starling and scarletchested sunbird.

The **Stevenson-Hamilton Memorial Library** on site houses a collection of books, memorabilia of the early years of the park and fine wildlife paintings.

From the rest camp visitors can embark on their own **game-viewing drives**, or a **guided bush drive** (*see* p. 168).

GAME-VIEWING DRIVES

BERG-EN-DAL

Visitors can travel north along the Skukuza/Malelane road or east along the Crocodile River road.

BERG-EN-DAL TO AFSAAL (75 KM): On leaving the rest camp, head for the viewpoint at **Matjulu**, an enormous granite

The reception centre at Skukuza, the Kruger's largest rest camp.

Cheetah are distinguishable from leopard by their round markings.

The Wolhuter Hiking Trail was the first to be opened and honours the legendary ranger, Harry Wolhuter.

The road initially winds next to the Sabie River and then swings in a southwesterly direction to reach the **Gomondwane wind-mill**. Further south, the road follows the course of the usually dry Vurhami River, passing near to the site where a trading store, **Sardelli's Shop**, was built in the 1890s. A short way on is the **De Kuiper Memorial**, where an expedition under Frans de Kuiper (the first whites to enter the area in search of a route between Delagoa Bay and the interior) was ambushed by local warriors in July 1725. After the Vurhami River a turnoff provides access to a viewpoint overlooking the **Gezantombi Dam**.

The **Hippo Pool** in the Crocodile River is rewarding for hippo sightings. Visitors walk with an armed guard to a viewpoint overlooking the pool, and are shown the nearby rock paintings.

An alternative return route to Lower Sabie is along the **Nhlowa road** (S28) – good for white rhino, buffalo, lion and cheetah.

PRETORIUSKOP

Several short drives around Pretoriuskop (over a distance of 30 km) are ideal for early morning or late afternoon game-viewing.

ALBASINI RUINS DRIVE (57 KM): From Pretoriuskop, drive towards **Shabeni Hill**, encircled by a loop road where you might well spot red duiker and oribi (both with a limited distribution in the park). Continue to the **Albasini Ruins** where João Albasini, the first European to settle in the area, built a trading store and house in the second half of the 1840s. The partly restored ruins and a display of artefacts can be seen at the site.

Backtrack on the **Albasini road** past the **Mestel Dam** to join the **Napi road**. Turn left and soon you will pass the grave of the Voortrekker, Willem Pretorius, after whom the outcrop is named.

VOORTREKKER ROAD DRIVE (102 KM): This drive initially follows the route used by transport riders between Delagoa Bay and Lydenburg during the 1870s and 80s, and is linked to the classic story of Jock of the Bushveld (*see* p. 179). Several plaques serve as reminders of those adventurous times. Among them are Jock's birthplace, **Josikhulu Drift**, where a trader, Thomas Hart, was murdered in 1876 and the **Mitomeni Spruit Camp Site** where riders used to overnight. From Afsaal continue north along the H3, follow the Napi Road back to Pretoriuskop, stopping at the **Transport Dam**, **Napi Rocks** and the **Shitlhave Dam**.

SKUKUZA

The roads radiating from Skukuza are ideal for self-guided game drives of a few hours to a full day.

SHIRIMANTANGA HILL DRIVE (37 KM): This circular route from Skukuza is ideal for the early morning or late afternoon. Take the Napi road and the S114 to the **Muhlambamadube Loop** (S112). A turnoff leads to the top of **Shirimantanga Hill** where James and Hilda Stevenson-Hamilton's ashes were scattered. To return to camp, follow the Skukuza/Malelane road north to the **Napi road** junction. Three kilometres beyond the junction a road branches off to a viewpoint on **Granokop** with its expansive vistas of the surrounding bushveld. The remaining 11 km follows the first section of the onward route.

LOWER SABIE ROAD DRIVE (100 KM): From Skukuza the main road to Lower Sabie follows the densely vegetated course of the Sabie River, frequented by elephant, buffalo (herds of up to 800), waterbuck and bushbuck. Many riverside viewpoints enable visitors to observe hippos and crocodiles in the Sabie River, and leopard are often spotted in the dense vegetation near the **Nkuhlu picnic site**, 20 km from Skukuza.

Return to Skukuza along the **Salitje Road** (good for giraffe, blue wildebeest, Burchell's zebra) which joins the H12. From here, backtrack 15 km along the Lower Sabie Road or take the Skukuza/Tshokwane road along the course of the Sand River for 6 km.

GUIDED BUSH AND NIGHT DRIVES

Visitors to Berg-en-dal and Skukuza can hire officials to take them on a guided game drive to

HARRY WOLHUTER

The classic tale of how Harry Wolhuter, one of the first rangers of the Sabie Game Reserve, killed a lion with his knife has become a bush legend. The incident took place in 1904 northeast of Tshokwane. A lion pounced on Wolhuter's horse, unseating its rider. Wolhuter dropped his rifle, but managed to plunge his knife into the lion's shoulder and throat. When the lion backed off, Wolhuter climbed a tree, fearing the return of a second lion that had gone after his horse. The lion did indeed return, but, after continuous harassment by Wolhuter's dog, eventually retreated. To keep himself in the tree should he lose consciousness, Wolhuter tied himself to a branch and was in great pain when his party caught up with him. Wolhuter's knife and the skin of the lion he killed are displayed at the Stevenson-Hamilton Memorial Library at Skukuza.

Lilacbreasted rollers are common residents of thornveld savannah.

Plaque to Jock of the Bushveld, immortalised in the famous book.

areas of the park usually closed to tourists. Groups are limited to a maximum of seven. Reservations must be made at least a month in advance through the Information and Environmental Education section (*see* At a Glance, right).

Night drives provide an opportunity to see some of the park's nocturnal animals – a variety of smaller cats, aardvark, porcupine and honey badger. These two-hour drives are conducted by conservation officials with powerful spotlights to scan the bush.

WALKS AND TRAILS

Visitors have a choice of a self-guided walk in Berg-en-dal, a guided walk at Pretoriuskop and three wilderness trails. Although game-viewing forms an integral part of the wilderness trails, their aim is to provide a better understanding of the complexities of nature. Trails (limited to a maximum of eight) run from Friday to

Monday, or Monday to Thursday, starting mid-afternoon and ending after breakfast. They are conducted from a base camp under the supervision of an armed trails ranger and a game guard.

BERG-EN-DAL: The 2,5-km self-guided **Rhino Walk** follows a paved walkway along the fence of the rest camp; 1,6 km is suitable for wheelchairs. Most of the nearly 100 tree species endemic to the area can be seen. Larger mammals often spotted are kudu, waterbuck, mountain reedbuck and bushbuck. The first 600 m has been designed with the visually impaired in mind – braille information boards and animal skulls are provided, as are plants which can be touched and smelt.

In addition to game-viewing on foot, the **Bushman Wilderness Trail** has the added attraction of a rich archaeological heritage (most of the Kruger's 115 rock art sites are in the south of the park). The rugged landscape here is dominated by massive granite outcrops. The **Wolhuter Trail**, the park's first wilderness trail (1978), honours the legendary Harry Wolhuter (*see* box, p. 168). This area supports one of the highest concentrations of white rhino in the Kruger. Other big game species often seen are elephant, buffalo, lion and leopard.

PRETORIUSKOP: Guided three-hour walks are conducted during school holidays in the Hlanwini Breeding and Quarantine Camp, south of Pretoriuskop. Among the species you might see in this 300-ha camp, enclosed by a predator-proof fence, are the

rare Lichtenstein's hartebeest and tsessebe. The **Napi Wilderness Trail** is conducted in the undulating terrain between Pretoriuskop and Skukuza rest camps. In addition to frequent sightings of white rhino, trailists might also encounter black rhino, elephant, buffalo, lion, leopard, cheetah and wild dog.

The Bushman Trail leads through the park's southwestern corner.

The central Kruger National Park, between the Sabie and Letaba rivers, is renowned for breeding herds of elephant and plains animals such as blue wildebeest and Burchell's zebra. Stalking the grazers and browsers are the predators, among them lion, leopard, cheetah and wild dog.

How to get there
Satara Rest Camp, 92 km north of Skukuza, can be approached along the park's main north–south road, or via Klaserie (take the R40 north from Nelspruit for 125 km) and Orpen Gate, 48 km to the west. Access to Olifants and Letaba rest camps, 54 km and 86 km north of Satara respectively, is also along the main north–south road, or the town and gate of Phalaborwa (continue north along the R40 from Klaserie for 97 km). Directions between the rest camps are clearly indicated throughout the park.

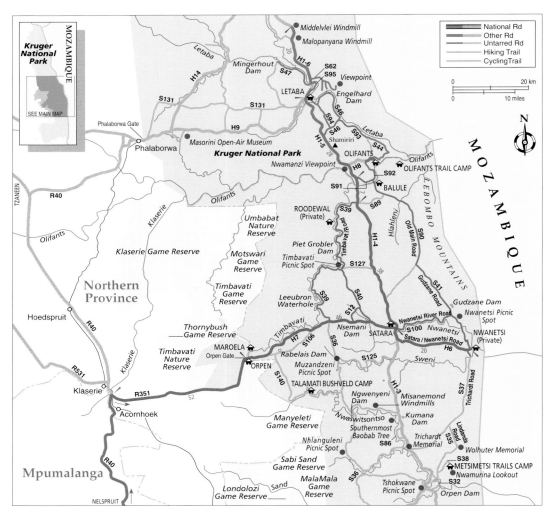

Other conspicuous trees include clumps of lala palm and the common cluster fig (or sycamore fig).

Wildlife is prolific, and herds of elephant, buffalo, blue wildebeest, impala and Burchell's zebra are common. Other species include giraffe, buffalo, kudu and klipspringer (in rocky areas). Shadowing the game are lion and other predators. Hippo and crocodile abound in the Olifants River.

Birding can be rewarding, with saddlebilled stork, bateleur, bat hawk, lilacbreasted roller, Burchell's starling and Marico sunbird likely to be ticked. An observation platform with a pay telescope in the camp offers excellent views of animals quenching their thirst in the river below the camp. Visitors can plan their own **drives** (*see* pp. 172–173), or join a **guided early morning** or **night drive**, conducted by officials.

SATARA

The Kruger's second largest rest camp, Satara lies in one of the best grazing areas of the park. It is situated on the extensive plains which characterise the landscape between the Sabie and Olifants rivers, amidst a savanna of marula, leadwood and knob thorn trees. Along the Timbavati River, to the west of the rest camp, some fine specimens of umbrella thorn and apple-leaf trees can be seen.

The highly nutritious **vegetation** attracts the park's largest concentration of **game** and supports herds of grazers such as blue wildebeest, Burchell's zebra, and one of the highest densities of giraffe. Elephant, buffalo, kudu, waterbuck and impala are common. **Predators** are also abundant – more lion occur here than anywhere else in the park.

The diversity of **birds** to be seen include openbill and marabou storks, hooded and white-backed vultures, secretarybird, kori bustard, wattled and Burchell's starling and redbilled quelea.

Unlike many camps, Satara does not overlook a dam or river, but the restaurant overlooks a waterhole outside the fence. An extensive road network around the camp allows visitors to plan their own **game drives** (*see* p. 171).

OLIFANTS

Close to the Lebombo Mountains, the Olifants Rest Camp is perched on a cliff on the northern bank of the Olifants River, near its confluence with the Letaba River. The view from here is unrivalled by any other camp. The camp lies between the **knob thorn** and **marula savannas** to the south and the **mopane shrub veld** dominating the eastern half of the park north of the Olifants River.

LETABA

This rest camp is set on a wide horseshoe bend along the southern bank of the river after which it has been named. A vast expanse of **mopaneveld** covers the plains to the north, south and east of the rest camp, while mixed **mopane** and **red bushwillow veld** dominates the vegetation west of the rest camp. Dominating the **riverine** vegetation are tall common cluster (sycamore) fig, sausage and Natal mahogany trees.

More lion occur in the central Kruger than anywhere else in the park.

Game to be seen includes giraffe, buffalo, kudu, waterbuck, blue wildebeest, impala and Burchell's zebra, and breeding herds of elephant. Tsessebe, sable and eland are some of the species with a restricted distribution in the park which occur here.

This area's **birdlife** includes the secretarybird, African fish eagle, bat hawk and kori bustard. Various kingfishers, the lilacbreasted roller, green pigeon, cinnamon dove, redbilled oxpecker and the greater blue-eared starling also occur.

One of Letaba's major attractions is the **Elephant Hall** in the Goldfields Environmental Education Centre (*see* box, right).

Visitors can go on **game drives** on routes of their choice (*see* p. 173), or a **guided bush drive** with a conservation official.

GAME-VIEWING DRIVES
SATARA
Satara's central location allows for game drives, in all directions, from a few hours to a full day.
TIMBAVATI RIVER DRIVE (142 KM): This drive explores west of Satara. Game abounds and among the animals you might see along the drive or at the waterholes are elephant, giraffe, kudu, blue wildebeest, impala and Burchell's zebra, as well as lion, leopard, cheetah and wild dog.

KRUGER'S LARGE TUSKERS

Renowned for its large tuskers, the Kruger is one of the few areas in Africa where elephants with both tusks weighing over 45 kg still occur. In the late 1970s the park's large tuskers became known as the 'Magnificent Seven'. By 1985, four of these, Shingwedzi, Shawu (his tusks of 317 cm and 303,5 cm are the longest ever recorded in southern Africa), Mafuyane and Ndlulamithi, had died of natural causes. Kambaku had to be shot when he was wounded outside the park and Dzombo was shot by poachers, but fortunately his ivory was recovered. These six elephants' tusks are the focal point of the Elephant Hall in the Goldfields Environmental Education Centre at Letaba. The only survivor of the Magnificent Seven, João, lost both his tusks in a fight in 1984 and they have not been found yet.

Since the demise of six of the Magnificent Seven, several more large tuskers (that had been overlooked earlier) have been identified. Also on display are the heaviest pair of tusks ever recorded in the park (75 kg and 55 kg), which were carried by Phelwane.

The exhibition, covering 400 m² depicts aspects of the elephant's life history – behaviour, population structure and dynamics, and reproduction.

Follow the Orpen/Satara road to its junction with the S40; continue to the **Ngirivane waterhole** (rated among the best in the park) before continuing along the S12 to the Orpen/Satara road and its junction with **Timbavati road**. Except for the first few kilometres, the road runs along the eastern bank of the Timbavati River, passing **Leeubron**, another rewarding waterhole. About 31 km after leaving the Orpen/Satara road is the **Timbavati picnic site**, with tables and benches shaded by a tall nyala tree.

Drive north on the Timbavati road, passing the **Piet Grobler Dam** and the turnoff to the

The spectacular view from Olifants Rest Camp is unrivalled by any other in the park.

Numbering over 150 000, impala are the most abundant large mammals in the park. Waterholes usually reward with good game-viewing.

Roodewal Private Camp (access for residents only), for 29 km before joining the H1-4 linking Satara and Olifants. From here you can return along the H1-4, or backtrack to the Timbavati picnic site and continue along the S40.

NWANETSI RIVER DRIVE (70–90 KM): This drive traverses the open country east of Satara. The road initially meanders along the northern bank of the Nwanetsi River, but you might see giraffe, waterbuck, blue wildebeest, impala and bushbuck. This is ideal leopard country where you could also see lion and cheetah.

On joining the **Gudzane road,** it is worth your while to make a detour to the **Gudzane Dam** (which is a good spot for water birds) before continuing south to the **Nwanetsi picnic site** which overlooks the scenic Sweni River gorge. The nearby **Nwanetsi Camp** is a private camp and access is restricted to residents only.

Before heading back to camp continue for a short way south on the **Trichardt road** to the causeway crossing the Sweni River, a good spot for water birds and crocodile.

From the picnic site either return to Satara along the H6 (stop off en route at the **Sonop** and **Shishangane windmills** to check for game), or take the Gudzane road north and then the S90.

OLIFANTS
Two circular drives are ideal for a short early morning or late afternoon drive, but longer drives can also be taken.

OLIFANTS AND LETABA RIVERS DRIVE (52 KM): This drive traverses the triangle formed by the confluence of the Letaba and Olifants – which support the highest number of hippo in the park.

From the camp, the S44 first follows the Olifants River with its fine stand of fever trees, enormous common cluster (sycamore) figs and tree euphorbias. A highlight of this section is the viewpoint overlooking the Lebombo Mountains to the east, the bushveld plains to the south and the rest camp to the southwest.

The road then swings away from the river in a northwesterly direction and after a few kilometres winds alongside the Letaba River. Elephant are common along this section and you might also spot nyala (more common further north) and leopard.

Return to the camp along the S46 and the H1-5 which passes **Shamiriri**, an outcrop eroded into fascinating shapes.

OLIFANTS RIVER DRIVE (52 KM): This route follows the horseshoe bend of the Olifants River, southwest of the camp, and then continues to the Bangu windmill.

Take the H8 and then the S92 to the low-level bridge across the Olifants River where you might see giraffe, buffalo and kudu. From there the road climbs steeply and you soon

---

MASORINI OPEN-AIR MUSEUM

The Kruger has many cultural links with the past such as **Makahane** (an Early Stone Age and Late Iron Age site near Punda Maria), **Thulamela** in the Pafuri region (*see* p. 177) and **Masorini**, 11 km east of Phalaborwa Gate. Masorini was occupied by Late Iron Age ancestors of the baPhalaborwa (Eastern Sotho) until the 19th century and

smelting furnaces, forges and implements indicate that the baPhalaborwa engaged in metal-working. The museum consists of an information centre where artefacts are displayed, reconstructed huts on the terraced hillside and a Later Stone Age site. There are also picnic sites and a walk is conducted around the museum (*see* p. 177).

The Late Iron Age site at Masorini Open-Air Museum.

pass **Balule**, a small rest camp of six huts situated on the southern bank of the river.

From here the drive continues on the Satara/Balule road, crossing the Hlanhleni River before reaching **Bangu windmill** where herds of Burchell's zebra and blue wildebeest, as well as giraffe, are often seen. Backtrack to the low-level bridge and continue on the S91 to join the H1-5 after 5 km. A short way on you reach the **Nwa-manzi Viewpoint** with its splendid vistas of the Olifants River.

LETABA

Short early morning, late afternoon and day drives can be taken from this camp.

MINGERHOUT DAM DRIVE (95 KM): This drive seldom fails to live up to its reputation for good game-viewing. It goes north from Letaba on the H1-6 for 4 km (look for waterbuck, bushbuck and leopard) and then follows a

An overnight hut at the Olifants Wilderness Trail Camp.

4-km loop (S95) along the river. On joining the H1-6, continue along the S47 (the Letaba River Road) to **Mingerhout Dam**.

Along the road to the viewpoint overlooking the dam there are numerous riverside loops. Watch out for elephant, hippo, giraffe, buffalo, eland, kudu, waterbuck and large numbers of crocodile. You could also come across leopard and lion here.

Backtrack to the H1-6 and, after crossing the Letaba River, continue north to **Malopanyana** and **Middelvlei** (often frequented by tsessebe) windmills. On returning to the rest camp, take the S62 which splits into three roads leading to the northern bank of the Letaba River and a viewpoint

overlooking the **Engelhard Dam** – a good observation site for hippo and crocodile.

ENGELHARD DAM DRIVE (35 KM): From Letaba follow the S94 for 3 km and continue on the Letaba River Road (S46) to the **Engelhard Dam** wall, 8 km from the camp. The dam attracts many water birds and you might see several heron species, openbilled stork, African spoonbill, wattled plover and African jacana.

The road follows the river and you have a good chance of seeing elephant, buffalo, kudu and waterbuck. Six kilometres beyond the dam wall you reach three viewpoints overlooking the river and, 2,5 km on, the junction with the S93. Continuing on the S46 you can either take the S94 back to camp or join up with the H1-5.

WALKS AND TRAILS

Three guided wilderness trails are conducted in the central region of the park (*see* p. 169 for more details of the trails in the park).

TSHOKWANE (departs from Skukuza): Undulating savanna dominated by marula and knob thorn trees, ravines and gorges characterise the area northeast of Tshokwane where the **Metsimetsi Trail** is conducted. The Nwaswitsontso River flows all year, attracting a variety of game (including large numbers of elephants) during the dry winter.

SATARA: The **Sweni Trail** is conducted southwest of Nwanetsi in an area renowned for its large herds of buffalo, Burchell's zebra and blue wildebeest. Larger predators trailists might see include lion, cheetah and spotted hyena. Giraffe, impala and both species of rhino also occur in the area.

LETABA: With landscapes ranging from the Lebombo Mountains in the east to plains and the magnificent Olifants River gorge, the **Olifants Trail** is rated as the most scenic wilderness trail in the park. In addition to large numbers of crocodiles and hippos, the area supports healthy populations of elephant, giraffe, buffalo, waterbuck, Burchell's zebra and blue wildebeest. Lion are also frequently sighted. The trails camp is situated on the southern banks of the Olifants River near its confluence with the Letaba River.

Relaxing after a day on the Olifants Trail, the most scenic in the park.

PHALABORWA GATE: The open-air museum at Masorini (*see* box, p. 172), a Late Iron Age site, 11 km east of Phalaborwa Gate, can be explored by joining a guided walk, accompanied by a tape recorded commentary. The walk ascends the terraces, where the baPhalaborwa lived and worked, to the summit of the hill boasting spectacular views over the surrounding mopane veld.

The vegetation of the northern section of the Kruger National Park differs markedly from that of the central and southern areas. Dominant in the east is a vast expanse of mopane shrubveld and to the west the vegetation is characterised by mixed bushwillow and mopane veld. The area supports numerous breeding herds of elephant and is the favoured habitat of several rare animals. One of its main attractions, however, is its prolific birdlife, especially along the Luvuvhu River in the Pafuri area.

How to get there
Mopani Rest Camp, 45 km north of Letaba, can be reached along the park's main north–south road, Phalaborwa Gate being the nearest entry point (take the R40 north for 225 km from Nelspruit). Shingwedzi and Punda Maria are 61 km and 131 km north of Mopani. Punda Maria can also be reached via Louis Trichardt and Punda Maria Gate or Pafuri, the northernmost gate. Directions between camps are clearly indicated throughout the park.

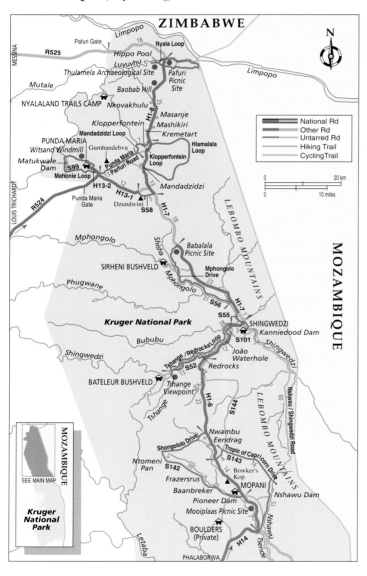

The flower of the impala lily, a thickset succulent shrub.

animals are Burchell's zebra, blue wildebeest and impala. **Predators** include lion and cheetah.

A variety of **water birds** (whitebreasted cormorant, herons, African spoonbill and African fish eagle) are attracted to the Pioneer Dam. Other **birds** seen in and around the camp include grey lourie, lilacbreasted roller, redbilled, yellowbilled and ground hornbills, arrowmarked babbler, and greater blue-eared and glossy starlings.

Visitors can watch game or birds from the **viewpoint** overlooking the dam, or **walk** next to the dam (*see* p. 175). The camp's roads are ideal for **self-guided game drives** (*see* pp. 175–176) and guided **night drives** are conducted (*see* p. 177).

SHINGWEDZI

With its old-world charm, this camp on the banks of the Shingwedzi River is especially attractive in winter when the red and white flowers of the impala lilies about the camp are in bloom.

The mopane shrubveld **vegetation** of the area is typical of this part of the park. Elephant, giraffe, kudu, waterbuck, impala

and Burchell's zebra are common; you might also come across sable, tsessebe, nyala and leopard. The **bird hide** on the Shingwedzi River and **Kanniedood Dam**, southeast of the camp, is a good spot for birding. Among the birds you could tick are darter, Goliath and greenbacked herons, yellowbilled stork and African fish eagle.

In addition to **self-guided game drives** (*see* pp. 175–176), visitors can join a **guided night drive** (*see* p. 177) on which nocturnal creatures may be seen.

PUNDA MARIA

The park's northernmost camp lies in an area with the richest diversity of **vegetation**: sand forest and tall mopane woodlands to baobab 'forests' and lush riverine forests along the Luvuvhu. Especially attractive is the Pride-of-De-Kaap, with salmon to brilliant red flowers from November to March, and the flame creeper with masses of flowers in September/October. The sand forest north of Punda Maria is one of the few places in South Africa where tropical dry forests occur. Typical species include the small copalwood, the pod mahogany with its large, dark brown pods, the green thorn and the red-heart tree.

Among the **game** often seen are elephant, buffalo, Burchell's zebra, impala, and nyala (especially common in the Pafuri area). Other species to look out for include eland, sable, suni, lion,

MOPANI

One of the newest rest camps, Mopani fronts on the Pioneer Dam, built in the course of the Tsende River. The camp is surrounded by flat countryside dominated by **mopane shrub savanna** to the east and mixed **red bushwillow** and **mopane veld** to

the west. Lala palms, knob thorn, apple-leaf and leadwood trees are prominent along river courses.

The area is noted for its white rhino, herds of elephant and buffalo, and **antelope** with limited distribution in the park – Lichtenstein's hartebeest, eland and sable. Among the more common wild dog and samango monkey, a shy inhabitant of the riverine forest along the Luvuvhu River.

One of the area's main attractions is its **birdlife** – look out for Arnot's chat in the mopane woodlands. Visitors can take self-guided **game drives**, and the camp has a short **nature trail** (*see* p. 177).

GAME-VIEWING DRIVES
MOPANI
Various routes – from short early morning/late afternoon to full-day drives – can be taken.

SHONGOLOLO DRIVE (64 KM): This drive (S142) hugs the Tsende River for 10 km, passing **Baanbreker** and **Frazersrus waterholes**, going through mopane and bushwillow veld to **Ntomeni Pan**.

In addition to more common species (Burchell's zebra, blue wildebeest and impala) you may see elephant, white rhino, buffalo, eland, sable and lion. At Ntomeni Pan the road swings northeast to join the H1-6 after 14 km. From here, the most direct route back to camp is south, along the H1-6. En route stop at **Nwambu**, **Eendrag** and **Bowker's Kop waterholes** to check for game.

TROPIC OF CAPRICORN DRIVE (57 KM): From Mopani head north on the H1-6 for 12 km and follow the S144 to its junction with the Tropic of Capricorn road (S143) which meanders through mopane veld. You might see South Africa's rarest antelope, Lichtenstein's hartebeest, which

Burchell's zebra are plentiful in the park and can be seen in fair numbers along the Shongololo Drive.

became extinct in this country earlier this century and was reintroduced into the park in 1985. In addition to more common animals, you might also encounter eland, roan, sable and tsessebe, and predators (lion and cheetah).

Later you join the **Nshawu/ Shingwedzi road** to **Nshawu Dam**, home to a good waterbuck population. Continuing southwest, the road follows the Nshawu River, passing three windmills. Join the H1-6 and go north to the **Mooiplaas picnic site** (overlooking a waterhole in the Tsende River), before returning to camp.

SHINGWEDZI
An early morning/late afternoon game drive to **Kanniedood Dam**, a few kilometres downstream of the camp, is especially rewarding.

TSHANGE/REDROCKS DRIVE (67 KM): From Shingwedzi, head for the H1-7; after 3 km turn right onto the S52, a delightful circular drive along the **Tshange/Redrocks Loop**. The area is within the home range of a small pack of wild dog (*see* box p. 176). You may also see the endangered roan (in the 1980s there were about 350 in the park, but today they number less than 50, mainly through

drought). Look out for Sharpe's grysbok, a small antelope which favours thorny scrub at the base of rocky outcrops. In South Africa it is restricted to the northeast of the Northern Province.

After winding along the northern bank of the Shingwedzi River for about 16 km the road doubles back. Turn right after crossing the Shingwedzi River and follow the short detour to the **Tshange viewpoint** with its superb vistas over the surrounding countryside (ignore the turnoff to the **Bateleur Bushveld Camp** as entry is restricted to residents).

The baobab tree is found mainly in the northern section of the park.

BAOBAB TREES

In South Africa the baobab is confined to the north of the Northern Province, mainly north of the Olifants River and the Soutpansberg.

The well-known baobab north of Tshokwane is the southernmost specimen in the Kruger. Further north baobabs are a characteristic feature of the landscape: in the Pafuri area they form 'forests'.

The trunk with its fluted, pinkish-grey bark reaches huge proportions: specimens of over 15 m in height with a circumference over 30 m are not uncommon. The baobab has an extremely long lifespan:

research shows that very large specimens could be between 3 000 and 4 000 years old.

This deciduous tree is especially conspicuous in the dry winter when its thick stem and tapering branches form the grotesque shape which led to the ancient belief that the tree had been planted upside down. Between November and mid-December hundreds of wax-like white flowers hang from the branches, each lasting only a day. The oval fruit is relished by baboons and a refreshing drink is made from the white pulp which contains tartaric acid.

WILD DOGS

The wild dog, one of Africa's most endangered carnivores, probably numbers fewer than 5 000 in the wild. Together with the riverine rabbit and the roan, it is one of the country's three most threatened mammals; its only viable population is found in the Kruger.

To determine the number in the park, a Wild Dog Photographic Competition was launched by the Endangered Wildlife Trust in conjunction with the National Parks Board in 1988. More than 5 000 photographs were submitted, enabling researchers to identify individual animals, since each dog has a unique coat pattern.

Other information assisted in determining the home ranges of the park's wild dogs. A total of 28 packs (358 wild dogs) were found in the park and adjoining reserves. Packs ranged from 3 to 24, averaging 12. The northern district supports almost 47% of the population and the central region just over 25%. A second competition, held in 1995, identified 434 wild dogs in 32 packs, also in the Kruger and adjoining private reserves.

Wild dogs hunt in packs: research has shown that impala constitute three-quarters of their diet, followed by kudu calves, duiker and steenbok.

The wild dog has largely been exterminated in Africa.

Return to the Tshange/Redrocks Loop, turn right and drive for nearly 11 km to a loop with a viewpoint looking down onto the bright red formations after which Redrocks are named. On joining the H1-6, turn left. As you head back to Shingwedzi stop at **João windmill** and take the detour onto the S101 past a viewpoint above the Shingwedzi River.

MPHONGOLO DRIVE (80 KM): Travelling north from Shingwedzi along the H1-7, a 3-km detour along S55, which follows the course of the **Mphongolo River**, might be rewarding. Game often seen here includes buffalo, waterbuck, impala and elephant.

On rejoining the H1-7, turn left and continue to the turnoff to the S56. The road winds through mopane veld before continuing along the Mphongolo River, passing through an area renowned for its breeding herds of elephant. You might also encounter buffalo, kudu, waterbuck and impala. The road follows the river for 17 km and continues along the Shisha River, passing the turnoff to the **Sirheni Bushveld Camp**. After 8 km it rejoins the H1-7 at the **Babalala picnic site**, frequented by eland, sable and reedbuck. Return to camp along the H1-7.

PUNDA MARIA/PAFURI
The roads in the northern part of the park offer a variety of drives.

MAHONIE DRIVE (28 KM): The Punda Maria sand forest can be explored along the circular **Mahonie Loop** west of the camp. Follow the H13-2 for 3 km and turn right onto the S99. Look out for suni, a small antelope; in the Kruger it occurs only around Punda Maria.

About 12 km beyond the junction you pass the turnoff to **Matukwale Dam** and double back, passing **Witsand windmill**, opposite a rocky outcrop. The outcrops north of the camp are the only habitat of the yellow-spotted rock dassie in the Kruger. Beyond the park, they are restricted to a few isolated mountains in the Northern Province. Further along the road passes the **Maritube Dam** and 4 km on reaches the camp.

PAFURI DRIVE (150 KM): Follow the H13-2 for 3 km north towards Pafuri; turn left onto the Punda Maria/Pafuri road, passing **Gumbandebvu**, an enormous sandstone outcrop. The **Mandadzidzi Loop** branches off to the right; 4 km on is the **Klopperfontein Loop**. Turn left and continue to Klopperfontein. On this stretch you might see elephant, buffalo, tsessebe, sable, nyala, lion and the rare Lichtenstein's hartebeest (a herd of 15 was released in 1990).

On joining the H1-8, turn left and go north, passing through mopane scrub typical of this area. After passing the waterholes at **Kremetart**, **Mashikiri** (look out for wild dog), **Masanje** and **Nkovakhulu**, the road skirts **Baobab Hill**, named after the ancient baobab landmark (*see* box p. 175).

Seven kilometres north of Baobab Hill the **Nyala Loop** splits off to the left and a short way on left again, continuing along the Luvuvhu River to the **Hippo Pool**. As the name of the loop suggests,

The elephant is the largest land mammal; bulls weigh up to 6 tonnes and reach a height of 3,6 m.

nyala are plentiful, as are baboon and vervet monkey. You might also spot buffalo, kudu, waterbuck, bushbuck, lion and bushpig – a nocturnal species found mainly in the far north of the park.

Thulamela, the outcrop near the turning point of the Nyala Loop, is an important archaeological site. Indications are that it was inhabited between the 15th and late 17th centuries. Among the finds were gold beads and a section of a gold bracelet. The site has been developed into an open-air museum which can be viewed on a guided walk (*see* below).

Dwarf mongooses occur mainly in the western half of the park.

To the east of the H1-8 a loop road winds along the river for 3 km to **Pafuri picnic site**. This is a birder's paradise where you might tick African finfoot, white-crowned plover, tambourine and cinnamon doves, Böhm's and mottled spinetails, racket-tailed and broadbilled rollers, wattle-eyed flycatcher and longtailed starling.

From the picnic site the road continues along the **Luvuvhu River** with fine specimens of jackal-berry, nyala, ana, sausage and baobab trees. There are several short riverside loops which wind though the riverine forest, the only place in the park where samango monkey occur – a secretive species more often heard than seen. Close to the Mozambican border the road doubles back, passing through a forest of fever trees, to reach the H1-8 21 km from the start of the loop.

Head back south on the H1-8 (the **Hlamalala Loop** is good for Lichtenstein's hartebeest and roan) until you reach the junction with the S58 which winds past **Dzundwini**, a massive sandstone outcrop surrounded by dense mopane woodland. Leopard are occasionally seen here and if you are lucky you might spot the pack of wild dogs that ranges in the area. Just over 1 km after turning onto the S58 a road branches off to the left, revealing fine vistas of the mopaneveld as it ascends Dzundwini. Also occurring in the area are lion, elephant, buffalo, sable and Sharpe's grysbok. From the junction of the S58 with the H13-1 it is a mere 16 km to Punda Maria.

NIGHT DRIVES

Many of the park's animals are nocturnal, emerging only when visitors must be in the camps. Two- to three-hour night drives, conducted by conservation officials, offer an opportunity to see animals such as aardvark, genet, civet, African wild cat and nocturnal birds (dikkops and nightjars).

WALKS AND TRAILS

PIONEER: A short walk leads from the camp's reception area to its perimeter fence along the dam. It consists of two sections. The right-hand leg goes over level terrain with many benches overlooking the dam and ends at the swimming pool 15 minutes later. The route to the left is over more uneven terrain, but offers magnificent views of the dam.
PUNDA MARIA: This is one of the few camps with a defined trail. The **Paradise Flycatcher Nature Trail** starts at the reception complex and winds through the vegetation in the camp.

See p. 169 for more information on wilderness trails.

The **Nyalaland Trail** leads through an area renowned for its scenery, baobabs and fever trees, where many rare plants, animals and birds occur. Game includes elephant, hippo, crocodile, buffalo and nyala. Birdlife includes mottled and Böhm's spinetails, Pel's fishing owl and tropical boubou.
PAFURI: Guided walks to Thulamela are presently conducted on an ad hoc basis for groups

Mopani Rest Camp fronts onto Pioneer Dam.

only (this will be changing at an unspecified date). In the course of this walk visitors view the remains of a Late Iron Age settlement, linked to the Great Zimbabwe empire. There is a display with information on the early inhabitants, artefacts, and photographs of the excavation, and information on the area's geology and ecology. The walk takes place on **Thulamela Hill** among centuries-old baobabs, offering fine views over the forests of the Luvuvhu River.

NORTHERN KRUGER NP AT A GLANCE

MAIN ATTRACTIONS
Wilderness atmosphere, game-viewing, bird-watching, Lowveld trees, archaeological sites, wilderness trails.

BEST TIMES TO VISIT
See p. 169.

PERMITS/BOOKINGS
See p. 169.

OPENING TIMES
See. p. 169.

MOPANI
Accommodation: One self-contained donor house for 8; 104 self-contained cottages/huts for 3 or 6.
Facilities: Shop (groceries, curios, liquor), restaurant, swimming pool and petrol.

SHINGWEDZI
Accommodation: One self-contained donor house for 7; 79 self-contained cottages/huts for 2–4; 55 caravan/camp sites, with kitchen units and hot/cold-water ablutions.
Facilities: Shop (groceries, curios, liquor), restaurant and petrol.

PUNDA MARIA
Accommodation: 23 self-contained cottages/huts for 2 or 4; 50 caravan/camp sites with two kitchen units and hot/cold-water ablutions.
Facilities: Shop (groceries, curios, liquor), restaurant and petrol.

BUSH CAMPS (Bateleur and Sirheni)
Self-contained units. No shops or restaurants.

WILDERNESS TRAIL
Four rustic 2-bed huts (with bedding), dining area, communal ablutions. Fee includes meals.

PICNIC SITES (Mooiplaas and Babalala)
Gas braai facilities, braai places, soft drinks and wood for sale, toilets.

ENQUIRIES
National Parks Board Reservations, PO Box 787, Pretoria 0001; tel. (012) 343-1991, fax. 343-0905; PO Box 7400, Roggebaai 8012; tel. (021) 22-2810, fax. 24-6211.

41 THE ESCARPMENT

Stretching south from its junction with the Strydpoort and Wolkberg mountains near Tzaneen, the Escarpment is a 250-km rampart of sheer cliffs. One of South Africa's top holiday spots, it is known for its scenic grandeur – its views, rock formations, waterfalls and the Blyde River Canyon.

How to get there
Sabie, about 385 km east of Johannesburg, is an ideal base from which to explore the Escarpment. From Johannesburg take the N4 past Middelburg, Belfast and Machadodorp; continue along the R36 to the historic Voortrekker town of Lydenburg. From here the road passes the Gustav Klingbiel Nature Reserve on the left-hand side, and continues over the Long Tom Pass to reach Sabie 56 km beyond Lydenburg.

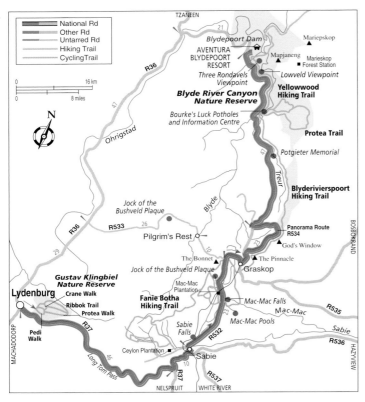

➡ The 140-km Summit Route starts at Lydenburg, passing some of the country's most beautiful scenery. Highlights include the Long Tom Pass, the Panorama Route, The Pinnacle, God's Window, Bourke's Luck and the Blyde River Canyon Nature Reserve. Part overlaps with the Waterfall and Digging for Gold routes (see pp. 182 and 184).

SUMMIT ROUTE

Nestling among the pine-clad slopes of the Drakensberg Escarpment, Sabie (see p. 185) is surrounded by enchanting plantations and mountain scenery. In common with many other towns and settlements in the area, a settlement sprang up here following the discovery of gold in 1880.

To supply the timber needs of the gold-mining industry, plantations were first established in the area in 1876. Since then vast areas of Mpumalanga have been afforested and Sabie is today the centre of one of the largest single concentrations of commercial plantations in the world. Covering 300 000 ha, it is an important centre of the area's timber industry. A visit to the **Forestry Museum** in Ford Street provides a fascinating insight into the development of South Africa's forestry industry.

Driving north towards Graskop from Sabie on the R532, you pass the **Sabie Falls** (see p. 182) outside town. The road passes through extensive pine plantations and after 10 km passes the turnoff to the Mac-Mac Pools and Falls (see p. 182) a short way on.

On the left-hand side of the road near the turnoff to the Mac-Mac Forest Station a bronze plaque commemorates **Jock of the Bushveld** (see box, p. 179).

This is one of several plaques along the old routes followed by the legendary Staffordshire terrier and Percy FitzPatrick.

The Mac-Mac picnic site is a short way on. As the road climbs to a rocky outcrop known as The Bonnet, a relict patch of indigenous forest on the slopes of Stanley Bush Kop comes into view. Ignore the Pilgrim's Rest (see p. 186) turnoff at The Bonnet and continue to **Graskop**, named after the grassy hillock on which a mining settlement was established in the 1880s. The forestry town, close to the edge of the Escarpment, is also known as 'The Window on the Eastern Transvaal'.

Continuing on the R532, turn off onto the **Panorama Route** (R534) 2,6 km north of Graskop. A short way on is the signposted turnoff to the 30-m-high **Pinnacle** towering above the densely-wooded Driekop or Pinnacle Gorge. The Pinnacle (an isolated column of weathered quartzite often mistaken for granite) lies at the southern end of the **Blyde River Canyon Nature Reserve** (see p. 180), which centres around the Blyde River Canyon.

From the Pinnacle the Panorama Route winds close to the edge of the Escarpment, with several viewpoints overlooking the Lowveld. At **God's Window** the cliffs plunge over 700 m to the Lowveld. On the edge of the precipice platforms with safety railings afford uninterrupted views of the magnificent scenery and indigenous forests of yellowwood, lemonwood, ironwood, wild peach and assegai clinging to the slopes. In the foothills, the forests are replaced by pine plantations as far east as the eye can see. The Escarpment was formed 2 000 million years ago when magma intruded the floor of a shallow sea (the Transvaal Basin). The magma's weight caused the centre of the basin to subside, forcing the rim's edges upwards.

From the parking area at God's Window a path leads up to the **Rain Forest**, with ferns, mosses and stunted yellowwoods draped with old man's beard, on the 1 730-m-high Quartzkop. Clivias covering the forest floor are especially attractive when they bloom between October and December.

Rejoin the R532, which winds through pine plantations interspersed with belts of eucalyptus trees, planted as windbreaks. Look out on the right for the **Potgieter Memorial** 19 km after you rejoin the R532. The stone memorial overlooks the site where the main party of Voortrekker leader Andries Potgieter camped in 1844 while he and a few men searched for a route to the sea. Fearing that the group had perished, the main party decided to return to Potchefstroom and named the river where they were encamped the Treur River (River of Mourning). When Potgieter and his men caught up with them shortly after they had set off, the river they were about to cross was named the Blyde River (River of Rejoicing). After crossing the Treur River the road passes through grassveld, 5,5 km later reaching **Bourke's Luck** (see p. 179), the main access point to the Blyde River Canyon Nature Reserve.

From Bourke's Luck, the road runs along the western boundary of the reserve, with magnificent views of the **Blyde River Canyon**. Here the Blyde River has created a 32-km-long canyon which is 700 m deep in places. From the **Lowveld viewpoint** on the edge of the canyon, visitors can enjoy awe-inspiring views of the canyon, ranked among southern Africa's greatest natural marvels. More stunning views of the canyon, the Blydepoort Dam and the Three Rondavels await visitors at the **Three Rondavels viewpoint** a short way on. Dominating the scenery are the Three Rondavels, reminiscent of traditional African huts. Also known as the Chief's Wives, the quartzite-capped peaks are flanked by the 1 631-m-high Mapjaneng (Chief). Further east lies Mariepskop (1 944 m), named after Maripi Mashile, a Bapedi Chief, who took part in a battle against the Swazis in 1864, during which the latter were defeated.

➡ *Bourke's Luck, the main access point to the Blyde River Canyon Nature Reserve, is 66 km from Sabie along the R532. The turnoff is signposted on the right.*

BOURKE'S LUCK

At the junction of the Treur and Blyde rivers, the swirling waters of the two rivers, aided by boulders and pebbles, have scoured magnificent cylindrical potholes into the yellow dolomite rock. Two footbridges span the Blyde River Canyon, with a third bridge overlooking the potholes.

Ironically, Tom Bourke, the prospector after whom the potholes were named, did not discover gold in the potholes, nor

As the Blyde River cut through the Escarpment, it left behind the quartzite-capped Three Rondavels.

did he strike it rich when the main gold-bearing reef south of the river was discovered adjacent to the property he had acquired at the turn of the century.

Not to be missed at Bourke's Luck is the **Visitor Information Centre**, with its outstanding

Water, aided by pebbles, has scoured these potholes at Bourke's Luck.

JOCK OF THE BUSHVELD

The adventures of Jock of the Bushveld are chronicled in one of the classics of South African literature. First published in 1907, *Jock of the Bushveld* gives a spell-binding account of the experiences shared by the tan-coloured Staffordshire terrier and his master and author of the book, Percy FitzPatrick, who was a transport rider between Lydenburg and Delagoa Bay (now Maputo) between 1885 and 1889.

Jock was born in 1885 near Ship Mountain in what is now the Kruger National Park. The runt of the litter of six, he was the only pup left when FitzPatrick adopted him. However, Jock soon proved his intelligence, agility and bravery. During his four years in the wilds he had numerous close encounters with game. In one of them, he lost his hearing when a wounded kudu ewe kicked him on the jaw. His adventures came to an end in Barberton in 1889 when FitzPatrick lost over 40 oxen to drought, heat and *nagana*. He was forced to abandon two wagons with most of their cargo during a return trip from Delagoa Bay. By an ironic twist of fate, Jock was shot dead a few years later when he was mistaken for a marauding dog suspected of carrying out night raids on a chicken pen. The following morning the real culprit was also found dead, killed by Jock.

LONG TOM PASS

The 46-km-long Long Tom Pass, which winds across the Drakensberg between Lydenburg and Sabie, is steeped in history and is one of South Africa's most scenic passes.

Sections of the original pass, built in the 1870s to link Lydenburg and Delagoa Bay (now Maputo), can still be seen from the modern pass. Known as the Old Harbour Road, the pass followed a treacherous route over Mauchsberg, the highest peak in the Drakensberg, in a series of hairpin bends and dangerous descents over the Devil's Knuckles and down the Staircase and Die Geut (The Gutter) – a steep chute.

The name Long Tom recalls one of the last battles of the Anglo-Boer War when the retreating Boer forces deployed two 155-mm Creusot artillery guns in the pass against the pursuing British forces commanded by General Redvers Buller in September 1900. The British forces originally gave the nickname of Long Tom to these guns.

A replica of one of these artillery pieces can be seen 3,4 km east of the 2 150-m-high summit of the pass. From the summit, the pass drops in a series of sweeping curves down to Sabie, losing 1 100 m in altitude over 8 km.

exhibits on the geology and the various ecosystems of the nature reserve, as well as points of socio-historic interest. There are picnic sites with braai places and toilets at Bourke's Luck.

➡ To reach the Blyde River Canyon Nature Reserve from Sabie, take the R532 north for 66 km, past Graskop and God's Window, to Bourke's Luck. The turnoff to the reserve is signposted to the right. The signposted turnoff to Aventura Blydepoort is also along the R532, 14 km north of Bourke's Luck.

BLYDE RIVER CANYON NATURE RESERVE

Covering about 27 000 ha, this reserve stretches northwards for 57 km along the Escarpment. It was primarily proclaimed to preserve the area's scenic beauty.

The **mammals** visitors might see include kudu, klipspringer, grey rhebok, common and red duiker, bushbuck and bushpig. The loud grunts of the hippo in the Blydepoort Dam are often heard by trailists on the day walks which traverse the slopes above the dam (see p. 181). The reserve is also the habitat of five of southern Africa's six primate species – thick-tailed and lesser bushbabies, baboon, and both vervet and samango monkeys.

Birdlife is prolific; to date 360-odd species have been recorded between the Long Tom Pass and the Blydepoort Dam. Among them are the brownheaded parrot, the colourful Knysna lourie and its close relative, the purple-crested lourie, chorister robin and the olive bush shrike. Birds of prey include black and crowned

The Escarpment's rugged edge has been created by erosion and the variable hardnesses of underlying geological strata.

eagles, jackal buzzard and lanner falcon. A noteworthy species which breeds on the cliffs near Bourke's Luck is the bald ibis.

The **vegetation** of the reserve ranges from dense indigenous forest in the canyon to mountain grassveld with the occasional tree fern alongside streams. Typical species of the grassveld include proteas (there are seven species in the reserve), cabbage trees and the Transvaal milkplum, which favours rocky areas. Two of the proteas, the Blyde River sugarbush (*Protea laetans*) and the Transvaal mountain sugarbush (*Protea rubropilosa*) are considered rare and can be seen growing on a rocky ledge below the Three Rondavels viewpoint.

Aventura's **Blydepoort Resort** is set in unsurpassed surroundings adjacent to the nature reserve. Visitors can enjoy the overwhelming beauty of the area from two viewpoints (accessible by car).

The reserve is traversed by three trails and Blydepoort Resort provides access to a number of short day walks in the nature reserve (*see* below).

WALKS AND TRAILS

Walks and trails to suit the interest and level of fitness of everyone criss-cross the Escarpment.
GUSTAV KLINGBIEL NATURE RESERVE (from Lydenburg to Sabie): The 20-km, two-day **Ribbok Trail** starts at the Lydenburg Museum and leads through the reserve, where trailists overnight in huts. The 5-km **Pedi Walk** leads to the ruins of an settlement which was inhabited by the ancestors of the Pedi people. The **Crane Walk** covers 9 km, initially following the Pedi Walk route and then continues to a dam and a vulture restaurant. The **Protea Walk** is named after the dense stands of proteas through which the trail passes. Trailists enjoy splendid views of their surroundings on this 12-km route, winding past old forts built by the Boers during the Anglo-Boer War.
CEYLON FOREST STATION: South Africa's first National Hiking-way Trail, the **Fanie Botha** winds mainly through pine plantations, occasionally interspersed with grassveld and patches of indigenous forest. The five-day trail

winds for 79 km to God's Window, but there are also shorter two-day options. For details of the Loerie Walk *see* p. 183.
GRASKOP: On the highly recommended 7-km **Jock of the Bushveld Trail**, starting at the Graskop Tourist Camp, trailists follow in the footsteps of Percy FitzPatrick and his faithful canine companion (*see* box, p. 179). An added attraction are rock formations resembling a sitting hen, wolf, sea-horse and vulture respectively.
BLYDE RIVER CANYON NATURE RESERVE: God's Window is the starting point of the **Blyderivierspoort Hiking Trail**, which meanders for 65 km through the reserve to Swadini in the Lowveld. Complementing this trail are two circular overnight trails, starting at Bourke's Luck: the **Protea Hiking Trail** is a four-day route

Protea rubropilosa, one of seven protea species in the reserve.

covering 41-km and the **Yellowwood Hiking Trail** covers 25 km in two days.

Day walks of 2 to 5 km can be taken in the nature reserve, from the Aventura Blydepoort Resort. Highly recommended is the 2-km **Tufa Trail** in the Kadishi Valley with its fringed pools and tufa waterfalls. These porous rocks are formed when carbon dioxide from the calcium-rich water originating in the dolomite hills further upstream is extracted by mosses, resulting in a buildup of calcium.
MARIEPSKOP STATE FOREST: Various trails start at the Mariepskop chalets. An easy 20-km circular hike (with shorter routes) goes through indigenous forest (yellowwood, Cape wild fig, black ironwood, cabbage tree and white stinkwood). During a steep 8-km hike up Magalieskop (1 688 m), only for the very fit, bushbuck, red duiker, samango monkeys and Knysna louries may be seen.

42 WATERFALL ROUTE

The crystal-clear mountain streams of the Escarpment, endowed with an abundance of rainfall, have created a variety of waterfalls, from small curtains and thin veils of water to high waterfalls with sheer drops. These cascading splendours are unrivalled anywhere in South Africa.

How to get there

The charming forestry village of Sabie is an ideal base from which to explore the many waterfalls of the area. Sabie, 385 km east of Johannesburg, is reached by travelling along the N4 past Middelburg, Belfast and Machadodorp and then continuing along the R36 to Lydenburg. From here the road continues over the historic Long Tom Pass to reach Sabie 56 km beyond Lydenburg.

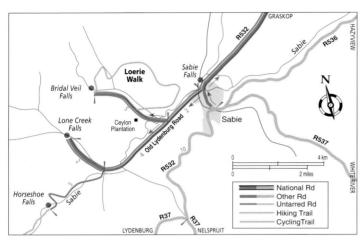

TREUR RIVER BARB

With only two populations in Mpumalanga, the Treur River barb is one of the rarest fresh-water fish in the province. This 10-cm-long olive-brown and silvery-white barb came to the attention of scientists in 1958 when it was discovered in the Treur River near Bourke's Luck. Following the introduction of trout and bass into the rivers of the Escarpment in the 1960s, the small barb fell prey to these predators and by the late 1960s no trace could be found of the Treur River population.

However, a population was discovered in 1967 in a 4,5-km section of the upper Blyde River. This population owed its existence to a 20-m-high waterfall which prevented trout from moving further upstream, and to measures taken by the landowners, Mondi Timber, to improve the habitat alongside the river.

In 1994 several hundred of these minnows were netted and reintroduced into the Treur River, where a waterfall will protect them from predation by exotic species.

➡ *The many splendid waterfalls of the Escarpment can be explored along a scenic 80-km one-way drive from Sabie and can be combined with Tour 41 (see p. 178).*

WATERFALL ROUTE

Four waterfalls can be viewed in close proximity to Sabie. Three of these are reached by travelling north along Main Street and then turning left into the old Lydenburg Road. Turn right after 2,5 km onto a gravel road which leads past the Ceylon Forest

Station to the Bridal Veil Falls parking area about 3,8 km beyond the turnoff.

From here it is a short walk through a patch of indigenous forest of yellowwoods, wild peach and water berry trees to the base of the **Bridal Veil Falls** – a gossamer screen of water cascading 70 m over the cliffs into a pool.

Retrace the approach route and turn right onto the old Lydenburg Road half a kilometre after the Ceylon Forest Station. Continue for 3,1 km on a gravel road and

turn right onto a tar road which ends at the parking area near the **Lone Creek Falls**, 2,7 km on. A tributary of the Sabie River plunges 68 m over a sheer cliff into the Lone Creek – a name dating back to the colourful gold-mining days of the 1870s. Picnic facilities and toilets are provided at the scenic parking area.

The **Horseshoe Falls** in the Sabie River are reached by returning to the old Lydenburg Road. Turn right and continue for about 4,2 km to the falls. Although they are not very high, the setting of the twin streams, in a patch of indigenous forest, makes a visit worthwhile.

Return to Sabie and follow the R532 towards Graskop, stopping on the outskirts of the town at the bridge over the 70-m-wide gorge formed by the Sabie River. The viewpoint below the bridge overlooks the deep chasm into which the 46-m **Sabie Falls** plunge.

Continue towards Graskop along the R532. The road winds through pine plantations to reach the turnoff to the Mac-Mac Pools about 10 km after leaving Sabie. Situated on the grassy slopes of Mac-Mac Bluff, the pools are in a tributary of the Mac-Mac River. After cascading over a low rock wall, the stream wends its way through a series of small pools made deeper by a series of low cement walls. Picnic facilities with braai places and toilets are provided and the pools are especially popular in summer when visitors can cool down in the sparkling water. The 3-km-long Secretarybird Walk is signposted at the pools.

A viewpoint overlooking the **Mac-Mac Falls** is a short way on. The 56-m-high falls were originally a single-drop waterfall, but during the search for gold during the 1870s the crest was blasted, splitting the waterfall in two. The mining settlement which sprang up here was reputedly named Mac-Mac by President Burgers: during a visit to the area in 1873, Burgers expressed surprise at all the Scotsmen living at settlement and named it Mac-Mac.

Shortly after the Mac-Mac Forest Station, the **Green Heritage picnic site** is on the right-hand side of the road. Until a few years ago it was shaded by tall Mexican cypresses, planted in 1924, but they had to be felled because of disease and indigenous trees have been planted. Starting at the picnic site is an easy 1,6-km one-way walk to the **Forest Falls** (*see* Walks and Trails below) where the Rooilelie River drops 18 m over a wide rock ledge into a crystal-clear pool. On the opposite side of the picnic site there is a short ramble to an inviting swimming pool and the **Maria Shires Waterfall** – a small cascade (*see* Walks and Trails below). The falls were named after the wife of Joseph Shires (Senior), who once owned land at Mac-Mac and wattle plantations in the area. The grave of Maria Shires can be seen along the shorter walk.

Continuing towards Graskop along the R532, you pass the turnoff to Pilgrim's Rest (*see* p. 186) and about 3 km further on you cross a small stream on a **Natural Rock Bridge** (signposted). About 7,6 km north of Graskop, the turnoff to the **Lisbon Falls** is signposted along the R532; the falls themselves are 2,4 km on. Above the 95-m-high falls, the Lisbon River forms a series of pools, before cascading in three separate falls over cliffs draped in shrubs into a deep pool. Picnic facilities are provided.

Also worth visiting are the nearby **Berlin Falls**, where the Watervalspruit has formed a narrow chute through the lip of a sheer, lichen-encrusted rock wall.

Watervalspruit plunges over the Berlin Falls into a pool enclosed in an amphitheatre of lichen-covered rock.

The Berlin Falls are reached by crossing the Lisbon River above the falls and continuing for 2,1 km to the signposted turnoff to the left. The falls are 400 m on. During the dry winter, the 80-m-high falls are often only a thin ribbon of water, but after heavy rains the water thunders through a chute onto a ledge, causing the water to spread out along the width of the cliffs before plunging into the pool below.

WALKS AND TRAILS

The indigenous forests and pine plantations of the Waterfall Route are crossed by several trails.
CEYLON FOREST STATION: The **Loerie Walk**, a 13,5-km route with a shorter option, initially winds through pine plantations before passing the Bridal Veil Falls. Here the path ascends steeply through indigenous forest before continuing through pine plantations. The **Fanie Botha Trail** also starts here (*see* p. 181).
MAC-MAC FOREST STATION: From the Green Heritage picnic site visitors can set off on the **Forest Falls Walk**, a 3,2-km circular ramble through pine plantations. The return route winds through indigenous forest along the Rooilelie River, a tributary of the Mac-Mac River. The picnic site is also the starting point of a short, 15-minute circular ramble to the **Maria Shires Falls**. The **Prospector's Hiking Trail** (*see* p. 187) starts at the Mac-Mac Forest Station and leads to Bourke's Luck.

The Sabie River skirts around and over rocks at the Horseshoe Falls.

(see p. 186)

(see p. 181)

(see p. 187)

WATERFALL ROUTE AT A GLANCE

MAIN ATTRACTIONS
Waterfalls, relics of the gold-mining era of the previous century, scenic picnic sites.

BEST TIMES TO VISIT
Throughout the year. Average daytime temperatures on the Escarpment are pleasant, but mid-winter minimums of close to zero are not uncommon. Most rainfall is recorded between November and March.

CEYLON AND MAC-MAC FOREST STATIONS
Permits/bookings: None required for the Loerie or the Forest Falls walks.
Opening times: Sunrise to sunset, throughout the year.
Accommodation: None.
Facilities: Braai places at start of Forest Falls Walk.

MAC-MAC POOLS
Permits/bookings: No bookings are required.

Opening times: Sunrise to sunset, throughout the year.
Accommodation: None.
Facilities: Picnic place, swimming area, Secretary Bird Nature Walk.

WATERFALLS
Facilities: Picnic places with toilets at Bridal Veil, Horseshoe, Sabie and Libon falls.

ENQUIRIES
SAFCOL, Private Bag X503, Sabie 1260; tel. (01315) 4-1058 or 4-1392, fax. 4-2071.

TOURIST INFORMATION
Lowveld and Escarpment Tourism, PO Box 5018, Nelspruit 1200; tel. (01311) 55-1988, fax. 55-1350.
Sabie Tourism, PO Box 494, Sabie 1260; tel. and fax. (01315) 4-3492. **Graskop Tourism,** PO Box 171, Graskop 1270; tel. (01315) 7-1316, fax. 7-1798.

43 DIGGING FOR GOLD

The Drakensberg Escarpment and foothills from Barberton northwards to Pilgrim's Rest are characterised by extensive tracts of mountain grassland, patches of montane indigenous forest and exotic plantations of pine trees. One of the most beautiful parts of the country – with scenery ranging from the undulating Barberton mountainlands to the splendour of the Escarpment – this region boasts a diversity of endemic flora and is home to one of South Africa's most endangered birds, the blue swallow.

How to get there
Barberton, 405 km east of Johannesburg, is an ideal base for exploring the Gold Route, retracing the hectic search for gold during the previous century. From Johannesburg follow the N4 to Nelspruit; from here take the R40 for 45 km to Barberton.

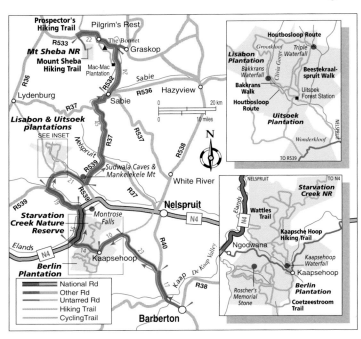

BARBERTON

Situated in the De Kaap Valley at the foot of the Makhonjwa Mountains, Barberton is a picturesque town whose streets are lined with jacaranda and flamboyant trees. Its name honours Graham Barber, who discovered gold in 1884 in a narrow creek southeast of the town.

Relics of Barberton's colourful and romantic gold-mining history abound in the town, including the façade of the first gold stock exchange in South Africa (dating back to 1887) and the Lewis and Marks Building, the first double-storey building in the then Transvaal. In the surrounding mountainlands, claims and names like Eureka City, Sheba Mine and King Solomon's Mine are reminders of the Barberton gold rush.

The name Barberton also recalls the adventures of Jock of the Bushveld (*see* p. 179); a bronze statue, sculpted by Ivan Mitford Barberton, can be seen outside the town hall. Another reminder of Jock's travels is a plaque on the spot (10 km north of Barberton on the R38 to Kaapmuiden) where an employee of Fitz-Patrick, Jantje, was attacked by a wounded buffalo and thrown into an umbrella thorn tree, which became known as **Jock's Tree**.

Spectacular **flowering plants** such as the Barberton daisy and the Pride-of-De Kaap (*Bauhinia galpinii*), with its deep salmon-orange flowers, grow in the area. Between May and August the yellow-white flowers of the dense concentrations of Barberton mountain sugarbushes (*Protea comptonii*) create a colourful display on the slopes of the Saddleback Mountains.

Several **rare plants** such as the Barberton Lowveld sugarbush (*Protea curvata*) are also found here. This bears striking deep red-pink flowers in June and July and is confined to a few hills in the mountains around Barberton. Also of interest is the Barberton cycad (*Encephalartos paucidentatus*), endemic to Barberton and Piggs Peak in Swaziland.

THE BLUE SWALLOW

The blue swallow, with its metallic blue-black plumage and elongated tail streamers, is one of the four most endangered bird species in South Africa.

It is an intra-African breeding migrant which arrives in South Africa from as far north as Zaïre in September to breed and heads northwards again in April.

The main reason for the decline of the blue swallow is the afforestation of montane grasslands, denying them access to their nests which are made in holes in stream banks, potholes and dongas.

During a survey conducted by the Endangered Wildlife Trust in 1984, only 46 positive and 17 possible nesting pairs were located in South Africa and Swaziland.

In 1986, 470 ha of montane grassland south of Kaapsehoop (known as Blouswaelvlakte or 'blue swallow plains') was set aside by the former Department of Environment Affairs, to ensure the survival of South Africa's biggest colony of blue swallows, at the time numbering about 12 pairs (the most recent count is 10 breeding pairs, or about 28–30 birds in total). Although more nesting pairs have since been recorded in KwaZulu-Natal, the blue swallow remains one of South Africa's most endangered birds.

The lure of gold has long lingered in the mountains of Barberton.

The area is also of **geological** significance as the basement rocks of the Barberton mountainland are among the oldest in the world. Dating back 3 400 million years, these rocks contain the oldest forms of life yet discovered on earth – rod-shaped microorganisms and blue-green algae.

With its combination of geological, botanical and mining points of interests, the Fortuna Mine Trail (see p. 187) should not be missed.

➡ *To reach the gold-mining settlement of Kaapsehoop from Barberton, follow the R40 for 18 km towards Nelspruit; turn left onto the Kaapsehoop road and follow it for 23 km to the T-junction with district road 799. Turn left here to reach Kaapsehoop 10 km on.*

KAAPSEHOOP

Abandoned houses and shops, the ruins of the government building and old street names are reminders of the days when Kaapsehoop, on the edge of the Drakensberg Escarpment, was a prosperous mining settlement.

Although Tom MacLachlan claimed as early as 1874 that he had discovered gold at De Kaap, it was not until 1885 that the De Kaap Goldfields were officially proclaimed. Thousands of prospectors, miners and fortune-seekers flocked to the area and in its heyday the settlement boasted a government building, two hotels, several bars, a school, post office and an assortment of houses.

Much of the area is covered in pine plantations, but relict patches of **indigenous forest** occur below the Escarpment to the south and southeast of the settlement.

Over 200 **bird species** have been recorded in the area, including one of South Africa's most endangered birds, the blue swallow (see p. 184). Among the species to keep an eye out for are the secretarybird, longcrested and crowned eagles, purplecrested lourie, blackcollared barbet, Natal robin, orangethroated longclaw and the olive bush shrike.

Mammals which trailists on the Kaapsche Hoop Hiking Trails (see p. 187) might see include baboon, vervet monkey and rock

Barberton nestles in a valley covered by the purple flowers of jacaranda trees.

dassie. Also known to occur in the area are common and blue duiker, oribi, bushbuck, klipspringer and bushpig.

➡ *From Kaapsehoop follow the gravel road westwards for 14 km to the junction with the N4. Turn right and continue to the turnoff onto the R539, 5 km after passing the Montrose Falls. Turn left here and take the P2-10 6,6 km further on to reach the turnoff to the Sudwala Caves after another 1,2 km.*

SUDWALA CAVES

Situated in the Houtbosloop Valley running through the foothills of the Drakensberg Escarpment are the Sudwala Caves – a maze of passages and caverns extending deep into the bowels of the Mankelekele Mountain. This underground treasure chest was created millions of years ago when carbon dioxide-rich water dissolved the limestone in the dolomite rock.

The main chamber, the P R Owen Hall, has a diameter of 67 m and the highest point of the dome-shaped roof is 37 m above the floor of the cave. Adorning the caves are curtains of stalactites hanging from the roof, a stalagmite called the Weeping

Madonna, a 14-m-high stalagmite called the Rocket Silo, and grotesque formations such as the Screaming Monster.

The adjacent **Dinosaur Park** gives visitors an impression of the fearsome creatures which roamed the earth millions of years ago. Life-like models of the tyrant lizard (*Tyrannosaurus rex*), the largest terrestrial predator ever known, and the thunder lizard (*Brontosaurus*) are displayed in realistic surroundings. Also to be seen is a display depicting the development of the horse family and two South African mammals

The Sudwala Caves with their stalagmites and stalactites.

which became extinct in the 19th century, the quagga and the Cape or black-maned lion.

➡ *From the Sudwala Caves, return to the T-junction with the R539, turn left and follow the R539 for 15 km and continue along the R37 to reach Sabie 30 km further on.*

SABIE

The search for gold in Mpumalanga was initially focused on the mountains around Sabie. In 1871 alluvial gold was discovered at Spitskop, some 23 km south of Sabie. Thousands of prospectors, miners and fortune-seekers rushed here when further discoveries were made nearby at Hendriksdal in 1872 and Mac-Mac in 1873. Most of the alluvial finds were disappointing and, with the opening of more promising goldfields at Pilgrim's Rest (1873), Barberton (1884) and the Witwatersrand (1886), most of the miners abandoned their claims.

The discovery of reef gold at Sabie in 1895 was by pure accident. While Thomas Glynn, owner of the farm on which Sabie was subsequently established, and some of his friends were practising target shooting in the upper reaches of the Sabie

River, a bullet struck a rock face and revealed a gold-bearing reef. The Glynns-Lydenburg Gold Mining Company was floated and, between 1897 and 1950, 1,2 million ounces of gold were extracted from the mine.

The **Sabie Forestry Museum** in Ford Street in the centre of town depicts the growth of the timber industry in South Africa.

➡ *From Sabie, follow the R532 towards Graskop (see p. 180) for 23 km and turn left at The Bonnet onto the R533 to reach Pilgrim's Rest 8,5 km further on.*

PILGRIM'S REST

The romantic gold-mining history of Pilgrim's Rest dates back to 1873 when Alec Patterson loaded his personal belongings onto a

The picturesque village of Pilgrim's Rest.

wheelbarrow (a habit which earned him the nickname Wheelbarrow Patterson) and left the Mac-Mac goldfields. Patterson headed for a valley 15 km northwest of Graskop and discovered gold in the Pilgrim's Creek. A gold rush was sparked when another digger, William Trafford, also discovered gold in the area and a shanty town sprang up virtually overnight.

There are several apocryphal explanations of how the mining settlement was named – the most common being that when Trafford settled there he exclaimed, 'The pilgrim is at rest'.

Within a year 1 500-odd miners were working claims in the area and Pilgrim's Rest became South Africa's first large gold-mining town with 18 bars, 21 shops, three bakeries and two banks. Early mining activities were centered around alluvial mining – panning the streams with sluice boxes and cradles – but in 1881 a mining rights concession, awarded to D H Benjamin, put an end to small-scale mining at Pilgrim's Rest.

In 1974 the then Transvaal Provincial Administration assumed ownership of Pilgrim's Rest and, unlike most other historic mining towns, it has been preserved almost in its entirety. At the **Digging's Museum** on the eastern outskirts of town, demonstrations are given of the alluvial mining techniques used by the early miners.

The focal point of the town is the Royal Hotel and its historic bar, which used to be a Roman Catholic Church in Maputo before it was dismantled and transported in sections to Pilgrim's Rest in 1893. Nearby is the **Miner's House** – a period museum representing a miner's house between the years 1910 and 1920.

Downtown is the **Reduction Works** which has also been turned into a museum. Built in 1896, the complex once consisted of 60 stamp batteries (where the final crushing of the gold ore took place), the mine workshops, smelting house and the manager's office. Guided tours are conducted daily (see p. 187).

MOUNT SHEBA NATURE RESERVE

This secluded 400-ha nature reserve below the 1 958-m-high Mount Sheba protects one of the few remaining large stands of indigenous forest in the Mpumalanga Drakensberg. Among the 110 species of **trees** which have been identified are fine specimens of real and Outeniqua yellowwood and ironwoods (some estimated to be 1 500 years old), the Cape chestnut, cabbage trees and red pear. The forest is also renowned for its rich diversity of ferns and mosses.

A network of trails (*see* p. 188) gives access to the forests, home to the thick-tailed bushbaby, samango monkey, red duiker and

bushpig. Oribi, blesbok and grey rhebok are found in the mountain grassveld and the rocky escarpment is the favoured habitat of baboon, rock dassie and klipspringer.

Birdlife includes the jackal buzzard, Knysna lourie, chorister robin, bluemantled flycatcher, gorgeous bush shrike and Gurney's sugarbird, as well as four sunbirds – malachite, lesser and greater doublecollared, as well as the black sunbird. Nestling in an amphitheatre surrounded by lush indigenous forests high above Pilgrim's Rest in the reserve, the Mount Sheba Hotel is a fine country hotel, renowned for its tranquillity and rustic atmosphere.

The forests of the Mount Sheba Nature Reserve boast no fewer than 110 indigenous tree species.

At the western end of town is the four-arch **Joubert Bridge**. Built in 1986 with dressed dolomite, it was named after the Mining Commissioner at the time, J S Joubert.

WALKS AND TRAILS

BARBERTON: The 2-km **Fortuna Mine Trail** trail meanders through typical Lowveld vegetation. About 100 different tree species have been labelled in the area. A highlight of the trail is the walk through a 600-m-long tunnel (a strong torch is essential), built in the early 1900s to transport gold-bearing ore from the Fortuna Mine to the mill. This section takes trailists through some of the oldest rock formations in the world.

UITSOEK PLANTATION: The network of trails in the Houtbosloop Valley offers trailists a choice of

The Barberton daisy occurs in the mountains around Barberton.

a two-day, 29,5-km hike along the **Houtbosloop Route** or two 11-km day routes – the **Bakkrans** and the **Beestekraalspruit** walks. On the second day of the Houtbosloop Route, the trail leads through a delightful patch of indigenous forest and criss-crosses the Houtbosloop River several times.

BERLIN PLANTATION: Two circular overnight trails, which comprise the **Kaapsche Hoop Hiking Trails**, traverse these pine plantations, southwest of Nelspruit. Several old diggings, an overgrown miner's house and other relics along the trail routes serve as reminders of Kaapsehoop's heyday. One of South Africa's most endangered birds, the blue swallow, breeds in the area of the Berlin Plantation (*see* box, p. 184).

MAC-MAC PLANTATION: The history of the Escarpment is linked to the search for gold and relics can be seen on the **Prospector's Hiking Trail** between the plantation and Bourke's Luck (*see* p. 179). The six-day trail over 69 km has shorter options.

MOUNT SHEBA NATURE RESERVE: The reserve is traversed by a network of well-maintained walks – from the relatively easy **Golagola Walk** (a delightful 2-km ramble along a mountain stream in the indigenous forest) to more strenuous

walks. One of the most scenic is to **Marco's Mantle**, a waterfall which plunges into a forested gorge. A highlight of the 5-km circular walk is a section along a ledge behind the waterfall, which plunges into a magnificent pool, passed on the return leg.

(*see* p. 179)

DIGGING FOR GOLD AT A GLANCE

MAIN ATTRACTIONS
Historic gold-mining villages, Sudwala Caves, Dinosaur Park, blue swallows, walks and trails.

BEST TIMES TO VISIT
Throughout the year. Average daytime temperatures on the escarpment are generally pleasant, but in mid-winter minimum temperatures of close to zero are not uncommon. Most of the area's rainfall is recorded between November and March.

BARBERTON
Permits/bookings: **Fortuna Mine Trail:** No permits are required.
Opening times: **Fortuna Mine Trail:** Sunrise to sunset.
Accommodation: Visitors are well catered for and accommodation ranges from hotels and guest houses to self-catering cottages and caravan/camp sites. Contact Barberton Publicity (*see* below).
Enquiries: **Barberton Publicity,** PO Box 33, Barberton 1340; tel. (01314) 2-2121, fax. 2-2121, extension 161.

SUDWALA CAVES
Permits/bookings: Advance reservations not required. Fee payable at gate. Groups of 15 or more to book a few days in advance.
Opening times: 08h30–16h30 throughout the year. Tours of the Crystal Chamber are conducted on the first Saturday of each month.
Accommodation: **Sudwala Lodge:** Hotel and timeshare; sixteen 2-bed en suite rooms, fully catered. **Reservations:** PO Box 30, Schagen 1207; tel. (01311) 6-3073, fax. 6-3077.
Facilities: Restaurant, curio shop, toilets.

Enquiries: PO Box 48, Schagen 1207; tel. (01311) 6-4152.

DINOSAUR PARK
Permits/bookings: Advance reservations are not required. An entrance fee is payable at the gate.
Opening times: Throughout the year 08h30–17h00.
Accommodation: **Pierre's Place:** Bed and breakfast; 3 double en suite rooms. PO Box 140, Schagen 1207; tel. (01311) 6-4134.
Facilities: Restaurant, curio shop, toilets.
Enquiries: PO Box 140, Schagen 1207; tel. and fax. (01311) 6-4134.

PILGRIM'S REST
Permits/bookings: Museum tickets and bookings for guided tours at Information Centre.
Opening times: **Digging's Museum:** Demonstrations daily at 10h00, 11h00, 12h00, 14h00 and 15h00 throughout the year, weather permitting. **Reduction Works:** Guided tours from Monday to Saturday at 10h30 and 14h00; 10h30 on Sundays. **Anglade House Museum:** Guided tours from Monday to Saturday at 10h30 and 14h00. **Town museums (House Museum, Dredzen Shop and House Museum and Pilgrim and Sabie News Printing Museum):** 09h00–13h00 and 13h30–16h15. **Information Centre:** 09h00–12h45 and 13h15–16h30. All museums and Information Centre are closed on Christmas Day.
Accommodation: Ranges from rooms in the Royal and European hotels (with en suite facilities) to authentic

miner's cottages furnished with antiques. **Pilgrim's Rest Hotel:** PO Box 59, Pilgrim's Rest 1290; tel. (01315) 8-1100.
Enquiries: Pilgrim's Rest Information Centre, Private Bag X516, Pilgrim's Rest 1290; tel. (01315) 8-1211, fax. 8-1113.

MOUNT SHEBA NATURE RESERVE
Permits/bookings: No bookings required for day walks.
Opening times: Day walks: Sunrise to sunset.
Accommodation: Twenty-five suites in hotel and twenty self-contained timeshare cottages, sleeping four to six people. Contact **Mount Sheba Hotel** and **Nature Reserve,** PO Box 100, Pilgrim's Rest 1290; tel. (01315) 8-1241, fax. 8-1248.
Enquiries: Mount Sheba Hotel and Nature Reserve, PO Box 100, Pilgrim's Rest 1290; tel. (01315) 8-1241, fax. 8-1248.

KAAPSCHE HOOP & PROSPECTOR'S HIKING TRAILS AND HOUTBOSLOOP ROUTE
Permits/bookings: SAFCOL (*see* below).
Accommodation: Huts with bunks and mattresses.
Facilities: Drinking water, fireplaces, firewood and toilets are provided at Kaapsche Hoop, Prospector's and Uitsoek. No fires at Lisabon hut.
Enquiries: SAFCOL, Private Bag X503, Sabie 1260; tel. (01315) 4-1058 or 4-1392, fax. 4-2071.

TOURIST INFORMATION
Lowveld and Escarpment Tourism Association, PO Box 5018, Nelspruit 1200; tel. (01311) 55-1988/9, fax. 55-1350.

44 MAGOEBASKLOOF AND WOLKBERG

Magoebaskloof is a lush, subtropical paradise of evergreen indigenous forests, verdant tea plantations, aromatic pine plantations, flamboyant trees and azaleas. Nearby lies the breathtaking Wolkberg – one of the few true wilderness areas left in South Africa, and only accessible on foot.

How to get there
Below the Drakensberg Escarpment in the Northern Province, Tzaneen is centrally located for exploring the beauty of the Magoebaskloof. It is about 485 km northeast of Pretoria and is reached by following the N1 to Pietersburg, the R71 (over the Magoebaskloof Pass) for 91 km and the R36 for 8 km.

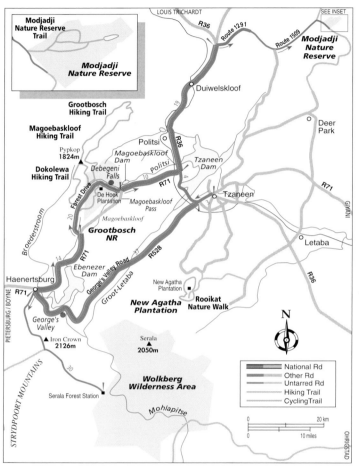

MAGOEBASKLOOF

At the northern extremity of the Drakensberg, Magoebaskloof lies between Haenertsburg on the edge of the Escarpment and Tzaneen in the Lowveld. The Magoebaskloof Pass, which winds down the Escarpment, losing over 600 m in 5,5 km, is one of South Africa's most scenic routes and is linked to two spectacular drives, George's Valley and the Forest Drive.

➤ The 60-km circular route along George's Valley and the Forest Drive is highly recommended, passing through tea plantations, orchards, pine plantations and indigenous forests. From Tzaneen take Agatha Street and continue along the R36, to the George's Valley off-ramp, on the left.

GEORGE'S VALLEY AND FOREST DRIVE SCENIC ROUTE

Winding along the Letaba Valley, the George's Valley road (the R528) passes through banana and mango plantations, and citrus orchards, with rows of neatly-planted pines on the valley slopes. The gently curving road mostly follows an easy gradient, and then winds steeply to **George's Valley**, dominated by the Iron Crown (2 126 m) and the Wolkberg Wilderness Area (*see* p. 189) to the left. About 28 km along the George's Valley road, you pass the turnoff to the **Ebenezer Dam** (stocked with bass, bream, sharptooth catfish and trout; fishing and watersports are allowed) and **Haenertsburg** (renowned for its cherry blossoms and azaleas during the September Spring Festival) is 6 km further along R528. Gold was discovered here in the 1880s, but mining proved uneconomical and miners soon abandoned their claims. The headquarters of the Zion Christian Church are at the village of Moria, near Boyne, about 19 km west of Haenertsburg on the R71.

Tea thrives along the slopes and foothills of the Escarpment.

The road through Magoebaskloof cuts across the Escarpment and is one of the most popular scenic drives in South Africa.

At Haenertsburg turn right onto the R71; after 14 km turn left onto the **Forest Drive** – a 20-km drive through pine plantations and the Grootbos Forest (the largest indigenous forest north of the Vaal River), which has been declared a nature reserve. Among the diversity of trees are yellowwoods, white stinkwood, lemonwood, ironwood and forest bushwillow. Delicate epiphytic orchids cling to the trees and masses of clivias grow in their forks.

The forests are home to **mammals** including samango monkeys, red duiker, bushbuck, leopard, and a healthy population of bushpigs. **Birdlife** is prolific and among the over 300 species recorded to date are the crowned eagle, African goshawk, Knysna lourie, terrestrial and yellow-streaked bulbuls, chorister and starred robins, paradise flycatcher and the blackfronted bush shrike.

Shortly after the old De Hoek Forest Station, starting point of Magoebaskloof's hiking trails (*see* p. 191), is the turnoff to the **Debegeni Falls**, where a tributary of the Politsi River cascades, in a series of 24-m-high falls, into a pool. Picnic places with braai

facilities and toilets enable visitors to enjoy the scenery. Resist the temptation to slide down the smooth rocks below the main falls – four people have died in accidents since 1981.

After 3 km rejoin the R71; from here the road winds past the **Magoebaskloof Dam** (fishing is not allowed) and passes extensive tea plantations en route to Tzaneen.

➡ *From Tzaneen follow the R71 into Haenertsburg. Leave Haenertsburg at its southwestern edge along a gravel road and keep left at a fork 14 km out of the town. At a four-way intersection about 6 km on, bear left and continue for about 25 km to the Serala Forest Station (which gives access to the Wolkberg), ignoring two deviations to the right.*

WOLKBERG WILDERNESS AREA

This 17 390-ha conservation area is one of the few remaining mountain wildernesses north of the Vaal River. Situated where the eastern extremity of the Strydpoort Mountains merges with the northern extension of the

Debegeni Falls is named after the pool into which it plunges.

189

THE MODJADJI CYCADS AND THE RAIN QUEEN

Of the 29 South African cycad species, the Modjadji cycad (*Encephalartos transvenosus*), growing on the slopes above the Rain Queen's kraal, is probably the most famous and has enjoyed the protection of successive generations of Rain Queens. With stems of up to 13 m high, they are the tallest cycads in South Africa.

Cycads belong to a group of plants bearing naked seeds (Gymnosperms) and male and female plants occur separately.

Modjadji cycads are the tallest cycads in South Africa.

The golden-brown cones of the female plants are enormous, weighing up to 34 kg.

The history of the Lobedu people living in the area goes back some 400 years when Dzugudini, the daughter of a Shona chief, and a handful of followers, fled from Zimbabwe after she gave birth to an illegitimate child.

The Lobedu were initially ruled by a king, but since the early 1800s have been ruled by a dynasty of queens, the Modjadji or Rain Queen. Belief in the ability of the Modjadji to make rain (a secret art which, legend has it, was brought along by the fleeing Dzugudini) earned her the respect of all southern African tribes and safeguarded the Lobedu from attack.

Surrounded by legend, the Rain Queen inspired Sir Henry Rider Haggard's classic novel *She*. She is not permitted to marry (but may have children) and she has to commit ritual suicide when she can no longer rule.

The call of the Burchell's coucal evokes the spirit of the bush.

Drakensberg, it is a wilderness of high peaks, forested valleys and grassy hills dotted with proteas.

Common duiker and bushbuck are the two most common **antelope**, but reedbuck, grey rhebok and klipspringer also occur. Among the other **mammals** to keep an eye out for are baboon, samango and vervet monkeys and bushpig. The ear-piercing shriek of the thick-tailed bushbaby (a nocturnal animal) is an unmistakable sound of the night.

The **birdlife** is not as prolific as that of the bushveld further east; to date some 160 species have been recorded. However, birders may see a number of noteworthy

species, including the bat hawk, martial eagle and blackfronted bush shrike. Other species include the secretarybird, crested guineafowl, Burchell's coucal, southern boubou and Marico sunbird.

The mountain scenery and wilderness atmosphere are hard to match and Wolkberg is, not surprisingly, popular with trailists (*see* p. 191).

➡ *From Tzaneen follow the R36 towards Louis Trichard, passing the 24 000-ha Tzaneen Dam, to reach the fertile Duiwelskloof Valley 22 km later. After a further 6 km turn right onto route 1291. After about 4 km bear right; after 6 km turn left onto route 1509. Continue for almost 11 km and turn right. The Modjadji Nature Reserve is about 4 km on.*

MODJADJI NATURE RESERVE

Covering 530 ha, the Modjadji Nature Reserve provides protection for the world's largest concentration of any single cycad species (*see* box, left). To enable visitors to explore the cycad 'forest', trails have been laid out (*see* p. 191). Picnic places with braai facilities overlook the Lowveld.

Looking towards Motale, a 1 639-m-high peak in the southern part of the Wolkberg Wilderness Area.

Roadside stalls in Magoebaskloof offer good value for money.

WALKS AND TRAILS

MAGOEBASKLOOF: From the De Hoek Forest Station, the **Magoebaskloof Hiking Trail** offers two circular three-day trails – the 36-km **Dokolewa Hiking Trail** and the 50-km **Grootbosch Hiking Trail** which goes through the indigenous Grootbos Forest.

NEW AGATHA: Named after the caracal (a regular visitor in the rainy season), the 11-km **Rooikat Nature Walk** winds through indigenous pigeonwood, white stinkwood, wild fig, assegai and water berry forests. Views of Krugerkop, the Devil's Knuckles and the Letsitele Valley reward trailists. Chances of seeing caracal are slim, but samango and vervet monkeys, baboon, bushbuck and even bushpig might be spotted.

WOLKBERG WILDERNESS AREA: Since this is a wilderness area, no facilities are provided and backpackers determine their routes. Popular destinations include the tufa waterfall in the Klipdraai River, the Mohlapitse River, Devil's Knuckles, Serala Peak and the Wonderwoud, a patch of montane indigenous forest.

MODJADJI NATURE RESERVE: A network of circular trails covering about 12 km traverses the reserve. From the parking area the trail winds through the cycad forest downwards to the thorn and grassveld area in the western section of the park, where game such as nyala, waterbuck, blue wildebeest and impala can be seen. Two loops along the main trail provide shorter options.

Many indigenous forests have had to give way to plantations.

MAGOEBASKLOOF AND WOLKBERG AT A GLANCE

MAIN ATTRACTIONS
Beautiful indigenous forests and scenery, magnificent scenic drives and walks, Modjadji cycads.

BEST TIMES TO VISIT
Throughout the year. The area enjoys a subtropical climate; summers are hot and humid with rain between October and April. Winters are dry and warm during the day, but cool in the evening. Mist can occur on the mountains throughout the year, but is especially common during the summer rainy season.

TZANEEN
Accommodation: Tzaneen Information (*see* below).

EBENEZER DAM
Permits/bookings: Contact Northern Province Waterboard (*see* below).
Opening times: From sunrise to sunset, throughout the year.
Accommodation: Fully-equipped, self-catering guest house for 6 people.
Facilities: Public picnic area, braai, toilets.
Enquiries: **Northern Province Waterboard,** Private Bag X104, Haenertsburg 0730; tel. and fax. (015276) 4200.

GROOTBOSCH NATURE RESERVE
Permits/bookings: **Forest Drive:** None required. **Debegeni Falls:** Obtainable at gate. **Dokolewa and Grootbosch hiking trails:** SAFCOL (*see* below).
Opening times: Daily sunrise to sunset throughout the year.
Accommodation: None in the reserve, except overnight shelters for hikers, with bunks and mattresses, firewood, running water and basic ablution facilities.
Facilities: **Debegeni Falls:** Picnic places.
Enquiries: SAFCOL, Private Bay X503, Sabie 1260; tel. (01315) 4-1058 or 4-1392, fax. 4-2071.

WOLKBERG WILDERNESS AREA
Permits/bookings: The Officer-in-Charge, Serala Forest Station (*see* below)
Opening times: Office: 07h30–16h00. **Wilderness:** Daily sunrise to sunset throughout the year.
Facilities: Picnic facilities at Serala Forest Station; no facilities in wilderness area.
Accommodation: Small camp site with cold-water ablutions only at Serala Forest Station.
Enquiries: **The Officer-in-Charge, Serala Forest Station,** Private Bag X102, Haenertsburg 0730; tel. (015272) ask for 1303.

MODJADJI NATURE RESERVE
Permits/bookings: Entry permits are obtainable at the gate.
Opening times: 07h00–16h00 throughout the year.
Facilities: Picnic sites with braai places and ablutions.
Accommodation: None.
Enquiries: Letaba Tourism (*see* below)

TOURIST INFORMATION
Letaba Tourism, PO Box 129, Haenertsburg 0730; tel. (0152) 76-4307, fax. 76-4386. **Tzaneen Information,** PO Box 24, Tzaneen 0850; tel. (0152) 307-1411, fax. 307-1507.

HIGHVELD AND BUSHVELD

Extending westwards from the Drakensberg Escarpment until it merges with the bushveld, the Highveld is a landscape of seemingly endlessly waving grasslands, punctuated by only two mountain ranges, the Witwatersrand and the Magaliesberg.

The focal point of the Highveld is Gauteng, the hub of South Africa's economy and the country's most densely populated area. However, small tracts of the Highveld have escaped development and provide islands of peace amid the hustle and bustle of city life. In these areas herds of typical Highveld game – blesbok, Burchell's zebra and black wildebeest – still roam the grasslands, as they did before people were lured to the area in search of gold. Millions of years earlier, homonids lived on these plains and their remains can be seen in the valleys and the caves at Sterkfontein, which are among the richest archaeological sites in the world.

At the western margin of the Highveld, the grasslands give way to bushveld savanna of bushwillow, acacia and cluster-leaf trees. Situated where the flora and fauna of the arid west meet those of the wetter east, the savanna supports a rich diversity of game and birdlife, representative of both zones. Rising above the bushveld are the Pilanesberg, an extinct volcano, the island mountains of Madikwe and the sandstone cliffs of the Waterberg.

To the east of the Waterberg, where the Nyls River cuts across the featureless plains of the Springbok Flats, lies the largest flood-plain vlei in South Africa, Nylsvley. Its diversity of birds is unrivalled by any other wetland in the country. At Warmbaths there are numerous hot water springs, offering visitors a range of recreational activities and opportunities to enjoy the therapeutic qualities of the water.

The large parks in this region – Pilanesberg, Madikwe and Marakele – rank among the country's foremost conservation areas. There are also many other delightful nature reserves: dams such as those at Bloemhof on the Vaal River and Hartbeespoort, as well as Barberspan, are popular destinations with birders and watersports enthusiasts, from freshwater anglers to yachtsmen. There are numerous walks and trails to choose from, as well as opportunities for mountain biking, horse-riding, hang-gliding and ballooning.

Pilanesberg National Park has the third-largest white rhino population in the world and visitors to the park are often treated to spectacular sightings.

Stretching for about 125 km in an arc from just west of Rustenburg to east of Pretoria, the Magaliesberg is an 'island' of undulating quartzite ridges, crystal-clear mountain streams and forested gorges, surrounded by densely populated urban areas and intensively cultivated farmlands. With its spectacular mountain scenery and recreational opportunities, it is one of South Africa's prime holiday destinations.

How to get there
Johannesburg is a convenient starting point for a 300-km-long circular drive of the Magaliesberg. Johannesburg can be reached via the N1 from Cape Town and Bloemfontein, or the N3 from Durban and Pietermaritzburg. At Rustenburg, travellers can either link up with Tour 47 to Barberspan (see p. 200) or Tour 49 to the Pilanesberg National Park (see p. 204).

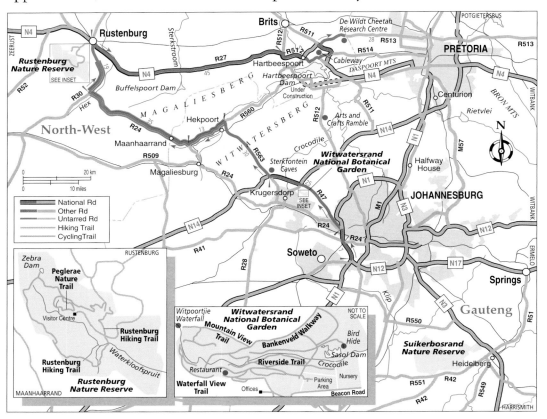

provide a nesting site for a resident pair of black eagles. A bird hide overlooks a small dam and there is an interpretative centre with displays on the history, flora and fauna of the area. There are several short walks that meander through the Bankenveld and cultivated gardens (see p. 197). A cafeteria serves light meals and refreshments on weekends and public holidays.

➡ *From the botanical garden, return to the R47 and continue to its junction with the R563. Turn right and continue on the R563 towards Hekpoort, turning right 2,3 km beyond the junction to reach the turnoff to the Sterkfontein Caves on the left after 1,3 km.*

STERKFONTEIN CAVES

Sterkfontein, a series of caves in the dolomite hills north of Krugersdorp, is the richest early hominid (ape-man) fossil site in the world and over 700 hominid fossils have been recovered from the caves over the past 60 years.

The Sterkfontein caves attracted worldwide attention following the discovery of the first adult remains of an ape-man, *Australopithecus africanus*, by Dr Robert Broom in 1936.

Other important hominid finds include the remains of the earliest member of the genus *Homo*, to which modern humankind belongs, and Little Foot – four foot bones of an early hominid. The identification in 1995 of these foot bones taken from the deepest part of the caves in the 1920s

The Witwatersrand Botanical Garden's Witpoortjie Waterfall.

➡ *To reach the Witwatersrand National Botanical Garden from Johannesburg, take the R47; 5,6 km beyond the Christiaan De Wet Drive intersection, turn left into Doreen Road. Then turn right into Malcolm Street which ends at the garden 2,5 km further on.*

WITWATERSRAND NATIONAL BOTANICAL GARDEN

The **Witpoortjie Waterfall** is the focal feature of the 225-ha Witwatersrand National Botanical Garden, north of Roodepoort. In addition to the typical Highveld **vegetation** – one of the few remaining patches of Bankenveld (see below) in densely populated Gauteng – which is protected in

its natural state, a cycad and a succulent garden have been developed. Also of interest is the delightful fern garden just below the waterfall where the Crocodile River cascades 70 m down a cliff.

Bankenveld is the name given by the pioneer white farmers who settled in the area. The Bankenveld vegetation is characterised by almost pure grassveld on the hill crests, low-lying plains and southern slopes, while the northern slopes support shrubs and trees.

Among the **birds** recorded in the garden are the lesser honeyguide, arrowmarked babbler, Kurrichane and Cape rock thrushes, whitebellied sunbird and the brownhooded kingfisher. The cliffs near the waterfall

The skull of 'Mrs Ples', the first found remains of adult ape-man.

provided the first evidence of hominids living in the Witwatersrand some 3,5 million years ago, half a million years earlier than previous hominid discoveries in South Africa. Thousands of fossils of other animals, including extinct baboons, hyena and sabre-tooth cats, have also been recovered from the caves.

Also of interest are the magnificent stalagmites and stalactites decorating the interior of the six underground caverns, formed millions of years ago when the dolomite was dissolved by carbon dioxide-rich water. The largest of the chambers, the Hall of Elephants, is 90 m long and 23 m high and there is also a large underground lake. Names such as the Bridal Arch, the Elephant, Fairy Hall and Lumbago Alley provide a hint of what visitors on a guided tour can expect to see (*see* p. 197). The caves are in the 20-ha Isaac Edwin Stegmann Nature Reserve, a property donated to the Witwatersrand University for scientific research and as a nature reserve.

➡ From Sterkfontein, return to the R563 and continue for about 22 km to its junction with the R560. Turn left and, 13 km further on, right onto the R24 which traverses the southern slopes of the Magaliesberg. At Olifantsnek the road climbs to a saddle in the range and then descends to Rustenburg, about 88 km from Sterkfontein.

MAGALIESBERG

The Magaliesberg was formed 2 000 million years ago when the centre of a huge inland sea, the Transvaal Basin, subsided under the weight of intruding magma, forcing the edges of the basin upwards. Rising 300 m above the surrounding landscape, the range forms a natural boundary between the Highveld to the south and the Bushveld to the north. As a result, the area sustains a wide diversity of plants and animals.

The **vegetation** found here includes white stinkwood, Transvaal red milkwood and Natal figs, which flourish in the sheltered kloofs. A profusion of Transvaal milkplums grow amongst the rocks, and stands of proteas, acacias, bushwillows and Transvaal beech trees are common throughout the range.

The Magaliesberg supports a wide variety of **birds**; its cliffs are home to three breeding colonies of Cape vulture, which is considered vulnerable. These colonies, at Roberts' farm, southeast of the Rustenburg Nature Reserve (20 breeding pairs), at Nooitgedacht near Hekpoort (30 to 40 breeding pairs), and at Skeerpoort, near the Hartbeespoort Dam (200 breeding pairs), are not open to the public. However, the sites are easily recognizable by the white-washed cliffs and the vultures are frequently seen soaring overhead. Among the other birds recorded here are Cape rock and short-toed rock thrushes, longbilled pipit, black and Alpine swifts, mocking chat and Ayres' cisticola.

Mammals are less conspicuous than birds and among the few larger species are leopard, mountain reedbuck, bushbuck, klipspringer and baboon. The range is one of South Africa's few remaining strongholds of the rare brown hyena, which is also relatively abundant in the Waterberg and the Kalahari Gemsbok National Park (*see* pp. 198 and 72).

To ensure the sound management of the range (mostly privately owned), the Magaliesberg was declared a natural area in 1977 and is managed as a protected natural environment. Although access is restricted, there are several accommodation establishments, offering a range of recreational opportunities ranging from walking trails to horse-riding.

➡ To reach the Rustenburg Nature Reserve from Rustenburg, turn off Van Staden Street into Wolmerans Street. Continue for 2,4 km. Turn left into Boekenhout Road and follow it for 5,5 km to the eastern entrance gate. Access through the northern gate is restricted to overnight hikers and visitors with reservations for the group camp.

RUSTENBURG NATURE RESERVE

Part of this scenic, unspoilt 4 250-ha reserve southwest of the town of Rustenburg lies on the farm Rietvallei which

Hartbeespoort Dam, at the foot of the Magaliesberg, is one of the Witwatersrand's favourite playgrounds.

originally belonged to President Paul Kruger. A distinctive feature of the Reserve is the extensive Rietvallei basin and part of the western boundary runs close to the cliff edge of the Magaliesberg.

Mammals such as the mountain reedbuck, klipspringer and common duiker, which occurred in the area when the reserve was proclaimed, have been supplemented with several other species, including Burchell's zebra, kudu, black wildebeest, red hartebeest, reedbuck, blesbok, impala and springbok. Also found in the reserve is the elegant sable, which came to the attention of zoologists for the first time in 1836 after a specimen was shot in the Rustenburg area by the British traveller Captain Cornwallis Harris. Carnivores are represented by the leopard, brown hyena, aardwolf, black-backed jackal and caracal, and several smaller species. Primates include the baboon, vervet monkey and lesser bushbaby.

With a **bird** list exceeding 230, bird-watching can be rewarding. Raptors recorded include black and martial eagles, the African hawk eagle, blackbreasted snake eagle and jackal buzzard. Birders may also tick off the whitebellied korhaan, Meyer's parrot, European and lilacbreasted rollers, whitethroated robin and Marico sunbird. Several species of swallow and swifts, as well as six lark species, have been recorded.

The **vegetation** varies from woodlands and thornveld to grasslands on the summit of the range. Over 115 tree species grow in the reserve; among these

Angling is a popular recreation at Hartbeespoort Dam.

are several acacia and bushwillow (*Combretum*) species, proteas, white stinkwood and Transvaal red milkwood. Conspicuous on the rocky ridges is the Transvaal milkplum and along the streams the common tree fern can be seen. Two Magaliesberg endemics, *Frithia pulchra* and *Aloe peglerae*, occur in the reserve.

Visitors can drive along the 6-km circular game-viewing route in the Rietvallei Valley and, for the more adventurous, a mountain-bike trail is planned. Outdoor facilities include an overnight trail and an interpretative nature trail (*see* p. 197). Picnic facilities for day visitors and camp sites for overnight visitors are adjacent to the visitor centre.

➤ *Approaching from Rustenburg, follow the N4/R27 for about 50 km and then continue along the R512 which becomes a single-lane road along the 59-m-high Hartbeespoort Dam wall. The road then passes through a 61-m-long tunnel and winds above the northern shores of the dam, passing the Hartbeespoort Snake and Animal Park. Turn left onto the R514 about 2,1 km beyond the park and left again to the cableway about 900 m further on.*

HARTBEESPOORT

Nestling in a valley between the Magaliesberg and the Daspoort range, the Hartbeespoort Dam is the focal point of one of Gauteng's most popular recreational areas. Built as an irrigation dam in 1923, the wall blocking the course of the Crocodile River has created an artificial lake covering 2 000 ha when the dam is full. The dam is the venue for a wide variety of **watersports**, ranging from yachting to waterskiing, and several long-established clubs are based there. **Angling** is popular too, and carp of up to 15 kg, enormous sharptooth catfish, yellowfish and banded tilapia are frequently landed.

A bird's-eye view of the dam can be enjoyed by taking a **cable-car** ride to the summit of the Magaliesberg where picnic places with thatch umbrellas are provided. On a clear day the skyscrapers of Johannesburg, over 50 km southeast, can be seen. The journey to the upper cable station, 378 m higher than the lower cable station, takes about 5 minutes. The Magaliesberg is a favourite site for **hang-gliding** and a launching site is situated near the upper cable station.

Aerial views of the magnificent Magaliesberg can be enjoyed by drifting over the range in a **hot-air balloon**. Flights are conducted daily throughout the year, weather permitting. Resorts on the shores of the dam offer a variety of recreational facilities. Farmstalls selling homemade produce and art and craft studios and galleries are situated in and around Hartbeespoort (*see* box, left).

➤ *To reach De Wildt from the cableway, turn left onto the R514. Continue for 2,6 km to the junction with the R27/R511. Turn left at the junction and bear right 1,3 km further on to join the R513 after 1,7 km. Turn right and pass the Margaret Roberts Herb Centre to reach De Wildt a short way on.*

CROCODILE RIVER ARTS AND CRAFTS RAMBLE

The Crocodile River Arts and Crafts Ramble takes motorists to some 15 studios, galleries and workshops along the scenic Crocodile River valley and the Magaliesberg area. Arts and crafts which can be viewed and purchased range from paintings and sculptures to pottery and woodwork. Ramble studios are open on the first weekend of the month, but most of the studios can also be visited by appointment. No set route is followed and motorists can determine their own routes from Johannesburg, Roodepoort and Krugersdorp from the south, and Hartbeespoort from the north. A map indicating the participating studios, restaurants, picnic places, trails and trout-fishing establishments is available (*see* At a Glance, p. 197).

The Magaliesberg offers ideal conditions for paragliding.

DE WILDT CHEETAH RESEARCH STATION

The name De Wildt is synonymous with that of Ann van Dyk, who, with her late brother, Godfrey, donated 50 ha of their farm to the National Zoological Gardens of South Africa in 1969 for the breeding of cheetah, a species already considered endangered at the time.

Until the mid-1970s, cheetah had proved extremely difficult to breed in captivity, but in 1975 a major breakthrough was made when the centre's first litter was born. Another milestone came in 1981 when a king cheetah cub was born to normal spotted parents, providing positive proof that it is a genetic variation and not a separate sub-species. In 1991 king cheetah parents had a full litter of king cheetah cubs.

Since its establishment, the centre has bred over 400 spotted cheetah and 30 king cheetah, receiving international recognition for its pioneering work in the field of breeding cheetah in captivity.

Other endangered species have also been bred, including the Cape vulture, wild dog, brown hyena, suni and South Africa's most endangered mammal, the riverine rabbit (*see* p. 80).

The animals are kept in large enclosures in near-natural surroundings and can be viewed on a two-hour guided tour. Visitors are driven around the centre in an open vehicle and stops are made along the way to feed the animals.

WALKS AND TRAILS

WITWATERSRAND NATIONAL BOTANICAL GARDEN: Visitors can explore the gardens along a number of short, delightful walks with descriptive names such as the **Waterfall View, Mountain View** and **Riverside** trails and the **Bankenveld Walkway**.
STERKFONTEIN CAVES: An hour-long guided tour of the caves is offered. From the main entrance visitors descend to the floor of the caves, 46 m below the surface, and explore the 400-m cavern. The caves are lit and easily negotiated most of the way. Sturdy shoes and light clothing are advisable.
RUSTENBURG NATURE RESERVE: There is a choice of two **overnight trails**, each covering 21 km

and lasting two days, or you can combine the two trails into a three-day route. The **Peglerae Nature Trail**, a circular 4,5-km interpretative route, is named after *Aloe peglerae*, endemic to the Magaliesberg. Points of interest along the route are explained in a brochure, obtainable from the visitor centre, and the trail serves as an ideal introduction to the ecology of the reserve. A 20-km day hike for day visitors and a trail for the disabled are planned.

A perfect way to enjoy the sunset at Hartbeespoort Dam.

WITWATERSRAND & MAGALIESBERG AT A GLANCE

MAIN ATTRACTIONS
Witwatersrand National Botanical Garden, Sterkfontein Caves, Magaliesberg (Cape vultures, birding, walks and trails), Rustenburg Nature Reserve (game-viewing, birding, trails and walks), watersports, freshwater angling.

BEST TIMES TO VISIT
Throughout the year. Most of the area's rainfall occurs as thunderstorms between November and March. In mid-summer maximum temperatures are high. In winter minimum temperatures are low, but pleasant in the day.

WITWATERSRAND NATIONAL BOTANICAL GARDEN
Permits/bookings: Fee payable at gate. Groups wanting a guide should book a week in advance through the Curator.
Opening times: 08h00–18h00 all year; no entry after 17h00.
Accommodation: None.
Facilities: Curio shop, education centre, information centre, cafeteria, public toilets, bird hide.
Enquiries: **The Curator, Witwatersrand National Botanical Garden,** PO Box 2194, Wilro Park, Roodepoort 1731; tel. (011) 958-1750, fax. 958-1752.

STERKFONTEIN CAVES
Permits/bookings: Advance booking not necessary; fee payable at cafeteria.
Opening times: Tuesdays to Sundays 09h00–16h00 all year; closed on Mondays (unless

public holiday), Good Friday and Christmas day. Guided tours every 30 minutes.
Accommodation: None.
Facilities: Cafeteria, museum with archaeological and natural history displays.
Enquiries: **Sterkfontein Caves,** PO Box 481, Krugersdorp 1740; tel. (011) 956-6342, fax. 660-5833.

RUSTENBURG NATURE RESERVE
Permits/bookings: No advance bookings for day visits.
Opening times: Daily 08h00–18h00 throughout the year. Day visitors are not allowed in after 16h00.
Accommodation: **Camp sites:** Braai facilities and hot/cold-water ablutions near administrative complex.
Group Camp: Seven huts (beds and mattresses provided, no bedding), hot/cold-water ablutions. **Overnight trails:** Two rustic overnight huts on each loop of the trail, water and toilets. Contact the Officer-in-Charge.
Facilities: Picnic places with braai facilities and toilets, visitor information centre, 2 walks for day visitors.
Enquiries: **The Officer-in-Charge, Rustenburg Nature Reserve,** PO Box 20382, Protea Park 0305; tel. (0142) 3-1050, fax. 95-0950.

HARTBEESPOORT
Permits/bookings: Hartbeespoort cableway: No advance bookings required (except for groups). **De Wildt Cheetah**

Research Centre: Book one day in advance.
Opening times: **Hartbeespoort cableway:** Monday to Friday 08h00–16h00, weekends and public holidays 08h00–17h00 (all through the year, weather permitting).
De Wildt: Tours at 08h30 and 14h00 on Tuesdays, Thursdays, Saturdays and Sundays.
Accommodation: Hartbeespoort Publicity Association (*see* below).
Enquiries: **Hartbeespoort cableway,** Tel. (01211) 3-0706. **Airtrack Adventures** (balloon trips over Magaliesberg), PO Box 630, Muldersdrif 1747; tel. (011) 957-2322, fax. 987-2465. **Bill Harrop's 'Original' Balloon Safaris,** PO Box 67, Randburg 2125; tel. (011) 705-3201, fax. 705-3203. **De Wildt Cheetah Research Centre,** PO Box 16, De Wildt 0251; tel. and fax. (01250) 4-1921. **Crocodile River Arts and Crafts Ramble,** PO Box 554, Lanseria 1748; tel. (011) 957-2580, fax. 957-2376.

TOURIST INFORMATION
Johannesburg Publicity Association, PO Box 4580, Johannesburg 2000; tel. (011) 29-4961, fax. 336-4965. **Rustenburg Tourist Information Centre,** PO Box 16, Rustenburg 0300; tel. (0142) 94-3194, fax. 2-0181. **Hartbeespoort Publicity Association,** PO Box 976, Hartbeespoort 0126; tel. (01211) 53-0505, fax. 3-1949.

46 WATERBERG

Rising 600 m above the vast Springbok Flats which stretch eastwards, the 15 000-km² Waterberg is so named because of its abundance of streams, waterfalls, pools and marshes. Encompassing the Sand River Mountains, Hoekberg range, Swaerhoek Mountains and the Moepel range, the Waterberg is a refuge to several rare and endangered species of game, as well as the world's largest breeding colony of Cape vultures.

How to get there

Nylstroom is an ideal base from which to explore the Waterberg which, with its brown, red and purple cliffs and deep ravines, is fast becoming one of South Africa's top eco-tourism destinations. To reach Nylstroom, 130 km from Pretoria, travel north on the N1 and turn onto the R33 at the Kranskop Toll Plaza. The town is 11 km further on.

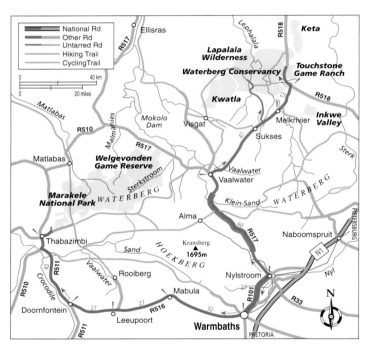

➡ To get to the Marakele National Park from Nylstroom, travel through Warmbaths to Thabazimbi along the R516 and R511. From Thabazimbi follow the Alma road for 3 km on gravel. Turn left and after 1 km you will reach the park headquarters.

MARAKELE NATIONAL PARK

Marakele (Tswana for 'place of sanctuary'), proclaimed in 1994, covers 44 000 ha of mountains, cliffs, deep river valleys and grass-covered hills at the western end of the Waterberg, and was originally known as Kransberg. Since the Waterberg is in a transitional zone between arid west and wetter east, species such as the gemsbok (of the west) and impala (favouring the east) occur. Likewise plants from both zones grow here.

Game brought into the park include reedbuck, red hartebeest, eland, waterbuck, impala, nyala, giraffe and hippo. Rare and endangered antelope – tsessebe, roan, sable – have been released. Bushpig, warthog, kudu, mountain reedbuck, bushbuck, klipspringer, steenbok and common duiker were found here when the park was established. Brown hyena and caracal also occur.

Marakele is set to become a Big Five park. First reintroduced was a herd of buffalo, then black and white rhino and, in September 1995, 40 elephant. Lion will be released once prey species (impala, Burchell's zebra, blue wildebeest) are sufficiently numerous. Leopard occurred naturally in the park when it was proclaimed.

Birdlife is prolific: 286 species have been recorded and the list is expected to top 400. Species vary from Gurney's sugarbird (a fynbos dweller) to the crimsonbreasted shrike (of the thornveld), and typical montane birds (Cape rock thrush). Of conservation importance is the Cape vulture colony on the cliffs on the park's southern border. Its 800-odd breeding pairs make it the world's largest Cape vulture breeding colony.

Vegetation consists of forests, deciduous woodlands, grasslands and proteaveld; over 400 plants occur here. Montane forests of real yellowwood, lemonwood, Cape beech and tree fuchsia grow in sheltered places. A profusion of ferns flourish along streams (over 30 have been recorded). Typical of the sour bushveld are the white seringa, red bushwillow, water berry and common wild pear.

The striking Waterberg cycad (*Encephalartos eugene-maraisii*), named after the Afrikaans poet and naturalist Eugène Marais, also occurs in the Wolkberg and the Middelburg area.

THE ROAN ANTELOPE

This striking antelope, with its greyish-fawn coat, curved horns and black and white face, is one of South Africa's three most endangered mammals (the other two are the wild dog and the riverine rabbit). Favouring open savanna woodland, it is largely restricted to the Kruger National Park and the Waterberg, and a number of private game reserves in the Northern Cape and North-West Province. The main reasons for their decline are the destruction of their preferred habitat by agricultural development and the fact that they are susceptible to diseases such as anthrax. They live in small herds of five to 12, but sometimes form herds of up to 80. Males reach a shoulder height of 1,4 m and weigh on average 270 kg, with females about 40 kg lighter. The roan is closely related to the sable and the gemsbok.

The Cape vulture frequents high cliffs when breeding.

The Lephalala River winding through the Lapalala Wilderness.

At the time of writing the park was still in its infancy and facilities limited to a tented camp on the Matlabas River. Situated in the Matlabas basin in the northwest of the park, where the river has made its way through the Waterberg, the camp has six four-bed tents and is accessible by 4x4 vehicle only. Visitors can explore the area along a 40-km network of 4x4 tracks , and guided night drives can be arranged. Another way to experience the beauty of the area is to join a guided four-day trail conducted along the tributaries of the Matlabas. Trailists provide and carry their own equipment. Overnight facilities are limited to a basic shelter. Plans are afoot to conduct environmental interpretation courses and a 4x4 trail.

➡ *From Nylstroom, follow the R517 to Vaalwater for 60 km; turn right onto the Melkrivier road. Turn left after 40 km and bear left again 5,5 km further on, continuing for 17 km to Lapalala's entrance gate.*

LAPALALA WILDERNESS
Lapalala is a 24 000-ha tract of wild country providing first-hand wilderness experience, rather than focusing on game-viewing.

One of Lapalala's objectives is breeding of rare and endangered **game**. In 1990 it became the world's first private conservation area to acquire black rhino. Two bulls and three cows, bought at the Hluhluwe Game Auction for a record R2,2 million, were later joined by five more and released in a 10 000-ha area. This area is sanctuary to other rare and endangered species such as roan and sable. Game such as white rhino, giraffe, gemsbok, kudu, blue wildebeest, red hartebeest, impala, Burchell's zebra and hippo can also be seen in the reserve.

The reserve is named after the Lephalala River (Sotho for 'the barrier' – probably a reference to times when it held more water). The river winds through the reserve for 35 km and partly forms a boundary with Touchstone.

Among the 275 **birds** recorded to date are several raptors (African hawk, black and martial eagles and the gymnogene). Other birds which might be seen include the African finfoot, Meyer's parrot, redbilled woodhoopoe, yellowbilled hornbill, Southern black tit, southern boubou and the redbilled oxpecker, reintroduced after it was last seen in the area in 1961.

The **Lapalala Wilderness School** plays a role in educating children about conservation. Since its establishment in 1985 thousands have attended its trails.

Lapalala has no game-viewing roads other than access roads, but **self-guided walks** at the six rustic camps allow visitors to explore their surroundings. Guided drives in open vehicles and walks are conducted from Kolobe Lodge and Rhino Camp. The **Rhino Trail** is a three-day guided wilderness trail. The **Rhino and Elephant Trail** is a combination of two days' trailing at Lapalala and three days in the Mashatu Game Reserve in Botswana (the group is transported to Mashatu).

➡ *From Nylstroom, follow the R517 to Vaalwater and go through Melkrivier to the junction with the R518. Turn left onto the R518 and left again at the Moerdyk signpost.*

TOUCHSTONE GAME RANCH
Touchstone Game Ranch, east of Lapalala, is the 17 500-ha habitat of 90-odd **mammals**, including four of the Big Five – white rhino, elephant, buffalo and leopard. Antelope include rare and endangered species such as roan, sable and tsessebe, and the uncommon black impala. Also occurring here are giraffe, blue wildebeest, kudu, cheetah, crocodile and hippo.

Accommodation ranges from self-catering to fully inclusive camps. **Game drives** in open vehicles, **guided walks** and **horseback safaris** are available.

WATERBERG AT A GLANCE

MAIN ATTRACTIONS
Spectacular scenery, game-viewing (rare and endangered species), bird-watching (largest Cape vulture breeding colony in the world), guided walks.

BEST TIMES TO VISIT
All year. Summer days are warm to hot with mild nights. Winters are mild and frost is rare. Most rain falls between September and March.

MARAKELE NATIONAL PARK
Permits/bookings: Advance bookings essential through National Parks Board (*see* below).
Opening times: Sunrise to sunset.
Accommodation: Tented camp with six 4-bed tents, each with ablution facilities.
Facilities: None, except at tented camp (park is still being developed).
Enquiries: National Parks Board Reservations, PO Box 787, Pretoria 0001; tel. (012) 343-1911, fax. 343-0905 or PO Box 7400, Roggebaai 8012; tel. (021) 28-2810, fax. 24-6211.

LAPALALA WILDERNESS
Permits/bookings: Lapalala Wilderness (*see* below).
Opening times: Sunrise to 18h30 (summer) and sunrise to 17h30 (winter). **Wilderness School:** 3 to 6-day courses for 9- to 18-year-olds, from February to December.

Accommodation: From rustic self-catering bush camps for 2 to 8, to Rhino camp (an exclusive 9-bed tented safari camp) and Kolobe Lodge with eight 2-bed thatched cottages. Accommodation at Rhino Camp and Kolobe Lodge includes meals.
Facilities: Game drives and guided walks from Rhino Camp and Kolobe Lodge.
Enquiries: Lapalala Wilderness, PO Box 645, Bedfordview 2008; tel. (011) 453-7645, fax. 453-7649.

TOUCHSTONE GAME RANCH
Permits/bookings: Touchstone (*see* below).
Opening times: Office open 07h30–17h00 all year.
Accommodation: One self-catering, luxury tented camp sleeps 6; one self-catering rock cabin sleeps 12; two catered camps sleep 8 and 12.
Facilities: Guided game drives in open vehicles, guided walks, horse-back safaris.
Enquiries: Touchstone Game Ranch, PO Box 57, Marken 0605; tel. (014) 765-0045, fax. 765-0108.

**TOURIST INFORMATION
Modimolle-Kranskop Tourist Organisation,** PO Box 583, Nylstroom 0510; tel. and fax. (01470) 2755. **Waterberg Tourism Authority,** Private Bag X136, Ellisras 0555; tel. (014) 763-2193, fax. 763-5662.

47 BARBERSPAN & OTHER BIRD HAVENS

On a flat plain in the North-West, Barberspan Nature Reserve is one of southern Africa's top bird sanctuaries. Thousands of water birds are attracted to the natural alkaline lake and to the Bloemhof Dam (a large man-made lake on the Vaal River), which both offer excellent birding.

How to get there
Take the R24 from Johannesburg (the N4 from Pretoria) to Rustenburg, the R52 to Lichtenburg and Biesiesvlei, and the N14 to Barberspan.

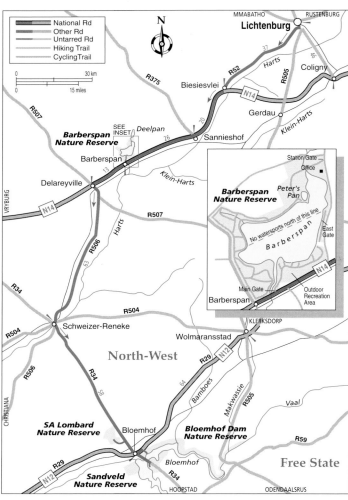

Lesser flamingos can usually be seen at Barberspan all year round.

BARBERSPAN NATURE RESERVE

The pan (11 km long and up to 3 km wide) is the largest of a series of depressions in a fossil course of the Harts River. It is fed by the river and when full (usually February/March) its depth varies from 1 m to 9,5 m.

There are many seasonal pans in the area, but Barberspan is the only one holding water all year. It is not only an important moulting area for **waterfowl**, but also a stop-over for **migrant birds**. The number of birds and species attracted to the pan fluctuate with the water levels. In the dry season (September/October) the pan supports up to 27 000 redknobbed coot, and numerous yellowbilled duck, redbilled teal, spurwinged and Egyptian goose and shelduck. However, when the seasonal pans are inundated by the summer rains, the birds disperse widely to breed elsewhere, returning as the pans begin to dry up. Mixed flocks of white and pinkbacked pelicans visit the pan in summer, and greater and lesser flamingos are usually present all year. Look out for the rare but frequently seen chestnutbanded plover.

The little stint is the most common Palaearctic migrant wader on the pan and large numbers of ruff are often present. Other migrants include ringed and grey plovers, turnstone, as well as marsh and curlew sandpipers. Species recorded in the grasslands include Swainson's francolin, grassveld pipit, orangethroated longclaw and pinkbilled lark.

The northern part of the pan and the reserve is conserved as a waterfowl habitat: no boating or angling is allowed. Visitors may drive on the 15-km road network and are free to explore on foot (no set trails). The southern part of the pan is a recreation area where **watersports** (sailing, boardsailing, canoeing) are permitted. Many angling enthusiasts come here – this is among the best freshwater angling waters north of the Vaal River. Sought-after species are smallmouth yellowfish, carp and sharptooth catfish. Others include banded tilapia, moggel, Orange River mudfish and three minnows.

Except for a few black wildebeest, springbok, Burchell's zebra and ostrich in the north of the 3 068-ha reserve, **wildlife** is limited to smaller species – Cape hare, ground squirrel, springhare, yellow mongoose, and the rare African striped weasel.

The **vegetation** is largely grassveld with thickets of sweet thorn, horned thorn, karree, common wild currant and Karoo bluebush.

BIRD MIGRATION

One of the main functions of Barberspan has been research on migratory birds, especially water birds, to enable ornithologists to gain a better understanding of their migratory patterns. Recoveries of ringed birds have produced some useful results. One of the migrant waders ringed at Barberspan, a ruff, was found dead in Russia six months later, having flown at least 10 000 km. A cliff swallow which was recovered had flown over 2 300 km, from Barberspan to Zaïre, in less than a week. Waterfowl recoveries have also been interesting. For example, yellowbilled ducks have been found to move extensively, but tend to restrict their movements between the pans surrounding Barberspan. Redbilled teals, on the other hand, cover long distances and recoveries have been made in northern Botswana, Namibia, Angola and Mozambique.

➤ *From Barberspan, continue on the R47 to Delareyville, the R506 to Schweizer-Reneke and the R34 to the S A Lombard turnoff. The reserve is 12 km along a gravel road.*

S A LOMBARD NATURE RESERVE

Antelope found in this 3 663-ha reserve include eland, gemsbok, steenbok and duiker. It has played a major role in the conservation of black wildebeest in the old Transvaal. Blesbok, red hartebeest and springbok are also bred here for resettling on farms and reserves.

Some 250 **birds** have been recorded in the area. Summer rains bring many ducks, geese, herons and other water birds to the four pans. Typical of the arid west are the Kalahari robin and rufouseared warbler. The black korhaan, doublebanded courser, grassveld pipit and several lark species are also seen.

➤ *From S A Lombard, take the R34 for 5 km to Bloemhof; the R29 towards Klerksdorp for 6 km to the signposted turnoff to the reserve.*

Whitebreasted cormorants whiten the dead tree on which they roost.

BLOEMHOF DAM NATURE RESERVE

This reserve on the northern shores of Bloemhof Dam in the Vaal River comprises 9 222 ha of water and 12 850 ha of grasslands.

It is popular with **watersports enthusiasts** and **freshwater anglers**; seasonally it supports a large waterfowl population. Since the dam is extremely shallow, its water level and consequently the number and species of birds fluctuate widely. Among the **waterfowl** attracted to the dam are whitefaced and yellowbilled ducks, South African shelduck and Cape teal, as well as Egyptian and spurwinged geese. The dam supports a large population of Goliath herons and, when the water level is high, Caspian terns breed on the islands. The many lark species to be seen include the melodious, clapper and spikeheeled larks. Look out for the Orange River francolin, kori bustard, Kalahari robin and the sociable weaver.

Typical highveld **game** (Burchell's zebra, black wildebeest, red hartebeest, blesbok and springbok) roam the grassy plains. Eland, white rhino, and gemsbok have also been reintroduced

➤ *From Bloemhof, take the R34 towards Hoopstad to the entrance on the southern side of the bridge over the dam. Turn right, taking the gravel road for 3 km to the office.*

SANDVELD NATURE RESERVE

On the southern banks of Bloemhof Dam, Sandveld has a land area of 14 700 ha and 23 000 ha of the dam. The 247 **bird** species recorded make this one of the Free State's most rewarding birding spots. Waterfowl and waders are attracted to the dam; the reserve is the habitat of the whitebacked vulture, yellowbilled hornbill, several lark species, Kalahari robin, crimsonbreasted shrike and the sociable weaver.

A road network traverses the game area. Species found here include springbok, gemsbok, eland, red hartebeest, Burchell's zebra and giraffe.

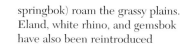

BARBERSPAN AT A GLANCE

MAIN ATTRACTIONS
Water birds, freshwater angling, watersports.

BEST TIMES TO VISIT
The dry winter is best for waterfowl as they congregate on waterbodies. Summer is best for Palearctic migrants.

BARBERSPAN NATURE RESERVE
Permits/bookings: Day permits obtainable at gate.
Opening times: Recreation area open all day throughout the year. Advise the Officer-in-Charge in advance of visit to northern part of reserve; open sunrise to sunset all year.
Accommodation: Basic camp sites with field toilets (none in reserve); contact Officer-in-Charge. Twenty 6-bed self-contained chalets; book through Barberspan Hotel.
Facilities: **Barberspan Nature Reserve:** Basic picnic sites only. **Barberspan Hotel:** Restaurant, bar, pool.
Enquiries: **The Officer-in-Charge,** PO Barberspan 2765; tel. (053) 948-1854, fax. 948-0101. **Barberspan Hotel,** PO Box 63, Barberspan 2765; tel. (053) 948-1930, fax. 948-0028.

S A LOMBARD NATURE RESERVE
Permits/booking: No fee. Advise Officer-in-Charge in advance of visit.
Opening times: Sunrise to sunset throughout the year.
Accommodation: None.
Facilities: Toilets only.

Enquiries: **The Officer-in-Charge,** PO Box 174, Bloemhof 2660; tel. (01802) 3-1953, fax. 3-1917.

BLOEMHOF DAM NATURE RESERVE
Permits/bookings: Permits to visit angling area at gate. Camp sites and visits to nature reserve through the Officer-in-Charge.
Opening times: Angling area all day; nature reserve sunrise to sunset all year.
Accommodation: Camp sites with toilets.
Facilities: Picnic/braai sites.
Enquiries: **The Officer-in-Charge,** PO Box 729, Bloemhof 2660; tel. (01802) 3-1706, fax. 3-1917.

SANDVELD NATURE RESERVE
Permits/bookings: Permits for day visits at gate.
Opening times: 24 hours per day throughout the year.
Accommodation: Camp sites with hot/cold ablutions. Nine chalets for 2 to 6 (all fully equipped, air-conditioned, self-catering). Book through the First Nature Conservator.
Facilities: Picnic sites, braai places and toilets; curio shop.
Enquiries: **First Nature Conservator,** PO Box 414, Bloemhof 2660; tel. (01802) 3-1701/2, fax. 3-1090.

TOURIST INFORMATION
North-West Tourism Council, PO Box 7727, Johannesburg 2000; tel. (011) 331-9336, fax. 331-9351.

201

The Nyl River flood plains, South Africa's largest flood plain vlei, have been called the jewel of South Africa's wetlands. Its bird list of some 400 species makes it a birder's paradise. Nearby are Warmbaths' thermal springs, one of the country's top holiday and recreation resorts.

How to get there
Warmbaths, an ideal base from which to explore the scenic attractions of the region, is situated 112 km north of Pretoria off the N1.

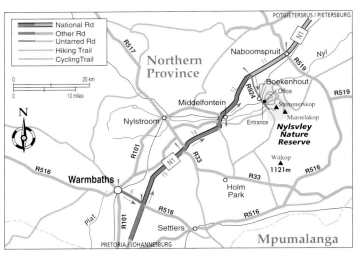

The blackcrowned night heron, one of 17 heron species at Nylsvley.

WARMBATHS

The town of Warmbaths owes its name and existence to the **thermal springs** which surface here. Rich in sodium chloride, calcium carbonate and other minerals, an estimated 22 000 litres of water flow to the surface every hour. The water temperature at the source of the spring is 52 °C, but is cooled down to 34 °C in the swimming pool and 40 °C in the rheumatism pool. The therapeutic effect of the springs

has attracted visitors for over 120 years and the resort is ranked among the most modern in the world.

For many visitors the resort's chief attraction lies in the **recreational activities** it offers. In addition to the outdoor swimming pools, there are supertubes and a wave pool. The more adventurous may want to experience the 170-m-long Rinkhals river-slide, with a drop equivalent to a six-storey building. Another attraction

is cable waterskiing on a specially built dam – the resort's circuit was the first in Africa.

The **hydro spa** is comparable with the best in the world; facilities include an indoor mineral pool, rheumatism pool and saunas. The spa offers hydrotherapy, massage bath treatments and saunas.

Game-viewing drives are conducted in the adjoining **Warmbaths Nature Reserve**. Among the animals to be seen are white rhino, impala, Burchell's zebra,

kudu, red hartebeest, waterbuck and warthog. Refreshments are served around a campfire on the night drives.

➤ From Warmbaths, return along the R516 for 9 km to the offramp onto the N1; continue north for about 43 km. Take the signposted turnoff to the Boekenhout station (R924) to reach the Nylsvley Nature Reserve entrance gate about 1 km after crossing the railway line.

NYLSVLEY NATURE RESERVE

Straddling the Nyl River, the 4 300-ha reserve lies within the river's 16 000-ha flood plain, a wetland which is about 50 km long and up to 6 km wide.

The flood plain is inundated by the waters of the Nyl River and its tributaries, which rise in the Waterberg to the west. The flood waters usually begin to spill onto the flood plain in December/ January and to recede in April. The extent of the flooding varies from year to year, but on average the flood plain is inundated in two out of every three years.

After good rains the shallow waters of the flood plain attract a multitude of **water birds**. The

For centuries people have recognised the therapeutic and recreational value of nature's warm water.

river's flood plains attract a greater diversity of water birds than any other wetland in South Africa and, in years of extensive flooding, support up to 80 000 birds.

To date some 104 water bird species have been recorded, including 17 species of herons and 17 species of ducks. Fifty-eight water bird species are known to breed on Nylsvley, which supports the largest breeding colonies of certain species in South Africa; among these are the squacco heron and the great white and black egrets. This is the only known breeding place of the rare rufousbellied heron in South Africa. Also occurring in large numbers are the little and yellowbilled egret, blackcrowned night heron and little bittern. Tropical species such as the dwarf bittern and the lesser moorhen are attracted to the flood plains.

During extensive flooding, up to 43 000 birds of the Rallidae family (rails, crakes, gallinules, moorhens and coots) are attracted annually to the wetlands. The vlei also supports large numbers of ducks, including whitefaced, whitebacked and yellowbilled ducks, and redbilled teal.

Nearly 300 of the 400-odd bird species recorded at Nylsvley are not dependent on the flooding of the Nyl River. Among these are woodland and brownhooded kingfishers, yellowfronted tinker barbet, whitethroated robin, seven cisticola species and the Marico sunbird.

Excellent birding can be enjoyed from a **hide** overlooking the flood plain on the adjacent farm, Vogelfontein, which was acquired and incorporated into the reserve in 1995. The hide is reached by turning left immediately after crossing the railway line and then taking the first road to the right. About 2 km beyond the turnoff the road crosses the Nyl River flood plain. A gate on the right provides access to the hide, a short walk from the road.

The wetland is a rich source of food for the water birds and is the habitat of 16 **fish** species, including the striped topminnow – a species with a limited distribution in South Africa. Most of the fishes are small barbs and minnows, which prey on mosquitoes, gnats and their larvae. The largest fish found in the Nyl River is the sharptooth catfish, which reaches up to 1 m in length. Also occurring on the flood plains are 18 species of **amphibian**.

Although the main attraction of the reserve is its birdlife, it has been stocked with several species of **game**, such as giraffe, Burchell's zebra, blue wildebeest, kudu and impala. Two rare antelope species, roan and tsessebe, are bred here for restocking farms and reserves elsewhere. Reedbuck, steenbok, common duiker and warthog are also found here.

The **vegetation** of the reserve ranges from flood plain grasslands, fringed by acacia savanna,

Purple gallinule are attracted to Nylsvley, particularly after flooding.

to woodlands of wild seringa, red bushwillow, peeling plane and silver cluster-leaf.

Despite its unique attributes, the Nyl River wetland has been overshadowed by other wetlands such as St Lucia and a mere 4% of the flood plain enjoys formal conservation status. Demands are being made on the water resources of the Nyl River and its tributaries by farmers building

dams in the Nyl River catchment, increased water requirements of Nylstroom and the possibility of afforestation. All these factors are threatening one of South Africa's most precious wetlands.

The network of tracks covering about 30 km west of the Nyl River is open to the public and, although there are no trails, visitors are free to explore the reserve on foot.

WARMBATHS & NYLSVLEY AT A GLANCE

MAIN ATTRACTIONS
Rich diversity of birdlife, thermal springs.

BEST TIMES TO VISIT
Birding at Nylsvley depends on the flooding of the flood plains, but is usually best between the hot months of December and February. Summer days are hot and most of the area's rainfall is recorded between November and April (late afternoon thunderstorms). Winter days are pleasant, but sub-zero temperatures and frost are common at night.

AVENTURA WARMBATHS
Permits/bookings: No advance bookings necessary for day visitors.
Opening times: Daily 24 hours throughout the year.
Accommodation: From one or two double-roomed self-contained cottages to luxury apartments and caravan/camp sites with hot/cold-water ablutions.

Facilities: Spa centre, outdoor and wave pools, supertube, squash, tennis, restaurant, ladies' bar, cafeteria, kiosk.
Enquiries: **Aventura Warmbaths,** PO Box 75, Warmbaths 0480; tel. (014) 736-2200, fax. 736-4712.

NYLSVLEY NATURE RESERVE
Permits: No entrance fee.
Opening times: Daily 06h00–18h00 throughout the year.
Accommodation: Camp sites with cold-water ablutions. Contact the Officer-in-Charge.
Facilities: Picnic sites with braai facilities.
Enquiries: **The Officer-in-Charge,** PO Box 508, Naboomspruit 0560; tel. and fax. (014) 743-1074.

TOURIST INFORMATION
Pretoria Information Bureau, PO Box 440, Pretoria 0001; tel. (012) 313-7694, fax. 313-8460. **Naboomspruit Publicity,** Private Bag X340, Naboomspruit 0560; tel. (014) 743-1111, fax. 743-2434.

White-backed ducks keep to reeds and vegetation for cover.

49 PILANESBERG NATIONAL PARK

Pilanesberg, rising 600 m above the surrounding plains, is the eroded remains of a volcano that was active millions of years ago. The volcanic crater rings are a natural boundary around the Pilanesberg National Park – renowned for its scenery, abundant game, diversity of birdlife and geology.

How to get there
Pilanesberg is 50 km north-west of Rustenburg (*see* p. 194). Day visitors may enter through any of the four gates, but overnight visitors must use Manyane Gate, near Mogwase. To reach Manyane from Rustenburg, follow the R510 towards Northam for 59 km and take the signposted turnoff to the left. The park entrance is 5 km on.

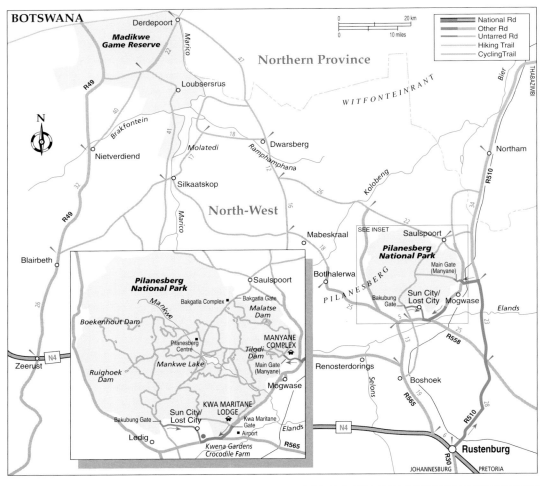

In under a decade Pilanesberg has been transformed from overgrazed farmland into one of the country's top wildlife areas. After its proclamation in 1979, Operation Genesis, involving the translocation of 7 000 animals, was launched. Set in an area where the arid western Kalahari and the moist eastern Lowveld overlap, the 58 000-ha park is home to a wide variety of animals and plants.

The geology and topography of the area have resulted in **vegetation** ranging from open grassland to densely wooded valleys. Typical tree species include the Transvaal beech, common hook-thorn, umbrella thorn, common wild pear and wild olive. Also found is the Transvaal red balloon tree, named after its bladder-like seed pod, which occurs only in a few populations in North-West. It grows up to 5 m high on stony hillsides and rocky koppies.

More than 35 large **mammals** and some 50 smaller species are known to occur in the park. It is sanctuary to the world's third largest white rhino population and has a healthy black rhino population. Other big game includes hippo, introduced into Mankwe Lake, elephant and giraffe.

Among the 19 **antelope** species are impala, kudu, gemsbok, waterbuck, red hartebeest, buffalo, sable, roan and tsessebe, as well as common duiker, klipspringer and steenbok. **Predators** include lion, leopard, cheetah, brown hyena and smaller species such as large- and small-spotted genets, bat-eared fox, black-backed jackal and caracal.

Lion were introduced to Pilanesberg in 1993, completing its count of the Big Five.

Hot-air ballooning over the Pilanesberg National Park offers a different perspective to game-viewing.

Five **viewing hides** allow close-range game- and bird-viewing. A tunnel of 180 m leads from Kwa Maritane to an underground hide overlooking a waterhole.

With a list exceeding 350, the park offers excellent **birding**. It is rich in **raptors**, including black, African hawk, martial and blackbreasted snake eagles. Up to 40 vultures have been spotted at the **Mothata Scavenger hide** near the Manyane tourist complex, where Cape and white-backed vultures are often seen.

Unlikely to escape attention is the grey lourie. Colourful species to keep an eye out for include the lilacbreasted roller, blackcollared barbet, crimsonbreasted shrike and the violeteared waxbill. Close-up views of more than 90 species found in Pilanesberg can be enjoyed in the **walk-in aviary** near the main entrance gate. Indigenous trees have been planted in the aviary; since the first birds released were hand-reared, they are used to people. Adjacent to the aviary is a water bird enclosure.

Geologically the area is unique (*see* box, below). A self-guided **geological auto trail** has been developed, offering insight into the geology. Points of interest are marked along the roads and are described in a booklet which can be bought at shops in the park.

The park can be explored on well-maintained **game-viewing roads**. Visitors can join a night drive, or an early morning or late afternoon game-viewing drive in an open vehicle. An exciting way of viewing the park and its wildlife is to take an early morning balloon flight. Drives are conducted by the various lodges and Pilanesberg Safaris (balloon trips over the park are offered). The park can also be explored on foot (*see* p. 206). Scenic **picnic spots** with braai sites are available.

➡ *The most direct access to Sun City from Pilanesberg is through Bakubung Gate in the south and the Kwa Maritane Gate. From Bakubung go south for 5 km, turn left and after 5 km left again to the* entrance to Sun City. From Kwa Maritane (open 24 hours a day), turn right and 3 km further on bear right, continuing for 3 km to the entrance to the Sun City complex, where you turn right again.

SUN CITY & LOST CITY

Set among the hills on the southern boundary of Pilanesberg, the opulence of the Sun City/Lost City complex contrasts with the tranquil atmosphere of the park.

Sparkling pools, lush lawns, waterfalls and rain forests with tropical palm trees have transformed the barren landscape into an oasis. A huge variety of birds are attracted to the gardens.

The thousands of trees, shrubs and flowering plants in the carefully landscaped garden below the Cascades Hotel include tropical palms and cycads. The paths through the dense forest offer glimpses of

ORIGINS OF A VOLCANO

Pilanesberg is in the second largest alkaline volcano in the world and has the most clearly defined ring structure. On approaching the park, visitors cannot fail to be impressed by this mountain tract rising up to 600 m above the plains. The complex covers 530 km² and consists of concentric rings of alkaline volcanic hills separated by valleys. The ring complex was formed between 1 250 and 1 420 million years ago as a result of volcanic eruptions, followed by periods of fracturing, collapsing and the intrusion of molten material. It is estimated that the volcanic rocks originally formed a 7 000-m-high volcanic cone, but most of the original volcano has been eroded, leaving only its roots exposed. It is likely that the main volcanic pipe was near Mankwe Lake.

Kudu and red hartebeest are among the 19 antelope species in the park.

the 12 waterfalls and cascades, which is the central theme of the 14-storey hotel.

The 25-ha **Gardens of the Lost City** are a botanical dream-world, depicting landscape themes, from the **Wet Tropical Forest** (masses of tree ferns, clusters of palm trees and wild figs), to the prehistoric atmosphere of the **Baobab Jungle**. The immense task of establishing the gardens is illustrated by the fact

that an 11- and 20-tonne baobab were transported from Messina, where they were threatened by road construction. At the **Dwarf Rock Forest**, stunted trees depict a semi-desert scene – in contrast to the **Orchid Forest** where 500 orchid plants can be seen.

The four hotels offer various activities: parasailing, windsurfing or the Valley of the Waves – a waterscape with a tropical beach, wave pool and water chutes.

MADIKWE GAME RESERVE

Madikwe covers 75 000 ha of bushveld, plains, cliffs and isolated island mountains 70 km north of Zeerust. It borders on Botswana in the north and west, the Marico River in the east and the Dwarsberg in the south. When proclaimed in 1991, much of the land was badly over-grazed. A rehabilitation programme was implemented to let the vegetation recover. Operation Phoenix (restocking with game) was the

largest programme of its kind in Africa, involving the reintroduction of 10 000 animals of 27 species. Madikwe boasts South Africa's second largest elephant population, and black and white rhino, lion, leopard and buffalo (the Big Five). It is sanctuary to wild dog, giraffe, blue wildebeest, springbok, gemsbok, kudu, impala, as well as a variety of birds. Its three lodges each offer guided walks and game drives.

➤ *Kwena is adjacent to (east of) the Skytrain parking area at the entrance to Sun City.*

KWENA GARDENS CROCODILE FARM

With its raised walkways around crocodile ponds, waterfalls and landscaped surroundings, Kwena Gardens Crocodile Farm near the entrance gate to the Sun City complex is undoubtedly one of the best in southern Africa. Guided tours are conducted regularly and, for those interested in finding out more about these fascinating reptiles, videos are screened. Feeding takes place at 16h30.

WALKS AND TRAILS

Early morning **game-viewing walks** of about three hours are conducted by Pilanesberg Safaris and the lodges.

Weekend **trails** with no set route are offered in the wilderness area by guides of the Gauteng branch of the Wilderness Leadership School, for groups of 6 to 8. Trailists sleep under the stars or in tents. Game-viewing forms an integral part, but the school uses a holistic approach, emphasising man's interaction with nature. Trails leave from Johannesburg late on Friday afternoons and return late on Sunday afternoons.

PILANESBERG NATIONAL PARK AT A GLANCE

MAIN ATTRACTIONS
Game-viewing, birdlife, walk-in aviary, unique geology, nearby Sun City/Lost City.

BEST TIMES TO VISIT
May to September as animals concentrate near waterholes. Temperatures are pleasant; sub-zero temperatures at night from May to August. In summer maximums average 35 °C; pack light clothing and rain-gear, as most rain falls between October and March.

PILANESBERG
Permits/bookings: Day permits at gate. Game drives and walks, hot-air ballooning, Pilanesberg Safaris (*see below*).
Opening times: April to August 06h00–18h00; September to March 05h30–19h00.
Accommodation: **Manyane, Mankwe, Bakgatla, Kololo and Metswidi camps:** Caravan/camp sites and safari tents to tented camps and self-catering cottages. Golden Leopard Resorts (*see below*). **Tshukudu and Bakubung Hotel:** No camping. Book at hotel (*see below*). **Kwa Maritane Game Lodge:** Luxury game camp. Book at lodge (*see below*).
Facilities: **Manyane:** Restaurant, bar, pool shop with groceries, liquor, curios. **Pilanesberg Centre:** Restaurant, curio shop, interpretative centre.
Enquiries: **Pilanesberg Safaris,** PO Box 79, Sun City

0316; tel. (01465) 5-5469/2-1561, fax. 2-1343. **Golden Leopard Resorts,** PO Box 937, Lonehill 2062; tel. (011) 465-5423, fax. 465-1228. **Tshukudu & Bakubung Hotel,** PO Box 294, Sun City 0316; tel. (01465) 2-1861, fax. 2-1621. **Kwa Maritane Game Lodge,** PO Box 6021, Rustenburg 0300; tel. (01465) 2-1820, fax. 2-1147. **Wilderness Leadership School,** PO Box 594, Sundowner 2161; tel. (011) 795-2439, fax. 795-4150. **Pilanesberg National Park,** PO Box 1201, Mogwase 0302; tel. (01465) 5-6135, fax. 5-6159.

SUN CITY & LOST CITY
Accommodation: Cabanas, Cascades and Sun City hotels, The Palace. **Reservations office,** Sun International, PO Box 784487, Sandton 2146; tel. (011) 780-7800, fax. 780-7457.

KWENA GARDENS CROCODILE FARM
Permits/bookings: At gate.
Opening times: 10h00–18h00 all year. Crocs fed at 16h30.
Accommodation: None.
Enquiries: PO Box 234, Sun City 0316; tel. (01465) 2-1262, fax. 2-1264.

TOURIST INFORMATION
Rustenburg Tourist Information Centre, PO Box 16, Rustenburg 0300; tel. (0142) 97-3111, fax. 2-0181.

INDEX